HOW CAN

Thank you for your interest in this ⟨...⟩er
of professional information for so⟨...⟩ ⟨...⟩d
financial institutions information.

From its inception in 1965, and through the acquisition of Probus Publishing Company, **Irwin** *Professional* has been known and respected worldwide for innovation, quality, and service in each of the key markets we serve. **Irwin** *Professional* is now positioned as the publisher of the largest and most diversified business and financial information product line in the book publishing industry. This position of strength and critical mass is vital in today's quickly evolving world of information delivery.

We have the information you need and can provide it in the format you require. To learn more about other **Irwin** *Professional* publications and to receive your copy of our complete products catalog, please take a moment to complete this form and return it to the **Irwin** *Professional* Customer Service Department.

Four easy ways to return this information:
• **Call** our Customer Service Department: toll-free 1-800-634-3966 extension 1956.
• **E-Mail:** ipro@irwin.com
• **Fax** toll-free: 1-800-926-9495
• **Mail** to Irwin *Professional* Customer Service, 1333 Burr Ridge Parkway, Burr Ridge, IL 60521

Be sure to include code **1956** with your request for additional information.

IRWIN
Professional Publishing®
code 1956

Name _____ Title _____

Organization _____ Address _____

Department/Floor/Suite _____

City _____ State _____ Zip _____

Telephone ( ) _____ FAX ( ) _____ E-mail _____

Did you purchase this book in a bookstore? Yes___No___ If yes, please indicate the store/ location._____

What is the name and location of the bookstore where you primarily purchase professional reading materials?
_____

Please indicate with a ✔ your areas of interest:
❑ Operations   ❑ Investment Management   ❑ Trust Services
❑ Compliance   ❑ Executive Management   ❑ Lending
❑ Fraud and Security   ❑ Human Resources   ❑ Finance and Accounting
❑ Retail Banking   ❑ Treasury/Risk Management   ❑ Other _____
Please send:
❑ the Irwin *Professional* Bank publication and products catalog
❑ my complementary issue of The Irwin *Professional* COMMUNITY BANKER
❑ information on upcoming seminars for financial institutions professionals
bankfm 2.96

BUSINESS REPLY MAIL
FIRST CLASS   PERMIT NO. 204   OAKBROOK, IL

POSTAGE WILL BE PAID BY ADDRESSEE

 IRWIN
Professional Publishing®
ATTN: PEGGY CONDON
1333 BURR RIDGE, PKWY.
BURR RIDGE, IL 60521-0081

THE BANKING REVOLUTION

Positioning Your Bank in the New Financial Services Marketplace

TOM HARVEY

To Kathy
With love & Thanks

11-20-96

A Bankline Publication

IRWIN
Professional Publishing®
Chicago • London • Singapore

A Bankline Publication

IRWIN
Professional Publishing®

© Richard D. Irwin, a Times Mirror Higher Education Group, Inc. company, 1996

Times Mirror
Higher Education Group

Library of Congress Cataloging-in-Publication Data

Harvey, Thomas W.

    The banking revolution : positioning your bank in the new financial services workplace / Tom Harvey.
      p.   cm.—(A Bankline publication)
    ISBN 1-55738-793-1
    1. Banks and banking—Customer services. 2. Bank management—Quality Control. I. Title. II. Series.
HG1616.C87H37   1996
332. 1'068'8—dc20   95–51288

Printed in the United States of America
1 2 3 4 5 6 7 8 9 0   3 2 1 0 9 8 7 6

*To my parents, Robert A. Harvey and Mary B. Harvey,
with love and thanks for teaching us that if something is
worth doing, we should do it the best that we can.*

CONTENTS

Chapter 3

What Happened?   77

Chapter 4

The Culprit   119

Chapter 7

The Challenge of Customers   225

The banking industry is undergoing fundamental change. As consolidation re-shapes the structure of the industry, market forces are causing industry leaders to dramatically rethink their strategies. As bankers approach the twenty-first century, they are faced with a global marketplace in which technology provides consumers with instant access to almost unlimited choices of financial services and service providers. In this new competitive environment, bankers are re-vamping their product lines and delivery channels to meet the new demands of a dynamic market.

In *The Banking Revolution,* Tom Harvey challenges the industry's tradi-tional thinking about structure and strategy. After he thoroughly details the evo-lution of banking, he calls for a revolution to "change the way bankers think and act." Harvey's prescription begins with leadership and focuses on quality and value. He supports his points by drawing from the works of several leading experts in quality, leadership, and management. He also uses many examples from his own experience as a banker, consultant, writer, and customer.

Today's bankers are faced with different issues than they were just a few years ago. Today, banks cannot survive unless they are market driven. Perfor-mance matters above all else. And resilience is a key characteristic of the win-ners. Today, banks face growing and often conflicting demands from sharehold-ers, customers, employees, and the community at large. In this environment, incremental change won't work. Dramatic change is called for and it must hap-pen now.

Harvey challenges the traditional conclusions drawn from management information and urges readers to "look at the numbers in a new way." Harvey's financial background is evident as he proposes sound and measurable ap-proaches to quality. "Attack the cost of poor quality. Redirect your energy to an understanding of what people do all day and eliminate the things that add no value to the customer. It's the change in thought, attitude, and action, but that is what has to happen."

As bankers prepare to compete in the next century, they will need to em-brace change and adjust to some new realities. They must understand the value of their human capital. Market-driven high-performance organizations will rec-ognize that their true competitive advantage comes from their people. Over the past several years, as the industry has focused on consolidation, people have too often been viewed as liabilities rather than assets. As the analysts insisted on improved efficiency ratios, bank executives responded by eliminating as many jobs as possible. Banks focusing on downsizing without regard for the unique skills and abilities of the people who are lost as their positions are eliminated will find themselves facing a dearth of talent. Attention must, once again, be paid to training and developing people. New competition will force new skills and abilities. Training and development must be a top priority.

To survive bankers need to better understand the individual needs of customers. In the future, only a very few banks will have the budgets to be household names nationwide and create products with real mass market appeal. The rest of the banks will find their success in carefully targeting those customers with whom they can build strong relationships and for whom they can customize products and services. Share of customer will replace share of market as the goal for most banks.

To paraphrase Mark Twain, the reports of the banking industry's death are greatly exaggerated. Commercial banks reported a record $13.8 billion in profits for the third quarter. This was the 11th consecutive quarter that bank earnings exceeded $10 billion. Ninety-six and eight-tenths percent of all commercial banks were profitable in the third quarter of 1995. Total bank assets grew by more than $59 billion in the third quarter to $4.23 trillion. Similarly, deposits grew by $24 billion.

Real progress is being made in the battle for new product and service authority. There is now bipartisan support in Congress for repealing the Depression-era law separating commercial and investment banking. Such a repeal will open the door for banks to offer their customers diverse and innovative products and services.

Banks' ability to be innovative also is enhanced by a new trend in Congress and among the regulatory agencies: reducing banks' regulatory burden. At last, policymakers have realized that, when it comes to efficiently serving bank customers, less regulatory red tape and paperwork is more.

The future is bright for those bankers who have a clear and compelling vision for their organizations, who listen to their customers and employees, and who create real value. *The Banking Revolution* will help any banker chart such a course. It will challenge you to change the way you think and act. In this rapidly changing environment, nothing less will do.

J. Douglas Adamson
American Bankers Association

When I started in banking as Manager of the Financial Controls Group at Union Commerce Bank, banking was a stable industry that was unaware of the monumental challenges that it would have to face in the next 20 years. As we watched Merrill Lynch promote its Cash Management Account (CMA), we did not understand that it had started the tremendous deposit disintermediation that continues to this day and did not realize that its introduction had changed banking in this country forever.

As the 1980s began, deregulation followed with the Depository Institutions Deregulation and Monetary Control Act of 1980 and the Garn-St. Germain Act of 1982. That produced fluctuations on the balance sheet and income statement, the likes of which had never been seen before as the cost of funds took some wild swings. Deregulation exposed the significant fixed- cost structure and the excess capacity that had characterized the industry. That in turn spawned Merger Mania I, which turned much of the industry upside down. As if that were not enough, during the mid- to late 1980s, there were enormous problems in the commercial real estate portfolio- which resulted in the massive cost cutting that dominated the headlines of *The Wall Street Journal* and *American Banker.*

As the 1990s began, the financial services industry was anything but stable, and it was becoming evident that the traditional ways that bankers were approaching their business would not work in the new environment in which they found themselves. That is where the idea for *The Banking Revolution* was generated.

At that time, I was working in the Finance Division at Society Corporation where I was responsible for financial systems, productivity and cost accounting, payroll and accounts payable, and a host of other things. The division had studied the early attempts at cost reduction, was not seeing the sustainable results that many bankers thought would occur, and was looking for a strategy that would really work. It then became very apparent that service excellence was the only answer to that question for two reasons. First, providing what customers wanted would increase their loyalty, lower the defection rate, and attract new customers, thereby generating greater revenue.

Second, service excellence means that fewer mistakes and errors are being made, which means that less people have to be on the payroll to correct them. That decreases cost. It looked to us like it was the best of all worlds. As we tested and quantified that hypothesis, we became convinced that it was the only way to go. However, the service excellence strategy was contrary to the way that most institutions were managed because it focused foremost on understanding the expectations of customers and then called for an organizational redesign to meet them. That would be a big change, but one that the banks would have to make.

In 1990, I became an entrepreneur and began working with banks and bankers, learning of their many challenges as they tried very hard to be competitive. From the outside, I watched them struggle, trying to meet a brand-new world with an outdated strategy. At the same time, I was able to conduct primary and secondary research about organizations in general and banks in particular and the behavior that would be necessary to succeed as the markets for financial services became more crowded each day. As a result, *The Banking Revolution* was designed to help bridge that gap. It concentrates on changing the structure and style of the bank from one that is internally focused to one that is dedicated to providing service that is the envy of the competition.

The book begins with the reason that change is required, namely, the serious and significant disintermediation that has occurred since the introduction of the Cash Management Account. The nonbank competition has made serious inroads into the banks' markets, which have been masked in recent years by the strong earnings streams that the rate scenario of 1993–1995 has provided. However, recognizing that rates will come back to more normal ranges, banks have some options on how to keep their earnings high. They can choose to cut costs again or they can begin to understand that service excellence is a sustainable profit strategy that may take longer to implement but will result in a robust, healthy institution.

In Chapter 2, there is an examination of the economics of such a strategy, including calculations of the cost of poor service and the negative impact that it has on the income statement. Many people will say that service excellence and quality cannot be quantified, but models are included throughout this section that enable the reader to do the computation for his or her own bank.

It is also necessary to understand the reason for the disintermediation, so Chapter 3 contains a short history of banking in this country since the Great Depression. Looking at past events provides some terrific insight into the reasons the current conditions exist. The legacy of the stability of the 1950s and 1960s may still prevail in the minds of many bankers now forced to deal with the turmoil that has been a part of banking throughout the recent past and will extend into the foreseeable future. What worked back then surely does not work now.

Chapter 4 gives a look at the impact of the history on the bank, with considerable space devoted to the way culture and tradition have prevented the industry from responding. Some bankers have declared the industry to be dead, but if we understand why banks and their bankers behave as they do, we have grasped the fundamental issue and can begin to deal with it. Survival and prosperity are indeed possible, but only if it is understood that the change is a fundamental one. It resides in the adoption of five basic organizational imperatives. In Chapter 5, we learn about the nature of change itself. In Chapter 6, we see the specific changes that have to occur.

First, there has to be a focus on the customer, not on the Overhead Ratio. Second, the bank has to take a longer-term view than the current look to the end of next quarter. Third, the hierarchy and the pyramid structure have to be dismantled, so that the bank can be as responsive as its competitors. Fourth, there must be a change from the command-and-control style of management to one of servant leadership. Finally, the bank must commit to continuous improvement of every one of its delivery systems.

In Chapter 7, we learn about customers, why they are important, and how to determine their expectations and perceptions of the service provided by the bank. A detailed research methodology is presented that enables the bank to isolate the specific places where customers think service levels can be improved. Having that capability enables the bank to pinpoint where resources need to be applied instead of spending hundreds of thousands of dollars, or even millions, on across-the-board cost-cutting initiatives that will not solve the problem.

With that understanding, the remainder of the book is devoted to what can be done to make the required change. In Chapter 8, we learn how to gather data about the bank itself, analyzing it to see why service problems are happening in the first place. A direct relationship between what the workforce does every day and the attitudes that customers have can be quantified and acted upon. Changing what people do correlates with the way service is perceived. They need to be empowered to serve their customers and to be accountable for what they do.

In Chapter 9, we take a look at a better way to attack service problems. There is an emphasis on teamwork and cooperation between various business units because everyone in the bank has to realize that they are dependent upon one another in the service of their markets. However, since each bank in this country is different from every other one, it is impossible and impractical to prescribe a universal antidote. There will be no set recipe or a paint-by-the-numbers that provides the specific action steps that, when completed, will guarantee success. *The Banking Revolution* requires thoughtfulness on the part of its readers. It poses questions to be answered and offers a methodology that, when implemented within the context of an individual situation, will go a long way toward competitive success. It asks the reader to think about his or her own situation and to use what is learned to improve it.

At the end of the book are some thoughts about the dilemmas facing the banks, the ways that current behavior contributes to them, and some ways to make changes so that the dilemmas may be eliminated. There is also an index in Chapter 10 that allows you to rate your bank's readiness to change.

Throughout *The Banking Revolution,* I have added some personal vignettes from my experiences in banking since my days at Union Commerce. There are also stories about friends, clients, and colleagues, some of whom are disguised, some not. All of them are offered as instruction because I hope that we can laugh at, and learn from, some of the things that we have done myself included.

There are also some challenges to conventional wisdom, for example, about the ability of mergers to create value. We are seeing some numbers that suggest that mergers really don't work and some statements from great banks like First Union and Fleet who have said that they are retreating from that strategy to focus on customer service. In this case and in all the others, where there is some evidence that says a challenge to a current practice is in order, it is my purpose to raise the issue for the reader to contemplate.

The objective of *The Banking Revolution* is to help the industry by presenting some new thoughts about the service of customers, the ways in which the organization behaves, and the relationship between the two. It asks for a commitment to excellence, the result of which is better service that yields higher revenues and lower costs. But it will take that organizational and personal change. If you are ready, let's get started.

Tom Harvey

ACKNOWLEDGMENTS

When my coauthor, Janet Gray, and I finished *Quality Value Banking* in 1991, I began to think more about the changes that the banking community was going to have to make. That marked the genesis of *The Banking Revolution* as it became very evident that America's bankers would need to see the attitudinal and behavioral change that was necessary to compete in the new banking environment and to understand why that change was needed. Thanks to Janet for starting me down this path; to Doug Adamson of the American Bankers Association and Mike Riley of the Bank Marketing Association for confirming the need for such a work; to my ever-attentive agent, Wendy Becker, for shaping the idea; and to my editor, Mark Butler, at Irwin Professional Publishing for all the help and encouragement as it became a reality.

As I conducted the research and worked on the manuscript, many other people deserve thanks and appreciation as well: The people of Union Commerce Bank, especially Tim Treadway, John Ramsey, Dick Wild, and Elaine Geller, all of whom taught me about banking in the first place. Bob Patrick and the staff at Society Corporation who gave me the chance to grow and experiment with new ideas. Bill Schrauth, Dawn Drewnowski, and the Service Excellence Council at the Savings Bank of Utica, New York. Dianne Doss, vice president of quality improvement, and Jane Sibler, vice president of finance, and the Quality Council at PNC Bank, Kentucky. Ned Richardson, Jack Kleinhenz, and the other members of the Fourth Federal Reserve District. Arnie Weaver, Don Radde, LeAnne Krokker, Maria Kibler, Dave Ellis, and the rest of the team at The Peoples State Bank in St. Joseph, Michigan.

Thanks also to Jim Caldwell, former president of the Wisconsin Bankers Association (WBA), for his vision and support of Total Quality Management; Jane Arnold, Susan Grigsby, Marie Anderson, Kim Kindschi; and others on the staff of the WBA and their "Total Quality Enhanced Bank" program. To Reed Brooks and Amy Sanderlin at Signet; George Nugent, Connie Remenschneider, and Chip Wyer at First of America. To Bob Rankin for his insight into the financial services industry; Jim Watt of the Council of State Bank Supervisors; Greg Golembe at Furash & Company; Mike Quigley of NationsBank; Dennis McDonald and Beth McGeough of Central State Bank in Muscatine, Iowa; Sheldon Everhart of UNB Corporation; and Jim Montague of CFI Genesys Solutions. Special thanks to John Gonas, formerly of Huntington Bank; Dave Sanders of National City Bank; and Bob Lias of BankOne. All provided invaluable assistance in the study and understanding of the impact of culture on organizational life.

I have great appreciation for the work of Dr. W. Edwards Deming, Dr. Joseph Juran, Dr. Peter F. Drucker, Dr. Leonard L. Berry and his colleagues, Dr. Peter M. Senge, and those who would help us understand organizations and the way they work. Thanks also to the many authors and writers whom I have quoted in these pages.

I would be remiss if I did not express gratitude to Scott Lange, not only for his friendship and support over the years, but also for his technical knowledge, which saved this work from a systems crash as the end neared. Thanks also to my ever-vigilant neighbor, Dorothy Kortepeter, who was always full of encouragement and optimism as the work progressed. Thanks to George and Ginny Bodwell, Cam and Julie Welsh, and Toby Kennedy and Sharon Freedman. Also to Jack Kluznik, Jack Lynch, Charlie Berkey, and Rick McLaren who got to hear pieces of the story on those long, Sunday morning runs. To Curt Oliver. And to Kevin McHugh of JKM Management Development for teaching me about organizational imperatives.

Many thanks to Mary Holmes, my colleague in *WIN Technologies,* for continually challenging the many concepts, theories, and conclusions that make up the work that you are about to read. Thanks also to friends at Irwin Professional Publishing, Kevin Thornton, Brian Hayes, and Patrick Mullen, throughout the last year.

Special thanks and love to my brother, Steve, and my sister, Barbara, who have always been there with laughter and fun; and to my son, Doug, whose growth and maturity continues to make me very proud and who has been very supportive of my work; and most especially, to my "best good friend," Paula, who has been an integral part of this endeavor and closer to it than anyone else. Thankfully, she understood the priority it has been for me, even when it tied up what most people would think was an excessive amount of time.

Without all of you, what follows would not have been possible. Thanks again, and I hope you like it.

T. H.
Shaker Square, Cleveland, Ohio
November 1995

CHAPTER 1

It's a New World Out There!

service *n.*

1. an act of giving assistance or advantage to another.

Banking in the United States will never be the same again. Banks, as we have come to know them, are obsolete. It's been coming since 1975, but it has been masked by other things. Now, this new world for America's bankers will necessitate several changes: changes in attitude, changes in behavior, changes in the very way they serve their customers. There is overcapacity in the industry, competition has emerged from the unlikeliest places, and technology is shaking the very structure and organizational style that have characterized American banks for the last 60 years. Those three factors—overcapacity, competition, and technology—and the reluctance of bankers to change have created an entirely different world of banking in this country.

This new banking environment will feature tremendous disruption. Nothing in it will stay still for very long. First, there will be almost total consolidation if the banks don't change. In the next 15 or 20 years, there could be only 3,000 banks instead of the present 11,000, with hundreds of thousands of people being displaced. One hundred or so of the surviving banks will be huge, approaching a trillion dollars in assets. NationsBank and Bank of America will lead the charge of these truly national banks. That's a far cry from what I grew up with, when the largest bank in the state had about $3 billion in assets. Is big better? The jury is out on that. The others will be small, $500 million on average, serving the needs of their communities.

The new world is also one of electronics, which has exposed the stifling, plodding structure and style of most American banks. With transactions effected over the wire from home or office, the need for bankers to handle them is eliminated, whether at the teller window or in the check processing department. That in turn impacts related companies such as the local courier service and even the regional Federal Reserve Bank, which won't have nearly as many checks to process.

In addition, new entrants with advanced products will come to market faster than banks. Microsoft is already here with its electronics. So are the private trust companies, mortgage companies, and the brokerages. These innovations will force the banks to change the way they serve their customers or they won't have any customers to serve. The same thing has happened in other industries; perhaps, that is the way it should be.

In the late 1980s, I was fortunate to hear the bank stock analyst J. Richard Fredericks of Montgomery Securities talk about this phenomenon at an *American Banker* conference. He called this phenomenon, appropriately, "Darwinian Banking"—survival of the fittest. His premise was simple: Only the banks that could fulfill the demands of their markets would survive and prosper. They cultivate and expand market share by fulfilling the needs of their customers, even when those requirements change. That results in financial strength. The survivors anticipate changes in their markets and adjust, always making sure that they keep customer satisfaction at the forefront of their thinking. "Fortress balance sheets" was the term Fredericks used.

Financial strength is, however, only the measure of organizational strength. Truly great numbers are representative of great performance and are not the result of accounting magic or aberrations in the financial markets. The message is very simple: Banks that can provide the best service to their customers will see their share of market increase and their profitability rise.

Banking will always be transaction based, but computers, not people, will accomplish them in the new world. Consumers will expect that debits and credits to their accounts, which they may have generated themselves, will clear accurately and on a timely basis with no great concern about the organization that makes it happen. Service will become the only differentiator for any financial services firm: giving assistance and value to its customers. Banking will become a "relationship business" as the transaction part of it will become routine and minimal in importance. But the banks will have to do it well. They will also have to have a workforce that can work with customers to establish, maintain, and increase their relationships with them if they are to survive and prosper. Will Spence, senior vice president of consumer financial services at the Wachovia Bank, phrased it well: "People buy their financial products from many sources. If you deliver excellent quality service, they're likely to buy more products from you."[1]

That's where the revolution comes in, because most bankers don't have a true service orientation. They have been order takers, but they can't do that in their new world. They have to adopt a new organizational and business philosophy which is very much different from the prevailing one. They will have to understand the expectations of their markets and will have to design and operate delivery systems that will enable those requirements to be met. Simply put: They will have to offer better service. It is a great opportunity!

WHAT HAPPENED?

In the summer of 1993, Bernard Baumohl opened his article in *Time*, "Are Banks Obsolete?" with:

> What would happen to the U.S. economy if all its commercial banks suddenly closed their doors? Throughout most of American history, the answer would have been a disaster of epic proportions, akin to the Depression wrought by the chain-reaction bank failures in the early 1930s. But in 1993 the startling answer is that a shutdown by banks might be far from cataclysmic.[2]

Hold it! Was Baumohl saying that we could witness the demise of the American banking industry and not feel it economically? Aside from a couple of million people who would be out of work and a few ancillary service providers such as Harland check printers and EDS that would feel the pinch, Baumohl is suggesting that there are new sources for loans and alternatives for deposits, which may mean that we don't need banking institutions as we have come to know them.

Business lending, once dominated by the U.S. banks, is now the playground of life insurance companies, brokerages, and finance companies, which now have 80 percent of the market. Time deposits in the banks fell from $1.09 trillion to $860 billion between 1990 and 1992, finding their way to the mutual funds and brokerage firms like Fidelity and Merrill Lynch. It was Merrill Lynch that started it, back in 1975, when it introduced the Cash Management Account (CMA). Merrill's innovation offered a higher rate of interest to consumers than the banks could pay and had some check writing privileges, but it did not have deposit insurance, a novel idea at the time. The American public basically said, "We don't care that these accounts are not insured by the FDIC. We want the higher rate." In a few short years, over $230 billion left the banks for the CMA and its clones.

It is this disintermediation that is a cause for concern. Deep inroads have been made into the conventional banking franchise on both sides of the balance sheet as traditional banking customers talk with their feet. Their message is very clear.

If banking customers are taking their business to Merrill Lynch, John Hancock, Prudential, Fidelity, American Express, General Electric Credit, and the rest, the negative organizational and economic impact for the banks is huge.

As deposits leave, they have to be replaced, typically with higher-cost funds, which decreases the net interest margin. As the deposits go, so do the loans, causing the banks to lose interest income. The fees related to those accounts disappear as well. As if that were not enough, the cost structure remains the same or actually increases as banks activate extra marketing efforts to try to recapture what they had lost.

This compression of the balance sheet and tightening of the income statement forces the banks into a predicament. Traditionalists and the analyst community say that they have to have better financial performance than the previous quarter and the last year; therefore they must generate more net income. They can either deploy investable dollars into riskier assets to generate that higher income stream or they can choose the old standby, cost cutting to reduce their expense bases. In these cases, the bottom line will improve in the short term. Or, they can examine their organization's structure and service delivery processes, streamlining both to ensure that their customers' needs are met, doing no more, no less. However, the latter strategy is a long-term one and the banks have to have profits now.

Typically, over the last 20 years or so, banks have tried the revenue side first. Remember the REITs, energy loans, HLTs, and commercial real estate loans that promised great returns but required rounds and rounds of cost cutting when they went bad? More recently, look at the rush to the derivatives market, which promised and delivered a very nice income stream as long as rates were favorable. But once they turned and losses started to be reported at places like BancOne and Bankers Trust, the cost cutting began. It looked very much like a repeat of the actions that were taken at Citicorp, Ameritrust, Manufacturers Hanover, and the others when those speculative deals of the 1970s and 1980s went sour. The issue is not a financial one per se as most bankers would suggest. Rather, it is one of organizational effectiveness and superior customer service that is ultimately reflected in the bank's financial statements.

With infrastructures and organizations that already are probably too expensive for core earnings of the bank to support, the disintermediation to the competition puts additional pressure on the income statement. It becomes a vicious circle. As customers continue to leave, earnings decline, but the structure is still in place so people are jettisoned. Even so, as the bank reports lower profits, the stock price suffers. Taken to the final conclusion, as we saw in the 1980s at the Bank of New England, the institution itself becomes subject to risk. In the words of Ed Furash, a banking consultant, "The banking industry didn't see this threat. They are being fat, dumb, and happy. They didn't realize that banking is essential to a modern economy, but banks are not."[3]

Oh? Ed Furash and Bernard Baumohl of *Time* seem to agree. That prompted some primary research. In an interview, the treasurer of a local company said rather matter-of-factly, "As far as I am concerned, I really don't need a bank anymore." She had transferred her personal accounts to Merrill Lynch and was very happy with the service provided. "Five years from now," she went on, "it'll be electronic banking all the way."[4] When I asked for a little background, she told me that she had moved all of her accounts from her local bank beginning in the early 1980s to institutions where she could get better rates and better service. Credit card, DDA, IRA, mortgage loan, a money market fund: She had moved all of them.

I realized, as I listened, that her story could be about any consumer of banking services in the United States. It just happened that she lived nearby and we had gone to the same graduate school. She could have been in New Mexico, Michigan, Georgia, or Oregon. She was telling me a universal story.

The changing nature of the industry was reflected in this one conversation. It was substantiated in many others. The message is: What kind of institution it is doesn't make any difference to the consumer. The one that provides the best service will win. In this case, Merrill Lynch was good at processing transactions and paid a higher rate on deposits, so that it received her transaction businesses. First National, the bank across the street, had taken the time to understand her company and its financial needs, so it won the lending business. Treasurers of large corporations have always thought this way, but now individual consumers can, too. They have so many different institutions from which to choose and so much information by which to evaluate them that they now can select the institution(s) that provide the greatest value. People used to have lifelong relationships with their banks and with their bankers. Electronics, the new competition, and interstate banking have put an end to that.

In this age of speed and innovation, consumers have come to expect this kind of responsiveness and creativity. Bank customers are no different. We go where we get value. In the words of the chairman of Aviation Methods, Roger McMullin, "Now, Merrill handles almost everything that we do here except for the payroll. They have all the resources of a bank, but they are not tied up in bureaucratic regulatory matters, so they can respond very quickly."[5]

The Wall Street Journal of July 7, 1993, carried an article, the headline of which read, "Merrill Lynch Pushing into Many New Lines, Expands Business Services." It began with an account of Gary Goldstein, president of The Whitney Group, an executive search firm, which was in the market for a $1 million credit line. Goldstein was quoted as saying that when the banks turned him down, he went to what was then a new provider of credit services, Merrill Lynch, which readily approved the loan. That was just the beginning for Mr. Goldstein and The Whitney Group. Merrill Lynch now arranges term loans, provides money market accounts, and manages the firm's retirement business. "They grab you with everything," said Goldstein. "Merrill has become a traditional banker to us."[6]

Apparently, to others as well. When *The Wall Street Journal* article was written, Merrill Lynch had client assets of more than $500 billion, or 2.4 percent of all U.S. financial assets. It managed over $115 billion in mutual funds and $71 billion in individual retirement accounts (IRAs), which was more than the top 102 largest banks combined. It was the largest underwriter in the United States, had $13 billion in insurance assets, and managed $5 billion in home mortgage loans. And Merrill Lynch did not have to worry about the regulations of the FDIC, the Office of the Comptroller of the Currency, or the Federal Reserve System. Further, it was able to cross state lines to provide its services well before the banks were allowed to do so. Thus, it was probably the first real "national" bank. Merrill Lynch had offices in all of the major cities in the United States and had pioneered the use of 800 numbers in its telemarketing efforts.

This kind of creative thinking and the lack of government regulation had enabled the firm to be flexible and to anticipate the needs of financial services customers wherever they might be. It provided a competitive advantage that the banks could not match. It also seemed to have a different cultural emphasis, the kind we saw in the Dean Witter commercials. "We measure success, one investor at a time."

THE REVOLUTION

That's what bankers have to do. Here's why: Banks no longer have to face the singular competitive pressures from First National from Across-the-Street, as they had for most of the 20th century. Nor did they just have to worry about Merrill Lynch, Fidelity, and Prudential. Even the advances of General Motors and AT&T were of diminished importance ever since Microsoft announced that it intended to acquire Intuit. That union, it was suggested, was to revolutionize the way in which financial services are provided.

By combining the economic, marketing, and technological strengths of Microsoft with the most well-liked software for managing personal finances, Intuit's Quicken, a completely new way of banking was opened to the consumer. In doing so, this innovative, technological combination rendered the banking infrastructure nearly obsolete. Even though the Justice Department successfully challenged the transaction and stopped the merger, others are soon apt to adopt and market the concept—and be sure that Microsoft will return.

This won't be a competitive battle based on services, rates, and fees as had been the case with the brokerage houses and AT&T. This will be a fundamental, basic behavioral change brought on by technology that will completely alter the ways in which consumers of financial services will do their banking.

The technology resulting from the proposed merger of Microsoft and Intuit would enable consumers to effect all kinds of banking transactions from a personal computer that is nowhere near the bank. They could pay bills, invest in mutual funds, or select equities, from home, the office, or a hotel room anywhere in the world. That made it unnecessary to write checks or complete transaction advices, and dollars would move swiftly and electronically through financial institutions. Deposits would be made electronically as well, effectively eliminating all paper from the conduct of basic banking activities. If there were materially fewer checks and deposits, trips to the branch would not be necessary.

What would then be the impact on the tellers and other branch personnel or on the back office at the bank with all of its high-speed, high-cost equipment that was needed to process all of the paper? With transactions moving from computer to computer, they would not be needed. To take it to the extreme, there was even talk that "digital cash" could be downloaded for use in stores and restaurants, a similar yet alternative service to the debit card.

As the transaction was announced, Microsoft Chairman Bill Gates said he was not a banker. In the traditional way of looking at it, he was right. From a different perspective, however, Gates became the prototype of the new banker as Microsoft, in one bold move, took aim on all consumers of all banking services, whether they were in Bar Harbor, Maine; La Jolla, California; Captiva Island, Florida; or Anchorage, Alaska. Microsoft was after the customers of *all* U.S. banks, not only those in the state of Washington where its corporate headquarters are located.

By offering these services, Microsoft planned to garner the market, enabling it to market even more automated services to its ever-expanding customer base, not to mention millions of dollars in transaction fees. That would make the bank, wherever it was, little more than a place to house asset and liability accounts that could be accessed from anywhere through a huge electronic switch. "Our [Microsoft's] goal is to revolutionize how people do their financial work. The most important customers for financial institutions don't work hours that allow them to go to bank branches."[7]

That kind of thinking is heresy in the banking business, but there are some people who see its implication very clearly. Some highly respected people in the industry are starting to talk about it, including Doug Adamson, executive director of Bank Programs and Professional Development at the American Bankers Association in Washington, D.C., and Dr. Lyle Sussman, professor of marketing at the University of Louisville. We first became acquainted when we were asked to participate in the annual conference of The Young Bankers Division of the South Carolina Bankers Association (SCBA) in April 1993.

In presentations that we prepared without knowledge of the others, all three of us spoke to the Young Bankers about the long-term effect of the disintermediation that was occurring in the industry and how it was being masked by the record earnings that the banks were enjoying at the time. We also talked about the behavioral changes that would have to take place for banks to provide the service that would allow them to attain a competitive posture. We also acknowledged that the customs and traditions that dominate the thinking of America's bankers might not allow them to make those required behavioral changes.

What would they have to do? For starters, we all suggested that they would have to turn their attention to understanding the needs and expectations of their customers and all consumers of financial services. They would have to understand what people want and need, both within their various customer bases and in the totality of their markets.

The next step would be to transform their organizations into fast-paced, dynamic revenue generators by abandoning the familiar command-and-control management style and the hierarchical organization structure that reinforces it, and organizing instead around their service delivery systems. Then, in an empowered environment, they would have to completely rethink the ways in which they provide those services that the financial marketplace demands in the most efficient and cost-effective manner because technology was making some startling advancements.

Until they did so, we told the Young Bankers, disintermediation would continue as their customers took their business to the organizations that provided the best service. The question for the banks would then become one of time and would they have enough of it. Each individual bank would have to answer that question on its own, depending where it was in terms of its competitive position, technological status, customer attrition rate, culture, and readiness and ability to change. However, what Lyle, Doug, and I did not know in the second quarter of 1993 was that by October 1994, that time frame would be shortened exponentially with the announcement that Microsoft had made the tender offer for Intuit. Home-based, electronic banking would be a reality very soon, and that called for immediate and dramatic change.

To be very clear about this, the quality of the service produced or the product manufactured is all that differentiates an organization, regardless of what it does. It could be a hospital, a dry cleaner, a local theater group, a computer manufacturer, a graduate school, a gas station, or a financial institution. For the banking industry, GMAC and General Electric Credit Corporation, among others, charge competitive rates on vehicles, houses, and other capital goods; AT&T, Ford, Sears, and American Express market credit cards with enticements to challenge the banks; and the brokerages pay more attractive rates for deposits. All of these relate to the idea that customers patronize the institutions that best service their needs. The better the service, the greater the number of customers. The greater the number of customers, the better the financial performance. In the words of Lands' End Chairman Gary Comer, "Take care of your people, take care of your customers, and the rest will take care of itself."[8]

This is brand-new thinking for most bankers who are used to a world of cost cutting, downsizing, and other such programs. But that is my purpose here, to stimulate some creativity. This is a revolution of thought, attitude, and action. It is one that asks for innovative ways of looking at the business that has not given much consideration recently to customers or the workforce. It asks bankers to put down their numbers and to concentrate, as Mr. Comer says, on these major stakeholders. It asks them to commit to a strategy of serving customers with excellence. This is the change that is necessary.

IF JAPAN CAN . . . WHY CAN'T WE?

Many companies in the manufacturing sector have made the change. For some, like General Motors, who were forced to make it by its new competitors from Japan, the jury is still out about how successful it will be. For others, like Motorola, who chose this new path consciously and who compete globally on quality, there is no question that a strategy of excellence works. The banks can learn from them. The concept, as it was for GM and other U.S. automobile manufacturers, is simple: If they are to survive, they will have to change. Motorola had been doing business that way for decades.

These companies and others, such as McDonald's, Disney, and Nordstrom's, have a commonality. They expect excellence from their people every day: doing their very best, each and everyday, to meet or exceed the needs of their customers. That is what the banks have to do as well.

Why? Because of the continuing disintermediation and the banker's new world, they have to rethink what they do and how they do it. Some already are, but for the most part they have to break out of their habits and customs and revolutionize the way they serve their markets. In spite of these innovations from companies like Microsoft, that will be difficult because they cling to the familiarities of past strategies, even though they might not be the right ones. They don't see that their new world requires a new response.

While they watched, Merrill, Microsoft, and foreign competitors like Dai Ichi Kangyo changed the banking world, much like what happened in the American automobile industry during the 1970s and early 1980s when cars from abroad began filling our parking lots. The Japanese with their Toyotas, Hondas, and Mazdas were in the right place at the right time as the OPEC oil embargo forced the price of gasoline through the roof, making these small, more fuel-efficient vehicles much more attractive to the consumer. We bought them for the gas mileage they promised, but we also discovered that the Japanese cars were very good. They didn't break down. They weren't recalled. And they were innovative, which helped make the experience of driving more enjoyable. We Americans flocked to buy them, just as it appears we are doing today with the services offered by the new banking enterprises.

There was a reason for the success of Japanese automobile manufacturers. Ever since the end of World War II, over 50 years ago, they had subscribed to the teachings of the late Dr. W. Edwards Deming. Dr. Deming was a statistician who developed and quantified the relationship of improved product quality, lower unit cost, and higher market share with increased financial performance. Asked by the Japanese to assist them in their economic recovery after the war, Dr. Deming began his work with a group called the Union of Japanese Scientists and Engineers (JUSE). At the time, Japan's production capacity was in shambles, having been devastated by the Allies. The task was to develop Japan's ability to produce goods that were good enough to be exported to the rest of the world in exchange for food and other items that it could not generate on its own.

In 1950, the managing director of JUSE asked Dr. Deming to give a course on quality in general, and statistical process control (SPC) in particular, to a group of Japanese workers and engineers. Statistical process control provides the ability to define acceptable standards of performance in any aspect of any worker's duties, so that actual results may be compared against them. Any outcomes that fall outside those defined limits of acceptability are easily identified for study and corrective action.

In July of that year, Dr. Deming gave the first of several lectures to a gathering of over 500. He told them:

> You can produce quality. You have a method for doing it. You've learned what quality is. You must carry out consumer research, look to the future and produce goods that will have a market ten years from now and stay in business. You have to do it to eat. You can send the quality out and get food back. The city of Chicago does it. The people of Chicago do not produce their own food. They make things and ship them out. Switzerland does not produce all their own food, nor does England.[9]

Dr. Deming knew that simply lecturing to this audience would not produce the desired result. He had to have the commitment of the management of the companies in which they worked. By the end of the summer of 1951, he not only had reached the engineers and other technicians, but also had gotten through to the leaders of Japan's largest companies. They had nothing to lose. They had lost it all in the war. They began to concentrate the energy and effort that had made their country one of the most powerful military machines in the world into a formidable economic competitor. "I told them they would capture markets all over the world within five years. They beat that prediction. Within four years, buyers from all over the world were screaming for Japanese products."[10]

Dr. Deming taught them the Deming Chain Reaction,[11] which is at the center of the concept of continuous quality improvement (see Exhibit 1–1). It is the framework supporting the logic that as errors and mistakes are eliminated, the quality of service improves while the cost to provide it decreases. Cost is

EXHIBIT 1-1

The Deming Chain Reaction

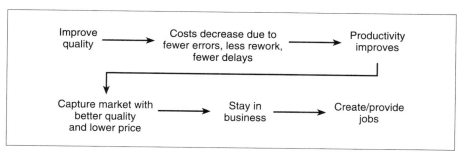

reduced because the bank does not have to have people on the payroll whose job it is to correct errors and mistakes. Therefore, there is better use of human and mechanical resources, which means that transactions can be processed more effectively and efficiently instead of devoting time and materials to correcting defects. The result is market acceptance and increased share.

As quality improves, productivity also increases. The bank is able to process more transactions with the same number of, or fewer, people and machines, thereby reducing unit cost even further. Ford Motor Company, which adopted Dr. Deming's teachings, provides evidence of this relationship. In the December 15, 1992, edition of *The Wall Street Journal* contained an article titled, "Team Spirit: A Decisive Response to Crisis Brought Ford Enhanced Productivity." It began, "Ford Motor Co. sold nearly as many vehicles in 1988 as it did in 1978—using half as many workers" and "about 7 1/4 hours of labor to produce stampings for the average vehicle, down from 15 hours in 1980."[12] Labor represents cost. Accordingly, the cost to produce the car now costs less by the equivalent of 7 1/4 hours, which in turn provides greater pricing flexibility and an increased ability to compete.

Assuming that there is demand for the service being offered, with higher quality and lower price, reflected by the cost reduction, the company is in a position to capture the market. It can retain and improve its relationships with its current customers and should attract new ones as well. Both provide additional revenues.

To achieve its goals, however, the bank must aim the improvement effort at reducing the number of daily mistakes and errors in the processes designed for providing service to its employees and customers. But we must think a little differently about what that means. It may mean rerunning a report that has an incorrect balance, or it may be re-reproducing a memo on the copy machine. It may be correcting a transaction that has been posted wrong to a customer account. In most cases, however, it is the process itself that needs fixing.

A word of caution: Just as the relationships in the Deming Chain Reaction are valid in a positive sense, they are equally true when things go wrong. As quality deteriorates, costs increase due to more errors and the time and energy needed to correct them. Accordingly, productivity decreases, adding to cost. The service, then, is of lesser quality and costs more, which tends to drive customers to competitors who can provide the service level that they want. Taken to the extreme, the bank or any company goes out of business as the final customers depart. Think about some of the most famous companies that have gone this route: Peoples Express, U.S. Steel, and the New York Central Railroad, to name a few.

During the 1960s and 1970s, the demand for Japanese goods exploded. They marketed products that worked and were cost-competitive, driving many U.S. manufacturers out of businesses that once had been their domain. Dr. Deming had given them the answer that applies to all organizations, even the banks: Improve the quality of goods and services to meet customer expectations by reducing errors and mistakes and sell them at competitive prices. With high quality and a fair price, Japanese products were in great demand.

Think about that logic. Producing goods of high quality costs less than those that are not. Which goods would more people buy? Something that works? Or something that needs repair? I don't think there is much question. It's the same thing in the services sector.

For some people in the United States, the competitive imbalance with the Japanese became a concern. In 1979, a television producer, Clare Crawford-Mason, was putting together a documentary that she was going to call, "Whatever Happened to Good Old-Fashioned Yankee Ingenuity?" The concept for the production was that the United States was being beaten soundly on several economic fronts by its Japanese competitors. U.S. automobile manufacturers were being beaten by Toyota, Honda, and Mazda; Ricoh and Sharp copiers were making their presence felt; U.S. television and VCR manufacturers were beginning to feel the pinch. The banks hadn't felt it yet, but they would. It was time, Crawford-Mason believed, to fight back.

As she conducted her research, she was referred to Dr. Deming and visited him several times at his home outside Washington, D.C. In those meetings, he explained the relationships of high quality, low cost, and increased market share. He also showed her the stories that had been written about him in Japan. She was astounded and was quoted as saying, "Here is the man who has the answer, and he's five miles from the White House and nobody will talk to him."[13]

As every good journalist does, Crawford-Mason needed someone to verify that Dr. Deming's principles worked, even with the parking lot full of Japanese cars. So she contacted one of his clients, William Conway of the Nashua Corporation, who provided all the support that she needed. He told her how the quality of his company's products had improved and how costs had gone down. And he agreed to appear in the documentary.

The final version of the film was complete. Ms. Crawford-Mason changed the name of it to *If Japan Can . . . Why Can't We?* At 9:30 P.M. on June 24, 1980, it aired on U.S. television in what has turned out to be one of the most successful programs of its kind. Dr. Deming discussed his principles during the show, while Conway reported that he was saving millions of dollars and improving productivity by using them. Following the broadcast, Dr. Deming's telephone began to ring. He was besieged by major corporations that wanted his help. Ford Motor Company called. So did General Motors, Hughes Aircraft, and Dow Chemical.[14]

The final results of the efforts of these companies to change will not be in for years, but for the near term they are beginning to be impressive. In April 1994, a *Fortune* article stated, "Only yesterday, Detroit's Big Three seemed helpless in the face of Japan's unrelenting gains in the U.S. market. Yet American companies have gunned their share of car and light-truck sales by three percentage points in the past three years, mostly at the expense of Japanese nameplates."[15]

Three percentage points may not seem like a lot, but considering the quality of their competition, the Americans were certainly doing something right. They had reversed the negative trends and had made some positive strides. It can be the same for the banks, which may not have realized the seriousness of the threat posed by the significant competition.

That same issue of *Fortune* contained another article, "Keeping Motorola on a Roll."

> Mention Motorola, the company that almost everyone loves to love, and the accolades fairly gush: titan of TQM, epitome of empowerment, tribune of training, icon of innovation, prince of profits. A leader in the worldwide revolution in wireless communication, this manufacturer of cellular telephones, pagers, two-way radios, semiconductors, and other electronic gadgets has become that most unusual of creatures—a big company that sizzles.[16]

For 1993, Motorola's sales increased by 27 percent, earnings improved by 127 percent, and savings from quality initiatives amounted to $1.5 billion, a portion of which the company turns back to its customers in terms of lower prices.

The results posted by Motorola and those starting to be realized by the Big Three automakers show that the commitment to excellence works. Look at the success that the Japanese have had. The banks can learn from them. The lesson? Produce and deliver a high-quality service, according to customer specification, at a fair price. Give your markets and your customers value. Clearly something is working for Motorola and the Big Three automakers. That something is the philosophical and behavioral commitment to being the best.

THE ECONOMICS

> To be very clear, the commitment to excellence and serving customers is a comprehensive organizational economic strategy.

This promise to serve is not limited to the people on the retail side of the bank who have been taught to smile and to call their customers by name. That is all well and good but doesn't go far enough. The entire transaction must be considered. Smiles do little when loan documentation is wrong; promises aren't kept; the ATM is down and you have an airplane to catch; the line is out the door; or you have to wait 15 minutes to talk to a customer service representative on the phone while being forced to listen to the bank's upbeat advertising.

Everyone in the bank, at all levels, has to understand that they have customers, people who rely on them for service. That means that they have to know what will satisify those customers. Then they must work together to design efficient organizational delivery systems, not functional ones, by which to meet those requirements, effectively eliminating everything else that precludes it. Better service results in more customers. More customers mean more transactions, which, as Dr. Deming suggests, lower unit cost and increase share. That means more bottom-line earnings.

Good in theory, but where's the proof? We saw some in Motorola's 1993 results. Further, the National Institute of Standards and Technology (NIST), the organization that oversees the Malcolm Baldrige National Quality Award process, conducted an experiment in 1994 to see if the theory held. In an academic exercise, it "invested" $1,000 in each of the companies that had won the Baldrige Award from the first business day in April of the year they won the award, holding the "investment" until October 1994. NIST also "invested" $1,000 in the Standard & Poor's (S&P) 500 Index. In this study, the winners of the Baldrige Award, companies that are committed to excellence, returned three times the advance of the S&P.[17]

In May 1991, the U.S. General Accounting Office published a report: *Management Practices: U.S. Companies Improve Performance through Quality Efforts.* It was an analysis of the data submitted by the finalists and semifinalists for the Baldrige Award for the previous two years. The most important of the results were:

- Product/service reliability increased by 11 percent.
- Error reduction of 10 percent.
- Decline in complaints of 12 percent.
- Lower cost of quality by 9 percent.
- Increased market share by 14 percent.[18]

Any organization would like that kind of outcome. For a financial institution, reliability is the most important service characteristic. Increasing it by 11 percent, for example, reflects better conformance to customer expectations. Meeting their needs means that fewer problems are occurring, which in turn means that there are fewer complaints from dissatisfied customers, which have to be acted upon. So, as the quality of the service increases, the bank will not have to pay people who make mistakes nor have to listen and react to unhappy callers. More important, it does not have to pay another set of people to fix and correct what has gone wrong.

That results in greater customer satisfaction and loyalty, which in turn creates repeat business and opportunities to cross-sell, both of which are revenue-enhancing activities, quite the opposite of continually raising fees or cutting costs across-the-board to keep the earnings at the levels desired by the analysts on Wall Street.

As Deming suggested and the NIST study and the GAO Report validated, companies committed to the continuous improvement of their service simply achieve better results than those that are not. They consciously design better ways to deliver service to meet the needs and expectations of their marketplace, decrease their unit costs by not making and having to fix mistakes, and, in doing so, increase market share. Those whose numbers were in the GAO Report offer some favorable supporting evidence because they had reduced their costs by 9 percent and increased share by 14 percent. Quite frankly, it is the best of all worlds.

Instead of closing their accounts and taking their loans, deposits, and fees to the brokerage, customers will remain loyal because the bank is providing the service they want. That halts the disintermediation and means that marketing expenditures can be aimed at finding new customers instead of persuading dissatisfied ones to stay. With a service quality strategy and the ability to deliver on it, the entire marketing effort becomes significantly easier.

At a time when the banks need a way to stem the tide of disintermediation and to increase earnings, the service quality strategy provides the answer. But it is not just the stuff that the people in marketing and the branch system talk about and that's as far as it goes. A service quality strategy has to permeate the entire organization, from the teller window to commercial loan operations to the security department to accounting. It is global in nature because each of these areas has customers to serve, and they might even be each other. Giving them what they want, when they want it, and in the format that they want, the first time and every time, eliminates mistakes and the necessity to have to correct them. Not only is it less expensive to do it right the first time, but also pleasing the customer increases self-esteem, decreases interdepartmental friction, and improves organizational cooperation.

Whenever I conduct a workshop or give a presentation at a banking conference, one of the semirhetorical questions that I ask is, "Does anyone know why the bank has an adjustment department?" As the audience ponders, there is always some self-conscious laughter, eyes roll to the ceiling, and whispers start. But the question is real. When operations and the branches continually make errors, the bank acknowledges and approves of them by allocating financial resources to the people in the adjustment department whose job it is to correct them. Common sense would tell us that the bank could reduce its operating costs if it eliminated the errors before they occur.

Since 1988, we have been conducting continual research into this side of the service quality equation. One of the more startling, yet consistent, findings concerns the number of mistakes and errors that are made and the number of unnecessary activities and tasks that are carried out in the bank every day. The first evidence came in early 1989, when I was director of strategic financial planning at Society Corporation. I attended a meeting at which Mike Hanson, then of J. D. Carreker & Company, told us that 30 percent of what we did was related to doing things wrong or to things that did not have to be done at all.

That meant we were wasting $0.30 of every dollar making and correcting mistakes or engaging in activities that had no customer value. Thirty percent is a big number. Because it is so huge, it was easy to be skeptical about it, but support comes from the law that created the Baldrige Award: "American business and industry are beginning to understand that poor quality costs companies as much as *20 percent of sales revenues nationally* [italics added] and that improved quality of goods and services goes hand in hand with improved productivity, lower costs, and increased profitability."[19]

Whether it is 30 percent of noninterest expense or 20 percent of sales does not matter. All that needs to be understood is that the cost of quality is huge in the United States, and its banking institutions are not exempt from it. Think of it from the perspective of being a consumer. Do you give your business to companies and stores that provide less than excellent service? Most likely not. It is the same way for your customers. They are looking for the place where they can get the service they want at a price that is acceptable, that's all. But it isn't happening.

A recent poll of 500 executives by the Lou Harris group indicated that 95 percent of them consciously incorporated quality as a part of their plans, which is exciting to consider at first blush. However, of the consumers studied in the same poll, 45 percent of them felt that quality is declining.[20] Here's why.

The pressure on earnings from Wall Street has driven bank management to squeeze as much cost out of their organizations as possible. Their balance sheets are under attack, as we have seen, and there is a market lid on the fees that can be charged. So, they assault the cost side. The problem with that is that, except for the people, expense levels are fairly fixed with the branches, computer systems, and main office complexes. So, the only thing they think they can do is remove the only variable cost they understand, and that is the people. When that happens, there are fewer people to handle the same number of transactions, which results in mistakes, frustration, frazzled nerves, and anxious looks for help.

A case in point. I went to my branch on the third of the month about 2:00 P.M. When I entered, I counted and found that I was the 17th person in the line. All I wanted to do was to get some traveler's checks. Four teller windows were open, of a possible 10. The branch manager and her assistants were sitting behind their desks, busily talking on the phone and shuffling paper, as customers waited to see them. A poster on the wall proclaimed that the customer comes first.

The line inched along. I reached the teller window 45 minutes later and asked for some traveler's checks. The young woman behind the counter looked at me and smiled. As I was signing the checks, I commented that it seemed to be a busy time. As she looked at the length of the line, the clock, and her manager in rapid succession, she replied anxiously, "Oh, I'm new here. I hope it's not always this way."

As I left the branch, 27 people were in the line, and there were no signs of it letting up. To keep expenses as low as possible, the bank had cut tellers, one of the most important groups within its workforce. In exchange, it got grumbling, disgruntled customers. Have I been in the branch since? No. Have I found other financial services providers that meet my needs better? Yes. Has the bank lost revenue? Yes. Has its cost structure changed? No. Does that put pressure on the income statement. In one, small way, yes. Did the cost cutting work? It depends on what management's objectives were. If they were to drive cost out, then it was successful. If they were to provide service that customers want and to have a chance to enhance relationships (i.e., profitability), then it was not.

THE CYCLE OF GOOD SERVICE

Heretofore, as shown in this basic example, most banks have paid lip service to the idea of service quality. The poster said one thing. The action said something quite different. For the most part, America's banks are not driven by customer satisfaction. Rather, it is a short-term financial view that is concentrated squarely on next quarter's earnings and the resulting impact on the stock price. Even while professing to be concerned about service quality—like the executives in the Harris poll and as the poster wanted me to believe—the behavior is driven by the bottom line. Banks do not understand that there is a direct relationship between the quality of service being offered and the bank's profitability, on both sides of the income statement.

E X H I B I T   1–2

The Cycle of Good Service

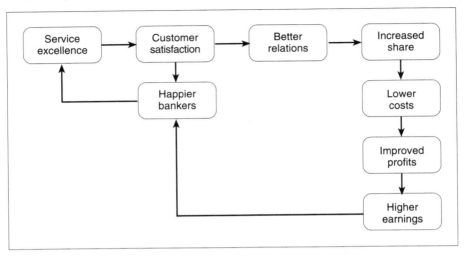

I know a bank that provides a great example of the way quality is viewed. On the same day that three improvement initiatives were kicked off, corporate headquarters circulated throughout the ranks of management a memorandum indicating that earnings for the year were projected to be too low and that expenses would have to be reduced by 10 percent. The bank now had two conflicting objectives: improve service levels and cut costs. Predictably, people who were being asked to participate on innovative quality improvement teams quickly changed their thinking to a mode of self-protection and survival. The prospect for real, sustainable improvement vanished.

Exhibit 1–2 is a simplification of the Deming Chain Reaction. It is called the Cycle of Good Service and shows the economic and behavioral relationships I am asking you to understand. There are two distinct, yet related, relationships as shown in the two circles. First, the smaller circle represents human behavior. In it, the people of the bank are providing the service that meets and/or exceeds the expectations of its customers. That is the definition of service excellence. When that happens, the relationship between the customer and the service provider is friendly and amiable, which is a positive experience for both. Both parties feel better about themselves. All things being equal, the customer is likely to return, bringing even more business. Service providers take pride in their work and try to ensure that everything they do pleases the customer. It is a very constructive behavioral reinforcement and good for self-confidence and self-esteem.

The larger of the two circles shows the economic relationships that result from providing excellent service. In this case, customer satisfaction leads to better relationships with the bank's current clients who are inclined to bring more of their business to it. That, by definition, increases market share, as does the influx of new customers who hear about the bank's legendary service levels.

Increased share means that more transactions are being processed, presumably with the same amount of fixed cost. That lowers unit cost and increases revenues, both of which lead to improved profitability and higher earnings. More earnings result in increases in the bonus pool, higher merit increases, and a higher stock price, which benefits all shareholders and the workforce that participates in the 401(k) program. Seeing the value of their personal portfolios rise due to their own actions and those of the rest of the team is another great reason for them to smile.

The financial benefits of the strategy can be significant; look at Motorola. When shared with the staff, the strategy provides a motivation to deliver even better customer service. On the personal side, people generally enjoy serving the needs of others. It makes them feel good about themselves.

Still, we cannot forget that the reverse of the Cycle of Good Service is also true, just as it is with the Deming Chain Reaction. Where the bank does not concentrate on satisfying the customer as the primary objective and is busy doing things that subtract from the customer's perceived value, both the financial and the nonfinancial rewards disappear. If the bank does not provide the service that people want, it will lose customers to the competition. Remember the inroads made by Merrill Lynch.

No business enterprise can exist without customers. Therefore, meeting customer expectation is the most important task for any bank, many of which have forgotten about it. The objectives are fundamental: First, as I have said before and it bears repeating, identify the requirements of the bank's customers and markets. Second, use that research to design streamlined delivery systems, using the latest in the ever-advancing technology. Third, adopt organization styles—perhaps very different from those to which today's bankers are accustomed—to support the service orientation.

To accomplish those objectives requires a different way of thinking from everyone in the institution. This is not just for workers. It is for everyone. It is an attitude that says, "Today and every day, I will do whatever I have to do to exceed the expectations of my customers."

Let me give you another example of how the absence of such a philosophy plays out. As I was interviewing members of the workforce of a bank's mortgage lending department, I noticed a pile of loan applications that had been through the credit and appraisal functions on the desk of a senior originator. I didn't think much of it at the time, but as I walked by the next day, I noticed that the pile was significantly higher. So, I asked the originator why the pile was growing. "Oh, my boss is on vacation, and she's the only one who can sign applications for the loan committee."

Having those applications sit on the desk, piling up for the 5 or 10 days that her supervisor was on vacation, meant that customers were kept waiting unnecessarily about the status of their mortgage loans, which is an anxious experience anyway. Unhappy customers have a tendency to talk about their unpleasant experiences, and it is this kind of service that opens the door for the competition. Furthermore, from the bank's perspective, it also meant that the loans were not being put on the books promptly, interest was not being generated, and fees were not being collected. All that had to be done to remedy the situation was to have alternative signing authority vested in another officer so that the process would not come to a screeching halt.

THE TRIPROL OF JOSEPH M. JURAN

Satisfying the expectations of customers is at the center of the philosophy of another of the masters of the quality movement, Dr. Joseph M. Juran. Like Deming, with whom Juran worked closely, Juran's teaching is at the core of the remedy for America's banks. Among the many new concepts he brought to the quality initiative is the idea of the TRIPROL, or triple role. The logic behind the TRIPROL is that each person in an organization functions in three different roles at various times. That is, each of us acts in a capacity of supplier, processor, and customer, depending on where we fit within a given process.

The TRIPROL begins with the following relationship. For people to do their jobs, they need input from someone else. Then they do something with that input, changing and enhancing it, thereby adding some value. Finally, they deliver it to the next person or department in the chain.

$$\text{Customer} \rightarrow \text{Processor} \rightarrow \text{Supplier}$$

In every process at the bank, this relationship is played out over and over. As a customer, you have to have information or materials from other people within the bank, so that you can fulfill your responsibilities. No one starts from scratch. It may be that you are in financial analysis and need accurate reports from data processing. As a credit analyst, you may need timely information from calling officers. As a trust officer, you certainly need the right data about your customers. Or, all you may need is a form, a legal pad, or a pen, which the purchasing department has supplied.

With that input, you act as a processor. You do something to it, whether it means opening an account for a retail customer, appraising a piece of property for a mortgage originator, or analyzing and formatting marketing demographics for senior management. You could be adding code to a computer program, interviewing a candidate for an open position, or running a proof machine at midnight. Acting as a processor also could be filling out an expense reimbursement form or one of those pink pieces of paper that announce, "While You Were Out."

When you are done functioning as a processor, you become a supplier and give the results of your work to your customers. You might be the CEO who has given a presentation to the board of directors. You could be from the mail room, having just made your morning's rounds or you could be a commercial lender who has called a good client with news of the approval of a needed line of credit.

Your customers take your input and do something with it, effectively becoming processors in their own right who look to supply their customers with what they in turn need in the performance of their own jobs. The totality of this systemic relationship is what Michael Porter termed the "value chain," as all economic activities in a service delivery system are identified and linked together.

The linkages in the chain are important as the subtlety in the concept of the TRIPROL relates back to the Deming Chain Reaction. If the input you give to your customers does not meet with their expectations, what happens? They have to either correct it themselves or give it back to you to fix. Both scenarios are expensive. For the TRIPROL and the Deming Chain Reaction to be as efficient as possible, every supplier must know and understand the expectations of his or her customers. If they don't, there is probably little chance that they will be met. When that happens, the Cycle of Good Service is interrupted and reversed, resulting in less than excellent service and higher costs and, once again, issues an invitation to the competition.

The chain reaction and TRIPROL are systemic in nature and encompass the entire organization as it serves to meet the expectations of its customers. They also apply to individual functions and activities within the bank's value chains, but the true value is not realized until their global application is understood. For example, it is all well and good for the people of the accounting department to commit to excellence. However, if their suppliers in purchasing and data processing are not equally dedicated, delivery of accurate reports and accounts payable checks may be materially more difficult.

Juran realized this connectivity, identifying it as the Big Q as opposed to the Little Q.[21] The difference between them is one of scope. Little Q concentrates on functional and departmental performance. Big Q is concerned with the organization as a whole and the processes within it as shown in Table 1–1.

It is important to understand this distinction now because quality is a pervasive organizational mandate. It is at the center of the banking revolution and is fundamental to its success. We must view service excellence as a cultural issue for the entire organization, not only for individual departments. Juran was one of the first to see this organizational relationship, teaching that everyone in the institution has an impact on serving customers, whether they are people inside the bank or the ones that walk in the front door to use the ATM.

T A B L E   1-1

Little Q and Big Q

Topic	Content of Little Q	Content of Big Q
Products	Manufactured goods	All products, goods, or services, for sale or not
Processes	Directly related to the manufacture of goods	All processes: operations, support, business, etc.
Industries	Manufacturing	All industries: manufacturing, service, government, etc., for profit or not
Quality viewed as a:	Technological problem	Business problem
Customers	Clients who buy products	All who are affected, internal and external
How to think about quality	Based on culture of functional departments	Based on planning, control, improvement
Quality goals are included:	Among factory goals	In company business plan
Cost of poor quality	Costs associated with deficient manufactured goods	All costs that would disappear if everything were perfect
Improvement directed at	Departmental performance	Company performance
Evaluation of quality based on:	Conformance to factory specifications, procedures, standards	Responsiveness to customer needs
Training in managing for quality is:	Concentrated in the quality department	Companywide
Coordination is by:	Quality manager	Council of senior leaders

As we examine the differences between Big Q and Little Q (see Table 1–1), it is easy to see the global nature of Juran's view. He said the quality pertained to *all* products and services, *whether for sale or not.* That means that people who do not have regular contact with the bank's external customers are just as responsible for excellence as those who do. Why? Because the cost of reworking errors and mistakes and the obstruction that they cause in the bank's operating processes are unnecessary and rob the bank and its shareholders and employees of economic value. Go back to the stack of mortgages that was piling up because there was no one around to approve them, which was probably a formality anyway. In this case, there was an internal failure between two parties inside the bank, which manifested itself in poor service for the ultimate consumer. That is what we have to avoid.

Juran also crossed another organizational boundary and applied quality to the services sector, where there is a key distinction. In a manufacturing situation, the consumer is influenced by the store or vendor only at the point of sale, which is presumably only once over several years. The product becomes the object that must be of quality because most of us cannot remember the name or the behavior of the person who sold us the product. It is the performance of the Maytag washing machine once we get it home that is important, not the salesperson at the appliance store who recommended it.

In a service environment like a bank, it is not only the services provided that are subject to customer scrutiny, but also the way in which the service is delivered. The banker has to understand that the way in which customers are treated, even when they use the ATM, is part of the services that the bank is offering. There is the financial side to the transaction and the human side, and both must be perfect. There is no distinction between them. As banking becomes more relationship based, this understanding becomes even more important.

Juran also drew the distinction between quality as a technological issue and a behavioral one for the entire business, again reflecting his systemic view of it. The commitment to excellence is a cultural theme that should be first on the agenda of everyone in the bank. In that way only will it be able to compete with the Merrill Lynches of the world.

Quality goals for education, process improvements, measurements, rewards, and the like become part of the entire organization, not just individual departments, as coordinated by the senior management of the bank. The implication is that quality cannot be delegated to the quality manager or quality analyst as some banks have done. It is the responsibility of the chief executive officer to lead the charge, effectively empowering the people at lower levels to define the expectations of their markets and to design the most efficient ways to meet them.

If continuous quality improvement is an organizational imperative for everyone within the bank, why hasn't it and the commitment to excellence been universally embraced by the U.S. banking system?

OSTRICH SYNDROME?

The primary issue appears to be one of skepticism about the whole notion, from the required behavioral change to the financial impact to be achieved. Although the nation's bankers can see the numbers about the advances of the competition, it does not seem like they put much stock in them, perhaps because the record earnings achieved in 1993 and 1994 have given them a sense of security. It looks like many bankers have the ostrich syndrome: closing their eyes, burying their heads underneath the pillow, and hoping that by morning the threat will go away. It won't.

There is a paradox here. Bankers are analytical people. They love their numbers. I know, since I used to be responsible for the accounting areas in two large commercial banks from which we shipped an awful lot of reports. One of the diseases that ran around was "analysis paralysis," as my friend Jim Andrews at Society Bank used to say. We would study the numbers every different way we could as everything we did had to be quantified. We wouldn't move unless the numbers said that we should. With that background, here's the paradox. Factual data suggest a change in customer behavior has occurred: disintermediation on the balance sheet and the advance of Microsoft and other new providers. The analysis of that data should trigger an innovative response from America's bankers, but they continue to clutch at the behavior that has worked in the past, seemingly ignoring that new information. They see it, but they don't believe it.

Let me give you an example. One bank that I know tracks how customers transact their business, whether at the drive-up window, the ATM, or at the teller window. The number of teller transactions has been decreasing; only 40 percent of all transactions are now processed inside the bank. Drive-up volume is declining a little, but ATM volume is increasing significantly. With these data, one would reason that customers are beginning to like automation and that electronic banking might be the next rational step for them. This change in consumer behavior, which they have quantified, suggests less reliance on the branch network and more on ATMs and home banking, but this bank is planning to build more branches.

This institution is not alone in that kind of thinking. The banking community, as a whole, apparently doesn't see what that holds for the future or it simply doesn't believe the current data. At a time when logic and foresight suggest less investment in brick and mortar, the total number of branches in the United States actually increased throughout the 1980s and early 1990s. Statistics from the FDIC show it (see Exhibit 1–3).

Instead of thinking of the future and competitors like Microsoft, bankers stuck to tactics that had worked in the 1950s and 1960s, but which are woefully inadequate today. Instead of building more costly branches, they should have anticipated where the financial services industry was going to be taken and then gotten involved with things such as interactive banking like Huntington Bancshares did. Banking is completely different these days, and there is a distinct possibility that America's bankers do not understand the threat. Even with this very serious danger, it is quite likely, as evidenced by Exhibit 1–3, that they prefer to remain in their century-old traditions, which certainly do not apply to the new banking environment.

There are other answers besides denial of the data. Maybe it is because bankers do not think they can do anything about their precarious position, preferring to blame Congress for failure to make all financial institutions subject to

E X H I B I T   1-3

Total Locations, 1988-1993

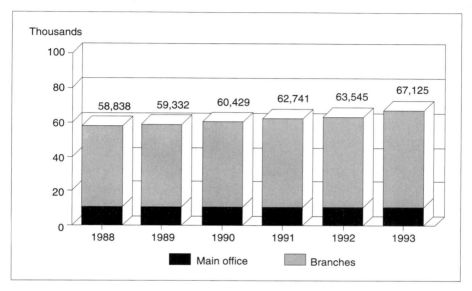

Source: Federal Deposit Insurance Corp.

the same regulation. Goldman, Sachs and Wells Fargo certainly have different rules to play by. It could also be that they are so wed to their mainframe systems that the prospect of banking at home with PCs connected to a huge switch is inconceivable. Or it may be that they have too large an investment in their systems, which would making changing them financially impossible.

Furthermore, the required external focus on customer satisfaction and market expansion by the entire organization may be contrary to the way they have always thought. They spend a lot of time defending their programs and divisional profitability against other members of management. Our experience suggests that too much time and attention is paid to it and not enough to the contribution of various banking relationships. Little thought is given to things such as market share data, accounts opened and closed, changing demographics and customer behavior, and product and customer relationship profitability—the things that are the real contributors to organizational financial performance. Roger Noall, chief administrative officer of Society Corporation, now Key-Corp, told me that the information we provided from finance dictated an internal view instead of an external one. His point was that we were so concerned about our numbers—justifying them and trying to make them look good—that we would spend a lot of time explaining variances from plan to each other instead of concentrating on pleasing our customers.

Teamwork, another prerequisite to success, has been squelched as the bank's structure and style have put people in organizational compartments that preclude effective communication and cooperation. Additionally, because of the pyramid organization structure, delivery systems appear to have been designed without the input of all of the people within them, meaning that the necessary linkages between them have not been established. People involved in the delivery of the same service to a customer may not know just exactly how they fit.

There is also an inordinate and unnatural amount of effort expended on cost cutting, with education and training always among the first to go. That scares people, stifles their growth, and leads to self-protection rather than creativity and innovation. The internal bureaucracy requires people to play a number of demotivating games, which detracts from the ability to serve. There is no doubt that few bankers understand the economics of quality and how expensive it is to provide poor service and how costly it is when customers decide to leave.

There is one last condition that seems to preclude it from happening in most banks. As in any organization, a service quality initiative will go nowhere without the endorsement and support of the bank's leadership. The question is, Why have more of them not seen how important it is?

If we remember that the commitment to excellence is a long-term strategy, it appears to contradict the short-term view that dominates the thinking of most bankers. This focus on the near-at-hand is caused by two very powerful stimuli. First, there is the desire to please the analysts. As far back as 1977 in finance planning and control at Union Commerce Bank, we had to present our forecasts and actual results to the gods of Wall Street, hoping that they would look favorably on us and make a market in our stock. Their influence continues to grow. Larry Frieder, professor of finance at Florida A&M University, said in a speech to the Bank Marketing Association's National Conference in September 1994, that banks used to be accountable to the regulators. Now "it's to the analysts." Instead of letting markets dictate the success and failure of the banks, Wall Street determines their fate. If the bank does well next quarter, the analysts write about the improved performance, spurring investment. Because the bankers own stock in their companies, seeing their personal fortunes improve makes next quarter's earnings really important.

More than that, the current incentive compensation systems within the industry reinforce the short-term outlook. Executive pay is tied so closely to short-term performance that there is no reason for a bank executive to think about the longer view unless the overall welfare of shareholders, employees, and their communities has any importance. Human nature is such that if you are getting "X" for a level of organizational performance, that's what you want to keep getting, or more. Therefore, there is no reason to invest dollars that will subtract from the bottom line (even if they can be capitalized) since it will end up in less compensation.

That's why cost cutting is so popular. It is easy to cut 10 percent to 15 percent of noninterest expense relative to growing share, which takes some time. If earnings for the year are going to be down, the quick solution is to slash some cost out to bring them back to the levels that the analysts want. But quicker is not always better.

The commitment to continuous quality improvement is for the long term and the rewards on that horizon will far outweigh those in the short term. Although most leaders would probably not admit it, this short-term view is the most serious and insurmountable of the impediments to quality in America's banks. It takes a courageous CEO to take that step.

I have often wondered what would happen if the bank would say to the analyst community:

> We're going to improve quality and service to our customers. In the process, we will lower costs and increase market share. It will take some time, but be patient with us. The financial results will be impressive and sustainable because we are in this for the long term.

"Banks think they deliver good quality service just because they don't get any complaint letters," says Bob Romano, managing partner with Romano & Sanfilippo, a service quality consulting firm in Escondido, California. "That's ridiculous. Dissatisfied people don't write letters. They just leave."[22] When they do, they take their loans, deposits, and fees to companies like Merrill Lynch. If we remember the lesson taught in the report of the General Accounting Office, offering a top-notch, first-rate, quality service is the best of all worlds. The companies in the sample lowered their cost by 9 percent while improving market share by 14 percent. It is hard to refute such data. It can be done, and it is being done.

THE TRANSITION

Some banks have been successful, however, in making the transition, and we can learn from them. P. Reed Brooks is senior vice president at Signet Bank in Richmond, Virginia. Reed and I served on the Advisory Board Company's Operations and Technology Council's Total Quality Management study in late 1993. He coordinates the service quality initiative at Signet and was gracious enough to be interviewed for this book along with Amy Sanderlin, who acts as team facilitator and teaches courses on quality improvement throughout the organization. The three of us talked about the importance of CEO involvement, and Reed said, "Service quality was clearly Bob Freeman's vision. He moved from president to CEO and started asking questions about it. We learned the basics and began educating people on the new service quality strategy. He's stayed the course in spite of criticism, and the stock's doing very well."[23]

I also spoke with George Nugent, Connie Remenschneider, and Chip Wyer of First of America Corporation. At the time of the interview, George Nugent was executive vice president and chief service officer, Connie was corporate quality service manager, and Chip was corporate quality service specialist. George reported directly to Daniel Smith, the chairman and chief executive officer of First of America. I asked about the beginnings of their service quality initiative. Connie responded, "The director of marketing, Bill Smith, was the advocate. He realized that quality would give us a competitive edge, so he formed a cross-functional task force to start looking at it. He wanted to get the bank organized around giving good service. It didn't come down from the CEO, but we knew we had his support."[24] It is, however, too bad it didn't last.

Arnie Weaver, president of Peoples State Bank of St. Joseph, Michigan, is another example. In response to changing markets and the recommendations of Executive Vice President Don Radde and Quality Analyst Maria Kibler, the bank, with Weaver's very evident support, embarked upon a change process focused on service. It started with education as workshops were made available to all employees, particularly the officer staff. The next step was to incorporate quality into the strategic plan. Market research, under LeAnn Krokker's direction, was used to formulate operating tactics with the management team meeting regularly to review progress. Then, the bank established an internal college, headed by Linda Lieberg, to teach everyone about the new direction. All of them indicate that they have just started on the journey, but are quite confident that it is the path to success.

In these three examples, it is evident that leadership is intent on changing the culture, to have a different outlook and to be the best. It takes courage to make that commitment. As I wrote in *Quality Value Banking,* "The key word is 'commitment'—long-term, unwavering, upheld-even-when-third-quarter-profits-are-down commitment."[25]

To compete in the new world means change—change in terms of individual and organizational behavior, triggered by the incredible technological advances that have been made in the recent past. It means abolishing the demeanor and deportment characteristic of America's bankers since the passage of the Federal Reserve Act in 1913 and the Glass-Steagall Act in 1933. However, reversing a behavioral model that has been ingrained in the way banking has been conducted is a serious and significant challenge. It may be easier to implement technological changes than to effect the organizational and behavioral ones.

It is changing from a focus on the internal workings of the organization, with all of its politics and game playing to see who can get ahead, to an attitude best described by one of our clients, Cliff Barlow at Peoples State Bank, who calls it "doorstep banking." What he means is that bankers have to take to the streets and the hallways to listen to their customers and to find out their expectations in the attempt to serve them better. It is a precursor of the concept of relationship banking, which will be the paradigm of the future.

The Banking Revolution is about organizational and personal change, transforming the bank, and changing its culture. It is not about the intricacies of technology. It is not about the economic vagaries of derivatives and the havoc they have caused banks like Barings and companies like Procter & Gamble. The subject is human behavior and what bankers will have to do personally and organizationally to survive in this ever-changing world.

We used to say that banking was easy. It really was when interest rates were set by the government and the money center banks, and the only competition was First National from Across-the-Street. That game is over. It ended when Merrill Lynch introduced the cash management account. And now there is the prospect of Microsoft. There is a brand new world out there: a world where consumers of financial products have a lot of new and different options and where service differentiates them. The banks have to duplicate the products at the very least; but to prosper, they will have to have an attitude and a culture of serving their customers better than any other institution. That's the revolution, and it's going to ask for change.

ENDNOTES

1. Katherine Morrall, "Service Quality: The Ultimate Differentiator," *Bank Marketing,* Oct. 1994, p. 36.
2. Bernard Baumohl, "Are Banks Obsolete?" *Time,* June 28, 1993, p. 49.
3. Ibid., p. 50.
4. Ibid., p. A14.
5. Conversation with Becky Montague, Cleveland, Ohio, Sept. 30, 1993.
6. Michael Siconolfi, "Merrill Lynch Pushing into Many New Lines, Expands Bank Services," *The Wall Street Journal,* July 7, 1993, p. A1.
7. Don Clark, "Microsoft Pact with Intuit Makes Gates a Power in Banking's New Digital Era," *The Wall Street Journal,* Oct. 17, 1994, p. A2.
8. Gregory A. Patterson, "Lands' End Kicks Out Modern New Managers, Rejecting a Makeover," *The Wall Street Journal,* April 3, 1995, p. A1.
9. Mary Walton, *The Deming Management Method* (New York: Perigee Books, 1986), p. 13.
10. Ibid., p. 14.
11. W. Edwards Deming, *Out of the Crisis* (Cambridge: Massachusetts Institute of Technology, 1986), p. 3.
12. Neal Templin, "Team Spirit: A Decisive Response to Crisis Brought Ford Enhanced Productivity," *The Wall Street Journal,* Dec. 15, 1992, p. A1.

13. Walton, The Deming Management Method, p. 18.

14. Ibid., p. 19.

15. Edmund Faltermeyer, "Competitiveness: How U.S. Companies Stack Up Now," *Fortune,* April 18, 1994, p. 55.

16. Ronald Henkoff, "Keeping Motorola on a Roll," *Fortune* April 18, 1994, p. 67.

17. Dirk Dusharme, "Baldrige Winners Take Stick," *Quality Digest,* May 1995, p. 9.

18. U.S. General Accounting Office, *Management Practices: U.S. Companies Improve Performance through Quality Efforts,* May 1991, pp. 23, 27.

19. 1992 Award Criteria, Malcolm Baldrige National Quality Award.

20. James Lordan, "Quality: Watchword of the 90s," *New England Banking Journal,* Spring 1991, front cover.

21. J. M. Juran, *Juran on Quality by Design* (New York: Free Press, 1992), pp. 11–12.

22. Morrall, "Service Quality" p. 33.

23. Interview with Reed Brooks and Amy Sanderlin, Signet Bank, Richmond, Va., Sept. 15, 1993.

24. Interview with George Nugent, Connie Remenschneider, and Chip Wyer, First of America Corporation, Kalamazoo, Mich., November 5, 1992.

25. Janet L. Gray and Thomas W. Harvey, *Quality Value Banking* (New York: John Wiley & Sons, 1992), p. 61.

CHAPTER 2

The New Opportunity

Business people are analytical. The controller sends out the monthly results to everyone in the company so that they can see how they did. It is a calling officer from the trust division who rifles to the end of her departmental income statement to see how much her customers contributed. It is the branch manager trying to see if his deposit levels met the plan. Numbers answer questions such as:

- How many loans did we book this month?
- What was the average rate?
- How did the demographics change?
- What was return on assets? Return on equity?
- How about earnings per share?
- What happened to the overhead ratio?
- What's total head count this month?

Numbers answer many more questions, most of them short term in nature. That is the heritage of the Industrial Revolution and the productivity increases that the machine age brought. Numbers tell companies what happened. They are also used to forecast future activity. It's also how Wall Street evaluates them.

In the mid-1800s, Frederick Taylor developed what came to be known as "scientific management," which was based on quantification of human activity. Everything that a person did could be broken down into definable and measurable tasks. Henry Ford, with his production line with interchangeable parts, added to the reliance on the numbers. Measurement became the symbol of the performance of the factory in the 20th century and remains so as we hurtle toward the 21st. Numbers are at the core of W. Edwards Deming's statistical process control, and we have all heard the phrase, "If you can't measure it, you can't manage it." So true.

Numbers and mathematics are the language of business. Customers order by numbers. Inventories are controlled by them. The value of the purchasing activity is represented by currency. Production runs are based on the amount of a product that is needed. Companies are valued using dollars. And of course the most important number is the stock price.

Bankers love their numbers as much as, or more than, other business people. When I was in charge of the accounting area in the bank, we had a group of people in internal reporting and another in external reporting. We also had groups of cost accountants, tax specialists, merger and acquisition professionals, financial analysts, budgeters, and forecasters, all of whom spent their days busily crunching numbers into their PCs and generating stacks of paper. I often thought we in finance should measure our productivity by the number of trees we used each month.

Every bank in the country measures profitability. Tax and securities laws require it. Other regulators need it, too. Revenues less expenses equals profits. Simple enough. Bankers calculate it for the entire organization and publish it in the annual report, so that shareholders, customers, employees, and the analysts can see how they are doing. They also rack up this organizational profitability on a quarterly basis, reporting it to the SEC, FDIC, Comptroller of the Currency, and Federal Reserve Bank. These regulators take the numbers and perform rigorous analysis to make sure that nothing is wrong or the least bit out of kilter.

Bankers also give the organizational results to the analysts and the rating agencies, the people on Wall Street who are so instrumental in influencing the price of the bank's stock. The attention that the analysts pay to the numbers and the recommendations that result from the analysis have caused bank managements to be ever watchful of the bottom line. It's hard, though, to play any game with one eye always on the scoreboard.

To complete the quarterly reports for the regulators and the analysts, the banks run their big, mainframe computers daily, generating a full balance sheet and income statement. We used to call it the "Daily Statement of Condition" and it had to be delivered to management by 10 o'clock every morning. I was never very sure of what they could do with it, even when they had it on time, but back then our assignment was to prepare it for their review. It was symptomatic of the short-term view.

The numbers are the basis for action. Inside the bank, numbers foster different strategies as management relies on them to guide future activities. Outside, investors use numbers to decide whether to buy or sell stock, and the regulators study them to see if they need to act. However, there is a huge assumption that accompanies this reporting of organizational profitability. It is historical in nature; it represents what is past. As such, there is nothing that can be done about it, but based upon those numbers—and seldom on things like consumer behavior—critical business decisions are made.

"WHAT CAN I DO WITH IT?"

To illustrate the point, a story follows that was critical to my thinking about management's reliance on this historical view. It first appeared in an article I wrote for *The Journal of Bank Cost and Management Accounting.* I have edited it slightly for relevancy.

> Late in 1986, after we [Society Corporation] had acquired and integrated Centran Corporation . . . we conducted another systems conversion, this time with our regional bank, which was headquartered in Dayton, Ohio. That conversion replaced all of the information sources that management of Interstate Financial, the acquired institution, had used in previous years and with which it was quite comfortable. . .
>
> Once the integration was complete, their CFO called and asked if I could visit with him and the CEO to review the monthly financial results. Since they were new at it, and it was my responsibility, I scheduled a meeting with them for the earliest convenient date. At the meeting, we reviewed some 40 pages of reports, profitability by region, sector within region, rates earned and paid, volumes of assets and liabilities, all compared to the plan; we looked at the net interest income and noninterest expense and their variances; I explained the charges from the management company for service rendered, the loan loss allocation, the corporate management allocation. But, after about an hour of this, the CEO said, simply, "That's great, but what can I do with it?"
>
> That was a question I had never considered before. What could management really do with the information that we worked so hard to produce?
>
> He continued, "Based on all of this, what action should I take? What behavior should I expect from my report points? You tell me that I'm favorable to plan in income. That's great, and I probably shouldn't do anything differently, right?"
>
> "Right," I said, feeling better.
>
> "Wrong," he countered. "Maybe there are cost reduction opportunities in the business sectors which would improve things. Maybe there are places where I can increase revenue streams. This pile of paper is great, but how does it help me to be more profitable? Where are my opportunities to get better?"
>
> "Huh?" He had me a little confused. We spent a lot of time and money on a management accounting system that apparently didn't serve the information requirements of management.

"All you give me," he continued, "is a snapshot of the last 30 days and the year compared to a plan that may or may not be any good. What can I do with it? It's just like baseball. If my kid makes an error, should he dwell on it? Seems unproductive to me. There's nothing he can do about it, and really, why should he? The only thing he can do is go on and make the next play. We, in management, look at the reports, give them a cursory review to make sure nothing major has happened, and go on. We can't do anything to change the results, so why pay much attention to them."

I was stunned! Maybe the executives don't really use the financial information we've been giving them. All that work for nothing. It doesn't help them sell more products, increase prices, decrease costs. It just tells them where they have been. Sort of like riding in the back seat of the old, family station wagon, from which you could only see the highway disappearing. A backward look, if you please, not looking at the road ahead and the curves and hills that are in front of the car. What you saw, looking at the road vanish, certainly didn't help in driving the car.[1]

Our regional CEO was unique. He was the only one who saw it this way. He was the only executive in the corporation who didn't exhibit elements of "analysis paralysis." He checked to make sure that the numbers verified what had happened and went on. As I thought about it, he made a lot of sense, but most bankers do not see it this way. It crushed my professional ego to hear what he had to say, but he was right. All we gave him was history. What did that help him do?

We thought we had an answer to that question. We'd give him more information about the past. We would calculate product profitability. We reasoned that every other sophisticated business knows what it costs to put its products in its stores; therefore we should, too. That would help our CEO in Dayton, we were sure. But there are some fatal flaws in the computation, most notably those concerning how the cost of facilities that support several services is allocated among them. Boy, would we argue about that! What percentage of the cost of the branch should be allocated to checking accounts? How much to savings accounts? Installment loans? What portion of operations should go to retail? To commercial? And on what basis? Then there was the matter of the revenue side. How would we account for waived fees, among other such profound questions.

The big question became the action to be taken if we found that a product was unprofitable. Could the bank stop offering checking accounts simply because they had little or no positive return? When all the arguing was over and we managed to come to some agreement on the cost allocations to different products, it was time to compute customer profitability. Someone had wondered aloud in a meeting if ABC Company was a profitable customer. That meant we had to know both the profitability of all services and the ones our customers used. Simple to say, very difficult to do. Here was still more arguing. If the product allocations weren't right (and they never were satisfactory for everyone), how could the measure of customer profitability be any better? Good point. Furthermore, the customer system was not set up so that we could guarantee that we had all of a particular customer's accounts under the right heading. I could have set up accounts under "T. Harvey," "Tom Harvey," and so on, which would make a profitability statement on me as a customer almost impossible. Addresses could be different; so could tax IDs. It was a big problem.

Unless specific cost accounting studies were performed for various services, the only numbers that really could be believed were the organizational ones. The others were too flawed. On the organizational side, though, the numbers had to be fairly accurate because they were reported to the regulatory agencies. However, when we provided information by business sector (e.g., retail, commercial), it was interesting watching people move the numbers around to their own advantage. I will never forget a meeting to discuss financial results in which the EVPs of retail and commercial gave presentations with numbers that were different from the official ones sent out by finance. The chairman just looked at me and said, "Well, which ones are right?"

After awhile, it seemed like all the numbers did was cause trouble. PCs made it worse. Everyone had his or her own spin. People would take numbers from the paper generated by the mainframe and key them into their machines to produce entirely different ones: a most unproductive task. We'd argue some more about these snapshots in time, not bothering to think about trends or what patterns might be emerging. What differentiates this approach from the traditional one is that the bank establishes relationships between strategies, behaviors, and the financial results. "Given the circumstances in the environment and what we did, how has the bank performed?" Not just at September 30, 1995, but over time. That stimulates even more thinking about behavior.

It also provides a database from which to forecast change. I am not talking about changes in asset and liability volume levels. I am speaking directly of behavioral change. "If we adopt a service quality strategy and if it takes 18 months for material improvements to be made, what will the income statement look like a year and a half from now? What things are we going to do? How much cost will be reduced? How much additional share will we have?"

This chapter is devoted to metrics and financial measurement. It asks you to start thinking about the numbers and their meaning in a different way. Don't rely on organizational profitability alone. View it with other information. Look at the numbers in a new way. The historical view is necessary for the regulators and it has some relevancy for the bank. But don't dwell on it, as "analysis paralysis" suggests. As we proceed, we will see some past results in a little different format. We will learn from them and move on. This is what you have to do in your banks. It is the lesson that I learned from our regional CEO in Dayton. The world is moving too fast for us not to listen and change.

THE FIRST CHANGE

Our premise in the banking revolution is change: change of thought, attitude, and action. In banking, the numbers guide all three. The first change is to start looking at some different, more meaningful numbers than a snapshot in time of their organizational, product, or customer profitability. Those numbers do not contain the information that is really necessary to manage the bank. Banks can only improve if they see, recognize, acknowledge, and deal with the current condition in the entire industry as it pertains to each individual one. Some of this might be old news, and some might dismiss it, but in the context in which it is presented, it provides ample evidence (1) that it is time to change how the numbers are viewed and (2) that other behavioral changes are necessary.

In the next few pages, we will be looking at some of the more critical numbers. They come from the Federal Reserve and the FDIC. I borrowed them to demonstrate the serious nature of the problem and the opportunity that awaits. They quantify what's happening in the new world. As you review the tables and exhibits that follow, think about what they mean but don't get too hung up on their implied precision. It makes no difference whether the industry earned $43.4 billion in 1993 or $46.7 billion. What is important is the behavior: Conditions were present that gave America's commercial banks higher earnings than ever before. Instead of simply proclaiming that everything is OK now that we earned so much, maybe our enthusiasm should be tempered in consideration of why it happened.

Optimism about the industry was buoyed by record earnings caused by unheard-of interest rate spreads. Rates charged on loans had not dropped as fast as those paid on deposits, which widened the margin between them to astronomical levels. Profits were $11.4 billion more than the previous mark of $32.0 billion set in 1992. It was an increase of 33 percent, which shows the abnormality. Bank earnings simply do not rise by one-third in any given year. It doesn't happen without an extraordinary circumstance, which is exactly what it was. Those earnings produced an average return on assets (ROA) for the industry of 1.20 percent, which was the first time a return over 1 percent was ever recorded (see Exhibit 2–1). That was a 30 percent increase in one year, which, even for the banker, should have been understood as an aberration, but wasn't.

For some more good news, there were no bank failures or any banks that had to be taken over by the government in the first quarter of 1994, the first time that had happened in over a decade, which is depicted in Exhibit 2–2.

The asset quality problems that had plagued the industry in the 1980s seemed to be over. It didn't look like any banks would have to take shelter with a merger partner due to their weakened financial position. No longer would they have to write off the risk-filled real estate loans, with their hopes of high returns, which had been put on the books when earnings were depressed just 10 years ago. The shadow of Barings and what its failure meant loomed on the

Return on Assets, 1989–1993

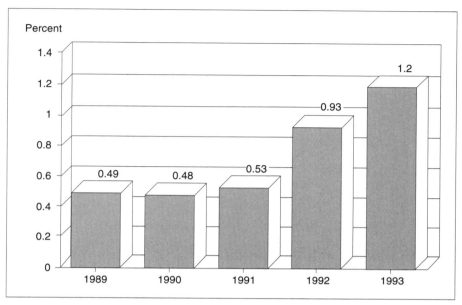

Source: Federal Deposit Insurance Corp.

Number of Failed/Assisted Institutions, 1989–1994, First Quarter

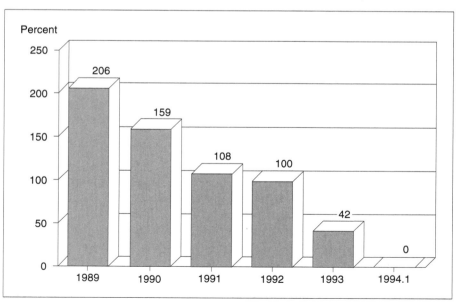

Source: FDIC Quarterly Banking Profile.

E X H I B I T 2-3

Total Loans and Leases, 1989–1993

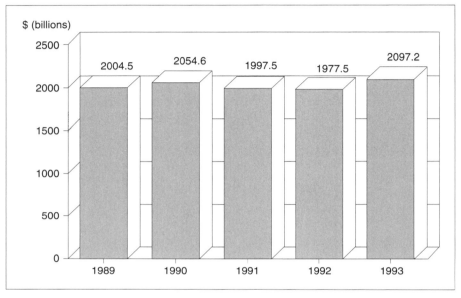

Source: Federal Deposit Insurance Corp.

horizon, but for the most part asset quality looked good. Earnings were way up and there was soundness in the banking system. If the review stopped there, it would be easy to conclude that everything was OK.

However, some disturbing news was being masked by this impressive performance. Commercial lending declined 7.5 percent between 1990 and 1992 (see Exhibit 2–3) as pension funds and insurance companies developed their own loan portfolios and U.S. corporations accessed the money markets directly. That is a behavioral change. This trend was reversed somewhat in 1994 as some banks showed nice growth, but the competition is fierce, forcing rate competition and some potentially uncomfortable risks. As that happens, bankers will experience a narrowing margin on a smaller loan portfolio in the future. That is what the consumers of these financial services are telling them. There are more alternatives for obtaining a loan than ever before, and they are being chosen. That's what this information suggests. It also calls for action. "Is this happening to us? If so, what can we do to stem the tide? If not, how can we make sure that it won't?" So, look at the trends in your portfolio and try to understand what the numbers mean in terms of the behavior of your customers. Then you can figure out what to do.

EXHIBIT 2–4

Total Deposits: Domestic Offices, 1989–1993

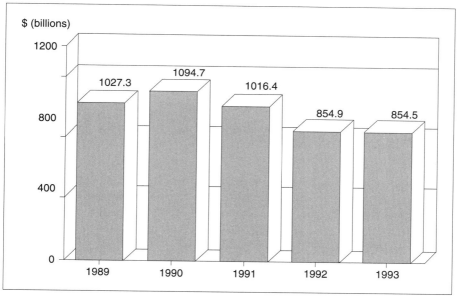

Source: Federal Deposit Insurance Corp.

Of equal concern is the liability side (see Exhibit 2–4). Time deposits in U.S. banks dropped by 21 percent from 1990 through 1992, as the mutual funds and stock market fueled the disintermediation. *Bank Marketing* reported in June 1994 that Americans had invested nearly $450 billion in mutual funds since 1990, three-fourths of which it was suggested will have to be replaced on the banks' balance sheets. The question is, Where will they find it?

Another problem on the liability side is the rampaging stock market. People are putting their savings into equities. And why not? The Dow Jones Industrial Average has climbed past 5,000, a number once considered inconceivable, and the value of personal and institutional portfolios increases as it goes up.

With higher rates being paid by the mutual funds and the tremendous appreciation in the equity markets, the banks have to realize that consumers really are not going to leave too much in their statement savings accounts. This is a new consumer behavior that should have been anticipated. Even though it was not, there's no time to wait. Bankers have to leave their offices, stare directly at the competition, and realize what the consumer is doing while they look at their own organizations to see how they can be restructured to let them compete. Any change in consumer behavior like this necessitates a change in the behavior of the banker.

> Since the banks [Society and KeyCorp] were actually combined last March, some key ratios have gone in the wrong direction for the bank. KeyCorp's return on assets dropped from 1.41% on March 31, 1994, to 1.28% on March 31 of this year. Its return on equity fell from 18.9% to 18.0% during the same period . . . KeyCorp has had a number of factors working against it since the merger . . . Interest rates rose sharply, causing the company to take $53.7 million in losses on its derivatives portfolio in the fourth quarter of 1994 and first quarter of 1995. The same rising interest rates cut into the company's net interest rate margin.[2]

It used to be that when the margin narrowed, the banks could increase their fees. Not any more, as consumers are getting tired of them. *Time*'s article, "The High Cost of Saving," was subtitled, "Customers grow irate as banks relentlessly jack up service fees and demand even larger deposits."[3] Again we have some hard evidence, represented by a new consumer behavior, that something is different. That should bring a new response.

Exhibit 2–5 displays the tremendous rise in the amount of noninterest income that the banks have generated over the past five years: from just under $45 billion in 1988 to almost double that in 1993. That is a huge increase in the charges levied on services that used to be free. Put a price on everything. That was the tactic developed in the 1980s. It may still be the thinking these days, even though customers are telling the banks something different.

Service charges on deposit accounts have been a direct contributor to this overall rise in total noninterest income, increasing 58 percent since 1988. Exhibit 2–6 demonstrates the increase that has contributed to consumer unhappiness.

> Maryellen Gordon is still fuming. When the Manhattan freelance writer opened a checking account at Manufacturers Hanover six years ago, she could keep as small a balance as she liked for a fee of $5 a month, and there was no charge for using the automated teller machines. Then Manufacturers Hanover merged with Chemical Bank in 1992, after which Gordon had to keep at least $3,000 in the bank to avoid being charged each time she used the ATM system. Enough was enough. Earlier this year, she took her money to a credit union where, for $2.50 per month, she can write as many checks as she wants—even draw her balance down to zero. "I probably had $25 taken out every month at Chemical," she recalls, "before I finally said, 'This is insane. What am I doing?'"[4]

Total Noninterest Income, 1988–1993

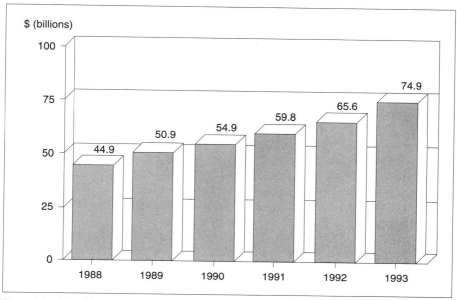

Source: Federal Deposit Insurance Corp.

Total Service Charges on Deposit Accounts, 1988–1993

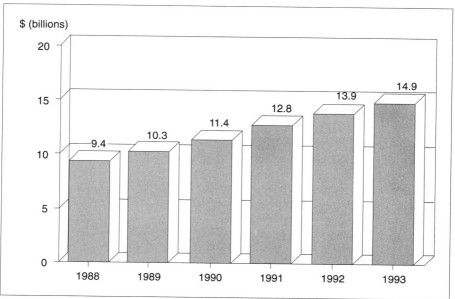

Source: Federal Deposit Insurance Corp.

EXHIBIT 2-7

How Some Bank Fees Have Risen, 1989–1993

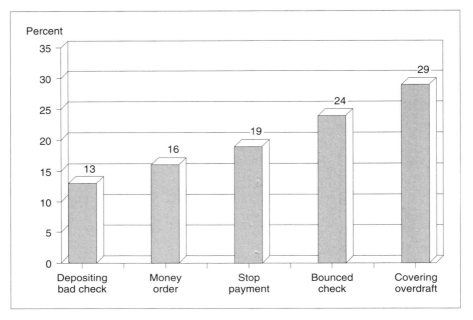

Source: Federal Reserve Bank.

USA Today also did a study on bank fees during the summer of 1994, the result of which is shown in Exhibit 2–7. No wonder consumers are upset. The paper included some of their comments:

> New Yorker Cheri Smith . . . who works for a publishing firm, can't afford the minimum balance. She pays $4 a month so she can write six checks or make ATM withdrawals on her account. After that, she is charged 50 cents per check and ATM use. "It's ridiculous; they charge you for taking *your* money out."
>
> Rep. Cardiss Collins, D-Ill., can afford to keep the minimum. But she did not know that if her balance at a Florida bank fell below the minimum, a $12 fee would eat what money remained.
>
> She learned the hard way when she tried to withdraw $300 and found that $300 wasn't left. When she replenished her account, she was hit with more fees: a $15 fee from the Chicago bank that wired the money and a $10 fee from the Florida bank for receiving the wire. "I paid $25 to have a lousy $300 wired to my bank," she says. "That's absurd."

EXHIBIT 2–8

Total Noninterest Expense, 1988–1993

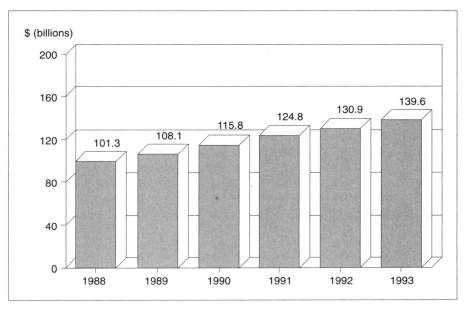

Source: Federal Deposit Insurance Corp.   •

"Banks have a license to steal," says Thomas McLoughlin, a Chicago re-
tiree who recalls when bounced checks cost 15 cents and depositing $300 got
you a toaster. "Put $300 in the bank now, and they charge you $3," he says.[5]

The bankers say that they have to charge customers to cover their expenses,
which is true. However their very cost structures are confusing. In 1993, noninterest expense grew again (see Exhibit 2–8), despite the draconian cost cutting
of the late 1980s. Only a few years ago the *New York Times, The Wall Street
Journal,* and the *Boston Globe* carried these headlines:

First Bank Systems' New Chairman Swings Ax and Tightens Purse Strings

Citicorp to Cut 4,250 Jobs over Two Years

Chase to Offer Severance to Employees

Fleet/Norstar to Cut 5% of Work Force

Ameritrust to Lay Off 780 in Move to Cut Expenses

Shawmut Posts Quarterly Loss, Will Cut Staff

E X H I B I T   2-9

Total Employees (FTEs), 1988–1993

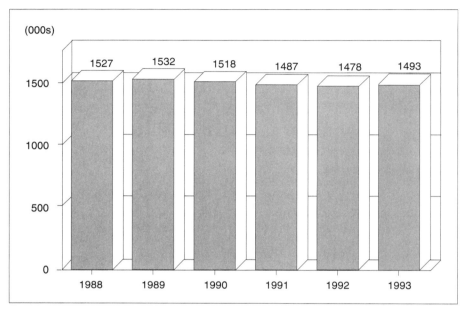

Source: Federal Deposit Insurance Corp.

They were not alone. In two surveys that we conducted for the National Association of Bank Cost and Management Accounting, 84 percent of over 400 banks had undertaken some kind of cost-reduction program between 1990 and 1994, but it does not appear that they were successful. Less than 5 percent of them had achieved savings of 10 percent or more while probably spending the same amount to conduct the program in the first place. In what is a most surprising statistic, according to the FDIC, total noninterest expense has increased 38 percent since 1988, from $101.3 billion to $139.6 billion in 1993, which is the period when the massive cost cutting was going on. It looks like it didn't work (see Exhibit 2–8).

At the same time, which makes it even more confusing, the number of banks decreased from about 14,000 to 11,400. With that, one would expect that overall costs and total head count would have come down. Costs have not been reduced, and head count has started to rise again as shown in Exhibit 2–9. After three years of modest decreases, the number of people working in the nation's commercial banks has increased to 1.493 million, a small expansion to be sure, but an interesting turn considering the continued public emphasis on cost containment.

EXHIBIT 2–10

Total Salary and Benefits, 1988–1993

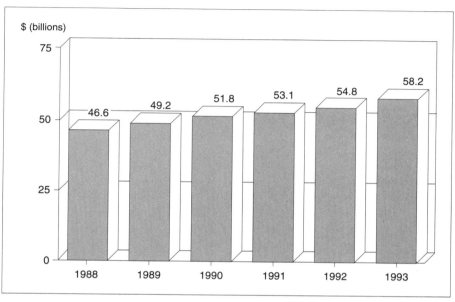

Source: Federal Deposit Insurance Corp.

An increase in the size of the workforce results in greater salary and benefit expense, which has grown almost 25 percent since 1988 and is the major contributor to overall expense growth. Even with the pressure to keep head count as low as possible, compensation expense has risen consistently every year (see Exhibit 2–10). That is caused by the automatic merit increases that all bankers have come to expect and by the expanded financial packages that are now enjoyed by many higher-ranking executives.

However, expenses are not only increasing on the "people" side. In spite of all the warnings about the new and different competition and their innovative ways to provide banking services, the number of banking locations in the United States also continues to increase. With the total number of banks decreasing, logic would suggest that there should be fewer branches, which is not the case. Those that remain are continuing to invest in "brick and mortar" while their new competitors are taking advantage of electronic distribution systems that render banks obsolete.

AT&T Corp. will offer consumers a bank-at-home system that operates on television screens. To use the system, consumers must purchase a $350 device that plugs into TV sets or lease the box for $13.95 a month. The service,

EXHIBIT 2-11

Operating Costs as a Percent of Bank Assets, 1989–1993

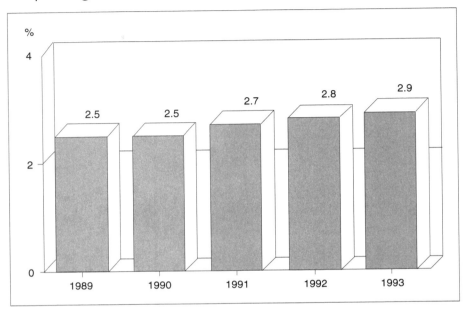

Source: *American Banker.*

AT&T Checkfree, allows consumers to pay bills electronically by entering commands onto a video program that appears on the TV. . . To make payments, consumers must provide bank account information to Checkfree and tell the company what merchants it wants to pay. The system should be available by late summer [1995].[6]

If the investment in branches and buildings brought an increased return, they might be justified, but expenses in America's banks are growing faster than the asset bases they support (see Exhibit 2–11). That says that they add a little more expense every time they put a loan on the books or invest in a branch, quite the opposite of the "economy of scale" that they want.

The banks that have been innovative with their electronics will achieve advantage over their banking competitors who continue to pour money into bricks and mortar, and perhaps even over Merrill Lynch, Fidelity, and all the rest. The crucial point to understand is the difference in the thought processes at some banks, such as Huntington and First Chicago, which have seen the future like AT&T and Microsoft have. Unlike the other banks, they are streamlining or modernizing their physical locations by installing electronic equipment that will make it faster and easier for their customers to transact their banking business. On the other hand, some financial institutions are continuing to focus on reducing expenses by cutting out jobs, not changing their delivery systems, which will make it even harder for their customers to deal with them. Once again, it is the thinking that has to be reevaluated and changed.

That's the crisis that Dr. Deming taught had to happen for substantial change to occur. Banks have to think about the welfare of their customers if they are to survive. Deposit disintermediation exists, forcing the banks to replace what is lost with higher cost funds, effectively narrowing the gross margin. Rates earned on loans also are narrowing, closing the margin even further. Fees, as noted, are under significant consumer pressure and may not be able to be raised, especially if the nonbanks cut them. Noninterest expense continues to rise as more people are hired and more locations are built while service quality continues to decline. Therefore, the income statement, which Wall Street uses to judge the effectiveness of the performance of the nation's banks, is under pressure in all four quadrants:

Lower interest income

Higher interest expense

Lower noninterest income

Higher noninterest expense

All that we hear is that everything is just fine. Business goes on as usual. It's *ostrich syndrome* again. Just put your head under the pillow for a few days and the problems will go away. Just ignore them. But it doesn't work that way.

Conversations with leading bankers across the country have made it evident that they don't think the threat is real. Not only is there significant disintermediation occurring, but also a major demographic shift. For the first time in history, the largest U.S. corporations have more relationships with foreign banks than they do with domestic ones, as reported in *The Wall Street Journal* (see Exhibit 2–12).

What does this mean? *The Wall Street Journal* interpreted it to be "another sign of the U.S. banking system losing its competitive edge,"[7] and that did not include the advances of the nonbanks such as Merrill Lynch, First Boston, and Dean Witter. The concern is one of competitive edge. It bears repeating that the banks used to be the only game in town. Now, however, every service that they offer has been duplicated by nonbanks and the foreign competition, often at a lower price, with better rates and higher quality. As *Business Week* suggests, all of this "could be the first sign of a problem in the making."[8]

There is an answer. There is a way to improve overall financial performance. Attack the cost of poor quality. Redirect your energy to an understanding of what people do all day and eliminate the things that add no value to the

E X H I B I T   2-12

Banking Relationships, 1987–1993

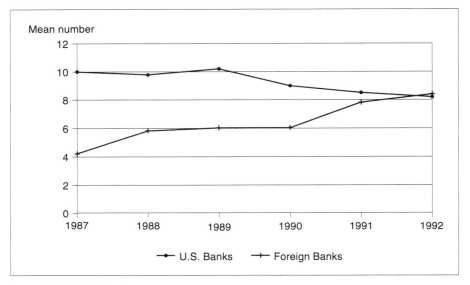

Source: *The Wall Street Journal.*

customer. It's a change in thought, attitude, and action, but that is what has to happen. So much of the waste in the bank's bureaucracy can be eliminated. As that happens, costs go down and share goes up. That is the new opportunity.

THE COST OF QUALITY

Philip B. Crosby introduced the subject of the cost of quality in the late 1970s with his landmark book, *Quality Is Free.* He had begun to apply the principles of Deming at ITT, where he was in charge of quality improvement. Back then, this was new stuff because service excellence was only starting to be the subject of conversation in American business. Not until 1980 did we see Clare Crawford-Mason's documentary, *If Japan Can . . . Why Can't We?* Two years later *In Search of Excellence* was published, and the Malcolm Baldrige National Quality Award did not appear until 1987. As a nation, we have had the relatively short period of slightly over 15 years to learn and understand how powerful a competitive weapon the commitment to quality can be.

Very few people, Crosby among them, understood the relationship of high quality and low cost that Deming taught. We still don't hear much about it, nor do many managers think of cost as representative of the behavior of the workforce or realize that what happens in the bank every day ultimately ends up on the income statement.

If bankers accept the notion that they must be focused on the singular goal of serving customers, they must look at their cost structures in that regard. America's bankers must examine their expense bases, asking the questions, "Why are we incurring this cost?" "How does it add value to serving our customers?" "Is there a better way?" This is a revolutionary way of looking at cost. It quantifies the daily actions of workers as they carry out their duties and responsibilities. It allows you to see the cost of what people are being asked to do in a very different way, and it enables you to see how that behavior relates to customer service. Most people equate salary and benefit expense with numbers of people, not with the activities, tasks, and functions in which people are engaged. In their way of thinking, if the bottom line fails to meet the plan or if expenses are too high, then people must go, which is exactly what has happened recently at such notable institutions as CoreStates, First Interstate, and even the venerable J. P. Morgan.

You must look at what is being done, not the absolute number of people on the payroll. It is not enough to look at the financial results and say, "Oops, too much expense, too many people, we have to cut." But that is what happens.

Here is an example from outside the banking arena:

> In late 1994, the Secured Asset Fund Earnings (SAFE) investment program of Cuyahoga County (Ohio) collapsed, resulting in a $115 million loss. As a result the county commissioners ordered all departments to cut expenses by 11 percent across-the-board to make up the loss.
>
> Having no choice, the county's departments began to comply. Management of a particular organization eliminated 700 jobs, some very essential people among them. To pay for losses in the portfolio, the people, who had no conceivable relationship to it, or had even heard of it, were let go. Because of fiscal irresponsibility on the part of politicians, qualified and competent professionals who brought needed service to the community were discharged. That service will now be missing.

To make the right move, you have to look at what people do and why they are doing it, avoiding the knee-jerk reaction to slash-and-burn in the organization. If an 11 percent budget reduction had to happen in the organization cited above, and the management had no choice, its first step should have been to look at the components of the cost structure, separating it into the two basic elements: the cost of conformance and the cost of nonconformance. Then it would have known what, and if anything, could be cut.

THE COST OF CONFORMANCE/NONCONFORMANCE

At this organization and in any other, the leadership would have had to look at the expense side of the income statement differently, as we will do now. It can be broken down into various kinds of behavior as the bank seeks to understand *why* the cost base is as it is. "Cost" can be divided into two main categories:

The cost of conformance.

The cost of nonconformance.

The cost of conformance, in behavioral terms, can be thought of as the expense that is incurred to reduce the possibility of failing in the customer's eyes, which is the worst thing that can happen, as we will see.

The cost of conformance is the desired state, that is, making sure that the service the bank is delivering to its customers meets or exceeds their expectations. It includes:

- Education of the workforce about new services.
- Having sufficient personnel to meet customer "wait time" anticipation.
- ATMs that are operational at times customers want them to be.
- Preparing and delivering accurate and timely statements.
- Answering and returning telephone calls in a timely fashion.
- Doing budgets once or, at the outside, twice.
- Conducting productive and thorough meetings.

Prevention

The cost of conformance is the expense associated with pleasing customers: understanding their wants and needs and doing only those things that satisfy them. One of its main components is prevention expense.

One of my clients defines *prevention* as "planning, meeting, or satisfying a need in advance." These are the costs of anticipation, the design of the desired behavior. *Prevention expense* is the amount spent to make sure that the bank delivers its service to its customers the way they want it, the first time, and every time thereafter. We call it DIRFT: Do It Right the First Time.

For example, the failure rate of a Xerox machine in the early 1980s was 10 percent, which meant that 1 copy out of every 10 had to be redone. If the cost to make a copy was $.02, the direct cost to make 10 copies became $.22, instead of $.20, and that did not include the "people expense" required to make the additional copy. Now, 2/10 of a cent doesn't sound like much, but think about a continual 10 percent overrun on *all* of the copies that are made in your organization. That gets expensive, but most people don't think about it that way. They do not relate it to the actions that reflect cost, albeit in the smallest of increments, but that is the change in their thinking that is needed.

At Xerox, the response was to listen to the complaints of its customers, to understand what they were saying, and to concentrate on prevention, particularly on the design of the machines. The company devoted time and energy to eliminating the possibility of unusable copies before they happened. As a result, users of Xerox machines spent much less time rerunning copies and grousing about how bad the machines were. In doing so, the overall defect rate dropped to 2 percent from 10 percent, and Xerox customers catapulted the company back to the forefront of the photocopier market. Because of increasing competition, even a 2 percent defect rate was unacceptable, so resources continue to be applied to ways to reduce it even further.

The crucial question for bankers is, What can we do to make sure that our customers are satisfied with the service we provide?

Inspection/Detection

The cost of conformance, though, is not limited to prevention. Also included in this category are some of the expenses that are incurred within the bank to ensure that what is being delivered to customers meets their expectations, or what it thinks they want. These are the costs of *inspection* and *detection,* which can be formal techniques or ones that have evolved or developed in response to a crisis. Some of the more formal ones, like the Audit Department, for example, have to be there for very good legal or regulatory reasons. Others, such as edit runs in computer programs to ensure that interest has been posted properly, have been adopted for sound business reasons.

Inspection and detection may have evolved over time as well, and may or may not be necessary. Think of the situation in finance where one person checks the work of an associate who is responsible for the accuracy of the numbers in the board report. The question has to be, is this action necessary or isn't it? If the answer to the question is yes, the next one to ask is, Why? Any that are considered unnecessary are candidates for elimination.

The bank must identify which inspection and detection techniques are valid and which are not. The review of loan documentation to make sure that it complies with all legal and regulatory requirements is a legitimate inspection function, as is ensuring that an invoice from a vendor matches the terms and conditions on the original purchase order. Balancing on the teller line at the end of the day is another, but there are excesses that happen every day.

This is where the 30 percent comes in and, as you wander around your organization, start looking for them. You might find one that resembles the situation that happened a couple of years ago at the meeting of the quality committee of a large and well-respected financial institution.

At this particular session, the manager of the trust department proudly announced that he and his people were committed to 100 percent accuracy. However, they had become suspicious that the statements sent to their customers were not correct. Even though they had not had any complaints about the statements, they instituted a program to make sure that the statements were right in the effort to provide the highest quality service.

As the manager of information systems rolled her eyes toward the ceiling, her counterpart from trust began to relate his story. Since the bank had started the quality initiative, he said, it was important to make sure that customer statements were correct. He had never questioned their accuracy before, but with the new emphasis on excellence, he wasn't sure that what was being sent to them was right. How, he had asked, could he report to the quality council that his service was of the highest caliber?

So, he continued, he had directed the head of the data processing department to send the statements and envelopes over to the main office and not directly to the bank's customers as they had done successfully for as long as anyone could remember. When they arrived, trust officers and administrative assistants spent hours checking them, stuffing them into envelopes, and taking them back to the mail room for delivery to their customers, which by this point was sometimes delayed by over two weeks.

After several months of reporting 100 percent accuracy to the quality council, someone finally asked, "Did these diligent members of your staff find any mistakes?"

"Well, no," the trust department manager answered. "We thought we found one once."

"Would they have really known one if they had seen one?" came the follow-up question.

After some prolonged and uncomfortable silence, and with some considerable thought, he admitted, "Probably not."

The crucial point in the story is that the trust department staff were looking at a perception that was not real. As a result, they had spent a lot of money needlessly. The energy and time it consumed resulted in unnecessary cost. People were being paid to do something that was not required. However, unless someone questioned this behavior, the cost would probably have gone unnoticed as long as it was within the budget. If the line item for salary remained under budget, nobody would have said anything.

In all likelihood, the behavior would have continued until that decisive quality council meeting when someone challenged it as unproductive and adding no value to the customer. As soon as the idea to check the statements was proposed, someone should have said, "Wait a minute, that just doesn't make any sense." The behavior of checking would not add any value and it would result in the delivery of statements later than customers expected. It was needlessly expensive and, even worse, it detracted from serving customers despite the good intentions. But nobody asked the question. Further, it only would have become apparent by looking at the behavior of the staff because traditional accounting systems would not have revealed the problem.

At a time when trust officers and their assistants should have been working with their existing customers and prospecting for new ones, there they were, sitting on the floor, searching for errors, all the while not knowing what one looked like. They should have determined whether the statements were factually wrong, how many were incorrect, if the same problem occurred on different days, and how long it had been happening. Doing so would allow them to pinpoint the problem, if there was one, and to correct it at its source and not to chase a problem that did not exist.

This invalid cost of *inspection* and *detection* can be eliminated, but only in terms of the behavior that it represents. That is why indiscriminate cost cutting doesn't work. That action only goes after expenses with no consideration for the behavior that those costs represent. Cost cutting always includes activities and functions that customers value.

The cost of nonconformance, then, is the expense incurred in performing tasks and assignments that add no value to the customer. These are the expenses that are involved in doing wrong things and in doing things wrong, even though the intention might be good. The motive of the manager of the trust department in the story was surely to provide excellent customer service by having accurate statements. The problem was not with that; rather, it was with the behavior he asked of his people.

Even with some *inspection* and *detection* costs being valid and necessary, others, such as those in the trust story, fall into the category of nonconformance. In our experience, we have found that bankers are notorious checkers. People are on the payroll simply to police the actions of others. It is as if no one trusts anyone else to do the job right the first time. Then the person hired as the "police person" also has to have his or her work checked by somebody else. In most cases, it is for no good reason, but an outgrowth of banking's traditional command-and-control management style.

Most of us would be surprised at the amount of checking that goes on in our banks every day to make sure that nothing goes wrong. We asked a client that was looking at the effectiveness of its mortgage lending process to classify its costs into prevention and inspection/detection. A process improvement team was assembled to work on the matter. The results of their analysis are shown in Table 2–1.

After they had compiled the list, the next challenge for this group was to identify the amount of time spent in each one of these activities. That would enable us to approximate the actual cost of this behavior and to eliminate as much of it as we could. Checking to make sure that things were being done right came out to be about 60 percent of the annual budget.

T A B L E   2–1

Mortgage Lending Prevention and Inspection/Detection Techniques

Prevention Techniques	Inspection/Detection Techniques
Accurate account/management information	ALCO portfolio review
	Application review by loan processor
Authorization policies	Appraisal reinspection
Automated applications/laptop PCs	Batch/proof of monthly transactions
Automatic payment processing	Coupon book order review
Convenient customer hours	Daily transaction balance
Insurance/investment policies	Data input review of new loans
Product training	Escrow reports
Service training	Executive committee review
Underwriting criteria	External audit review
	File maintenance input review
	Fixed-rate loan monitoring
	Foreclosure reviews
	General ledger reconcilements
	Hazard insurance tracking
	Internal audit review
	Legal reviews of title information
	Loan collection activities
	Loan collection reports
	Loan committee(s) review
	Mortgage insurance tracking
	Nonaccrual reports
	Payoff inquiry log and review
	Plot reviews on releases
	Preforeclosure inspections
	Quality control review
	Regulatory agency review
	Repricing reviews
	Review of closed loan file
	Review of investor reporting
	Secondary market review
	Transaction approval review
	Underwriting review
	Verification of consumer credit

An enormous amount of this kind of inspection is going on everyday in every department and operation of the bank. It results in unnecessary costs, lower earnings, and, ultimately, reduced shareholder value. It also lowers the trust level between people who are supposed to be teammates in the service of the bank's customers. The cost of nonconformance can be decreased only by doing an activity or task right the first time.

Failure and Correction

Sadly, however, errors do happen, even with all of this checking. The president of the bank was invited to see the results of the work of the client's mortgage lending team. We had made a flowchart of the various activities involved and had annotated the reasons for them. As he was looking at the flowcharts, I heard him say, "Prevention, inspection, correction, review, correction, inspection, failure, correction, inspection. We spend all this money on making sure errors don't happen, and THEY STILL DO!"

The dictionary has a rather harsh definition for the word *error:*

error *n.*
_____
something incorrectly done through ignorance or carelessness

I might add "through lack of instruction and/or education" or "because we have always done it this way," because most mistakes are not the fault of the individuals who have made them. In any event, errors do occur for a variety of reasons, and they must be fixed. We call these tasks *failure* and *correction* activities. They are by far the most expensive activities as far as the bank is concerned.

There are two types of failure and correction: internal and external. *Internal failure and correction* is defined as fixing something that has gone wrong before it reaches the final consumer. It happens all over the bank. Think about the number of times a report, letter, or memo has to be corrected before it is sent to the final recipient. Then think about what that behavior costs.

Here's a hypothetical story about internal failure that is based on a real circumstance. As we walk through it, think about the times you have seen a similar situation. It happened at a smaller institution, which was embroiled in a competitive battle with a couple of large regionals that had purchased the other independent banks in the area.

It begins with our bank—let's call it Farmers & Merchants—that outsourced its computer work to a reputable time-sharing vendor located 200 miles away. The vendor, XYZ Systems, was responsive and attentive to the needs of F&M and apparently of its other clients as well.

In essence, XYZ functioned as F&M's systems department. It took daily transactions over the phone lines each night, processed them, and provided reports the following day. Statements were rendered as required and were sent to F&M for mailing to the bank's customers. On this particular Wednesday morning, the bank's quality council was meeting when the manager of operations was called out of the room. She came back a few minutes later and announced, "The statements are wrong. They have the wrong interest calculation." What should the bank do?

Debate ranged from sending the statements, even though they were wrong, to the bank's customers so that they would be received on time to asking XYZ to change the interest calculation and to run the statements again. That would mean that the statements would be late, but accurate. A third party suggested that they "white out" the wrong numbers, type in the right ones, and send the statements out. That suggestion, thankfully, was quickly rejected.

The outcome of the conversation corrected this *internal failure*. The operations manager called XYZ, provided the correct calculation, and asked that the statements be reprocessed that same night. The corrected ones arrived two days later and were sent out. The majority of the bank's customers never knew there had been a problem.

The bank had provided the expected service but incurred a lot of unnecessary expense, primarily in terms of the incremental time it took to deal with the problem. Additional statements had to be ordered, but it was a small price to pay. Nevertheless, all of this corrective activity was unnecessary. It is represented by an increase in cost, but it is the behavior, not the cost, that is the point. If F&M and XYZ had taken the time up front to validate the computation, they would have avoided the failure and subsequent correction, the last two components of the cost of nonconformance.

Both parties were responsible for the problem. The hard part is being critical of your own behavior. It was very easy to rationalize that XYZ should be blamed, a blame which it should share with the bank, but these kinds of things happen all over the bank. If instructions had been clear, perhaps the entire problem never would have happened. Make a note right now to start looking at these kinds of things and see how many failures like this occur over the next week.

As you do so, assign a time value to the failure and correction. That will allow you to put a cost on it. Then begin to question the behavior of the people involved, even yourself. Ask them why the task could not have been done right the first time. Explain to them how expensive their actions are and how their time could have been used in preventive modes and not in failure and correction. Watch out for their responses because they might be a bit defensive.

At the conclusion of Chapter 2 is a worksheet that you can use to record the times that you see this kind of behavior, the time it takes, and the reasons people give as explanation. Once completed, it will make for some interesting reading after a week or so. Turn to it now and familiarize yourself with it. In the morning, make a copy of it and go to work.

The point of all this is simple, yet profound: The cost of poor quality is very real, and as you will see, failure and correction are very expensive.

The most damaging of the dimensions of the cost of quality is *external failure,* which means that a mistake has reached the customer. It differs from internal failure because the error left the bank; you can't get it back to fix it and customers begin to question your ability to provide the service that they want. In *Quality Value Banking,* we cited an example of external failure that is quick and to the point. At Quality Forum VII in New York in October 1991, the president of Ricoh, Hiroshi Hamada, told the audience and to those watching on television that after making a line of copiers available to the market and installing several of them, a defect was discovered. All of the copiers, those that had been sold to customers and those that were waiting in stores and Ricoh distribution centers, had to be recalled and reengineered to correct the mistake. Hamada estimated the cost of the error at each possible prevention and detection point:

Design phase	$35
Before production	$368
Before shipment	$17,000
Recall/correction	$590,000

The cost to fix the problem was nearly *17,000* times greater than the cost of preventing it in the first place.[9] That does not include the cost of the negative word-of-mouth advertising that occurred as Ricoh's customers grumbled to their friends and business associates. Just think about the number of people you tell about the poor service you receive at the grocery store, the damage the dry cleaner did to your favorite blouse, the recall of your minivan for a $.04 washer, and the length of the line at the post office. It is the same thing with customers of the bank.

Recently, I happened to be in the line at the post office. The gentleman in front of me sighed as the minutes ticked away, "This is just like the bank." Do people talk about the poor service they experience at your bank? You bet. The only consolation is that the bank across the street doesn't offer any better service so there isn't much choice, but there certainly is with Merrill Lynch, First Boston, and the more progressive institutions like Security First Network Bank, that were first in line on the Internet.

What do they talk about? There are hundreds of examples, but three will suffice. First, there is the story about the bank that paid one of its quarterly dividends *twice* on the same day. Think of what it cost to issue "stop payments" on a million duplicated dividend checks and the more than $250,000 cost of unnecessary postage. Then think about the bank's image among shareholders, many of whom were customers as well. Many of them wondered, "If they can't get the dividend right, what will they do with my accounts?"

Then there was the bank's marketing department that was asked to develop a flyer announcing an increase in NSF charges, which was to apply to all retail deposit accounts. The flyer was to be included in the July statements. Responsibly, marketing created the announcement, obtained the approval of the retail banking committee, had the printing done, and delivered the final product to the mail room. Not only did the fee announcement come as a surprise to the bank's customers, but it also was out of line with other banks in the area. After taking a considerable number of complaints, the fee was rolled back to what it had been before. A simple example, yes, but it happens all the time.

The last banking story is about ATMs. How many times have you visited one and the message on the screen indicated that it was being serviced? At 10:00 A.M. on Saturday or 45 minutes before flight time? Even though the woman you saw walking back to her car was shaking her head and grumbling about finding another ATM, you approached it, hoping that the same fate wouldn't happen to you. It seems that is impossible to get cash only at the most critical moments.

One more example of external failure. In response to an automobile recall notice, I took my car to the dealer to have a seat belt release fixed. It was done quickly and expertly, but I thought if 100,000 people have cars like mine and it costs $250 to correct the problem, that's $25 million which will be added to the price of the next line of cars that we will be asked to buy. The question then is, Will I buy a car that costs more and is potentially less reliable than others that are available to me? It is the same with banks because more alternatives are available to banking customers every day. External failure is deadly.

POOR QUALITY? IT IS EXPENSIVE!

Len Berry, a coauthor of *Service Quality,* is also professor of marketing at Texas A&M University. Len was the first person who I heard advance the notion that quality could be a profit strategy. In 1988, he gave a speech called "Principles of Service Quality" to the officers of Society Corporation in which he talked about the economic value of providing services that customers want and in the way that they want them. He told the group:

TABLE 2-2

Cost of Quality Estimate

20% of sales revenues	Malcolm Baldrige National Quality Award
30% of expenses	Ernst & Young
30% of expenses	McKinsey
40% of expenses	Philip Crosby
30% of manufacturing cost	IBM Corporation
30% of sales	Dr. J. M. Juran
17% of manufacturing cost	Dr. W. Edwards Deming
25% of noninterest expense	BancOne

Service quality *differentiates* one company from another. Whereas competing service organizations offer the same types of services, they do not offer the same service. Service excellence is the *one* strategy dimension that is both important to customers and difficult for competitors to duplicate. . . There are various costs of poor service, several of which are overlooked.

1. Loss of market share.
2. Higher employee turnover and recruiting costs.
3. The costs of correcting mistakes.
4. Higher marketing costs.[10]

At the time, I was skeptical of this innovative concept. Quality as a profit strategy? Then I learned about the 30 percent of noninterest expense that represented doing things wrong or activities that did not add any value to the customer.

That was the connection. If we were doing things wrong, it was costing the bank needlessly. More important, however, if that were the case, our customers probably weren't very pleased with the service they were getting and maybe they were starting to look for another bank or brokerage to take care of their financial needs. I began to play with the numbers; when I took 30 percent of noninterest expense for our bank, I found that it was more than we had earned the previous year. Now, who in their right mind would tell the chairman something like that? Neither he nor anyone else would believe it. So, I challenged the 30 percent number, did some firsthand research, and found some very consistent support for it (see Table 2–2).

E X H I B I T 2-13

The Cost of Quality

Noninterest expense, 1994	$500 million
Cost of quality	× 15%
Total improvement opportunity	$75 million
Tax effect	× 65%
Total potential benefit	$49 million

Whichever estimate we choose, it is still a big number. In the next several pages, we will work through the cost of quality calculation and will relate it to consumer behavior. At the end of this chapter is a set of worksheets titled "The Cost of Quality," which you can complete for your department and/or bank. It mirrors the series of steps that follow. The purpose is to demonstrate the kind of opportunities available for improvement.

Recognizing that the 30 percent figure for noninterest expense may be a little unbelievable, even though there is strong support for it, we will use 15 percent as the target for the waste and rework that can be eliminated. The initial computation is quite simple (see Exhibit 2–13).

By examining, changing, and eliminating behaviors that add no value to customers in a systemic way, this bank would be able to achieve savings of $49 million after tax. It had posted a return on assets (ROA) of 1.05 percent and a return on equity (ROE) of 16.10 percent. Adding the $49 million to 1995's net income and recomputing these ratios results in ROA of *1.38%* and ROE of *21.22%* as shown in Exhibit 2–14.

What does this mean? Simply this: If the bank is spending money to commit errors and make mistakes, and then to fix and correct them, it is incurring unnecessary expense. If it is spending needlessly, the cost to deliver service is higher than it should be. If that is the case, the cost to deliver can be systematically decreased, which provides increased margins and greater earnings.

Think about the adjustment department; it exists to fix a constant stream of mistakes and errors made by other people and their machines. Also, remember the trust department. It engaged in a series of unnecessary behaviors when it attempted to isolate errors that did not exist—chasing ghosts, as it were. Then think about the flyer that the marketing department developed, only to have the whole thing reversed. If the bank can eliminate those kinds of behaviors and can emphasize and reward accuracy the first time, the cost of quality as shown in Exhibit 2–13 will automatically decrease.

What usually happens in the bank? When a problem first occurs, additional resources are thrown at its symptom to the detriment of performance

E X H I B I T   2–14

Impact of Quality Improvement

	Before Improvement	After Improvement
ROA	1.05%	1.38%
ROE	16.10%	21.22%

somewhere else within the organization. In effect, it tolerates and acknowledges that transactions cannot be done right the first time and pays for additional people to fix them, causing a negative impact on the margin. As long as mistakes aren't reaching the customer, most people are happy, but there is a huge opportunity there. At a time when earnings are under increasing pressure, attacking the cost of poor quality is the only successful way to lower or contain expenses.

Everyone wants to keep costs as low as possible. Wall Street and management certainly do. Banks have tried to raise revenues and have now hit narrowing margins and the maximum levels of fees and other charges. The cost side is all they have left. To be competitive, it has to be kept as low as possible. "The shift clearly has been to wring out expenses," says James McDermott, an analyst at Keefe, Bruyette & Woods.[11] Carving out the cost of failure and correction achieves that objective, but in an entirely different way. It provides value to the customer and increases earnings. That has a very positive impact on the stock.

A few years ago, Sanford Rose wrote in the *American Banker* about the effect of a reduction in expenses on the stock price. He reported that First Manhattan Consulting Group's economic model suggested that modest cost decreases result in substantial appreciation in the price of a common share. Without going through all of the metrics, Rose stated, "By trimming just 35 basis points from its 275 basis point expense burden, the undifferentiated bank can achieve an improvement in overall stock valuation of between 60 percent and 65 percent."[12]

Hold on a second! Was First Manhattan saying that the effect of a cost decrease like the one shown in Exhibit 2–13 will be reflected positively in the bank's stock price? By 60 percent. If cost reduction is sustainable, which is what happens when the bank attacks the cost of poor quality, the appreciation in stock price is quite real.

The calculation in the *American Banker* assumed that a "mere 13 percent" reduction in expenses would result in a 60 percent to 65 percent increase in the share price. The model shown in Exhibit 2–13 shows that a pretax decrease of 15 percent is achievable simply by eliminating the costs of correction, failure, and some inspection/detection. The bank that can do that will see its expenses drop and its stock price grow, thereby enriching its stockholders. Further, it will also be providing better service to its customers, which results in fewer accounts being closed and even more earnings. What's the catch?

There is only one: Reducing the cost of quality is a longer-term solution than cutting costs across the board. If the bank wants to hype ROA and ROE in time for next quarter's earnings release, it will have to use the traditional slash-and-burn head-count reduction approach that has been the standard in banking since the mid-1980s. However, as we saw in Exhibit 2–8, these kinds of actions have not been successful in the past and, as noninterest expenses continue to grow, they are unlikely to yield any sustainable benefit in the future. What we need has to be totally different! Revolutionary!

> For years, for example, American manufacturers thought they had to choose between low cost and high quality. "Higher quality products cost more to manufacture," they thought. "They take longer to assemble, require more expensive materials and components and entail more extensive quality controls." What they didn't consider was all the ways that increasing quality and lowering costs could go hand in hand over time. *What they didn't consider was how basic improvements in work processes could eliminate rework, eliminate quality inspectors, reduce customer complaints, lower warranty costs, increase customer loyalty, and reduce advertising and sales promotion costs. They didn't realize that they could have both goals, if they were willing to wait for one while they focused on the other.* [Italics added.][13]

Reducing the cost of quality will not be as easy as cutting costs across the board, although it will definitely be more creative and more fun. It does take some serious thought and evaluation of each task and activity within the bank's myriad of processes to see what value they add to both internal and external customers. In doing so, there is none of the mental and emotional trauma associated with indiscriminate cost cutting. With the structured process that you will see, teams of people can identify the costs involved in prevention, inspection/detection, internal failure, and correction within six months and can begin to determine the contribution of each one to the bank's performance in service to its customers.

Because it is a new way of thinking, a certain amount of education has to take place. But once that is complete, instead of taking 10 percent across the top, they look for the following things:

- Duplication of staff, line, and production functions.
- Fragmentation in delivery systems.
- Bloated organizational hierarchies.
- Significant, repetitive rework.

- Reasons for employee turnover.
- Ineffective branch location and staffing.
- Multiple decision groups.

They have to do it within the context of the expectations of their customers. The typical cost reduction effort fails because it does not consider the value placed on various services by the customers who purchase them. The bank *has* to start with customers and work backward.

"THE BACK DOOR"

The fundamental premise is that eliminating the activities that result in the cost of poor quality means providing service that will meet the expectations of customers, will bring them back, and will attract new relationships. In "Closing the Customer Retention Gap," Terry K. Gilliam asks:

> How can improving customer retention by only 5 percent annually double profits in just five years? The answer lies in what we know about existing customers that stay with the bank versus new customers:
>
> - They cost less to serve.
> - They own more accounts per household.
> - They are the richest source of *profitable* new customers.
> - They attract staying employees and vice versa.
>
> All this adds up to a 100 percent earnings improvement from a 5 percent customer retention improvement. . . And, unless your service falters, your competition can't break the cycle . . . ever.[14]

As shown in Exhibit 2–13, the bank is spending $49 million to do wrong things, to correct them, and to provide services that are not in demand. Management of the bank really wants to increase its customer retention rates but cannot seem to do so even with the slickest marketing campaign that the advertising agency can suggest. It is no wonder. The bank has:

- Systems that generate error-prone statements.
- Customers who cannot get through to their relationship officers (who are off at meetings trying to figure out ways to cut costs) and always have to talk to the Voice Mail.
- Regular ATM servicing that takes place at 2:00 P.M., a time when there is considerable customer traffic.
- Branches that close at 4:30 P.M., a half-hour before everyone else gets off from work and would like to do their banking.

- A full parking lot when the branch is open and customers who have to leave their cars and walk through the rain and snow.
- An emphasis on efficiency, which means there aren't enough tellers, and those who are on the line show their frustration every time a customer shows up at the window.

The bank has competing objectives in this case. The marketers want more customers—a great and noble goal. The people in finance want reduced cost, which is the corporate philosophy. Therefore, resources are not expended to serve customers; even if the folks in the branches and operations want to provide excellent service, the attention paid to cost precludes it. It is a philosophy that has to change.

> Cost pressures are driving bank managers to keep a lid on salaries, cut staff, and demand greater productivity.
>
> These actions often sabotage service, as anyone can attest who has waited fifteen minutes to reach a teller, only to be treated as an annoying obstacle in the teller's race to push paper. Charging fees for services that formerly were "free," and cutting out expected services . . . tend to darken customer's perceptions of service, especially when banks fail to explain such actions clearly and honestly, as they usually fail to do.[15]

So customers leave, taking their loans, deposits, and fees to the competition, which is very glad to have them since they receive an unexpected, incremental revenue stream. We can calculate the impact of customer attrition, a phenomenon known as "the Back Door." Our objective is to figure out what it costs the bank when customers leave. It is a relatively simple concept. The resulting computation becomes another financial opportunity that is available to the bank from a strategy of service excellence. It shows what can be saved if the bank can determine why customers leave and then fixes the problem. It is a strategy of doing whatever is necessary to retain current customers.

The Economics of Quality Workbook at the end of the chapter can be used to calculate "the Back Door" in the sequence that follows. We will be using an example of the retail side of the bank, but the concept also applies to corporate banking, trust, private banking, and so forth. It makes no difference what the mix is. All that is important to understand is that it is very expensive when your customers take their business elsewhere.

Evidence suggests that about 20 percent of the typical bank's retail account base leaves every year; 40 percent of them do so because of poor service. Again, the caution is not to get hung up on the precision of the numbers. In your institution, it may be higher, it may be lower. Former chief quality officer at BancOne, Chuck Aubrey, had a plaque in his office proclaiming that 68 percent of the accounts that close do so because of poor service.

EXHIBIT 2–15

Replacement Cost Calculation: Deposits

	Rate
Average fed funds rate	9.4%
Minus average deposit rate	5.7%
Replacement cost	3.7%

By improving service, the bank can keep its customers from leaving, but what will it recoup? Let's walk through the calculation. The first thing to do is gather the following data:

- Percentage of accounts closed annually.
- Percentage of accounts closed because of service problems.
- Current fed funds purchased rate.
- Weighted average cost of funds.
- Weighted average rate earned on loans.

For demonstration purposes, assume that the 20 percent customer turnover rate and the 40 percent service quality rate are representative, and that the Fed funds rate is 9.4 percent. The assumption here is that for every deposit dollar that leaves, the bank has to replace it with fed funds. The controller has also told you that the weighted average cost of funds is 5.7 percent and the weighted average rate earned on the portfolio is 10.45 percent.

The key calculation is the *replacement cost*. In other words, what is the increment that the bank has to pay for funds over the weighted average deposit rate that it is currently paying its depositors? To obtain it, subtract the weighted average deposit rate from the Fed funds rate (see Exhibit 2–15).

Then follow the logic contained in Exhibit 2–16. The spread between the weighted average cost of funds and the replacement cost determines the margin impact. The narrower the spread, the less effect and vice versa. In this case, the bank loses $375 million in deposits, which equates to almost $14 million lost in the margin—all because the bank is not delivering its services to its customers the right way every time, which has caused them to go to Merrill Lynch or Paine Webber.

However, it doesn't stop there. If the customer closes the deposit account, the assumption is that the loan will go as well, and there is a material cost to that¡ (see Exhibits 2–17 and 2–18).

E X H I B I T 2-16

Margin Impact of Lost Deposits

Total deposits	$4.69 billion
Account turnover	× 20%
Closed due to service problems	× 40%
Lost deposits	$375 million
Replacement cost	× 3.7%
Lost margin	$13.9 million

E X H I B I T 2-17

Opportunity Cost Calculation: Loans

	Rate
Average rate earned	10.45%
Minus average rate on deposits	5.7%
Opportunity cost	4.75%

E X H I B I T 2-18

Margin Impact of Lost Loans

Total loans	$2.55 billion
Account turnover	× 20%
Closed due to service problems	× 40%
Lost loans	$204 million
Opportunity cost	× 4.75%
Lost margin	$9.7 million

Once the replacement cost is derived, the computation is easy (see Exhibit 2–18). Take the weighted average rate earned on the portfolio and subtract the weighted average cost of funds to determine the income that is being earned, then lost, when the customer walks out the back door. In this case, the portfolio earns 10.45 percent with the weighted average cost of funds being 5.7 percent, so the earning margin lost on every lost loan dollar is 4.75 percent. The bank loses $204 million of loans at an average rate of 4.75 percent, which equates to another $10 million lost in the margin. However, that's not all. Consider the fees

E X H I B I T   2–19

Fee Income Effect

Total fee income	$119.9 million
Account turnover	× 20%
Closed due to service problems	× 40%
Total lost fees	$9.6 million

E X H I B I T   2–20

Effect of Service Improvement

	Before Improvement	After Improvement
ROA	1.05%	1.63%
ROE	16.10%	24.77%

that are lost as well. Look at Exhibit 2–19. There is another $9.6 million, bringing the total lost to $33 million, which the bank could drop back to the bottom line. That is $21.5 million after taxes that, when added back to new income, produces the following ratios (see Exhibit 2–20).

There is no question that the analysts would look favorably at the bank with numbers like these, but we're not quite through yet. With $375 million in deposits and $204 million in loans going out the back door, the bank has to replenish them. That means it has to pay branch managers and loan officers to gather them when they could be spending their time scouting for *incremental* new business and keeping their current customers happy, not to mention cross-sell activities. Advertising costs increase along with marketing expenditures as the line areas scramble to replace the customers who have left.

Not only does the institution pay unnecessary costs to make and correct mistakes, handle customer complaints, reprocess statements, and so on, but it is also very expensive when customers decide that enough is enough and actually leave. Costs increase, margins decrease, and profitability suffers. Then the cost cutting starts and service suffers even more.

> The longest lasting of the self-defeating cost reductions is to let quality fail. Customers seem to talk more about failures than about successes. So, selling costs rise disproportionately on failure. And, as General Motors learned in a very painful way, customers are slow to forgive quality problems. Market share lost on quality is the hardest to recover.[16]

Unless the bank invests in the service attitude in all areas, not only the branches, the spiral will continue as shown in the reverse of the Cycle of Good Service. Poor service results in customer dissatisfaction, weakened relationships, decreased share, higher costs, lower profits, depressed earnings, and unhappy bankers, not to mention lower stock price. To preclude this unfortunate chain of events, the bank will have to increase the education budget, research customer expectations and perceptions, understand the real internal culture and environment, identify the dimensions of the cost of quality, and engage in process redesign. As we shall see, it will have to reorganize itself completely to support the new customer service orientation.

NUMERICALLY SPEAKING

The bank has to compute and report organizational profitability to its shareholders and the regulators. It is the law and the legacy from those who have gone before, and it makes good business sense. There must be accounting rules as recommended by the Financial Accounting Standards Board. There has to be a consistent way for the Securities and Exchange Commission (SEC) and the rest at the regulation community to evaluate performance and to spot potential problems.

If we think of numbers as representative of behavior, they must be actionable. We must be able to look at what they are telling us and to make the proper response, not just cutting 10 percent across-the-board to make up for a projected budget deficit but identifying in great detail where money is being spent needlessly. We have to find the consumers of cost, those things that are done that add no value to the customer, which, when stopped, will drop greater earnings to the bottom line.

As costs decrease, there is pricing flexibility. The bank may be able to have a more competitive price than the other banks and nonbanks in town while it also enjoys a higher margin on every transaction. Why? If it can reduce the cost to deliver the service that customers want while the other providers don't, a portion of that cost reduction can be passed on to the customer, the very strategy used by Motorola. When was the last time the bank reduced the fees it charges its customers? Wouldn't it be nice if it could while simultaneously maintaining or increasing the margin on each transaction? Reduce the cost of quality and that will be the result.

Then, because customers are happy, they develop a loyalty to the bank, maintain their deposit and lending relationships, and effectively close the back door. As Janet Gray and I were doing the research for *Quality Value Banking,* I had the opportunity to talk with Ed Bell, then president of the Ohio Bell Telephone Company and a director of Ameritrust. When I told him that we were writing a book on service in banking, he responded, "Is there any?" Banks are not known for their service. That is why there is such a great financial opportunity for those that can grasp it. Improving service is a win-win situation.

Nevertheless, improving service means working with customers. That means an external view. No more time for analysis paralysis. Here's the situation:

- Disintermediation is rampant.
- Technological advances favor the competition.
- Overcapacity is on the agenda of almost every banking conference.
- Unsuccessful approaches to cost management are tried and tried again.

Banks, for the most part, have not understood and adopted the economic and organizational power that a true service strategy can provide. Like our regional CEO in Dayton, check the numbers and make sure nothing cataclysmic has happened. Do this regularly but don't dwell on it. Turn your attention outward. Find out what your customers want. Determine what is being done in the bank that may be precluding it. Calculate what that is costing and what the opportunity is. Then go after it. Eliminate as many *failures* as possible. That means less need for *correction*. Look at all the *inspection*. Is it really necessary? Subscribe to DIRFT. It is the only answer.

Use your calculation of the cost of quality and the "back door" as benchmarks. They are the stake in the ground from which improvements in customer service are measured. Do not abandon the numbers. Use them to indicate where there are areas of opportunity, but always think of them in terms of the behavior that causes them. Change the behaviors and the numbers will change. Change the numbers and the behavior won't.

The Cost of Quality

BANK

Date	Behavior	Time Required	Time to Correct	Reason

The Economics of Quality

SCHEDULE 1
The Cost of Quality

Noninterest expense, 1994 _____

Cost of quality _____ × 15%

Total improvement opportunity _____

1—Tax rate × _____%

Potential savings—*to Schedule 3* _____

SCHEDULE 2
Performance Measurements, 1992

Net income, 1994—*to Schedule 3* $_____

Average assets $_____

Average equity $_____

ROA
Net Income 1994 / Average assets—
to Schedule 4 and Schedule 12 _____%

ROE
Net Income, 1994 / Average equity—
to Schedule 4 and Schedule 12 _____%

SCHEDULE 3
Performance Measurements, 1994

Net Income, 1994—*from Schedule 2*   _____

Potential savings—*from Schedule 1*   _____

Adjusted net income—*to Schedule 11*   _____

Average assets $_____

Average equity $_____

ROA
Adjusted net income, 1994 / Average assets—
to Schedule 4   _____%

ROE
Adjusted net income, 1994 / Average equity—
to Schedule 4   _____%

SCHEDULE 4
Performance Measurement Comparison

	Before— *from Schedule 2*	Estimated after— *from Schedule 3*
ROA	_____%	_____%
ROE	_____%	_____%

SCHEDULE 5
Replacement Cost Calculation: Deposits

	Rate
Average fed funds rate	_____%
Minus average rate on deposits	_____%
Replacement cost—*to Schedule 6*	_____%

SCHEDULE 6
Margin Impact of Lost Deposits

Total deposits	_____
Account turnover	× 20%
Quality problems	× 40%
Lost deposits	$_____
Replacement cost—*from Schedule 5*	× _____%
Lost margin on deposits—*to Schedule 10*	$_____

SCHEDULE 7
Opportunity Cost Calculation: Loans

	Rate
Average rate on portfolio	_____%
Minus average rate on deposits—*from Schedule 5*	_____%
Opportunity cost—*to Schedule 8*	_____%

SCHEDULE 8
Margin Impact of Lost Loans

Total loans	_____
Account turnover	× 20%
Quality problems	× 40%
Lost loans	$_____
Opportunity cost—*from Schedule 7*	× _____%
Lost margin on loans—*to Schedule 10*	$_____

SCHEDULE 9
Fee Income Impact

Total fee income	$_____
Account turnover	$\times 20\%$
Quality problems	$\times 40\%$
Lost fees—*to Schedule 10*	$_____

SCHEDULE 10
Total Financial Effect

Lost margin on deposits—*from Schedule 6*	$_____
Lost margin on loans—*from Schedule 8*	$_____
Lost fee income—*from Schedule 9*	$_____
Total before taxes	$_____
1—Tax rate	_____%
Total gross impact	$_____
Divide by 2*	$_____
Total "back door" effect—*to Schedule 11*	$_____

*"Closing the back door" completely may not be practical. For illustrative purposes, we suggest that the bank can close it halfway.

SCHEDULE 11
Potential Performance Measurements

Adjusted net income—*from Schedule 3* $_____

"Back door" effect—*from Schedule 10* $_____

Potential net income   _____

Average assets $_____

Average equity $_____

ROA
Adjusted net income / Average assets—
to Schedule 12   _____%

ROE
Adjusted net income / Average equity—
to Schedule 12   _____%

SCHEDULE 12
Performance Measurement Comparison

	Before— *from Schedule 2*	Estimated after— *from Schedule 11*
ROA	_____%	_____%
ROE	_____%	_____%

ENDNOTES

1. Thomas W. Harvey, "Cost Drivers: A Different Approach to Management Information in Banks," *Journal of Bank Cost & Management Accounting,* Summer 1990, pp. 5–6.

2. Dan Shingler, "Wall Street Not Yet Sold on KeyCorp," *Crain's Cleveland Business,* June 5, 1995, p. 6.

3. Jon Greenwald, "The High Cost of Savings," *Time,* June 20, 1994, p. 50.

4. Ibid.

5. Janet L. Fix, "Consumers Are Snarling over Charges," *USA Today,* Aug. 2, 1994, p. 2B.

6. "The Money Channel," *The Plain Dealer,* June 11, 1995, p. 4H.

7. Fred R. Bleakley, "U.S. Banks Lose Corporate Clients to Lenders Abroad," *The Wall Street Journal,* Sept. 29, 1992, pp. A2, A9.

8. Kelly Holland, "Take Our Money, Please," *Business Week,* July 18, 1994, p. 67.

9. Janet L. Gray and Thomas W. Harvey, *Quality Value Banking* (New York: John Wiley & Sons, 1992), p. 86.

10. Leonard L. Berry, "Principles of Service Quality," speech at Society Corporation, Aug. 1988.

11. Suzanne Alexander Ryan, "Fleet Financial to Reduce Staff as Much as 19%," *The Wall Street Journal,* March 9, 1994, p. A3.

12. Sanford Rose, "Raising Your Stock Price by 60%," *American Banker,* Nov. 7, 1989, p. 4.

13. Peter M. Stenge, *The Fifth Discipline* (New York: Doubleday/Currency, 1990), p. 65.

14. Terry K. Gilliam, "Closing the Customer Retention Gap," *Bank Marketing,* Dec. 1994, p. 51.

15. William H. Davidrow and Bro Uttal, *Total Customer Service: The Ultimate Weapon* (New York: Harper & Row, 1989), p. 6.

16. Donald V. Potter, "Success under Fire: Policies to Prosper in Hostile Times," *California Management Review* 33, no. 2 (Winter 1991), pp. 32–33.

CHAPTER 3

What Happened?

To achieve the benefits that the commitment to excellence promises, there will have to be change: change in the thinking, actions, and behavior of the nations' bankers. With any change in the competitive environment, they simply have to change what they do and how they do it. To understand the required change, though we have to be aware of the events that have shaped the industry and the economy as a whole during the last 60 years or so. We have to study the behaviors and actions that have influenced banking; that is, why the industry is as it is.

What follows is an economic and behavioral examination of the unique situation in which the United States found itself, particularly after World War I, in terms of its bankers and the population as a whole. During this century, the role of banking has experienced some wide swings as the people and the government have attempted to define what part banks should play in their lives.

THE FRENZY TURNED QUIET

We cannot view the disintermediation to the new competition in isolation. History is a great teacher. As with the numbers, we must learn from the past, not dwelling on it, but applying its lessons to the future. As such, we have to take a "big picture" view of banking to understand the cause-and-effect relationships that produced the current competitive situation in the industry. The time to begin that study is 1932. The stock market had crashed three years before; the New York Yankees had swept the Chicago Cubs in the World Series; the University of Southern California and the University of Michigan went undefeated in their gridiron campaigns, only to share the "national championship"; and Gene Sarazen won golf's U.S. Open for the second time.

In 1932, however, the Great Depression still gripped the country. Unemployment had reached one-quarter of the American workforce, personal savings had been wiped out, and thousands of banks had closed their doors. In July 1932, the stock market was valued at one-tenth of its value in September 1929. The people were mad and directed their anger at the nation's bankers. And with good reason.

During the late 1920s, the United States was riding a cash boom, partly because of the prevailing monetary policy but mainly because it had an operative productive capacity while Europe did not. In a theme that would be replayed 30 years later, the Continent had been devastated by World War I, while American soil had escaped the ravages of the conflict. This gave the United States a tremendous manufacturing and trade advantage because it was able to produce the goods that its people and those of Europe needed, and the economy raced ahead. The time was termed "the Roaring 20s," which was also an apt moniker for the financial markets of the time.

Those Americans with cash had their investment options, but the country's prevailing financial policies favored stocks and bonds. Wall Street was the benefactor, to the point where there was genuine concern that there might not be enough stock to go around. In mid-1929, *The Wall Street Journal* suggested, "There is a vast amount of money awaiting investment. Thousands of traders and investors have been waiting for an opportunity to buy stocks on just such a break that has occurred over the last several weeks."[1]

The market was on a roll. Prices were on the rise and with a limited supply of stock, there was no reason to suspect that the escalation would not continue. By 1929, there were 6,500 securities dealers in the United States where there had been 250 before World War I. These dealers and the banks fueled the expansion, encouraging their clients to purchase stocks on margin, that is, putting down $1,000 to buy $10,000 worth of stock. With these eager buyers, corporate America found that it was easier and cheaper to issue stock offerings to raise cash than to finance their growth with debt, so they began going directly into the financial markets, bypassing the banks and depriving them of the loans and resultant interest income that had heretofore been theirs.

That meant that the banks had to replace the lost revenues, and the stock market looked like a good place to do it. They jumped in, helping many average Americans get rich. The newspapers were filled with stories of the newfound wealth as the bankers like Charles Mitchell of National City Company, now Citicorp, encouraged and paid their brokers to make more sales with the promise of higher commissions. Seeing the outcome, average people wanted to share the wealth, buying stocks of all kinds and forcing prices higher and higher. It seems in retrospect that the nation's bankers forgot that they were trusted fiduciaries who were supposed to help their customers grow. "Bankers," as Ron Chernow pointed out in *The House of Morgan,* "took on the image of garrulous hucksters," as the market roared on.[2] Disaster, as we know, loomed on the horizon.

As 1929 progressed, there were some isolated, and ignored, cases of worry about the whirlwind on Wall Street, one of which was being nurtured in Washington, D.C. President Herbert Hoover was not a finance man, but he understood the potential downside risk of the speculation that was happening in the stock market. He began to think that maybe federal regulation to minimize the potential risk would be a good idea. Accordingly, he asked for advice from experts in the field who were, to no one's surprise, some of the nation's leading bankers. Predictably, they shunned regulation. It would cramp their style. Obviously, they dismissed the idea and reminded the president of the prosperity of the decade. Production was up as America's corporations replenished the world with what had been destroyed by war. As bankers, they were helping in their own way, creating wealth even for the smallest investor, so what was there to worry about?

Even with this self-serving advice, by October 1929 the president had become even more worried about the increasing speculation and contacted his banking advisors once again. It was very clear to him something was wrong. Hoover continues to receive a lot of bad press, even today, as he is charged with responsibility for the Great Depression. Maybe some of the criticism is justified because of his lack of action after the market crashed. On speculation, however, he had been right from the start. Speculation and the wild rise of the stock market was an unnatural economic phenomenon. There would have to be a corresponding correction, which would be severe.

The market was indeed out-of-control and there was nothing the president could do about it. The nation's bankers who argued incorrectly that it was part of the normal economic cycle continued to incite increased investment. True to the laws of supply-and-demand, prices rose higher and higher. With a lot of cash, a number of limited equities in which to invest, and the hope of getting rich in a hurry, investors, including the bankers (both professionally and personally), continued to buy in a feeding frenzy. Hoover saw the danger, but with the prosperity, who would listen? Why should they? They were amassing great paper wealth, so listening to a man who did not know much about the intricacies of finance, even the president of the United States, was absurd.

By the last week of October, some jitters became apparent. On the 23rd, the selling began. Westinghouse Electric lost 35 points, a lot today and even more 65 years ago. General Electric lost 20 the same day. The morning's activities saw a $10 billion paper loss. As prices plummeted, investors were destroyed. Their stock had lost its value, they had loans to repay, and there was no way that they could do it. On this Black Thursday, something had to be done or the collapse would continue, taking everyone with it.

In the midst of the panic, a consortium of bankers invested $240 million in the market to brace the fall. As they began to buy, there was some stabilization, and cautious statements began to come out from Wall Street that maybe the worst was over, praising the bankers' rescue. But there was an uneasy feeling in the consortium that even $240 million wouldn't be enough to stop the run.

On Friday the 24th, there was some selling, but nothing close to what had happened the day before. By Monday, however, the mood was one of fright as investors wanted to cut their losses and to get out as fast as they could. On Tuesday, October 29, selling proliferated; no one was buying, not even the bankers. They, too, were trying to salvage something of their own wealth. As prices plunged and took personal wealth along, the loans that had been taken out to buy the stock were suddenly in serious jeopardy. Millions of dollars of outstanding loans would go unpaid. This started a crisis in the banks that would be felt for a generation or more. It was clearly a disaster that would change the way the American people felt about their banks for some time. The 1920s had roared for the last time. So had the banks. As Ron Chernou writes, "The age had come to an abrupt, calamitous end. The crash was a blow to Wall Street's pride and its profits. As Bernard Baruch later said, 'The stereotype of bankers as conservative, careful, prudent individuals was shattered in 1929.' "[3]

In early 1930, the market showed a temporary correction and returned to its former value, but by early spring an unrelenting slide was under way. Hoover's answer was the same one that he had used in 1921 when, as secretary of commerce, he had been successful in curing a deepening recession. In a series of talks with the country's business leaders, the president convinced them to maintain compensation levels, to invest in public works, and to increase local welfare programs. His objective, as it had been a decade before, was to reverse the increasing deflationary trend which occurred as businesses had cut wages and jobs to lower their costs and to keep their prices competitive. However, as prices kept falling, the natural reaction of business was to cut more jobs and reduce wages even further, which effectively slashed the nation's purchasing power in the process. Without the ability to consume, much less to deposit any excess revenue in the bank, the economy ground to a screeching halt.

The issue was a lack of consumption. There simply was not enough consumer demand to equal the country's productive capacity that had developed since the end of World War I. With wages cut, jobs lost, and savings disappearing as bank after bank failed, disposable income was almost nonexistent. To illustrate the point, see Exhibit 3–1. In 1930, there were about 150,000 nonfarm foreclosures; in 1931, 200,000; 1932, 250,000; and in the first part of 1933, almost one-half of all residential mortgages were in default.[4] People could not work and earn a wage; therefore, they could not make mortgage payments. Consumer spending for cars stopped, new construction came to a halt, and demand for agricultural products withered away. Autoworkers, construction

E X H I B I T   3-1

Nonfarm Foreclosures, 1930–1932

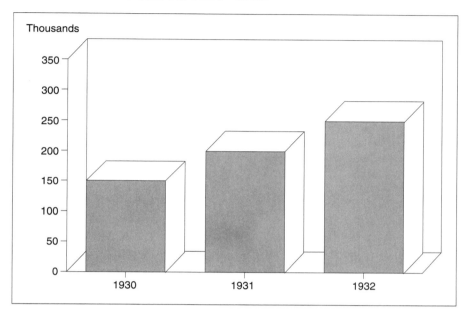

workers, and farmers, who may have had nothing to do with the crash of the stock market, suddenly found themselves victims of it as wages plummeted, jobs disappeared, and purchasing virtually vanished.

DEPRESSION

Terrible it was. Between 1929 and 1933, the gross national product plunged from $104 billion to $41 billion; 5,500 banks failed; stocks listed on the Big Board fell to 11 percent of their pre-Crash value; unemployment climbed to one-third of the American work force. It is estimated that the average income of American families dropped nearly 40 percent, from $2,300 in 1929 to $1,500 in 1933. Twenty-eight percent of the nonrural population was without any income. Welfare was virtually nonexistent, difficult to qualify for when it did exist, and then only provided pennies a week, which most people were ashamed to take anyway. Millions of young men crisscrossed the country on freight trains, desperately looking for work; millions more simply gave up.[5]

Not a pretty picture and one which most of us in this last decade of the 20th century cannot even fathom. Unemployment lines out the door and around the corner; soup kitchens dotting the avenues of the major cities; and "Hoovervilles," small shanty towns that sprang up to house the transient and the homeless. We have our problems now, with the homeless among them, but the sheer magnitude of the problems of the early 1930s puts the Great Depression in a class by itself.

It was extremely complicated as well. Blame was difficult to place. Everyone who played in this dangerous game should have shared in it. The individuals and organizations that saw their investments evaporate overnight certainly would not think that it was their fault even though they kept borrowing and buying. Congress, which would be subject to the wrath of the populace, surely could have been more diligent during the 1920s and would be in the years that followed. The bankers, who closed the doors of their institutions to their depositors, did not see anything wrong as they fueled the inflation of the stock market. Denial and finger-pointing were everywhere. The casualties, sadly, were all Americans, whether or not they had gambled unsuccessfully in the market. Personal fortunes had been lost, but what was worse was that those who had nothing to do with the Crash found themselves disadvantaged by it. Demand dried up, wages and jobs were cut, and nobody had any money to spend.

Hoover and the Republicans worked diligently at their program of "volunteerism," hoping that industrial America would come to the rescue to stimulate the much-needed consumption. It did, for a while. Wage levels were maintained through 1930 along with prices and employment levels, but it couldn't last. By the end of 1931, more than 1.7 million workers had suffered wage cuts. Demand just wasn't there, and capacity had to be reduced, greasing the slide into depression and hastening Herbert Hoover's exit from office.

In 1932, Franklin D. Roosevelt was elected president of the United States and promised the country a "New Deal," the prime objective of which was to restore employment levels. To achieve that goal, Roosevelt implemented economic programs that would have a permanent effect on the country whether they worked or not. The New Deal would change the way we thought.

The new president understood very well that the problem was one of lack of demand, and he had to find a way to prime the pump. The answer lay in the work of John Maynard Keynes, who advanced the justification for deficit spending as a way to stimulate economic growth. The only way to do that, he argued, was for government to start it. The reason was very clear: No one else had any money to spend. However, there was a problem with that in the United States. Most Americans were still suspicious of any federal intervention. Roosevelt knew that and thought he had found a way around it.

His first action was to sponsor the National Industrial Recovery Act, which created the National Recovery Administration (NRA), a cooperative venture between the country's largest corporations and government. The NRA authorized spending $3.3 billion toward the goal of full employment, but it was designed to rely principally on business activity to restart the economy. It didn't accomplish that objective, but what is critical to understand is that it changed America for good. It marked Washington's entry into our everyday lives.

Roosevelt was also convinced that Washington had to fix the banking system, which, in 1932, was in complete disarray. There was no other way to do it. Banks were closing right and left, taking the hard-earned savings of ordinary folks with them. There were too many small, undercapitalized banks dotting the countryside. The absence of branch banking precluded diversification, so that banks were at the economic mercy of their surrounding markets. Rural banks suffered as farm income dried up, while urban banks had the same problem when factories closed. Finally, the people began to change their opinions about their bankers as unethical and fraudulent behavior became public.

In January 1933, the Senate Banking Committee empowered an assistant district attorney from New York, Ferdinand Pecora, to investigate the events that led to the stock market crash, especially those within the banking industry. The banks had been the conduit for the run-up, selling their clients on the riches to be made, with greed and avarice the primary motivators. Pecora suspected this to be true and convened public hearings into the behavior of the banking community, especially of those in New York who had been closest to the action. The Pecora Hearings exposed their criminal behavior. The people listened eagerly and their anger grew; so did that of the House and Senate. They began to understand the conflicting roles that bankers played: accepting deposits, encouraging and facilitating imprudent investment, and making loans with the acquired stock as collateral. It was a vicious, greedy practice which the legislators would make sure never happened again.

If Pecora's hearings were not enough, Roosevelt sent the country and its bankers another message. Since 1929, thousands of banks had failed and bank holidays were declared in several states. On the day of Roosevelt's inauguration, the banks in New York were closed. Illinois followed. The American financial system stopped. On March 6, 1933, the president called for a three-day national bank holiday to let things cool off. He then extended that deadline until Monday, March 13. Skillfully, on Sunday the 12th, Roosevelt went on national radio to have a "fireside chat" with the American people in which he urged them to have confidence in their banking system. He let everyone know that he was in charge. No longer would the banks control their own destinies, ever again.

The American people must have listened to their president because, on the next day, deposits in the nation's banks exceeded withdrawals for the first time in years. Within the next month, Treasury Secretary William Woodin determined that more than 70 percent of the banks were fit to reopen, but Congress was determined to make sure something like this never happened again.

The result was the Banking Act of 1933, known as the Glass-Steagall Act, which would alter forever the ways that banks would operate in this country. This legislation was designed to safeguard the small depositor from the kind of collapse that had happened after the Crash. Congress wanted to make sure that there would never be a repeat performance in which so many banks closed and savings accounts disappeared. Glass-Steagall was concerned with the safety and soundness of the industry and was intended to ensure the conservatism of the nation's bankers. Control was placed on bank officers concerning what they could and could not do; national banks would have to have greater capital reserves; and banks would not be able to engage in both investment banking and commercial banking, a combination thought to be one of the primary causes of the inflationary spiral of the stock market. In effect, it legislated the bankers' behavior.

Interestingly, the Glass-Steagall Act applied only to the banks, not to independent brokerage operations. Congress apparently saw the banks as the primary culprits and wanted to put them under wraps to make sure that something like the Crash would never, ever, happen again. The exclusion of the brokerages would come back to haunt the banks in the 1970s, but in 1933 that didn't matter as long as the banks were completely restrained from behavior that could produce such a catastrophe. Glass-Steagall did just that and, as a by-product, it did one more thing.

Just in case the bankers somehow put the savings of their customers in jeopardy, the Glass-Steagall Act had a remedy: deposit insurance. With the creation of the Federal Deposit Insurance Company (FDIC), Congress established a safety net for the nation's savers, but in doing so, it showed the complete distrust it had for the banks. Even with restricting them to the business of taking deposits and making loans, Congress put in this insurance contingency in case the bankers somehow got themselves in trouble again. If the country's leadership had not been so suspicious or had not expected banks to fail once again, taking the depositors' money with them, they would not have designed an insurance fund to protect them. As such, the formation of the FDIC generated another new banking behavior although no one knew it at the time.

Because deposits were now insured against loss if the institution failed, the government would make the customer whole. Thus, the accountability of the bankers waned. They did not have to be as prudent in their lending practices and could, if they wanted to, pursue assets of higher risk, knowing full well that even in the worst case, the FDIC would pay off their depositors. This provision of Glass-Steagall was perceived to be very necessary to stabilize the economy in this most angry time and to bring order to the payment system. In that light, perhaps, it was appropriate, but it did open the door to a new behavior which, in the long run, Congress might have wanted to keep shut.

The basic aim of Glass-Steagall was to say to bankers, "You are never going to do again what you did in the 1920s." But it also told them they were no longer in charge of their own fate, which brought some serious problems. When things would change again in the 1970s, it became apparent that the Glass-Steagall Act and its enforcement provisions were so tight, there were serious questions about the bankers' ability to shed their traditions to adopt a new behavior that would let them engage in the new competitive environment successfully, even if they had been permitted to.

The Depression lingered on with little improvement. The National Industrial Recovery Act had given business and government control of wages, prices, and production levels, but it had done very little to stimulate consumption or to increase employment. Nor did it reflect the views of all sectors of the economy. Many business people across the country were not about to trade their freedom for intervention and control from Washington, even though the federal programs might have helped them recover. The independence that had characterized the American spirit since the beginning prevailed once again; on March 27, 1935, the Supreme Court ruled that the NRA was trying to regulate commerce that was not interstate in nature. Therefore, the NRA was unconstitutional and had to be dissolved.

Five months later, Roosevelt rolled out the Second New Deal. "The First New Deal characteristically told business what it must do. The Second New Deal told business what it must *not* do."[6] The New Dealers were not pleased that the NRA had been struck down, so they turned to the political left and started a course to oversee the redistribution of the country's wealth and power to the people whom the Depression had ravaged. In spite of the independent American spirit, the administration and the Congress decided in mid-1935 that it was time to take matters into their own hands. The following were some of the results of their efforts:

- The National Labor Relations Act (the Wagner Act), which rescued and gave some much-needed clout to the trade associations and unions.
- The Public Utility Holding Company Act, which broke up the interlocking organizational structures used by the utilities to control their subsidiaries.
- The Social Security Act, which was the first federal welfare activity.
- The Works Progress Administration (WPA), which put eight million people to work and funded 60 percent of the construction in New York City in 1937.

- The Tennessee Valley Authority (TVA), which gave power to the people at the local level to plan and build a system that would provide inexpensive electricity to the rural south-central United States.
- The Banking Act of 1935, which was to put the regulatory power of the federal government at an all-time high.

The Banking Act of 1935 strengthened federal control of the banking system, a tie that would never be broken again. Banking and government would be forever "joined at the hip." Under recommendations from Marriner Eccles, a Utah banker and advisor to the Roosevelt administration, the shape of the Federal Reserve System changed. It would move to Washington, D.C., from New York. That made bankers outside Wall Street happy because they did not like controls imposed by their brethren from Morgan, National City Bank, and the like. The Federal Reserve's structure also would change. The Federal Reserve Board would be replaced by a board of governors appointed by the president and confirmed by the Senate. The Open Market Committee would become the responsibility of the board of governors and regional representation and not that of the managers of the regional Federal Reserve banks.

From a behavioral perspective, the most important feature of the Banking Act of 1935 gave the Federal Reserve Board the power of setting interest rate ceilings. Regulation Q prohibited the banks from freely establishing the rates they would pay on deposits because the Fed now had the power to choose the maximum that could be paid. Behaviorally, however, it took the pricing decision out of the banker's hands, made all banks look the same (at least on the deposit side), and restricted the banker even more. It changed the basic mentality of the banker from businessman to order taker, which may have been the congressional objective, by effectively eliminating creativity and innovation.

The government thus created a behavioral pattern in which bankers always looked to Washington. They were being told what to do, the price they could pay, and the markets in which they could compete. As punishment for their transgressions of the previous decade, they were completely restrained. All that bankers were allowed to do was take deposits, paying a rate of interest set by the government, and make loans, generally at little more than the prime rate, which was set in New York by the money center banks. Just in case, there was deposit insurance. For the next 50 years, that would be the behavioral model.

The authors of the 1935 Act knew what they were doing, at least for the circumstances that they had to address. After its passage, the banks began to heal. In 1936, no national bank failed, but the country as a whole remained sick. Roosevelt rolled out the other programs in an attempt to stimulate purchasing, but it was World War II, not the New Deal, that pulled the country out of the Depression. While it is true that many of Roosevelt's reforms did not achieve the goals that he had set, it is important to understand that they stabilized the country, which was a necessary first step.

The NRA had failed to provide the necessary purchasing power to the economy. It had started to reverse the downward economic spiral, but did not achieve what everyone wanted. Tax laws had not redirected wealth as planned. Farmers continued to produce more than could be consumed, both at home where urban demand disappeared and with trading partners overseas who were in the midst of their own economic disasters. The banking industry had been normalized and brought some order to the economy. Some welfare relief had actually gotten to those who needed it. Labor standards were increased through the Wagner Act, the TVA was a great success and accomplished its objectives, and the WPA put a lot of people to work even though there were still nine million unemployed in 1940. The New Deal had enabled the country to survive the Depression and brought a new and more optimistic outlook to the American people. For that, we should be grateful.

Behaviorally, though, the New Deal began to change a time-honored tradition in this country. In spite of their independent spirit, the American people realized for the first time that a problem was too great for them, or their states, to solve. The Depression gripped the entire nation, and it would take national policy to escape from it. The trade-off came in the understanding that to escape the Depression required federal intervention, led by a charismatic president whose programs and doctrines returned much of the dignity that had been lost. Production was increasing, albeit slowly; welfare reform was in the works; the banking system was stable and forever connected to government; and most Americans now saw a glimmer of hope as the 1930s came to a close.

WAR

The Depression dominated the culture. How long it would have remained in the national conscience and impacted the economy had there not been war is a matter of some debate. Nonetheless, the outbreak of World War II proved to be the economic event that would regenerate the country. Even though the president had fought deficit spending, the advent of the war made it a national necessity. The United States entered into the war in the name of democracy and threw everything it had, and more, into its preservation. Starting in 1939, Congress opened its checkbook as never before. That makes one wonder what would have happened to the economy if it had done so five or six years before.

All of a sudden, nobody cared about the notion of deficit spending. We had a war to win. Congress authorized $64 billion for defense weaponry: planes, ships, and guns of all sizes. That doubled the gross national product (GNP) from $88.6 billion in 1939 to over $200 billion in 1945. During the five war years, 17 million jobs were created. At the same time, the budget deficit rose from $4.4 billion to over $57 billion. Seventy-five percent of the people paid income tax, a demonstration of their new earning power. Unemployment almost vanished, going from nine million in 1939 to less than one million in 1942. Five million women went to work. The average workweek increased by eight hours to 45.3 hours with the six-day week becoming commonplace.

With work came something new: wages. With memories of the Great Depression still vividly in mind, people wanted to buy all of the things of which they had been deprived in the previous decade. Salaries and wages were coming in, but there was nothing to buy, because rationing had become the order of the day as the nation supplied its war effort in the Atlantic and Pacific theaters. Tires, gasoline, heating oil, meat, and sugar could be had, but were in limited supply. Small appliances, automobiles, and large items such as refrigerators became scarce. There was nothing to do but invest what you had, either by putting it in the bank or by buying war bonds.

The United States was fighting a global war on two fronts, thousands of miles apart, and the world looked to it for leadership. As the war wore on, the American productive capacity was the only one capable of supplying the military and U.S. allies with the necessary supplies and equipment. Those partners and their enemies could not.

> We turned out fewer than 6,000 airplanes of all kinds in 1939 at a cost of $279.4 million. In 1944, the number of aircraft plants had doubled and their combined output was 96,369 planes, practically all of them combat types, at a total cost of $167 billion. In 1939, the aluminum industry consisted of a single company with an annual output of 300 million pounds, most of it going into pots, pans, and home appliances. In 1944, there were more than a dozen producers and fabricators in the field with a total ingot output of 2.3 billion pounds, all of it going into airplanes and other munitions. Steel production increased 85% during those years; coal, 55 percent; and the output of synthetic rubber, which in 1940 was little more than a laboratory curiosity in this country, went from zero to 900,000 tons.[7]

The real source of victory in World War II was not, as many have maintained, that "right was on our side" or even "democracy." We fought for those principles, but what enabled the Allies to emerge victorious was the ability to manage terribly complicated human, supply, communication, and transportation systems, both at home and abroad, better than any other country. The United States was able to work with its Allies to bridge some immense logistical gaps while the Axis Powers could not.

It was a lesson to be applied in peacetime, too, as the United States assumed the role of production house for the world, the likes of which had never been witnessed before. The giant American industrial machine was the greatest contributor to the ultimate outcome of the conflict. It fueled a national pride, even with the great sacrifices that the American people had been asked to make. However, a subtle change was gaining strength in the American culture. Just as we had looked to President Roosevelt for help during the Depression, we started glancing toward Washington for direction during the conflict. The White House and Capitol Hill controlled the business of business, as the war effort dominated the nation's production facilities. In doing so, our individualist, pioneer, independent, capitalist outlook was slowly replaced by bureaucracy, never to be regained again. The government managed the war effort on the battlefield and in the domestic economy, and would continue to increase its influence over the lives of all Americans in the years to come.

PEACE, HOUSES, AND CARS

The end of World War II provided the most unique economic circumstance in history for the United States, a situation which has largely been overlooked. It was a coincidental combination of military might, a dominating work ethic, and a very convenient geographic location that would propel America into a position of economic supremacy that would go unchallenged for the next 30 years.

Like World War I, the war that ended in 1945 had seen fighting in a lot of places, but not on American soil. Japan lay in ruins as the result of the horror of the new atomic weaponry. Devastation gripped England, Germany, France, and the rest of the Continent once again. From an economic perspective, American manufacturing capacity was still intact while that in the rest of the world was in shambles. Therefore, the United States was the only country with the ability to produce the goods necessary for the reconstruction of the war-torn world and for its own growth, which resulted in a domestic financial bonanza.

When the war ended in Europe and the Pacific, the American people were ready to enjoy life because they had endured and prevailed over the hardships of the Depression and the war. They were tired of it and wanted to forget. There were materials to be produced to retool the country and to assist the vanquished. There were also things, such as cars and refrigerators, to make. The economy was ready to make the change from a wartime capacity to a peacetime one.

At first, there was some overcapacity as the soldiers returned to the workforce. Housing was limited as well, and some economists were forecasting another depression. However, the returning troops were willing and able to work and brought two different perspectives with them that would give rise to the modern corporation. First, they carried the scars of the Great Depression with its uncertainty and poverty, and they wanted to avoid a repetition of that at all costs. Security was of the utmost importance to them. Second, even though the troops had been asked to perform the dirtiest imaginable human task between 1941 and 1945, they had been part of a successful, pyramid organization. They reasoned that big, militarylike organizations had achieved a great victory; therefore, they could provide that sense of security and success now that the war was over. "And, so, by the hundreds of thousands, American men exchanged their uniforms for gray flannel suits."[8]

William Whyte, author of the famous *Organization Man,* saw this phenomenon as a fundamental behavioral change in America. Whereas the spirit of the nation before the Depression and World War II lay in the unbridled individualism of the pioneers, by the early 1950s security was the key word. Members of the workforce sacrificed their individuality for a dependence on the government and the organization. The banks were even more secure because they really weren't subject to competition and could surf along the crest of the economic expansion with little or no risk.

During the war years, balances in savings accounts had risen from $40 billion to $150 billion and would continue to grow. Because of New Deal regulation, banking had become very predictable, almost monotonous. Routines were established within the boundaries of regulation that prescribed the desired, acceptable behavior. The word for the bank employee, above all other jobs and organizations, was "safe." When you joined the bank in 1950 at age 22, you expected to retire from it 43 years later, gold watch and all.

This behavior was rewarded generously as the generation that came home from the war became more financially successful than any other in American history. In fact, just as the profitability of the nation's banks was unnatural in 1993, the economic spiral that took place in the 1950s created wealth in a measure that will never happen again. Behaviorally, however, the message was one of work hard, stay out of trouble, and don't offer anything too creative—and the corporation will take care of you. Why not? The workforce had been through a lot, what with the Depression and the war. It was time to settle down and to enjoy life.

Did we ever! In addition to increased wages, Americans had their savings from the war years. With their savings accounts and a regular paycheck, they were ready to buy, buy, buy. Not only was there pent-up demand, but there were more of us. The population in the United States grew by 28 million in the 1950s as a result of the Baby Boom (see Exhibit 3–2). Beginning in the late 1940s and continuing through the next decade, there was a population explosion, the likes of which was mirrored only by the economic one happening at the same time.

More people, an attitude of consumption, money to spend, seemingly endless sources of energy and other natural resources, and a skyrocketing birthrate fired a demand for things that people had never thought of before: television, convertibles, electric dishwashers, boats, trips to faraway places by plane, not train. The banks played their role well: Take in the deposit, make the loan, get a fair profit. It really was safe.

In 1950, the United States began producing for another war effort, this time in Korea, that would not end until July 1953. Further, it continued to mold

EXHIBIT 3-2

Population Increases, 1920s–1950s

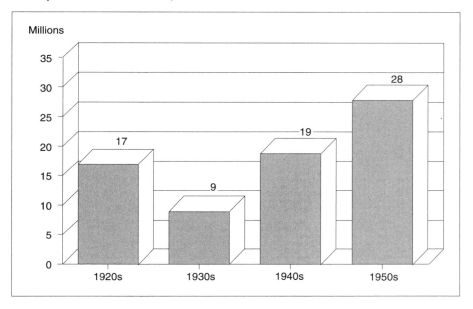

the steel and wire that was still necessary to rebuild the rest of the world devastated by World War II. With this demand from foreign shores and the increased need at home, the United States had to produce more. As U.S. corporations manufactured and sold their products, the money from sales rolled in, manifesting itself in higher wages and bonuses, which enabled the recipients to buy even more. Between 1945 and 1960, the number of automobiles in the country increased by 133 percent. In 1954 alone, Americans bought 1.5 million new homes, much to the delight of the banks' mortgage lenders. People were also fascinated by the gadgetry generated by wartime technology; 1.4 million power lawn mowers were purchased that same year.[9]

Half again as many people owned homes in 1960 as they did in 1950, but the old streets with their traffic lights and stop signs surely were not the way to get to suburbia. Americans had to have a network of freeways to make transportation faster and easier (the folks in Southern California may be somewhat skeptical of this development as they creep along I-405 and I-10 toward downtown Los Angeles every morning). In the greatest public works program ever, the new interstate highway system allowed people to live farther from the workplace, and when they got there, they were getting used to the comforts of life that the economic bonanza had provided. In the 1950s, more than 98 percent of

U.S. homes had a refrigerator; 90 percent had a TV; 80 percent owned at least one car; and by 1960, 20 percent owned two cars or more.[10]

That sparked more economic growth, and the suburbanites were there to receive its benefit because their annual income was almost double that of everyone else. The middle class expanded rapidly as the number of salaried workers increased 61 percent between 1947 and 1957. Explosive growth in the suburbs during the 1950s reshaped life in this country and for its bankers. As people moved away from the central city, taking their ever-increasing salaries with them, the bank had to follow, making it easy for the suburbanites to make that biweekly deposit. Bankers began building branches on every street corner to enable their customers easy access while competition continued for those valuable deposits. They couldn't compete on rate. Reg Q saw to that. Instead, they had to differentiate with location and service. This strategy, although very necessary at the time, would prove problematic by the time the 1990s arrived.

However, this incredible increase in consumption caused another behavioral problem. "The issue was not quality, but quantity—turning out enough sewing machines; washing machines; dryers; television sets; electric irons; barbecue grills; tricycles; and, above all, automobiles to meet the demands of millions of young couples who were moving to the suburbs."[11] Nobody seemed to care about quality. It wasn't important. If the product didn't work, people had enough money to get another one as per capita income increased by almost 50 percent in the 1950s. That only fueled production even more as America's factories raced to meet sales requests, which then resulted in more real wages. What people didn't realize was that because they did not demand quality, they surely would not get it, as the mind-set of the American producer changed again. The importance of a quality product would be forgotten until the early 1980s.

TRANQUILLITY SHAKEN

As the 1950s came to a close and the 1960s began, the economic machine hummed on, but the country would experience another drastic social and economic change. From the calm and tranquillity of the 1950s, the United States would endure the tragedy of confrontation at home and abroad that would threaten to tear it apart. Having been a child of the decade, it is for me easy to remember Vietnam; the student uprisings at Columbia University and at the 1968 Democratic Convention, among other places; the racial conflicts in Newark, Watts, and at home in Cleveland; and the assassinations of Martin Luther King, Jr., John F. Kennedy, Robert Kennedy. There was the music of the Beatles, a fancy for beer, and the beginning of the drug culture, with Haight-Ashbury as a haven for many. The difference between the 1950s and the 1960s would be like night and day.

The 1960s were a time of expansion for America's bankers, as they deployed themselves overseas, looking for new sources of deposits: Eurodollars they were called, and they were not subject to Regulation Q. It would not be the last time that bankers found ways to skirt the Glass-Steagall Act as they looked for better spreads and higher profits than the domestic law would allow. As the bankers took a more global view, they were not alone. The 1960s was the decade that refocused the attention of the American people from the quiet of Elm Street to the far reaches of a world they were not sure that they wanted to know, either at home or abroad.

With the economy enjoying its legacy of the 1950s, it was logical to believe that all that had to be done was to expand what already had been happening. Therefore, as he took office, President Kennedy concluded that he did not have to alter the financial policies that were in place. Everything at home had been good for 15 years and all indicators showed that there was no reason it would not continue. Little did the president know that production in the United States was slowing while the operative capacities of Japan, the United Kingdom, Germany, and France were being restored.

To compound matters, there was that place called Vietnam. The new president inherited a situation that in all reality he could not win, but military action in Southeast Asia seemed the best way to stop the spread of communism. Kennedy was determined to fight it, which meant more people and matériel. He did not live to see the outcome of that decision, but his successor, Lyndon Johnson, stayed committed to the course Kennedy had set. As the war escalated, the government spent more and more.

The strategy was futile, trying to save a country that did not want to be saved. President Johnson had two choices: to step it up or to withdraw. He chose the former. Significantly, he also rejected a plea from Congress to raise taxes to pay for the war, preferring to rely on deficit spending. It was an economic decision that would affect the country for the rest of the decade and, when combined with decreasing domestic production, signaled the beginning of the economic decline of the United States. What followed in the nation's financial world could scarcely have been imagined and would change it completely.

Between 1949 and 1973, average family income doubled. Times had been very good. Vietnam had continued the economic legacy of World War II and the Korean Conflict. Even though Americans did not like the idea of their sons and daughters fighting in remote places, war fueled the economy and those at home benefited from it. Like Johnson, President Richard Nixon failed to raise taxes to pay for Vietnam. This started the inflationary spiral that would characterize, and humble, the United States for years. The deficits incurred by the federal government to finance the war increased significantly. Similarly, the lack of a corresponding tax hike left consumers with high amounts of disposable income which they continued to spend, effectively driving prices up. By 1971, the inflation rate had reached 4.5 percent and the deficits weakened the power of the dollar in overseas markets.

> Taken as a whole, the Nixon years set the nation on a course of inflation that was to culminate in the blowout of the late Seventies. It began in 1969, when Nixon took office and continued Lyndon Johnson's policy of fighting a war in Vietnam without raising taxes to pay for it. To combat the resulting inflation, Nixon imposed government controls on wages and prices. Persuaded by Federal Reserve Chairman Arthur F. Burns, Nixon went against virtually all his other economic advisers. Yet, he took little interest in the controls and the wall of inflationary pressures building up behind them . . . In the end, when controls were lifted, price pressures exploded.[12]

OIL SHOCK

World War II left the United States as the leader of an international neighborhood while it also faced increasingly troublesome domestic issues. There was the separation of Germany, the conflict in Korea, the threat of Cuba, troubles in the Middle East, the Vietnam war, the opening of relations with China, and nuclear proliferation treaties with the Soviet Union. There had been peace in the 1950s and violence in the 1960s, but the 1970s brought a different kind of turbulence that led to fundamental economic and political change in the United States. Americans didn't know it then and are just starting to realize its significance, but 25 years ago there was little reason to be concerned as the economy hummed along.

> The massive changes have largely gone unnoticed, in part, because making sense of change is never easy in retrospect. But the invisibility of these changes can also be traced to the twenty-five-to-thirty-year period of uncommon stability after World War II. The Cold War. Americanization, industrialization, the rise of an economy based on mass production and consumption— each of these defining forces of that period was based on a particular form of simplicity, namely uniformity. There was uniformity in goods, uniformity in services, uniformity in production methods, and uniformity in persons. There was only one telephone company, two superpowers, three television networks, and four automobile manufacturers. Moreover, there was uniformity in the way that uniformity was promoted: It was imposed from the top down through large institutions.[13]

The large corporations and the burgeoning government that had been building to police them had control of American lives, again limiting their pioneering, independent, and entrepreneurial spirit. The large corporations to which the soldiers flocked after World War II grew and grew, but they all looked the same. Then there were the banks—large, bureaucratic organizations in and of themselves—which were also encumbered by the Fed's cost and price controls that made them even more similar. They, too, had grown in size as the economy zoomed ahead, continuing to build branches on every street corner of the new suburbs that were springing up. Their products were the same; their people looked the same; their facilities were the same. That's what regulation had done.

With the war in Vietnam coming to a close, production in the nation's factories slowed, and unemployment began creeping upward. The Organization of Petroleum Exporting Countries (OPEC) made it even worse. Government and business were not prepared or able to deal with what was going to happen.

OPEC rammed through a fourfold hike in oil prices in 1973, sending an inflationary wave through the world economy. No one foresaw the hike in energy prices and, in one of those "small picture" decisions, Chairman Arthur Burns of the Federal Reserve chose to accommodate the surge with monetary expansion. In doing so, he threw gasoline on the fires of inflation. The logic? As long as prices were going higher, we would have to have more cash to pay them. It was at that point that the United States really began to lose its competitive edge against Japan, which had chosen to hang tough against inflation.[14]

In the winter of 1973–74, heating oil and gas prices increased by one-third because the United States had become dependent upon the OPEC nations for its petroleum reserves and therefore had to pay their price. Our dependency on others was now complete, something that our self-sufficient, pioneering forefathers would never have believed possible. In 1970, the United States had spent $4 billion on foreign oil; by 1980, it was $90 billion. In the spring of 1974, lines at the gas station never ended and the price of a gallon doubled; I used to have the cleanest car in Cleveland because I found a car wash that promised a full tank with every wash and wax. "Americans could no longer shape their economic future alone. In this sense, one commentator concluded, 'The year 1973 should probably be taken as a watershed, sharply dividing the second half of the twentieth century.' Prior to that, America had exercised virtually unchallenged economic and military dominance in the world."[15]

The OPEC price increase changed our immediate behavior: Gasoline was now a precious commodity and its high price limited the use of our beloved cars. It also resulted in a major change in our purchasing attitudes. Gas-guzzlers with big fins in the back were to be history as we looked for cars that were economical, but the Big Three automakers were stuck in their paradigm, mired in their bureaucratic organizations, and unable to respond to Honda, Toyota, and Nissan. Finally, Detroit gave us the Vega and the Pinto about which little has to be said. It was the same position in which the banks of the 1990s find themselves, facing foreign competition with better products. It would take 20 years for Chrysler, GM, and Ford to begin to reverse the trend, but it would never be the same again. Just look out in the parking lot.

Influences from the Middle East and Japan changed the way Americans lived during the 1970s. The United States was also experiencing a phenomenon called stagflation, that is high inflation and high unemployment, which was compounded by decreasing production. Productivity averaged 1 percent per year compared with 4 percent in Germany and 5 percent in Japan. The economy wound down and made its presence felt in the nation's banks. They saw their earnings start to fall, realized that their core business couldn't restore them, and therefore invested in high-risk activities, hoping to stem the tide. The real estate investment trust (REIT) was the culprit this time, and high-risk investments were a scenario that would be replayed again and again.

To stimulate investment in real estate projects, Congress had freed the REITs from paying corporate income taxes in 1960. These trusts would borrow in the open market from investors and banks, using the proceeds to finance construction and other real estate projects. In the early part of the 1970s, they had borrowed over $15 billion from the banks and were then turning around and lending to developers without the usual restraints attached to such loans by the banks. They did not require things like personal guarantees or preleasing minimums, and building after building sprouted from the ground.

Then the recession of 1974 hit. Combined with overcapacity and high construction costs and interest rates, it caused a severe depreciation of real estate values and sent most of the REITs into bankruptcy. That meant, of course, that they could not repay their loans. By spring 1978, the banks had written off over $1 billion. The question that remained? If the REITs were lending to developers without the terms and conditions that the banks themselves imposed on their customers, why did the banks finance them? The only answer was in the front-end fees banks could charge and the promise of high return, a combination that would come back to haunt them again a few short years later.

This behavioral pattern would be repeated—just like the 1920s when the banks rolled the dice on the stock market—and that is the most perplexing thing. The banks undertake a high-risk strategy that is out of their area of expertise and get burned, to the detriment of their shareholders, customers, and employees. Then they replicate the behavior again and again. It has even happened in 1995.

The 1970s were, for most, an unsettling time. The baby boomers were entering the job market and found competition there that would haunt them for the rest of their professional careers. The affluence that many of them expected was giving way to the prolonged economic decline that had begun 15 years earlier. Average personal income began to slip in 1973. During the Eisenhower years, the average family's income rose 30 percent, adjusted for inflation. The same increase occurred in the 1960s, but from 1973 through 1980 it fell 7 percent.[16]

At the same time, housing prices would nearly quadruple from 1968 through 1989. In 1950, our parents paid 14 percent of their wages for housing. By

1973, it was 21 percent, and 10 years later, when it was our turn, it would take 44 percent.[17] As costs accelerated, so did the workforce, which grew by an estimated 1,500,000 people per year. There weren't many good jobs around either, especially with unemployment running about 9 percent. There was no growth in the 1970s. In 1973, the top fifth of American families enjoyed a mean average income of $68,278. Ten years later, it was $66,607.[18] This harsh new reality was beginning to dawn on people as they discoed to the beat of the BeeGees and watched Mary Richards and Lou Grant on "The Mary Tyler Moore Show."

THE BANKER'S NEW WORLD

The action of OPEC was a blockbuster, but there was another watershed event in the mid-1970s, a very quiet one that would add to the turmoil of the nation's financial markets. Merrill Lynch introduced the cash management account (CMA) in 1975, which, in essence, changed the game for bankers forever. It signaled the entrance of nonbank competitors into the cozy little world of the commercial banking system in the United States. The CMA and similar accounts offered by other brokerages provided interest on deposits in accounts with check-writing privileges. It was a checking account that paid interest. The trade-off was that it was not insured by the FDIC.

With soaring inflation on everyone's mind, getting additional revenue from your checking account was a great idea. Who cared if the funds on deposit weren't insured? To have Merrill Lynch pay 10 percent or 11 percent—compared with what was earned at the bank, typically nothing on checking accounts and maybe 5 percent on passbook savings—was certainly an attractive alternative. "From a standing start in 1974, money market . . . funds grew to nearly $80 billion in outstandings by the end of 1979 . . . Although to a depositor these funds looked like they were interest-bearing checking accounts [which were prohibited by regulation], the Federal Reserve ruled in the mid-70s that these funds were not checking accounts."[19] They would continue to grow.

With the Fed's ruling, the banker was disadvantaged. This was strange because logic would suggest that the Fed, the banks' bank, would not want its constituents subject to additional competition. But that's what the Fed did, and there was no way for the banks to compete with the CMA, or whatever the investment house chose to call it. Bank regulation wouldn't let them. Neither would their internal bureaucracy. America's bankers were stuck in the rut of regulation where:

- They couldn't conceive of paying interest on checking accounts.
- Their automated systems would not let them pay interest on checking accounts, even if they wanted to.
- Rates earned and paid were determined by somebody else.

That had been the behavior for some 40 years. It was representative of the way we bankers always thought. The Fed wouldn't let the banks compete so that was the mind-set we developed. It never occurred to us that we could choose another strategy since the Fed was the umpire of the only game in town.

In the days before the CMA, however, that was OK. The prime was around 7 percent and Reg Q said we could pay around 3 percent, so we made at least 4 percent on every lending transaction. Four percent was enough to cover our operating expenses, so there was no need to do anything differently. As long as loans were of quality, the 4 percent margin was guaranteed.

With a margin that grew every time $1 was added to the portfolio, life at the bank was good albeit a little boring. It was surely good enough to cover the cost of building branches, investing in mainframe computers and systems, and hiring more people to make sure nothing went wrong. All that changed when Merrill brought out the CMA, throwing the banks into chaos. In the mid- to late 1970s, they weren't alone. The economy itself was reeling.

By December 1980, the inflation rate was still in double digits, the prime rate had crested at over 20 percent as the Fed was trying to curtail spending, and the unemployment rate was uncomfortably high as well. In *Quality Value Banking* we told the story of Gerry Donovan, chief trader on the money desk at Union Commerce Bank. Gerry's story bears repeating as it showed the turbulence of the money markets as the Fed sought to destroy inflation. It also shows what happened when the prime rate actually rose to 21.5 percent.

> It was the middle of 1980. The trading room at Union Commerce was in a more frenzied state than usual. Typically, the traders would be looking at their Reuters screens, telephones cradled between the shoulder and the ear, with clocks on the walls showing the time in four American time zones. There would be empty Burger King wrappers, half-consumed Cokes, cigarette smoke so thick you could cut it with a knife, and paper ledgers on the chief trader's desk which showed the bank's current position.
>
> Because of some of its problems in the past, Union Commerce was a daily buyer of funds; that meant we did not have a deposit base that was sufficient to fund our lending activities. Gerry Donovan's job was to purchase funds in the open market at the best possible rate available, which was, we hoped, less than the average rate being earned on the investment and loan portfolios.
>
> It was a Tuesday, late in the day, when the phone rang. It was Donovan, more animated than I had ever heard him. He said that the money markets had dried up; there was no money; and that the bank was basically insolvent. He had tried to buy funds all over the world, but even at 21 percent, there were none to be had. We were in deep trouble, especially if our customers found out and started a run on the bank.
>
> Somewhat less important, we were also looking at the prospect of funding loans that were earning 12 percent with funds that cost us over 20 percent.

So, even if we survived the crisis, the financial results would be poor, at best, which would send a signal that we did not want to our shareholders, customers, and employees.

I called our chairman and explained the situation and the one option that we had: to admit our problem to the Federal Reserve Bank of Cleveland and to borrow the money that we needed, a practice which was very much frowned upon in those days. Humbly, we called the Fed which came to the rescue. We would do the same thing several times in the next month. We avoided the run.

This story demonstrated the seriousness of the inflation issue. In order to whip it, money would have to be tight and rates would have to be high. As the Fed implemented that policy, however, it hurt the banks because most of them were carrying loans on their books that were earning less than the cost of the money they had to buy to fund them. It didn't take special intelligence to figure out that if we were earning 12 percent on the portfolio and the cost of funds was 20 percent, we were losing 8 percent, a situation which obviously could not last long.

With unemployment and inflation high and a recession in full swing, capital expenditures slowed, factory modernization came to a halt, and worker discontent increased. If that weren't bad enough, the Japanese had begun to serve the needs of the world's markets better than any other country as competitive advantage swung to the Far East. In 1960, the United States had been responsible for 35 percent of the world's economic output; by 1980, it was 22 percent. In 1960, we had shipped 22 percent of the world's exports; by 1980, only 11 percent. By 1980, more than 70 percent of all American-made goods were competing directly with goods from abroad.

Disposable income fell by 3 percent per year from 1973 through 1981. Most people, including the nation's bankers, feared that double-digit inflation was becoming permanent. Workers in the nation's offices and factories began to think that they were at the top of a financial escalator that only went down. They became disheartened and demotivated as they began to realize that they would never accumulate the money their parents had. They looked at management and saw the salaries, bonuses, and stock options; they saw their own opportunities for advancement narrowing; and they began to feel that something was very different. That played right into the management thinking at the time as the caste system, promulgated by the hierarchal organization, was the way to keep the organization under control. If we narrowed what people did, weren't too liberal with officer titles, and kept the management club closed and exclusive, we could keep a lid on costs and could ensure that people did only what they were told to do, no more, no less. Routine, uniform, bureaucratic, and impersonal. That was the way to handle the economic reality of 21 percent interest rates, falling earnings, and a suddenly rambling stock price.

REAGANOMICS

The electorate spoke loudly in 1980, calling Ronald Reagan to lead it out of the misery of stagflation and looking to him for hope. The new president responded. In a reversal of the New Deal policies of Franklin Roosevelt, Reagan was determined to give control back to the people. The president sponsored a substantial tax cut, which he believed would stimulate short-term purchasing and long-term investment. That would provide growth for U.S. manufacturers and thus more real wages, with the hope of generating more tax revenue as well.

That was all well and good; however, he also endorsed the tight money policy of the Fed, which drove rates up and tended to limit spending as it tried to cure the ravages of inflation that the legacy of Vietnam and OPEC had brought. On the one hand, Reagan wanted the American public and its corporations to buy while on the other hand, the interest rate scenario was aimed at curtailing their spending. Rates simply had to come down and stabilize while spending continued.

Reagan championed free competition, urged the unshackling of industries beset by regulation, and felt quite sure that business knew more about competition than government. Such a strategy would result in better quality, more competitive pricing, and even more growth. Not thinking systemically, the Reagan administration did not realize that a sudden relaxation of federal regulation might cause more behavioral problems than it would solve, especially for those in the banking system who had always been told what to do and how to do it.

The president also promoted and defended democracy whenever and wherever possible. His administration would spend as much for defense as President Johnson had done for the war in Vietnam and, like LBJ, it didn't raise taxes to pay for it. Congress was also trying to spend on some of its favorite social programs, while at the same time, Paul Volcker, chairman of the Federal Reserve Board, was trying to keep spending to a minimum to quell inflation. The result was economic gridlock in Washington, so that in 1981 the country slid even further into recession. By February 1982, unemployment was still over 8 percent and the prime rate was just under 17 percent. The deficit stood at $128 billion for 1982 alone.

Reagan would follow a familiar path. He would try to spend his way out of the problem. By 1983, his policies had started to work, spurred on by the massive defense spending, and the economy rebounded. He also had beat inflation, which fell to 6 percent because interest rates remained high. The federal deficit got bigger and bigger, but nobody seemed to care as Reagan poured money into defense and special domestic projects. The question remains: Was Reagan shortsighted, too? Was he so concerned about the immediacy of his reelection that he encouraged the deficit spiral and did not worry about the long-term consequences?

DEREGULATION

Just think how you, as a banker, would have felt in 1979 when you heard Ronald Reagan campaign for deregulation. You'd have been overjoyed, even if you weren't quite sure what it all meant. "Oh, boy, now we can compete with Merrill Lynch." In response to the CMA, America's bankers had to level the playing field or the brokerages would take all of their customers. Either they had to be able to offer services that matched the CMA or the severe disintermediation from their vaults would continue, jeopardizing their very existence. The U.S. banking system could not simply go the way of the buggywhip and the horse and wagon.

Merrill Lynch; Goldman, Sachs; Fidelity; and the rest of the new competition offered the CMA or its equivalent. These accounts became very profitable because these organizations had three distinct cost advantages over the banks. First, they were not subject to the burdensome regulations of the banks. In one very small example, the amount of paper completed in U.S. commercial banks that was sent to the Fed, FDIC, Comptroller of the Currency, and the various state banking commissions was staggering. Paper cost was not cheap, but think about the people whose job it was to fill out the forms and to send them in. It would take four or five full-time people, plus the paper, plus the computers, plus the overtime—and you get the idea. Merrill Lynch wasn't required to do all that.

Second, and much more important, Merrill Lynch and Goldman, Sachs had modern delivery systems. They used telemarketing, advertising on television, computer networks, and other technology to acquaint potential customers with the benefits of the CMA and its clones. The banks, on the other hand, had branches dotting every street corner which were filled by people who were there to gather the neighborhood's deposits. Those branches and the cost to keep them operating were expensive. Think about the courier service, the lease cost, the people expense, the cost to plow the snow and cut the grass, insurance, and so on. The brokerages didn't have to have branches.

Third, the banks had to pay insurance premiums to the FDIC. Because the brokerages were offering uninsured accounts, they did not have the expense that the banks had. When we add the cost of the branch system to the expense of regulation, then factor in the additional interest expense caused by prevailing monetary policy, and the banks' net income was squeezed very hard. In an industry that had enjoyed a very calm ride since the 1940s, something was definitely different. Look at Exhibit 3–3 and Exhibit 3–4.

These two critical measures of performance show the problem. Merrill Lynch and the others were cutting into the banks' revenues while they also maintained a cost advantage, which they have done to this day. Hence, the need for the banking revolution.

E X H I B I T   3-3

ROA: 1979–1987

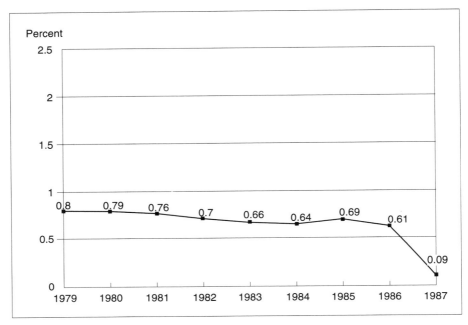

Source: Federal Deposit Insurance Corp.

The bankers of 1979 saw the disintermediation and pressed hard for the ability to compete, not understanding that because they had always had price controls they might be getting into some new and different territory. Nevertheless, they had to have the freedom to set their own interest rates; if they didn't, the brokerages would eventually drive them out of business. The first attempt to bring some equilibrium to the financial markets came in the form of the Depository Institutions Deregulation and Monetary Control Act of 1980, otherwise known as DIDMCA. This legislation contained the following major changes:

- Phased out Regulation Q interest rate limits over a six-year period, 1981–1986.
- Raised FDIC coverage from $40,000 to $100,000.
- Permitted all depository institutions to pay interest on checking accounts.
- Required that the Federal Reserve make its services available to all depository institutions.

EXHIBIT 3–4

ROE: 1979–1987

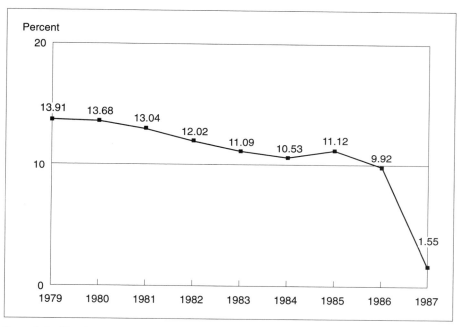

Source: Federal Deposit Insurance Corp.

This was all well and good, but having to wait six years to be able to compete on rates continued to put the banks at a disadvantage. The bankers wanted to get going, but they couldn't. DIDMCA allowed them to begin to fight back, but it did not go far enough fast enough. Perhaps Washington was suspicious of giving bankers too many new freedoms too soon. In any event, DIDMCA did not result in that level ground between banks and nonbank depository institutions.

The bankers knew it and lobbied hard, even if they may not have realized what was going to happen to them next. The outcome, two years later, was the Depository Institutions Act of 1982, otherwise known as the Garn-St. Germain Act, which sought to remedy the shortfalls of DIDMCA by making the following adjustments:

- Allowed the banks to introduce accounts that could compete directly with the CMA.

- Enhanced the power of the FDIC to save failing banks.

- Required that all depository institutions could offer the same rates, whereas previously the savings and loans could pay a higher savings rate.
- Allowed the S&Ls to offer both commercial and consumer loans.

The banks and thrifts jumped aggressively into the market, but they forgot one thing. With the ability to compete came an implicitly higher interest cost; the higher rates paid to their customers kept the pressure on their margins. Again, when combined with their cost structures, the banks were not out of the woods, by a long shot. They should have seen it coming; they should have realized that their antiquated pyramid structures and brick-and-mortar delivery systems were expensive and had been built for another time. They didn't, and earnings continued to suffer. By the end of 1984, more than $200 billion had been siphoned off into the CMA and similar accounts at other brokerages with only a little less than $300 billion remaining in the banks and S&Ls.

It was the end of one era and the beginning of another. From their cozy cocoons that were protected by Regulation Q, the banks found themselves looking not only at First National from Across-the-Street as the competition, but also General Motors, AT&T, Safeway Supermarkets, Sears, and American Express, in addition to Merrill Lynch. For the banking community, the 1980s were a whole new ball game. It used to be that the banking system had a monopoly on the financial services offered to the American public. Suddenly and swiftly, every service that they offered, including deposit insurance, was now offered by somebody else. What is more, chances were pretty good that the new competition had a more efficient cost structure which gave it another advantage. Better products and lower prices, Deming told us, will indeed create a market.

LATIN AMERICA, OKLAHOMA, WALL STREET, AND NEW ENGLAND

The late 1970s and 1980s saw a state of frenzied activity in the banking industry. There were a lot of things going on at the same time as bankers grappled with the profound changes that were rattling their industry. The important thing to understand is the banks' behavior as they sought to restore their bottom lines to their former status. They would try to increase revenues, to find economies of scale, and to cut costs, but they would never look at the real culprits: the blocks and barriers of ineffective organization structure, strategies that did not address the real issues head-on, and behavior that precluded the delivery of world-class service.

It had begun years before. As Merrill Lynch was attacking the liability side of the balance sheet, there were some assaults on the asset side as well. Many of the largest banking customers in the United States had found the

Eurodollar, Eurobond, and commercial paper markets where they obtained loans directly from investors, effectively bypassing the banks. Loan portfolios declined, interest income dropped, earnings decreased, and even more pressure was put on the bottom line and stock price. " 'You've got a chronic asset-quality problem,' [said] a Fed policy maker. 'You've got too many loans chasing too few profitable alternatives.' It's that problem that drives the banks so heavily into Third World loans, leveraged buyouts (LBOs), and commercial real estate—the areas now giving them such problems."[20]

"Welcome to Latin America," the sign said. Many U.S. banks, most of them from New York, had been encouraged by the federal government to make loans to the developing nations of the world. The banks believed that they had a promise from Washington that if the loans went sour, the government would back them up. It was a great proposition: high earnings and no risk, just like the prospect of the REITs a decade before. Therefore, the banks lent huge sums to Brazil, Mexico, and other Latin American countries to enable them to import those goods that would assist in the creation of a self-sufficient economy, thinking of course that no sovereign nation on earth had ever gone broke.

As they tried to build productive capacities, the Latin American countries developed a voracious appetite for borrowed funds. Competition in these markets drove the banks to some very generous terms and conditions, so that by 1981 the top 15 debtor nations owed U.S. banks $334 billion which carried annual interest payments of $44 billion, two rather sizable sums.

The ability to pay the interest and to reduce the principal was solely dependent upon each country's ability to generate income. As long as they could sell their products in the world's markets, they could generate sufficient funds to service the debt, but when the recession hit, that ability was severely hindered. As in the Great Depression, the problem was one of insufficient consumption. It became apparent to U.S. banks that the debt would not be repaid. That left them with billions of dollars of nonearning assets on their books, which put even more pressure on their income statements. Bank depositors were not at risk because of the FDIC's safety net, but shareholder value suffered. Throughout the 1980s, the banks added more and more to their reserves for bad debts of developing nations, which reached over $14 billion by the end of 1987. If that were not enough, some of the nation's bankers had chosen another path: trying for the quick buck, disdaining the idea of the risk-reward trade-off.

The sign read, "Welcome to Oklahoma City." It was just like the story of the stock market, the REITs, and the Latin American developing nations—the promise of wealth in exchange for risk that either the bankers did not see or chose to ignore. As such, we need to take one last look at Penn Square, another example of how the banks have taken less than prudent action, resulting in massive losses and failure. Instead of a perfectly Darwinian U.S. economy, in which those who make the mistakes are punished with bankruptcy, the FDIC was there to make sure that the depositors of the nation's banks would never lose their savings. If a bank had a problem, the depositor would be made whole by Uncle Sam.

The story began in Oklahoma City, which had become the home of Penn Square National Bank in 1960. By early 1975, Penn Square had assets of $35 million, which suddenly grew to $100 million within the next four years, spurred on by investment in oil and gas. As long as the wells continued to produce, everything was fine. Benjamin Klebaner documented what happened in *American Commercial Banking.*

> Rig operations dropped by 40 percent between December 1981 and July 1982, but Penn Square's loans soared from $239 million to $421 million. Participations sold to other banks grew to $2.1 *billion.* By July 1982 Continental Illinois had acquired $1.13 billion, and Seattle First National $378 million. Chase Manhattan (long renowned as an oil lender) had $275 million, 58 percent was charged off by 1985. Michigan National Bank lost almost half of its $199 million in Penn Square loans. Among these gullible lenders, only Chase Manhattan survived intact.[21]

Oil prices fell through the floor. In 1982, the price of a barrel stood at an artificially high $42; a year later OPEC cut it to $28.50. In a repeat of the debacles with REITs and loans to developing nations, the banks were hung out to dry by borrowers who could not make enough money to service their debt. In Texas, a lot of new signs went up. Chemical Bank of New York acquired Texas Commerce; First Interstate took over Allied; MCorp became part of BancOne; and Republicbank and Interfirst joined to form First Republic, which was subsequently taken over by NCNB, the predecessor of NationsBank. Additionally, Seattle First was forced to merge with Bank of America, but the world waited to see what would happen to Continental Illinois.

Continental Illinois was the sixth largest bank in the country in 1981. It had grown tremendously in the 1970s as Roger Anderson, its chairman, encouraged his officers to make loans. Len Barker, now with KeyCorp in Cleveland, had been with Continental during the expansion and told me that it was "Go! Go! Go!" Management knew of the risks of participating in the Penn Square loans, but they saw a chance to make that quick buck, effectively rolling the dice that nothing would go wrong. However, there were two main problems. First, Continental Illinois had grown so fast that it had not taken the time to train its lenders in the art of credit risk. Second, the bank's internal control systems were ignored when they began to indicate there was a problem. Any experienced officer could have seen, as Barker recounted, that there is little sense in making energy-related loans at a time when prices were falling. Continental is an example of what can happen when greed becomes more important than customer service.

Anderson's petroleum-related portfolio continued to grow. By 1982, as we have seen, it had $1.13 billion of Penn Square's participations on its books. When OPEC cut the price, Penn Square went under, leaving Continental with 7.7 percent of its total loans on nonperforming status. The problem became apparent in May 1984. Continental's depositors saw that the very capital structure of the bank was at risk and started withdrawing funds. An electronic run was soon under way, starting in Hong Kong, moving to London, and finally coming home to the United States.

It was a good thing that the FDIC understood the domino effect of what was happening because it moved quickly to shore up the capital base of the failing bank. Continental was bigger than all of the banks that went bankrupt in the Great Depression put together. Therefore, drastic measures were in order. The FDIC bought $4.5 billion in bad loans, encouraged the major banks to lend another $5.5 billion, and invested $1 billion in preferred stock to prevent the bank from bankruptcy and taking its 2,000 small correspondents with it. These actions also prevented some serious problems at some larger banks such as the Bank of America, Manufacturers Hanover, and Continental's hometown neighbor and rival, First Chicago, in addition to some 50 Midwestern banks that had "more than their entire bank capital on deposit at Continental . . . *That's* why it was worth saving."[22]

Continental Illinois survived the scare; its depositors were saved from risk. However, the bank never recovered and was sold to Bank of America on January 28, 1994. Other banks would not be so lucky. The same fate that awaited Penn Square reached Abilene National Bank, Oklahoma National Bank, First National Bank of Midland, and First National Bank of Oklahoma City. Fifty-two banks were claimed by the crisis in 1985, 84 more failed in 1986, and 120 closed their doors for the last time in 1987, all the result of misguided strategy from nearly a decade before.[23]

The Continental Illinois affair showed a basic flaw in the banking system. Glass-Steagall stated that banks must operate in their traditional markets and could not expand into new ones such as insurance and other types of investment products. That meant that banks could not compete with brokerages, which were now offering products like, and better than, the banks'. With the banks' burdensome cost structures, the disadvantage would continue to increase, forcing bankers to find new sources of revenues within those established markets. Higher revenue in banking means more risk. Clearly, neither Brazil and Mexico, nor Texas and Oklahoma, were the promised land.

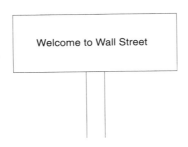

"Welcome to Wall Street," the sign read. Oh, the fees that a deal like RJR Nabisco could bring! Banks that got involved in financing such ventures could make 1 percent to 2 percent of the value of the transaction. That meant anywhere from $260 million to $520 million for the RJR deal. A nice piece of change when banks were scrambling for earnings that said to the enterprising young banker of the 1980s, "The higher the value of the deal, the more the bank makes. The more the bank makes, the more I make. Hmmmmm."

Commercial banks had financed leveraged buyouts, mergers and acquisitions, and recapitalizations starting in the 1970s. There would be a few deals every year, but starting in 1986 it got a little crazy. Between 1986 and 1989, an average of 300 deals were made each year, representing billions of dollars that changed hands.

The problem with these transactions was that they were driven by the investment bankers, not by the organization's market expertise and growth. They were caused by Wall Street financiers who tried to figure out how much they could get for the surviving restructured company, either by selling off divisions, changing product lines, moving to areas where labor was cheaper, or other such tactics. When one group determined it could get "x" for the acquired organization, the ego of the other group drove them to find "x + 20 percent," which then drove the third one to find "x + 20 percent + 20 percent more," and so on. That fostered a bidding war; the price of a share of Kraft went from $59.50 to $102.00 in the first 12 days of the takeover battle.[24]

When the owners of companies, like anyone else, saw the kinds of appreciation that were taking place in the financial markets, they reasoned that they might as well cash in on the deal too, hanging on for the highest possible price. So were the bankers who financed the deals. They had a lot of money to lend, and they would get those wonderful fees. Prices went skyward, just like they had on Wall Street some 60 years before.

There would be a limit. The restructured company would have to be able to provide a return sufficient to pay for the transaction. By 1990, it was apparent that many of the resultant companies could not do that. As with the oil and gas lending, the REITs, and the loans to developing countries, if the borrower could not service the debt from the bank, trouble loomed ahead. The Bank of Boston, for example, invested $2.5 billion in leveraged buyouts (LBOs), one-fifth of which were rated "substandard," as of November 1989.[25]

During the 1980s, more than 100 of the companies listed on the Fortune 500 list were acquired or were the subject of an LBO. In a scene that would also be played out in the nation's banks, corporate America was changing. The books are not closed on the exposure suffered by the banks in these leveraged transactions and the resultant restructuring, but that is not the real issue. What matters is the behavior of the banker who, driven by the chance to raise fee income, passed the point of prudency again. It was as though the lessons of the past had not meant anything.

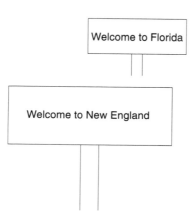

"Welcome to New England," read the next sign. A little further on, one proclaimed, "Welcome to Florida." The pressure for earnings continued to outweigh common sense and the lessons of history. The red ink from losses incurred in Latin America, energy-related loans, and the highly leveraged transactions wasn't even dry when commercial real estate became the hot ticket for the nation's banks. While only the big banks financed Henry Kravis, Ted Forstmann, and the other LBO specialists, all of them plunged headfirst into the commercial real estate market, to the tune of about $400 billion by the end of the 1980s. Commercial real estate loans offered a new opportunity to raise interest income.

There were plenty of places to find it, and the stampede was on. The Economic Recovery Tax Act of 1981 had made it advantageous taxwise for people to invest in real estate projects that, in turn, allowed developers to find money easily. The building boom was on. That meant the price of land appreciated; an increase in the number of projects meant a shortage of skilled labor, driving wages skyward; construction materials were in short supply; all of which contributed to higher-priced properties. As the value of buildings increased, so did the rents because the developers had to cover their mortgage payments. It was just like the stock market run-up of 60 years earlier, and the banks played a contributing part.

Consider the plight of First American Bank & Trust of North Palm Beach, Florida. The bank used real estate as the vehicle in its effort to grow. It increased its real estate portfolio by 70 percent between 1984 and 1986, which was more than 50 percent of its entire loans, obviously violating the rule of diversification. Taking advantage of Florida's expansion, there were condominiums, malls, and office towers to build, and First American was right there ready to help. *Business Week* reported that "in the rush to grow, loans were often approved without financial statements and personal net-worth histories . . . loan documentation was woefully inadequate."[26] Operations were a problem as well, as internal control systems broke down, making it hard to find problems, like it had been at Continental a few years before. Losses piled up as developers could not pay interest or repay principle and First American became the 205th out of 206 banks "to close in 1989, the worst year for bank failures since the Depression."[27]

Previously, a developer would have to assure the bank that 90 percent of the building was leased before the project could start. The process used to be to find the land, then the architect, then the contractor, then the tenants, and then the financing. During the frenzy of the 1980s, that somehow got turned around as banks, hungry for the front-end fees and resulting interest payments, made commitments to the developers first. That meant that a building could rise from the ground without any tenants at all in a worst-case scenario. Thus, as more expensive buildings went up, rents would follow until they became too high and potential tenants would find alternative leasing arrangements in less pricey neighborhoods.

As that phenomenon occurred, vacancy rates began to rise. Banking ob-
server Lowell L. Bryan reported that vacancy rates rose from 5 percent to 20
percent between 1980 and 1990, with the supply of available space increasing
by 200 percent while rents were kept artificially high by developers who were
trying to get their money out. That told others that the market was still strong
when, in reality, it was weakening by the day.

As with the other scenarios described in this section, the banks were OK
until the sources of revenues of its borrowers began to fall, which is what happened in the mid-1980s. Rents began to drop even as more space was becoming
available. That meant more unused capacity and a further decline in the price
that could be charged in a classic supply-and-demand situation. With rates
dropping, interest payments stopped. Loans went on nonaccrual and finally had
to be charged off. The wreckage was universal as the following reports in the
press indicate.

> The massive job cuts double [Citicorp's] previous estimates, underlining the
> tough times hitting the banking industry. [Chairman John] Reed also said that
> Citicorp's troubled real estate loans, its main scourge and a problem crippling
> scores of U.S. banks, should peak next year [1991].[28]

> First Chicago's restructuring follows similar cost-cutting efforts at Citicorp,
> Chase Manhattan Corp., and Security Pacific Corp. as well as announcements
> of merger plans that are expected to produce layoffs at Chemical Banking
> Corp., Manufacturers Hanover Corp., NCNB Corp. and C&S/Sovran Corp.
> Most of these banks have made big cuts in their corporate lending business
> which has been hurt by thin profit margins and a rising tide of soured loans,
> particularly on commercial real estate.[29]

> Shawmut National Corp., citing deterioration in the New England real estate
> market, reported a fourth quarter loss of $215.7 million, said it plans to cut its
> work force 10 percent, or about 1,200 employees.[30]

> At June 30, [1990], past-due real estate loans plus foreclosed properties rose 52
> percent to $1.75 billion, from $1.15 billion at March 31. In the first half, Chase's
> net income sank 64 percent from a year earlier to $96 million, or 44 cents a
> share, as its provision for losses on bad loans grew 50 percent to $450 million.[31]

> "Unquestionably, the earnings of Ohio banks, including Huntington and Na-
> tional City and BancOne and Ameritrust, clearly have been nicked because of
> increases in loan-loss provisions—and about half of that is caused by real es-
> tate," said Elmer Meszaros, an analyst with Roulston & Co.[32]

> Hurt by the collapsing real estate market and the recession, the Pittsburgh-
> based concern raised its provision for credit losses by $175 million. Mellon
> said the increase reflects a rise in assets not earning interest, particularly bad
> real estate loans which jumped by $103 million, or 18 percent, from the end
> of the third quarter.[33]

Bank of Boston has just recorded a $125 million loss for third quarter, after setting aside $370 million to cover a mounting pile of troubled loans . . . What happened? To some extent, Bank of Boston's troubles are simply the result of the cooling of the once-torrid New England economy. But the bank had made itself especially vulnerable to such a downturn by shoveling millions of dollars into loans to neophyte developers, builders who ran into big trouble when home buyers turned cautious.[34]

Federal regulators yesterday took over Bank of New England Corp., the region's third largest bank holding company. The Federal Deposit Insurance Corp. assumed control of Bank of New England, the holding company's $13.2 billion core, Connecticut Bank & Trust Co., which has $7.7 billion in assets, and the $1.1 billion Maine National Bank.[35]

It was the pressure for earnings that drove many of the nation's banks to take these kinds of unnecessary risks. Customers were walking out the door to visit the new competition and the regulatory climate would not let the banks play on the same field. Many of the banks rolled the dice and lost and then had to jettison people and assets to survive.

We began to see headlines that proclaimed the great benefits to be achieved from this new and different approach to earnings improvement. It was an interesting tactic. The market dictated the cost of funds. Fees were running into the same problem; besides, the customer was getting tired of them. There weren't any more opportunities to raise interest income. The only thing left was to cut costs. That was the logic.

SLASH-AND-BURN

As the real estate woes gripped most of the nation's banks and profitability suffered, bank stock prices reflected it. Wall Street didn't like what it was seeing as bank after bank reported losses in the late 1980s and early 1990s. Trading of the stock was brisk because many investors wanted to unload their shares, fearing, like the Bank of New England, they would become worthless. Chase and Citicorp lost 50 percent of their market value in the second and third quarters of 1990. Prudential Securities took a sell position on them as well as on such stalwarts as Chemical, Manufacturers Hanover, First Chicago, First Interstate, First Union, Wells Fargo, PNC, and Norwest. In total, money center banks lost about 35 percent of their share price compared with the S&P 500, which lost only 9 percent.[35]

It was time to cut expenses and cut they did. The problem was, however, that the banks cut not knowing if what was being taken out actually provided benefit to their customers. Cost reduction became the rage as CEO after

CEO saw the stock price dive. From First Interstate in Los Angeles to Chase Manhattan in New York, banks underwent the trauma of these indiscriminate slash-and-burn, cost-cutting efforts. What made it even more emotional was that companies other than banks were doing it, too.

The nation's business periodicals carried stories about the cost reduction programs at McGraw-Hill, IBM, Shearson, AT&T, Ohio Bell, General Electric, Eastman Kodak, Du Pont, Apple Computers, and on and on. Whether it was called "restructuring," "downsizing," "rightsizing," or what have you, the 1980s saw a behavior that may not have been totally justified. It may well be that these huge companies did have some bureaucratic bloat and that some cost reduction was required, but more likely the cuts were made to shore up profits to satisfy the analysts on Wall Street. It didn't work.

Dr. Donald E. Rosen, a psychiatrist who directs the Professionals in Crisis at the Menninger Clinic, said that those who survive "are lethargic, feel empty, [and are] no longer able to take satisfaction in what they once enjoyed . . . They have a deep questioning of the tasks they perform."[37] They no longer like to go to work. It's called survivor syndrome.

All the while, management is talking about teamwork and pulling together for the long term in an empowered environment. The literature suggests, and I can vouch, that after a cost-cutting exercise, very few people in the workforce trust their management anymore. If workers have seen their friends displaced, what is to prevent management from doing it again, only the next time they may be on the list. That gets very expensive as people hunker down to protect themselves and work on their résumés when they could be writing business proposals. Those who are lucky find a new position and leave, taking their talent and experience with them. That's good, says the cost cutter, because "we won't have to pay salaries and benefits anymore." What about lost sales?

MERGER MANIA I

The 1980s saw another phenomenon that was new to bankers: acquisitions and mergers. As I wondered then and still do now, what made them think that mergers were good? We always talked about the great economies of scale to be achieved, but with the serious limitations on bank cost accounting systems, it was very difficult, if not impossible, to tell whether or not they were being accomplished.

> As I was riding home on the transit one winter day in 1980, I asked a veteran banker if mergers would ever hit our industry like the ones we had been reading about in the manufacturing sector.
>
> "Of course not," came the reply. "The Fed would never allow it."
>
> A year later, I was in charge of merging Union Commerce Corporation into Huntington Bancshares. This hostile takeover demonstrated the volatility

that struck the industry as the fierce battle for Union Commerce was one for which neither organization was prepared. On July 23, 1983, Union Commerce disappeared.

It was a harbinger of things to come as bank after bank pursued the merger strategy. They thought that by merging with another institution, they could gain those "economies of scale." They could consolidate operations and staff departments, taking advantage of the reduced people cost. Thousands of bankers were terminated. I was never quite sure that the consolidations really did provide economic value; intuitively, I thought they should provide the ability to drive down unit costs. After all, with so many duplicated positions, how could they not?

We watched as BancOne left its Columbus home and acquired organizations in Texas, Wisconsin, Arizona, and Indiana; as Wachovia, First Union, and NCNB would divide the southeast; as New England became the target for Shawmut, Fleet, and Bank of New England; as National City and Huntington sought to expand outside the state of Ohio; and as BankAmerica ventured up to Washington to save the troubled Seafirst. While all of this was going on, I was hard at work at Society integrating 3rd National, Dayton; Harter Bank, Canton; and Central National, Cleveland; with Trustcorp and Ameritrust right around the corner. Like cost cutting and lending to speculating real estate developers, mergers seemed to be the latest in a long line of fads that the nation's bankers pursued. Oh, but these were providing value. Or were they?

The shareholders of the target were surely enriched. Criticism, however, was levied at CEOs who paid entirely too much for the new franchise, with studies showing many of the deals were not delivering what had been promised. " 'On paper, all these deals look pretty encouraging,' says Judah Kraushaar, an analyst with Merrill Lynch & Co. But he adds, particularly for deals assuming big revenue gains, 'the risk of some of these deals not being 100 percent executed [as planned] is going to grow.'"

The mergers had the same effect as the cost cutting. Behavior became defensive and self-protective. Little risk would be taken, even at a time when the new competition was sweeping away the bank's customers. It would turn the workforce inward as they tried to wring out as much cost as they possibly could, but that strategy may have backfired. You see, while everyone at the bank was figuring out how to "do more with less," the competition was expanding its marketing efforts. At a time when bankers should have been out in their markets working with their customers, they were in their merger task force meetings, filling out forms, or trying to determine whom they could do without. I know . . . I was there.

One thing I will admit curiosity about: Why do bankers pursue these fads? Is it because they are afraid to be left behind by somebody else who has tried something new? Cathy Mitchell, then vice president at National City Bank, called it a "lemming syndrome," meaning that the bankers would follow any new strategy that a competitor had devised, even to a less than desirable end. If that is the case, why haven't more of them copied Merrill Lynch?

In the early 1990s, as in the 1930s, the banking industry had serious problems, but no one offered a long-term, sustainable solution. The bottom had fallen out of the commercial real estate market, cost cutting was rampant, the deposit insurance fund had been depleted by the savings and loan fiasco, 8 percent of the nation's banks were on the problem list, more banks had failed in the 1980s than in any decade since the 1930s, and competition was everywhere. These struggles were expensive because the rating agencies downgraded the banks' bond ratings, resulting in the banks having to pay higher interest rates. ROA, for the industry, continued to fall, going from .80 percent in 1979 to .53 percent in 1991. It was not a pretty picture as Washington and Wall Street wondered what to do.

The interest rate spread would not last as the cost of funds would catch up, narrowing bank earnings. Cost cutting would still be the emphasis as bankers sought to prop them up. Of course, there were still derivatives, those misunderstood financial instruments that caused real problems for KeyCorp, Bankers Trust, PNC, BancOne, and the rest. It was reminiscent of REITs, energy-related loans, HLTs, loans to developing countries, and commercial real estate. An improperly supervised employee-trader proved it was possible to bankrupt a major institution such as Barings.

> In one humiliating blow, [Nick] Leeson's huge trading loss wiped out the blue-blood investment bank's $900 million in capital and prompted the Bank of England to put Barings into bankruptcy. The collapse also sent shivers down the spines of bankers around the globe. "With so much money moving around so quickly, this is the kind of thing all of us worry about," says First Chicago Corp. CEO Richard L. Thomas. "It's stunning to think that a 233-year-old institution can be brought to its knees overnight."[38]

NOW WHAT?

What I have tried to do in this and the previous chapter is to provide an understanding of why the banking industry is in crisis, even though it does not think it is. Banking is an integral part of the U.S. economy and is now forever connected to the federal government. From 1933 to 1980, it was regulated as to what it could do, where it could do it, and the prices it could charge. In a big hurry, that very quiet and cozy world changed. There was the CMA, exploding technology, new entrants into the industry from nearly everywhere, the falling apart of the real estate market, and the necessary reduction of costs. The problem is that in this very different competitive and economic environment, the behavior, save the rhetoric, remains the same.

We continue to hear:

"Build expensive branches and other facilities to gather deposits."

"Invest in high-risk misunderstood securities with the hope of the big return."

"Keep the efficiency ratio as low as possible to please the analysts."

"Make sure that the hierarchy is intact."

"Be on the lookout for merger partners, even big ones, where we might be able to get some economies of scale."

"Let's declare victory over this service thing and move on."

Only in a few places do we hear bankers call for a completely new and radical way of dealing with their new environment.

So far, we have seen the problem and the opportunity. We need to understand, however, why the problem exists so that we can do something about it. In the remainder of *The Banking Revolution,* I will present the root causes of the problem, notably the existence of inflexible structure and misguided strategy, and will conclude it with a prescription to remedy it.

Before we begin the next leg of this journey, read a quote about Ed Crutchfield, CEO of the progressive First Union of Charlotte, North Carolina, that puts the matter into perspective.

In a decade, its [First Union's] assets have climbed tenfold, to $75 billion. The stock trades at 45 3/4, roughly eight times projected 1995 earnings, compared with nine times for the industry. Last year, First Union earned $4.73 a share, almost double 1989's level, and this year it likely will report $5.20.

So, why isn't Crutchfield smiling?

Because, he says, like a lot of bankers, he pursued the wrong strategy. "While we were busy buying other banks and congratulating ourselves," says Crutchfield, "someone else—Merrill Lynch, GE Capital, Fidelity, Schwab, and Goldman, Sachs—were out there stealing our best customers by the tens of thousands.

"I was in denial," says Crutchfield, recalling the day three years ago when colleagues showed projections that cast doubts on his buy-and-build strategy. "But, those charts corroborated what I was feeling in my bones, that banking as we know it is a dead business."[39]

On June 19, 1995, however, Ed Crutchfield smiled as he was being interviewed on CNN. First Union had just acquired First Fidelity, giving it a substantial foothold in the northeastern part of the country in addition to its existing presence. Merger Mania II was just around the corner. In the most telling statement, Crutchfield said that his company was planning a migration of another sort. This trip was to be a technological one: from branches to PCs. The revolution was on!

ENDNOTES

1. Lloyd Wendt, *The Wall Street Journal* (Chicago: Rand McNally, 1982). p. 201.
2. Ron Chernow, *The House of Morgan* (New York: Atlantic Monthly Press, 1990), pp. 303–4.
3. Ibid., p. 320.
4. Anthony J. Badger, *The New Deal: The Depression Years, 1933–40* (New York: Noonday Press, 1989), p. 33.
5. Paul Leinberger and Bruce Tucker, *The New Individualists: The Generation after the Organization Man* (New York: HarperCollins, 1991), p. 128.
6. Arthur Schlesinger, Jr., quoted in *The New Deal,* ed. Carl. N. Degler (Chicago: Quadrangle Books, 1970), p. 17.
7. Cabell Phillips, *The 1940s: Decade of Triumph and Trouble* (New York: Macmillan, 1995) p. 140.
8. Leinberger and Tucker, *The New Individualists,* p. 29.
9. Ibid., p. 30.
10. Ibid., p. 125.
11. Ibid., pp. 29–30.
12. "Nixon: A Tattered Economic Legacy," *Business Week,* May 9, 1994, p. 102.
13. Leinberger and Tucker, *The New Individualists,* p. 306.
14. "Nixon: A Tattered Economic Legacy," p. 102.
15. William H. Chafe, *The Unfinished Journey* (New York: Oxford University Press) p. 447.
16. Leinberger and Tucker, *The New Individulest,* p. 277.
17. Lowell L. Bryan, *Bankrupt: Restoring the Health and Profitability of Our Banking System* (New York: HarperBusiness, 1991), p. 54.
18. Paul Duke, Jr., and David B. Hilder, "Banks' Woes at a Time of Economic Gloom Are Cause of Concern," *The Wall Street Journal,* Nov. 1, 1990, p. A12.
19. Benjamin J. Klebaner, *American Commercial Banking: A History* (Boston: Twayne, 1990), p. 230.
20. Lewis T. Preston, quoted in Chernow, *The House of Morgan,* p. 659.
21. Klebaner, *American Commercial Banking,* p. 231.
22. Bryan, *Bankrupt,* p. 112.
23. Christopher J. Chipello. "Bank of Boston Faces the Perils That Await Eager 'Superregionals,'" *The Wall Street Journal,* Nov. 17, 1989, p. A1.
24. Gail DeGeorge, "Portrait of a Classic Bank Collapse," *Business Week,* July 16, 1990, p. 150.
25. Ibid.
26. Reuters, "Citicorp to Cut 4,250 Jobs over Next Two Years" *The Plain Dealer,* December 8, 1990, p. D2.
27. Peter Pae, "First Chicago Cuts 1,000 Jobs, Takes a Charge," *The Wall Street Journal,* July 25, 1991, p. A6.
28. Lawrence Ingrassia, "Shawmut Posts Quarterly Loss, Will Cut Staff," *The Wall Street Journal,* Jan. 24, 1991, p. A5.
29. Robert Daniels, "Chase to Offer Severance to Employees, Take $30 Million 3rd-Quarter Charge," *The Wall Street Journal,* Aug. 13, 1990, p. A4.
30. Miriam Hill, "Real Estate Woes Hitting Banks Hard," *The Plain Dealer,* Dec. 23, 1990, p. 1-E.

31. James S. Hirsch and Michael J. McCarthy, "NCNB Net Fell, Mellon Had Loss in 4th Quarter," *The Wall Street Journal,* Jan. 21, 1991, p. A5.

32. Chipello, "Band of Boston Faces the Perils," p. A1.

33. Kenneth H. Bacon and Ron Suskind, "U.S. Recession Claims Bank of New England as First Big Victim," *The Wall Street Journal,* Jan. 7, 1991, p. A1.

34. Gary Weiss, "Bottom-Fishers Are Eyeing the Banks," *Business Week,* Nov. 12, 1990, p. 119.

35. *Quality Digest,* Nov. 1994, p.9.

36. Quoted in Lee Smith, "Burned-Out Bosses," *Fortune,* July 25, 1994, p. 44.

37. Kelley Holland and Sam Zuckerman, "A Bank-Eat-Bank World—With Indigestion," *Business Week,* October 30, 1995, p. 130.

38. Paula Dwyer, et al., "The Lesson from Baring's Straits," *Business Week,* March 13, 1995, p. 30.

39. Paul Gibson, "Denial and Destiny," *Financial World,* Oct. 11, 1994, p. 33.

CHAPTER 4

The Culprit

Based on what we have seen so far, there is good reason to believe that Ed Crutchfield is right. Charles S. Sanford, retiring chairman of Bankers Trust of New York, came to the same conclusion as far back as 1987 and began changing his bank. Mergers and consolidations will continue at a rapid pace; the latest guess is that there will be only 9,000 banks in the country by the year 2000. Further, technology advances will be staggering, if what we have seen in the past five years is any indication. There is tremendous disintermediation going on, new entrants are flocking to the banker's markets, and a behavioral heritage may preclude bankers from becoming truly competitive. Banking, as Crutchfield and Sanford have said, may be a dead industry, but there is a chance.

We are seeing a tremendous paradigm shift in the financial services industry of which modern, creative bankers can take advantage. To be successful, though, they will have to change radically; those who are unable to make the shift will find it very difficult to compete. As I study the banks, the message that comes through is clear: If you can serve your markets and your customers better than anyone else, you will prosper and survive. If you don't, your organization will be very vulnerable to the onslaught of nonbank and foreign competition.

What do we do? That is what the remainder of *The Banking Revolution* will describe. We need to understand why the industry has the problems it has: Simply, it is an *attitude* that has caused the significant disintermediation from the banks to the new breed of bankers and brokers who aggressively market their services. We must also be aware of the underlying reason for that attitude, so that the proper diagnosis can be made and the cure prescribed.

DISINTERMEDIATION AND THE NEW COMPETITION

I will be as abundantly clear as possible about why the condition exists. We know what the symptoms of the problem are: (1) disintermediation and (2) the new competition. We also know how the condition evolved over the last 50 or 60 years to let it happen; we saw the benefits that can be achieved with a new service-oriented strategy in Chapter 2; and now we will learn where the problem really resides and why it has been allowed to fester so long. Then we will learn what can be done about it.

> The root cause of the disintermediation to the competition is the interlocking relationship of the culture of banking companies in the United States and their traditional organizational structure and style.

To compete in both the near and long term, the banks' structure and style will have to undergo revolutionary change. That will not be as easy as it sounds because of the way banks have been managed and have operated since the passage of the Glass-Steagall Act in 1933.

Before we learn about the changes that are necessary, we must understand the root cause of the issue. We cannot simply treat the symptom; we have to cure the problem at its source. John Ramsey, then CFO at Union Commerce Bank, taught me that lesson in 1978. When we would think that we had solved a problem, John would make us work all the way back through the process to see where the issue and its cause really resided. Then, and only then, were we able to cure it.

Let me give you an example of how *not* to approach it. A bank that we know was experiencing an increase in the number of telephone calls that were coming into its customer service area. The customer information system dutifully recorded and tracked the increase and produced some nice graphs that showed the upward trend. Reviewing the reports, the manager realized that the number of calls had increased and saw that the standard telephone response time was not being met. Customers were put on hold for seven or eight minutes and the abandonment rate was almost off the chart.

Not being schooled in the John Ramsey approach, the manager came to two conclusions. He reasoned, "If we are going to have this number of calls coming in, if we can't answer them according to the bank's performance standard, and if I don't want to get a bad service rating, I will need more telephone lines and more people," and off he went to see the head of retail banking with his recommendation.

The request seemed very logical to his boss: More calls coming in and a slower response time could only mean authorizing more telephone lines and more people. After calling the folks in the telecommunications department, it was on to Human Resources. The lines went in at a substantial cost, and people were added on first and second shift, also at considerable expense. More calls

Root Causes of Service Quality Gaps

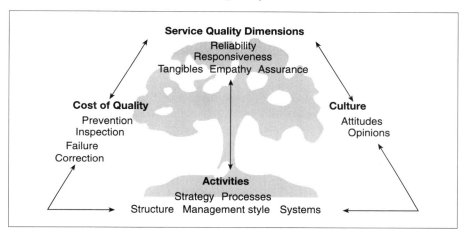

came in, but that was OK since they were being handled within the standard time—for a while. Slowly though, the reports began to show response time deteriorating and the abandonment rate increasing. To the manager's way of thinking, that could only mean two things: even more lines and more people.

Most banks solve their service problems like the one in the story. They throw money and people at them instead of finding their root causes and fixing them right there. I am not sure that the bank in our story ever did analyze *why* the number of calls continued to increase, because obviously something was broken elsewhere within the bank. I am sure that noninterest expense was higher than it had to be and that customer satisfaction levels were lower. Before you decide on a solution, make sure that you have the right problem.

THE RELATIONSHIP

As we have been working to understand the implications of culture on service quality, we developed the diagram (see Exhibit 4–1) which is the *key* relationship in the banking revolution. It is very simple in concept but difficult to implement, primarily because it is a different way of looking at the organization and challenges the prevailing culture.

The diagram says that any gaps between what customers expect from the bank and their perceptions about what they actually receive are caused by what the people of the bank do every day. There is nothing really profound there. It is not rocket science. To be clear, service quality problems do not exist in and of themselves as the manager in the previous story believed. The root causes of service quality problems are found in the activities, tasks, and functions that occur on a daily basis. That means things are occurring in the banks that have caused the significant disintermediation to the new competition, which may be very difficult to identify and correct. The fundamental cause is culture, but let's take it from the top.

At the top of the tree are the five dimensions of service quality—reliability, responsiveness, assurance, tangibles, and empathy—first identified by Len Berry, David R. Bennett, and Carter W. Brown in their book *Service Quality*. For now, you need to understand that measuring the expectations and perceptions of your customers and calculating the gaps between them will tell you where they think you can improve. The gaps start pointing you toward the root causes of the organizational issues that are precluding the delivery of excellence.

Any shortfalls between customer expectations and perceptions do not exist in a vacuum. Deficiencies in service delivery, where the bank is not meeting the expectations of customers, are a function of its culture, which consists of the attitudes and opinions that the workforce brings through the front door every morning. If the culture does not foster a genuine desire to deliver excellence for the customer and all members of the bank's workforce, it is virtually guaranteed that it will not be delivered.

What is culture? Simply, it is the way things are done in the bank every day and the philosophy that guides those actions. It is how the organization expects the people to behave. It is the institutional habits. For example, if the culture rests on the efficiency ratio, people will work very hard, trying to deliver service in a cost-conscious way. They will think of expense first, rather than the customer. They may cut corners, and they will be focused internally on the bottom line. However, if the culture is one of service first, the bank's staff will think more about delighting the customer, rather than what it costs. If your bank emphasizes and pays for productivity, it will be a most productive place. If, however, the emphasis and compensation system are based on excellence, the result will be excellence. The bank can decide for itself which one it wants.

It is the bank's culture that influences the attitudes and opinions of the workforce, which are then manifested in the way they serve customers. Typically, the culture has been prevalent for a long time; that means changing it, as we will see, is a very difficult thing to do.

As Exhibit 4–1 shows, culture does not contain the specific root causes of service problems although it is the primary reason for them and it gives some clues about where they might reside. This is where it starts to get complicated. By looking at the culture, we can see what thinking guides the daily activities, tasks, and functions in which the people are involved. We can understand the philosophy that influences what the workforce does in the performance of their duties. We must also understand that culture does not exist by itself. It is directly related to and is shaped by the bank's structure and style, which create the strategy, systems, and processes that direct the thinking and the work of the people. Which came first, the culture or the structure and style? It doesn't make any difference because they cannot be separated.

This interlocking relationship between culture, structure, and style influences and shapes the delivery of service. However, the specific reasons for gaps between the expectations and perceptions of customers are found in what happens, Monday through Friday, from 8 A.M. to 5 P.M. For example, if the people in commercial loan operations have found that they have some serious service quality gaps and at the same time maintain that they have too much to do, we need to find out the exact areas in which customers think there is room for improvement, what the staff is doing, and why they are doing it. In this case, we would most likely find that management has decreed (style) that regardless of the number of new loans that are originated, staff levels in operations (structure) have to remain constant, both of which are cultural issues. Yet, the people who work there are swamped and customers aren't happy.

Thus, culture is a prime contributor to style and structure, yet style and structure contribute to culture. Both then influence and are influenced by daily activity. They reinforce each other and it is tough to break them apart. However, that is what must happen.

To complete the loop, daily activity contributes to the culture; produces a certain level of service, whether acceptable or not to the customer; and can be classified into the four dimensions of the cost of quality (see Exhibit 4–1). In this new and perhaps complex relationship, the cost of quality measures what people do and corresponds directly to the severity of the service quality gaps: the higher the gap between the expectations and perceptions of customers, the higher the cost of quality. Why? Because of the mistakes that are being made and the incremental cost it takes to correct them.

It is incumbent on the management of the bank to understand the interrelationship of these four elements of their service delivery systems. To close the gaps, to delight customers, and to lower the cost of quality, the bank has to change its culture, structure, and style and the daily activity that result from them.

A PARADIGM SHIFT

Joel Barker is a futurist. He looks at changes in behavior and determines, as best he can, what they will mean in the future. He wrote a book about this, *Paradigms: The Business of Discovering the Future,* in which he defined the word "paradigm [as] a set of rules and regulations (written or unwritten) that does two things: (1) it establishes or defines boundaries; and (2) it tells you how to behave inside the boundaries to be successful."[1]

As we proceed through this book, we will use that definition, but we must recognize that it contains two entirely different thoughts. First, it says that a paradigm tells you the game that is being played, and then it tells you what you have to do to win (i.e., the behavior). As you look at the tree in Exhibit 4–1, consider this question:

What is the purpose of an organization?

I ask of you: What is the purpose of your bank? Not the mission statement that's on the walls, but why does your bank exist? Ninety-nine percent of the bankers in this country would respond, "to increase shareholder value." That's what Harvard and the other business schools have taught their students since the 1950s. That's what all businesses in the United States have stressed, and that includes the banker. The economic expansion of the 1950s and 1960s left a legacy of maximizing shareholder wealth, which the business schools helped to perpetuate. It is what I was taught throughout my banking career, and it is still being taught today.

We are going to start to bridge the gap between the banker's historical way of doing business to the revolutionary behavior that will be required going forward. Let's take a minute to examine this banking paradigm in consideration of our definition. If the organization exists "to increase shareholder value," the rule that it establishes is to focus on the bottom line and earnings per share. It becomes the philosophical driver in other words, the culture. Everyone in the, bank knows that financial performance is important, above everything else, and the behavior that it creates is also bottom-line driven and doing whatever is possible, or required, to improve it.

That's why the go-go bankers at Continental Illinois bought the participations of Penn Square; that's why the lenders at Bank of New England and all the others changed the way they did business so they could go after more risk-filled commercial real estate projects; that's why Nick Leeson gambled and lost Baring's; that's why banks charge those high fees for services; that's why cost cutting is so popular; that's why there could be a combination of NationsBank and Bank of America; and that's why all the other mergers are a subject of conversation. From my formal and informal research, there is no escaping this driving, cultural force: a preoccupation with the bottom line. Presumably, higher earnings mean higher dividends and a higher stock price. The First Manhattan model proves it, but based on current performance, even as earnings are way up, we haven't seen either dividends or stock price improve very much. The markets are not rewarding the current behavior. That is why it is time for a new paradigm.

Here it comes! When I hear the common response, "to increase share-holder value," I counter it. I would suggest that:

> The purpose of any organization is service to all of its stakeholders, starting with customers and employees, and finishing with stockholders.

Here's why: Without customers neither of the other two groups is needed. If your bank has no customers, there is no work and therefore no need for anyone to do it; nor is there any need for capital. Accordingly, business must be based on serving customers. Everything in the organization must be pointed toward services from the attitude of the people to the delivery systems that are in place. The customer simply must come first, but there is a huge problem: The structure and style (culture) of most banking organizations won't let it happen.

Bob Waterman, coauthor of *In Search of Excellence,* has just written another excellent book, titled *What America Does Right: Learning from Companies That Put People First,* in which he captures the spirit of what I am advancing here: "Corporate cultures that tend to put their three constituencies—shareholders, customers, and employees—on the same plane, as opposed to putting shareholders first, are perversely the ones that do best for shareholders."[2]

Heresy, you say. Let me try something on you that I really want you to think about. It's a theory, and I really hope that I am wrong about it. I met recently with a friend of mine who has been close to the banking industry for over 20 years and knows the importance of customers. We talked about the banking revolution; he played devil's advocate, saying that he really thought a lot of bankers put their customers and employees before their shareholders and all that implies. I conceded that maybe some of the smaller community banks like The Ohio Bank did, hoped he was right about the larger ones, but remained firmly convinced that most banks in the country do not.

We explored that a little. If banks really do put customer service first, then why do they cut costs—that is, the people whose job is to serve customers? The emphasis on cost cutting instead of revenue enhancement means that banks are trying "to do more with less." However, here is another new, yet documented, relationship: With fewer people to deliver expected service, there is less and less service really given.

> Consider Zenith Electronics Corp., clobbered for years by cheap foreign-made televisions. The Glenview (Ill.) consumer electronics company has halved its payroll since 1985 to 6,200 . . . But analysts say that the chronic downsizing has now left Zenith without the manufacturing wherewithal to meet demand for its hot new product, the flat computer screens it sells to Compaq Computer Corp. and Groupe Bull. A spokesman for the company concedes that Zenith has "cumulative backlogs" it hopes to reduce in coming months.[3]

We have all heard the stories, and I have even recited a couple of them, about the length of the line in the branch as it increases because there are fewer tellers to help out. But what happens in areas like new product development? If banks have been downsized, can they respond to the advances of Merrill Lynch? Why aren't branches open during "people hours" instead of "banker's hours"? If banks did put customer service first, why is there so much disintermediation to the competition? Why do they continue to raise fees to the dismay and anger of their customers?

We hear that brokerages and others who have entered the financial services marketplace have advantage in terms of price and distribution channel. OK, but if the banks had cultures that favored innovation and a passion for customer service as the new competition arrived, they would have anticipated it and had plans in place by which to keep their franchises. That is not what happened.

Look at First Chicago, which I held up as an example of what banking will be like in the future. In late April 1995, television station WGN reported that First Chicago would charge customers $3 every time they transacted their business with a teller. First Chicago's primary argument for this action is a preoccupation with cost because it is cheaper to use an ATM than to see a teller. What does that do for service? What it says is this: When customers need the most help, they have to pay the most for it.

My friend and I continued our dialogue. With a culture based on cost, maybe it is true that the banks don't put the welfare of their customers first, but surely they are concerned about the welfare of their employees.

"Hmm," he thought, "a cost-based culture also affects the employee base." The people who are left after a cost-cutting initiative typically have more to do with the same amount of time and resources and with no corresponding increase in compensation. That's demotivating. I know. I've been there. Further, their sense of security is shot. They begin to think that they are to be next, which limits their creativity and innovation. It also causes them to start networking with friends and relatives all across the country about possible job opportunities elsewhere, which takes them even further away from serving their customers.

Furthermore, there is the negative psychological impact of the pyramid structure that puts people in boxes and effectively restricts them from any semblance of creativity. Working in a box becomes repetitive, ordinary, and dull. Doing the same thing day after day becomes a chore. It's demotivating. People cannot use the full measure of their talent. They just put in their time from one pay check to another, and I suspect they are not having very much fun. Yet, that's the organizational style that grew out of the structure, as we will see.

We concluded that maybe the workforce isn't the emphasis either. Therefore, it has to be shareholders. We agreed, "Sure, with all the cost cutting going on and earnings being what they are, it's the stockholder who is being enriched." On the other hand, bank stock prices have not done that well recently. When the rumor first surfaced about KeyCorp buying First Chicago, I called an analyst friend who said, "The deal makes sense, but Key's stock won't support it." KeyCorp isn't alone, and First Chicago got together with NBD.

I have maintained that indiscriminate cost cutting does not work and results in "cost creep," the outcome of which actually lowers the earnings from what was expected. Another culprit is the awarding of contracts to some of the senior people, which guarantee a certain amount of compensation regardless of the bank's performance level. Reminds me of the contracts in baseball where even if you hit .200 and make a bunch of errors, you still get paid a guaranteed amount this year *and* next year. Also, the executives have the "golden parachutes" in case of a takeover. These elements of executive compensation are expensive and detract from earnings which in turn decrease shareholder value even more.

It is also curious that even with the great earnings of 1993 and 1994, bank stocks have not risen as fast as the Dow-Jones. That means that the market doesn't value what the banks are doing, and their stocks reflect it. If the focus is not on customers—and it is not on employees and shareholders—where is it?

I will leave the answer to you, but I am suggesting where it should be, on the right side of the tree shown in Exhibit 4–1. It's in a culture and an organization that realizes the importance of *all* of its stakeholders—customers, employees, and shareholders. There is great benefit to be gained from this revolutionary paradigm shift. Just look at the performance of those companies that put the focus on the shareholder behind the other two.

> Over an eleven year period, from 1977 to 1988, Harvard business professors John P. Kotter and James L. Heskett studied the nature of corporate values as they related to company success . . . Specifically, their sample of big, established companies that fit this category did 4 times better in revenue growth, almost 8 times better in job creation, 12 times better on stock prices, and an astounding 756 times better in net income growth.[4]

Although it may not be true for all banks, my hypothesis, based on experience and observation over the last 15 years or so, is this:
• Many banks have not been able to understand the value of the customer due to the regulated and economic environment in which they existed from 1933 through 1986, the prevailing thought that business existed to "maximize shareholder wealth," and the cultural focus on the bottom line that they foster.
• Due to disintermediation, adherence to a costly organization structure and style of doing business, and the pressure for earnings from the analysts on Wall Street, banks have not been able to withstand the American fad of downsizing and putting their trusted employees on the street to the detriment of the morale of, and the ability to provide service by, those who are left.

- Therefore, because bank cultures have not emphasized customer service and have effectively demotivated their remaining employees, the new competition has made profound financial inroads, thus preventing banks from maximizing shareholder wealth.

Profitability follows organizational performance, plain and simple. Just look at Motorola. To achieve them, the banks will have to change their thinking radically if they want to survive.

A DINOSAUR STORY

There is an old story about the Last Annual Convention of the Royal Order of the Dinosaurs. I do not take credit for it, but it serves to illustrate the point. The delegates had come from miles around, arriving at the chosen swamp right on time. When they had gathered, the Grand Poobah Dinosaur, a brontosaurus, I think, lumbered up to the podium. He looked out over the assembly of his friends and colleagues, adjusted his spectacles, and unfolded a piece of paper. After a sip of water, he began:

"If we don't change . . ."

That was all he said as he returned to his place with the others.

The moral of the story, plainly, is that the evolutionary nature of business dictates that the banks have to change. They should have changed already. Ask Ed Crutchfield.

What has to change? First, structure and style, the two biggest contributors to culture. The bigger culprit of the two is style because it creates the behavior and perpetuates the structure. To change the structure, the style has to change. Before we get into that behavioral shift, we have to understand the structure that we are dealing with, how it sustains the culture, and the way it influences the style.

Most modern banks have embraced the pyramidal hierarchy. Even the smaller banks used it, as shown in Exhibit 4–2.

It was not a new idea. The corporate pyramid was, in all actuality, the idea of Adam Smith, economist, philosopher, and author of *Wealth of Nations,* published in 1776. The concept of the structure that Smith envisioned was adopted 100 years later by the manufacturing concerns that emerged from the Industrial Revolution in Europe and the United States and has remained the prevalent one to this day. In those days, it was a great model by which to get things done in business. A look at history shows that Smith probably got the idea from the military.

The hierarchal form of organization had been used more than two thousand years ago by great warriors such as Alexander the Great. The leader decided what to do and told his generals, who told their majors, who told their

E X H I B I T   4–2

Typical Bank Organization

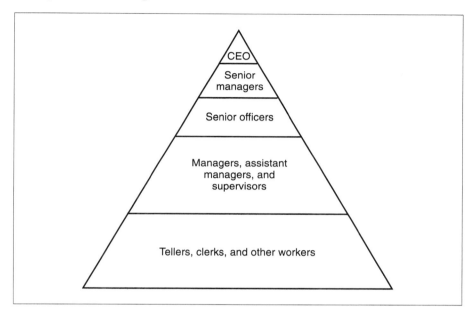

lieutenants, who told their sergeants, who told their spear carriers. It was a one-way command-and-control strategy that guaranteed a discipline that orders would be followed. The church has used the same structure, but thank goodness the parish priest doesn't carry a spear.

Adam Smith wrote it down and applied it to business. In the concept of the specialization of labor, Smith maintained that a group of specialists, each making a small part, could produce more of a product on a daily basis than an artisan who created the entire thing. He based this theory on the notion of familiarity with the task and the ability to do it better with experience. If one could learn a task and was reasonably handy, that task could be performed better and better with practice. If the worker had to learn only one task, it would be considerably simpler than having to learn and execute two or three.

That makes sense. Let's use a baseball example. If all I have to do is learn how to play second base, I can practice there until I become very good at it, assuming of course that I have the brains and talent in the first place. But, if I have to become proficient as a catcher, as a pitcher, *and* as a second baseman, I have to learn several different skills. Practice time on each of them is limited and I probably won't be as good at any of the three as I am at being a second baseman, a specialist.

Smith's logic was grasped by Frederick Winslow Taylor in the mid-1880s. Taylor called the idea scientific management, and it was he who put people in their "boxes." If machines could produce the same things over and over again, he reasoned then human beings could be trained for the regular repetition of the same, small tasks as well. That would guarantee increased productivity, limit any creativity or deviation from what was expected by management, and would go a long way toward maintaining the status quo.

There were four main concepts that made the pyramid of scientific management work. First, tasks were made so simple that errors could not be made. Next was the idea of "unity of command" in which a worker had only one boss. Presumably, the worker would have one set of instructions that were consistent and provided a pretty good idea of what he or she was supposed to do. In case a mistake was made, the boss was there to remind the worker of the proper way to do it. Third was the notion of "chain of command." Because each person in the organization only had one boss, the chain of command facilitated instruction and reporting. The last concept was "defined span of control," which meant that supervisors could have only a specific number of people reporting to them, perhaps five or six, so that they could maintain control. I can remember meetings in which we were asked to redraw the organization chart and people would say, "You can't do that. You can only have five people reporting to you and that includes Yvonne [my secretary]."

These customs would govern organizational thinking to this day, but there were a couple more that had to be added. As the United States grew and demand for products increased, manufacturing processes became increasingly complicated. That made it more difficult to communicate about what was expected, which nurtured the creation of a new breed of businessperson, the professional manager. This person came on board to ensure that there was good communication and information flow and that the end product met the company's specifications; in essence, to command and control the work of others. But it also had a side effect. It added a layer between the owner and the worker, hence the beginning of bureaucracy, and it made functional production more routine. It added control but did little to add value because the incremental cost in most cases outweighed the benefit. However, times were good, demand was high, and profits would pay for the additional people.

Thus, the typical business organization looked a lot like the one depicted in Exhibit 4–2, with various layers of people responsible for specific tasks. Their job descriptions said so. However, as things got more complex, there had to be further division. At General Motors, there were a Buick division, a Pontiac division, a Chevrolet division, a Cadillac division, and an Oldsmobile division. Other GM subsidiaries were responsible for making parts. Therefore, not only was the organization broken vertically, up and down the pyramid, but also it was broken horizontally (see Exhibit 4–3).

EXHIBIT 4–3

Typical Corporate Structure

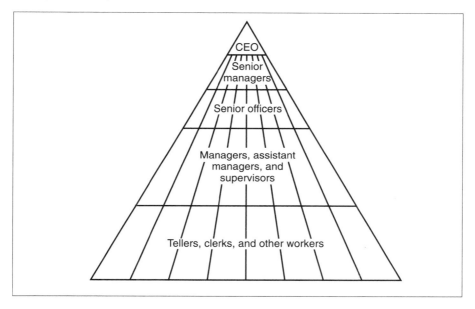

By breaking the organization into smaller and smaller pieces, people were compartmentalized and isolated from their superiors and subordinates (if they had any) as well as from their peers in other parts of the organization.

As a case in point, I was visiting the operations division of Irving Trust before it became part of the Bank of New York, researching the proof system that they used. Conveyer belts snaked their way through the department with proof operators taking work from the baskets that rode on the red line, punching it into their machines, and returning it to a basket on the yellow line for that which had been completed. I asked the manager of the area what was behind the red door through which the work came.

The response? "I don't know."

The next logical question was, "Well, where is it going when the operators are done with it," as I pointed to a yellow door on the far side of the department.

"I don't know."

This department existed to process paper into the proof machines. No more, no less! It did not matter to anyone inside it where the work came from or where it was going. Everything was so structured and orderly that it became routine.

Nothing varied from day to day. That's the way management wanted it. So did the controller, the auditors, and the regulators.

They were called procedures, doing it by the book. Each specialist/department was given a very small piece of the process to perform. That made it less likely for mistakes to be made and easier for the manager to control, making the entire process very efficient. As long as the organization was small, that was all right, but if it grew, keeping track of everything would become more cumbersome and difficult. That meant more control systems, that is, more layers of people who were employed only to tell people what to do and to make sure that they did it, but who surely did not inspire a lot of trust.

With the productivity and consumption boom that followed World War II, the resulting wages and security more than offset any personal inconvenience caused by the structure and style of the organization. It is also important to remember that this was all that businesspeople knew, and, in essence, it was just like the army had been. Nobody talked about teamwork, empowerment, reengineering, or leadership. Some of these concepts hadn't even been invented. It was the hierarchy with an emphasis on control that was the prevalent style for most American companies, including the banks. Orders issued from the top were repeated down through the organization while managers and information systems were developed to make sure that nothing went wrong.

The banks added another wrinkle. We had our layers of management and still do, and we had our divisions—commercial, trust, retail, finance, marketing, and so forth. That separation was not enough. We had to divide the labor even more. What did we do? We created the operations division, which would report to a different senior executive. This unit would contain commercial loan operations, installment loan operations, international loan operations, demand deposit operations, and the time and savings department. It might even have facilities, security, telecommunications, purchasing, and the vault. The bank's service delivery systems were segregated even more.

In our bank, the commercial lenders reported to the chief lending officer while the people in commercial loan operations reported to the cashier. This meant that two internal groups reporting to the CEO were involved with delivering the same service to the same customers. Each one had its own rules and procedures, which nearly always made it difficult to communicate and cooperate with one another even though they were part of the same bank. There were also the natural rivalries between commercial and retail, marketing and finance, and audit and everybody else, with trust sitting all alone. It was really strange, in retrospect, as we fought against each other, not thinking too much about the competition or the customer. It is a wonder that anything got done. A friend in a major bank holding company calls it "walking in mud, up to my knees. Slippery, deep mud, that sucks when you pull your feet out."

In their smash book, *Reengineering the Corporation,* Michael Hammer and James Champy said that historically there was some benefit to be achieved with the pyramid. They suggested that in a stable or expanding economy, it worked fine. If more capacity was needed, the corporation added people at the bottom, shoving a few of the more talented ones up the ladder into supervisory roles and so on. Further, training was made easier. The simpler the task, the easier it was to learn it. With the emphasis on control, compartmentalization facilitated budgets and reports at the cost center level, so that everyone could see their variances from the plan. Even so, compartmentalization does not facilitate the delivery of service.

The typical corporate structure (see Exhibit 4–3) was also expensive. That is what really hampers the financial performance of the banks. All of that infrastructure, the boxes, and the hierarchy result in significant operating expenses at a time when the banks cannot afford it. It also precluded constructive dialogue with peers as divisions, departments, and individuals competed with one another for resources. Thanks to Adam Smith and Frederick Taylor, people got boxed in, and they lost sight of the business of the bank and how they fit in.

It is true that as the economy and the bank expanded, people could be added and productivity would improve, but there were some inherent flaws in the thinking of Adam Smith and Frederick Taylor. First, if there were four people involved in a process, and each one specialized in a function within that process, there would have to be good communication between them for the process to run smoothly. The first worker would have to know what the second worker wanted and how it was to be delivered for it to work; that is, the first one would have to know the expectations of the second and then produce accordingly.

The second worker would have to know what the third wanted, and the third would have to know the expectations of the fourth. Very likely, they would have to cross organizational lines that had been established to provide good control and to preempt good communication. What we did was to create a structure that made it quite difficult to deal with one another. When life was simpler the pyramid perhaps did work, but as things have gotten more complicated the result of the principle of specialization of labor has become organizational fragmentation, because invariably there are breakdowns in those vital exchanges of information.

The second flaw? People are not machines. Peter F. Drucker said it best: "The human being does individual motions poorly; as a machine tool, he is badly designed."[5] As a species, we think too much to be cast in the mold of repetitive work. The more tedious the task, the more the mind starts to wander. "Take time each day to daydream," a wise philosopher once said. In that repetitive environment, it would be just that, a day . . . dream. Whether it is an officer thinking about the PTA meeting or an analyst pondering the first tee, it's the same. If we are not concentrating on the matter at hand, error rates tend to increase.

We humans like to be in control of what we do, to analyze it, to think about it, even if we can't change it. Few of us really like to be told what to do, but that was the underlying rationale of the specialization of labor and its application, scientific management. Nevertheless, Adam Smith's concept and Frederick Taylor's interpretation of it became the model for the corporations of the 1800s and 1900s and is still in use today. The pyramid and its hierarchy are the structure; command and control is the style. They reinforce and complement each other, but they have outlived their usefulness.

> The reality that organizations have to confront, however, is that the old ways of doing business . . . simply don't work anymore. Suddenly, the world is a different place. The here-and-now crisis of competitiveness that American corporations face today is not the result of a temporary economic downturn or of a low point in the business cycle. Indeed, we can no longer even count on a predictable business cycle . . . as we once did. In today's environment, nothing is constant or predictable—not market growth, customer demand, product life cycles, the rates of technological change, or the nature of competition.[6]

The problem is one of timing. The world of the banker changed faster than the banker's ability to change banks' style or to adopt a new structure. It is also entirely possible that even if bankers had wanted to, their cultures would have prevented change from actually happening. Having been raised in an environment controlled by regulation in which the restrictions were more severe than they are for most businesspeople, bankers embraced "command and control" and built hierarchies to carry it out. Even the smallest banks used the model because that was the only one around. In 1982, it all changed and it has been changing ever since. The issue therefore has become an inability to cope with the new world because the bankers' paradigms of structure and style were so strong. They are the behavior that the banker knows: structured, compartmentalized, with orders generally coming from the top. As we start the revolution to change the culture, it is these traditions, the habits—if you will—that have to change first.

THE FOUNDER OF THE BANK

We're going to see how all of this happened in banks through a short story about their founders. Whether you are at Citicorp in New York, at NationsBank in Charlotte, at Bank of America in San Francisco, or at First National from Across-the-Street, what I am about to describe happened at one time or another in your bank's history. I have done this exercise with many groups of bankers, but this particular group won the prize for creativity as it progressed.

Picture a typical room at which conference presentations are given. The screen is down, a lectern is at the front of the room, a flip chart is positioned to the right of the screen, tables and chairs have the conference notebooks strewn upon them, and bankers are waiting to see what's going to happen next.

"We're going to develop a story about the founder of the bank," I tell the assembled group of bankers. "He was a fine, upstanding citizen who went around to his friends in town, telling them that he'd like to start a bank and asking them if they would patronize the new institution." As I am saying that, I draw a box at the top of the flip chart, writing the letters "CEO" inside it.

"Investment begins, and soon the founder has enough capital to satisfy the state and the Fed, so he decides the time is right to open the doors of this brand new bank. He's taking in deposits for his customers and investing them very prudently in high-quality loans and securities, earning a very nice spread between the two. He feels comfortable making car loans and mortgage loans, and even did a construction loan for the owner of the hardware store. But soon the founder is working 18 hours a day, six days a week; he hasn't seen his family except on Sundays for six months. Oh, he's making a lot of money, but he's tired and decides he needs some help. So he hires a lender to ease that burden." I draw a box below and to the left of the one marked "CEO," inserting the word, "Loans." I connect the two boxes with a line (see Exhibit 4–4).

"Business continues to be good, but the founder is having trouble keeping track of everything. So he hires a finance guy to keep things straight and under control." Another box on the chart, this one marked "Finance," connected to CEO by a line.

"By this time, the founder realizes that he may have some trouble maintaining deposit growth, so he decides to hire somebody to help him build and run a branch." A fourth box on the chart, marked "Branches," another connective line.

"The business grows," I tell them. "He's got a lot of loans to make, deposits to take in, funds to invest. How's he going to accomplish that?"

"Needs an investment guy," someone hollers from the audience. Another box, another line to the CEO.

"What else does he need?" I ask.

"Probably needs some lending specialists. How about a mortgage guy, an installment guy, and a commercial guy?"

"OK," I respond, "who will they report to?"

"To the box marked 'Loans,'" comes the reply. Three boxes under the one identified as "Loans." Three more connecting lines.

EXHIBIT 4-4

The Founder of the Bank

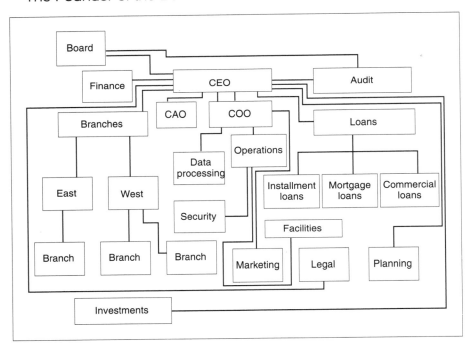

"Hey," I hear, "he's got to have somebody to process the work. How about an operations department?" There is some laughter in the room.

"Who's operations going to report to?"

"The COO," is the response.

"We don't have a COO," I say, looking at the chart.

"Oh, yes we do," says a guy in the front row, "just draw another box under the one for the CEO." "Operations" goes under the COO. More laughter.

"Gotta have more branches, maybe we should make districts or regions out of them." The chart is quickly filling up, but I put three or four branches on it with lines up to "Branches."

"He's got to have data processing."

"Who's that report to?" I ask.

"COO." Another box, another line.

"Who else does he need?"

"Gotta have a marketer," I hear. "Reports to the CEO."

They are getting the hang of this, I think to myself, as I draw another box and another line.

"How about Facilities?"

"Reports to?" I respond.

"COO."

"Hey," I say to them, "the COO has got a lot on her plate. What are you going to do about that?"

"Chief administrative officer," comes the reply. "Reports to the CEO." More boxes, more lines.

"Need a security department."

"Need a wire transfer department." More boxes, more lines. The chart has become filled with them, like the one shown in Exhibit 4–4.

"We need an auditor," as everyone laughs.

"Oops, the auditor reports to the board, and we don't have a board of directors."

A new box above the CEO for the board with one to the side marked "Audit."

"Who's missing?" I ask and the department names come flying out of the audience.

"Personnel." "Statement rendering." "The mail room." "Controlled disbursements." "Planning department." "Legal." "Gotta have special projects." "Yeah, and work measurement, too." "Are we going to have a trust department?"

"Who else is missing?" I keep asking. After about half an hour after I drew the first box, I hear the word, "Customers."

What happened? In a short amount of time, these bankers, at my insistence, had helped me build a big, confusing bureaucracy with lines and boxes everywhere. By the time we finished, there were about six layers, and we had not reached the branch manager level. We had also built vertical "silos," the chain of command for retail, commercial, trust, operations, and administration. As I accentuated the vertical and horizontal lines with my red marker, it was easy to see how the hierarchy was created, complete with its compartments for the people.

To the credit of my friends in the story, they played along very well as we built the chart. In a serious yet lighthearted way, we had fun as they told me where to draw the boxes and lines. Nevertheless, there was a lesson to be learned: The bankers of the past had created pyramids and hierarchies just like their brethren in industry. It was what Adam Smith, Frederick Taylor, the church, and the army had taught them. Also, there was an important realization as we neared the end of our session: Any organization, including one that exists to offer financial services, has to start and finish with customers. Its structure and its style (culture) have to concentrate on meeting their needs.

THE NEW MODEL

I am always amazed at stories like that in Chapter 1 about Clare Crawford-Mason and her television documentary on Dr. Edwards Deming. The film examined the competitive disadvantage at which the United States found itself in the late 1970s, with the conclusion being that if U.S. corporations had listened to Deming and had implemented the lessons that he taught, they would have avoided the fall into economic mediocrity. Many U.S. companies, Motorola among them, adopted his principles, hunkered down for the long term, and are enjoying financial prosperity. What surprises me is that only a few, in the whole scheme of things, have listened to and acted upon what is a winning strategy. Maybe they think it is too hard.

On the other hand, it is curious that until the mid-1980s, we had never heard the word *downsizing*. All of a sudden that's all we heard about. Companies were "downsizing," "rightsizing," and cutting back left and right. If those actions had been made with customers' expectations in mind and with process innovation the result, I would endorse them. What I am afraid has happened is a reaffirmation of the belief that shareholder wealth has to be maximized. Therefore, there is a continual rush to downsize in the pursuit of the bottom line. That relegates the fulfillment of the needs and requirements of customers coming in second, or even third.

In what is an organizational mystery, the answer lies in what Deming started teaching in the 1950s. It has not been endorsed and adopted, while company after company, bank after bank, has sped to cut back and most likely has not achieved what it thought it would. It appears that it is easier to command and control a downsizing than it is to help people change their thinking to a philosophy centered on helping others.

Another master of the study of organizational structure and style gave corporate America a model for success at the time of the draconian cost cutting of the 1980s, but it too has been all but ignored. Peter Drucker described the organizational model for the 21st century in early 1988. The following insight appeared in the *Harvard Business Review*.

The typical large business 20 years hence will have fewer than half the levels of management of its counterpart today, and no more than a third the managers. In its structure, and in its management problems and concerns, it will bear little resemblance to the typical manufacturing company, circa 1950, which our textbooks still consider the norm. Instead it is far more likely to resemble organizations that neither the practicing manager nor the management scholar pays attention to today: the hospital, the university, the symphony orchestra. For like them, the typical business will be knowledge-based, an organization composed largely of specialists who direct and discipline their own performance through organized feedback from colleagues, customers, and headquarters. For this reason, it will be what I call an information-based organization.[7]

Drucker continued, using the symphony orchestra as a primary example. If the New York Philharmonic or the Cleveland Orchestra were organized like our corporations, there would be a senior vice president conductor of the brass; an executive vice president conductor of the strings; assistant vice president conductors for the bassoons, clarinets, and flutes, each one of whom would report to the senior vice president conductor for woodwinds. Who knows, there might even be a bass drum conductor who had not yet reached officer status, but was on the fast track.

I hope that this example serves to illustrate the point. Each professional in the orchestra is competent, responsible, and accountable for his or her own performance. There are section heads who are the acknowledged leaders, but there is only one conductor and only one symphony. Everyone has the same music and is expected to play it perfectly. If not, there is immediate feedback from colleagues and headquarters (the conductor), and ultimately from the audience, the orchestra's customers.

Why haven't the concepts of Deming and Drucker been more readily adopted in corporate America—where all of the first violins play the same part without the aid of their own conductor, acting as a team, to fulfill the expectations of their customers, and where the cellos and the basses do the same? They are certainly less expensive and are designed to produce better output because people are held accountable for their own actions. Given those outcomes, it makes a great deal of sense. The answer lies in our understanding of the banker's culture and a return to the work of Joel Barker, author of *Paradigms*.

Barker draws a distinction between pioneers and settlers. The settler is always looking at the horizon of a new place, a new technology, a new organization structure, or a new culture, asking the question, "Is it safe out there?"

"Of course," comes the reply from the pioneer, "it's safe out here," but it is only safe because the pioneer took the risk and went out to make it safe.[8] Barker suggests that the pioneers are those who choose to change and to adopt a better way as an act of the heart and not of the head. They don't need reams and reams of data; they need only enough to be satisfied that their chances for survival and prosperity are pretty good. When they obtain it, they have the gumption, as we have seen in recent Nike ads, to "Just Do It."

Settlers wait to see if it is safe, which is why they wouldn't adopt something revolutionary like Deming and Drucker called for. Why are banks settlers and not pioneers? For the answer, we have to go back to the style and structure that were adopted during the time of regulation, which has remained the prevailing culture ever since.

With their vertical and horizontal compartmentalization, banks found it was virtually impossible to develop a fundamentally new and different behavior. The structure would not let it happen. There were too many layers to fight through and too many silos to enlist in your cause, when they were trying to get you to endorse theirs. To make it worse, the suggestion of an information-based, team-oriented, cohesive organization instantly caused trouble because it was trying to replace a culture that simply doesn't want to hear about it and would resist it mightily.

I have talked about Merrill Lynch and Goldman, Sachs before. They aren't perfect, but they were the pioneers in the new banking paradigm. They used computers and telemarketing, effectively making the new territory safe. However, when the banks asked the question, Is it safe? and were told that it was indeed safe, they apparently did not believe it because there are more branches and other physical locations dotting the landscape of America than ever before. The brokerages attacked the fundamental paradigm: the style and structure that characterized financial institutions. They even changed their focus toward the customer. Why else would they call you at 6:30 P.M. on Tuesday to ask for your business just as you sat down to supper?

For the banks, as I have maintained, the revolution starts right here. There has to be structural change and the adoption of a new way of doing business. In doing so, we are attacking the old paradigms head on. These traditions will resist. They will fight back. But they cannot continue to govern the thinking of America's bankers who will find it hard to become pioneers. Their culture, their structure, and their style have never let them do it before, but they will have to do it now to survive. The banks aren't going to change their structures overnight; they won't change their businesses; they can't change 60 years of tradition; but they can change their style and then perhaps the other necessary changes will follow.

> The message is clear. If you want to be one of the first into the new territory, you cannot wait for large amounts of evidence. In fact, you must do exactly the opposite. If you want to be early, you must trust your intuition, you must trust your nonrational judgment and take the plunge; make the leap of faith to the new paradigm.[9]

Can bankers leap on faith? That, too, will be hard for these risk-averse conservatives who are so caught up in their numbers that their focus is internal, not on the outside where competitors and customers reside. This analysis-paralysis has to be overcome, and fast.

The problem is compounded by the fact that most bank CEOs probably don't see much reason to change. They don't see any life-threatening crises out there that would force a new behavior or call for a new structure. Here's the call. Ever since 1975, disintermediation has slowly eaten away at the banker's franchise, which is personified in The Parable of the Boiled Frog.

> If you place a frog in a pot of boiling water, it will immediately try to scramble out. But if you place the frog in room temperature water, and don't scare him, he'll stay put. Now, if the pot sits on a heat source, and if you gradually turn up the temperature, something very interesting happens. As the temperature gradually rises from 70 to 80 degrees F., the frog will do nothing. In fact, he will show every sign of enjoying himself. As the temperature gradually increases, the frog will become groggier and groggier, until he is unable to climb out of the pot. Though there is nothing restraining him, the frog will sit there and boil. Why? Because the frog's internal apparatus for sensing threats to survival is geared to sudden changes in his environment, not to slow, gradual changes.[10]

Perhaps human beings have the same internal apparatus. It took a crisis to scare the U.S. automobile industry. It took one to move Xerox back to competitiveness. Maybe the banks need a big shock, something that will jolt them out of the comfort of their traditional structure and style. They have to start thinking systemically, looking at the "big picture," and seeing what's happening.

THE ORGANIZATIONAL IMPERATIVES

When they do, they will see, as Ed Crutchfield did, that the big shock has already occurred. It's called disintermediation. To do anything about it, as Ed Crutchfield did, America's bankers have to admit that it is a problem. At the top of the house, the leadership has to recognize that the new competition and the resultant disintermediation are, in fact, a crisis. There need be no blame, no finger-pointing, no accusations of failure. What has to happen is an honest assessment of the current situation, the aim of which is to take advantage of it.

> If managers want to change an organization's culture, they must first have a solid grasp of the present situation, how it was formulated, and how it is operating. They need a clear idea of where they want to go, how they're going to get there, and the probable consequences of the attempt. This is not to discourage organizational change, but rather to make it possible. Without clear thinking on these issues, the organization will merely thrash in confusion, everyone babbling about change while they keep banging up against the forces of reality.[11]

We have to understand where we have been and why we were there before we can take the proper actions to move forward. It will not be easy. In my experience, when one tells the leadership that their structure and style are the problem, one can expect a fairly defensive reaction. After all, it is a threat to their management technique, to their very being, that there may be a crisis looming "out there" and they have missed it. That's why it is so important to assess the situation honestly, to understand why it is as it is, and to make the necessary change to move forward.

Over the past five or six years, hardly an issue of *Business Week, Forbes, Fortune,* or the *Harvard Business Review* has not had an article or expose on some form of downsizing, rightsizing, restructuring, reinventing, reengineering, or whatever you choose to call it. They all imply tinkering with the structure that is already in place when a radical change is needed. The prescription that follows attacks the root of the problem: the culture. What has become apparent during the research of this book is that, much like the boiled frog, people get so used to being in their surroundings that when it is time to change, they can't do it.

In a survey of 531 executives whose companies had undertaken a restructuring, 43 percent indicated that a "dysfunctional culture" was the major barrier to success. At least they were trying to do something, but their structures and styles wouldn't let them.[12] But that is exactly what has to happen.

Like the dinosaur, banks that don't change their cultures— that is, their structures and their styles—will find that some other economic entity will come along and do it for them. Darwinian Banking, Richard Fredericks calls it. I am afraid that with earnings where they are and with the banker's paradigm as strong as it is, the ostrich syndrome may be prevailing. You say, "Maybe, just maybe, if I ignore it long enough, it will go away." I'm sorry to disappoint you, but Merrill Lynch, Fidelity, Schwab, GM, AT&T, and the others are not going to go away.

There has to be a new breed of banker in this country, one that may hearken back to a model used 100 years ago. That model was based on service and doing what the customer wanted, no more, no less. These bankers knew that if they did that, the bottom line would take care of itself. They had no structure to speak of. Frederick Taylor's models were in their infancy and nobody back then was likely to think they applied to banks anyway. With hardly any structure and a style that was based on service, many banks prospered.

At the outset, understand that the revolution will not happen overnight. I have said that before. It will take between three and five years to change the culture, but the longer the banks wait, the longer it will be before they are successful. Indeed, the prediction for significant consolidation in the industry raises the question of whether the banks have enough time. One thing is clear: If they choose not to start, they definitely will not have time.

I am going to address the issues of structure and style together because both are so intertwined they cannot be changed by themselves. I will talk about pioneers and settlers, boiled frogs and dinosaurs, but I hope what comes out of the remainder of *The Banking Revolution* will provide a blueprint for success. It will not be easy because of cultural resistance, but to be in control of your destiny is worth the effort.

> It must be considered that there is nothing more difficult to carry out, nor more doubtful of success, nor more dangerous to handle, than to initiate a new order of things.
>
> *Machiavelli*, The Prince

A CUSTOMER FOCUS

The first cultural imperative is an attitudinal switch, the very concentration of most banking professionals. First, they must put customer satisfaction at the top of the list. It must be a real commitment and not simply window dressing. Banking professionals must turn outward to emphasize market share and not earnings or some internal productivity measure. They must answer the questions, "What do my customers want?" "What would my markets like?" "How can I provide it?" and "How will we know when we have succeeded?" I have suggested that the current banking paradigm causes a focus on earnings, which forces most bankers to spend time reviewing and justifying their numbers when they should be out in the market, trying to increase share. That's what has to change.

As a case in point, I spoke recently with a senior vice president in the commercial lending division of a major regional bank. When I asked how things were going, he responded that he had been working on a paper about his division's performance for the last three or four days and it had to be done by the weekend, just three short days away. "On his (the Boss') desk by close of business Friday," my friend said wryly. Now, not only do we have a fine example of command-and-control here, but we also have six or seven days when this well-respected commercial banker was in his office writing a report. I submit that the bank would have been better off if he had been working in the market.

One day later, I discussed customer service with another friend in a different bank. He told me that his bank's planning process was so detailed that he had to take the time to budget the actual number of lunches with customers in the coming year and the exact number of miles he would drive to see them, performing some detailed calculations that the budgeting system required. (Who's working for whom?) In response to my question about the amount of time it took to go through the exercise, without pause he said, "About six months." The lesson here is the same. His numbers will be used by his superiors to command and control his behavior, hanging out there over his head, as he tries to work with his customers. Should he spend more than planned, odds are there will be questions about it in terms of cost, not about the revenue that the additional investment generated. Furthermore, six months is a long time to be away from your customers.

Then, there was the trust officer who was told in October that he could not visit with his customers anymore that year because he was over his travel budget and had to make it up. It didn't make any difference to management that he was well ahead of plan on the income side or that the competition's trust officers were going to have a field day. He was over budget, period.

In 1954, Peter Drucker wrote *The Practice of Management.* The line that keeps coming back to me from this classic work is: "There is only one valid definition of business purpose: *to create a customer.*"[13] With all of the cost cutting and the pernicious influence of Ivan Boesky and others of the 1980s, it seems that the financial world forgot this maxim. We are here to take care of the needs and expectations of our customers. That is, in essence, a matter of culture.

What does the culture of your organization emphasize? The efficiency ratio? Service excellence? Something else? Remember the stats about Motorola cited earlier: sales increase of 27 percent in 1993, earnings improvement of 127 percent, savings of $1.5 billion from quality initiatives. Here's one more: their quality objective—three defects per million opportunities. They call it Six Sigma as they strive for complete customer satisfaction. Motorola's culture is squarely focused on customers and providing the products and services that they want. It isn't the only one. Bruce Berg, president of Home Depot's Southeast Division, says:

> Our culture helps us act in the proper way without going through several channels. It plays a role in the decisions like, "Am I free to make this decision?" The culture of the company is "This is going to cost money, but what does it cost to get customer loyalty for life?"[14]

It is time for the banker to spend more time thinking about ways to please the customer instead of filling out forms for the boss. The style will have to change and so will the compensation system. If the bank is paying people to fill out forms and to write reports justifying their numbers, then that is what will happen. But if the bank wants to increase market share, that is what it will have to pay its people to do.

SERVANT LEADERSHIP

Second, and right beside the first, the prevailing leadership style has to change. Command-and-control, like the pyramid structure, does not fit today's fast-paced banking environment. Management's most difficult task will be to let go of the workforce, empowering the people, to use an oft-quoted phrase. What does this change mean? It means that managers throughout the organization must become *servant leaders,* a term originated by philosopher and author, Robert K. Greenleaf. A servant leader, Greenleaf writes, serves others first and then makes a conscious decision to aspire to lead.[15] It is not thrust upon a technician from above; it is not something an MBA is told to do. It is an internal quality, based upon self-awareness and self-confidence, that causes others to want to follow.

Peter M. Senge, author of the pioneering work *The Fifth Discipline,* takes it a step farther when he suggests that the leader should function as designer, steward, and teacher. This is the leader who is "responsible for building organizations where people continually expand their capabilities,"[16] creating something new, and inspiring people to learn and to grow. Note his words. He has not said anything about restructuring, downsizing, cost cutting, or reinventing. He uses words like "builds," "expands," "creating," "inspiring," "learn," and "grow." All of these words are positive and uplifting, quite the opposite of those used in most institutions and by most authors today.

Harvard professor Shoshanna Zuboff, author of *In the Age of the Smart Machine,* says:

> The 21st century company has to promote and to nurture the capacity to improve and to innovate. That idea has radical implications. It means learning becomes the axial principle of organizations. It replaces control as the fundamental job of management.[17]

As such, it will be a significant paradigm shift as banker goes from settler to pioneer and from commander-in-chief to servant leader. Why does that have to be? In a bureaucracy, nothing new will ever happen. Bureaucrats build boxes to preserve the status quo and then command and control behavior. Because of their heritage, they have preserved the status quo, both in terms of structure and style. We saw the reasons for this before. Their behavior caused the government to slap on regulations. They also had the tradition of Frederick Taylor's structure and style. The water in the pot was starting to get warmer.

The only way that a bank can move, therefore, is if the leadership changes the course, encouraging the others to follow. Their heritage says that before anything is done, they look to the boss for direction; that is what most bankers do. Thus, for boxes to be opened and for people to be empowered, it has to begin at the top. If the culture is going to change, the leaders have to change it. They can't order it. They can't just say, "Go, change," and revert to their old ways. They must live it. "A leader says: 'I will go; follow me!' knowing that the path is uncertain, even dangerous."[18]

THE LONG-TERM VIEW

That is the world in which we live right now. Uncertain at best, dangerous at worst. However, instead of ignoring it and hoping it will get better—ostrich syndrome—bankers can take charge of their situations, influencing and directing their own futures. To do so, the next thing they will have to change is the attention that everyone pays to the short term.

This will be a very difficult challenge. Getting the senior people of the bank to think about the long term is a change of fundamental behavior. It is the paradigm with which they grew up, have mastered, and have been paid for. It is this quarter's earnings against last quarter's, against the plan, against last year's, against what they told Wall Street they would make. That has been the measuring stick, with very little attention paid to growth patterns over time. In what may be another controversial statement, I would contend that the job of management is to take the franchise that they have inherited and to make it better, and that means over the long haul.

During the fourth quarter of 1994, I had a delightful conversation with Dennis McDonald, president of the Central State Bank, which has been doing business in Muscatine, Iowa, since The Great Depression. Dennis had called to talk about how to approach service quality improvement. My first question to him was, "Just what do you want to accomplish?"

His response was refreshing. "Tom," he said, "I want to improve this place [the bank] just like my predecessor did and just like his predecessor did." When I asked how he defined "improvement," he replied, "Taking care of the changing financial needs of our customers and helping the community to grow." Old-fashioned? Midwestern? You bet. But I'll wager that the Central State Bank with Dennis McDonald at the helm will do very well.

What differentiated McDonald from many other bankers was his long-term outlook. He sees the changing demographics of the community; he understands that the technology of only a few short years ago is now obsolete; he realizes that interstate banking is here to stay and that other regulations will continue to impact his business; and he is concerned about service to his customers, employees, shareholders, and community. Does he care about the short term? I suspect that he does, but not to the degree that most bank presidents do. The word that keeps coming to mind about Dennis McDonald is *foresight,* a primary requisite of leadership.

Greenleaf has a great definition of foresight. He said that foresight was "regarding the events of the instant moment and constantly comparing them with a series of projections made in the past and at the same time projecting future events—with diminished security as projected time runs out into the indefinite future."[19]

Perhaps a synonym for foresight would be anticipation: being able to anticipate the changes in customer and community demographics, seeing trends in the industry and understanding their implications, and questioning the role of technology and knowing what it can do in the future. Evaluating previous projections in terms of current performance and then gazing out into the future takes time, but that is the perfect way for the leadership of the bank to spend it. Gary Hamel of the London Business School and C. K. Prahalad of the University of Michigan's business school call this "opportunity management." What they mean by that is spending a significant amount of time understanding the forces that shape your industry and developing strategies and competencies that enable you to influence it.[20]

Foresight, anticipation, opportunity management. I think what each is saying is to study what you thought was going to happen in terms of what did happen and then to use that information to chart the course for the future. Using the principles of systems thinking, see where you have been, where you are, and where you are going. If the banks had applied these principles when the CMA came out, or when Penn Square was peddling loan participations, or when real estate deals looked too good to be true, they might have been able to avoid the devasting financial ramifications that they caused. Further, as they saw the new competition with its new technology and structural paradigm, they could have seen that disintermediation was going to occur and could have taken preventive actions instead of merging with others or cutting costs. The job of the leadership is foresight, as shown by Dennis McDonald, charting the course to improve the long-term value of the franchise.

THE HORIZONTAL ORGANIZATION

David Robinson, president of CSC Index, says, "Changes in operating models are tectonic shifts of the business world. They don't happen very often, but when they do, they flatten the unprepared." The half century of dominance of the functional hierarchy as the model for organizational design is about to be superseded.[21]

The recent literature has contained various descriptions of the "horizontal organization," with every one of them calling for a flattening of the hierarchy. Flatten or be flattened is the message. The bank should not be organized simply for the sake of being organized, according to the Taylor model that has certainly outlived its usefulness. The pyramid structure is antiquated; technology and a better understanding of human behavior have seen to that. Working under the premise that the customer comes first and abandoning the command-and-control attitude, they must organize in such a way as to emphasize customer satisfaction. Consumers of banking services do not care what hoops you have to jump through to solve a problem or to open an account. They want it done accurately. They want it done now. I asked another friend why I couldn't access my business account through the ATM. "Because the system isn't set up to handle that," was the answer.

I read that to mean, "The system won't let me." Who is working for whom? Is the system working for the bank or is the bank working for the system? This is not a technical issue; it is an organizational issue that says that the bank is making it hard for the customer to do business with it.

Turn back to Exhibit 4–4, "The Founder of the Bank." Draw a red circle around it and a diagonal line from top right to bottom left. Get rid of it. Now, how hard is that to do? Basically, what I would like you to do is what they did at Olin Pool Products: two layers, one titled "coach" and the other "teammate." The result is a horizontal organization. You might call it nonhierarchal, networked, or clustered, but whichever term you use, leave the pyramid behind.

Organize the bank around its value chains, a concept fully explored by Michael Porter in *Competitive Advantage*. Porter defined a *value chain*:

> The value chain disaggregates a firm into its strategically relevant activities to understand the behavior of costs and the existing and potential sources of differentiation.[22]

Basically, a value chain is all of the activities involved in putting a service in the hands of your customers. It crosses the traditional boundaries of the pyramid organization structure as cross-functional teams of people work together to fulfill their customers' expectations.

Starting with those expectations, they can work backward to identify the tasks and functions that add value to the service, the ones that they don't know which become candidates for elimination, and the ones that should be rearranged for a smoother transaction flow. This is where you will find some natural opportunities for cost reduction and for increasing market share as well.

Michael Porter identified five primary activities that are common to every value chain:

- Inbound logistics
- Operations
- Outbound logistics
- Marketing and sales
- Service

He also isolated four generic support activities that are needed as well:

- Purchasing
- Technology
- Human resource management
- Infrastructure

Included under infrastructure are functions such as planning, finance and accounting, legal, government affairs, and general management. There is potentially a lot of fluff in them and they must be examined accordingly. That also applies to the other eight. Questions to be asked are: What are we doing? Why are we doing it? Can we do it a better way?

As J. M. Juran taught us in Chapter 1, each person in the chain functions as a supplier, a processor, and a customer. In these functions, they must know the expectations of those who are dependent on them to ensure that what they do is acceptable. It is the linkages between people and departments that are crucial. If they are coordinated and have good communication, there is a smooth transfer. If they are not, the bank incurs additional, unnecessary cost. It is the optimization of the entire value chain that is important, not that of an individual or a functional group.

The first step in the journey toward a horizontal organization is the identification of the bank's vital value chains. Why do we want the organization to be horizontal in the first place? The answer to that question revolves around bureaucracy, speed, and expense. To be responsive to your customers and markets, you have to be fast these days. You can't wait for approval to come from finance, where analysis-paralysis may be the rule, or for someone in operations to make necessary systems modifications. This kind of arrangement, also called the adaptive organization, allows the teams to work closely with suppliers and customers as they organize around the things that have to get done and in the order in which they must happen.

This probably already happens in the "shadow" organization that is typically found in large bureaucracies. In the shadow, some enterprising people who need to get things done in a hurry can't wait to go through layers and up and down silos. Therefore, they have developed their own network of people who they know can also get things done. For the most part, they ignore the formal reporting system. It works, but it's expensive because formal structure could be blown up with value chains taking its place.

To identify the chains, determine how they relate to the bank's strategic objectives. Does it contribute to our mission and goals? If so, how and then how much? Once identified, each one becomes the responsibility of the head coach, recognizing that only two layers, a la Olin, is probably a stretch at the outset. Titles become descriptive: Head Coach of Retail Customer Satisfaction. The appropriate people are put on the team: contact people; operations folks; and somebody from legal, accounting, and systems. The selection criteria vary by value chain and by banking organization. It all boils down to what makes sense. When the team knows what it is supposed to do, it establishes its own performance targets based on the expectations of its customers, and sets off to meet them.

The horizontal organization enables the workforce to provide service that meets the expectations of the bank's customers, increasing market share. Further, it is less expensive to operate, lowering noninterest expense. I have maintained that a service quality strategy is the only one that guarantees financial success. A flattened structure, void of boxes and silos and organized around value chains, is what makes it happen.

KAIZEN

What we are talking about here is also a fundamental change in style: the way the people of the bank think and deliver service. They have to understand the needs of their markets and the expectations of their customers. They have to have the right people in place to deliver the required service. They have to be empowered with authority to do whatever is necessary to provide that service. They must work with each other to make sure that their "handoffs" are smooth. They need education in the importance of the principles of service excellence. They have to have sufficient information about their customers to set their performance targets. And they must be rewarded accordingly for meeting them.

People at the bank must also be committed to what the Japanese call *kaizen,* continuous improvement of every activity within every process within the bank every day. Think about the CEO who walked around every day asking, "What have you done today to improve the service to our customers?" Pretty soon everyone in the organization knew that this question was going to be asked, so they began making sure that they had a good, positive answer. That's *kaizen.* World-class performers believe in it and work toward it. Just look at Honda, Nissan, Toyota, and Motorola.

There is a certain amount of rebellion that has to occur to make this happen. "An inquiring mind and a healthy disregard for rules" is the way one of my clients puts it. However, to overcome the culprit of culture, structure, and style, above all there has to be a leader committed to the transformation who says, "Come along, follow me." When you hear it, come on deck and start throwing the tea into the harbor.

ENDNOTES

1. Joel Arthur Barker, *Paradigms: The Business of Discovering the Future* (New York: HarperBusiness, 1992), p. 32.
2. Rahul Jacob, "Corporate Reputations," *Fortune,* March 6, 1995, p. 65.
3. Elizabeth Lesly and Larry Light, "When Layoffs Alone Don't Turn the Tide," *Business Week,* Dec. 7, 1992, p. 100.
4. Robert H. Waterman, Jr., *What America Does Right: Lessons from Today's Most Admired Corporate Role Models* (New York: Penguin Books USA, 1994), p. 26.

5. Peter F. Drucker, *The Practice of Management* (New York: Harper & Row, 1954), p. 283.

6. Michael Hammer and James Champy, *Reengineering the Corporation,* (New York: HarperBusiness, 1994), p. 17.

7. Peter F. Drucker, "The Coming of the New Organization," *Harvard Business Review,* Jan.–Feb. 1988, p. 45.

8. Barker, *Paradisms,* p. 71.

9. Ibid., p. 83.

10. Peter M. Senge, *The Fifth Discipline* (New York: Doubleday/Currency, 1990), p. 22.

11. Jack Asgar, "Paradigm Lost," *Training,* Nov. 1993, p. 94.

12. Robert J. Ellis, "Breaking through the Cultural Wall," *Wyatt Communicator,* Fall 1994, p. 3.

13. Drucker, *The Practice of Management,* p. 37.

14. Jacob, *"Corporate Reputations,"* p. 60.

15. Robert K. Greenleaf, *Servant Leadership* (New York: Paulist Press, 1991), p. 13.

16. Senge, *The Fifth Discipline,* p. 340.

17. Quoted in Thomas A. Stewart, "The Search for the Organization of Tomorrow," *Fortune,* May 18, 1992, p. 93.

18. Greenleaf, *Servant Leadership,* p. 15.

19. Ibid., p. 26.

20. Gary Hamel and C. K. Prahalad, "Seeing the Future First," *Fortune,* Sept. 5, 1994, p. 66.

21. Rahul Jacob, "The Struggle to Create an Organization for the 21st Century," *Fortune,* April 3, 1995, p. 90.

22. Michael E. Porter, *Competitive Advantage* (New York: Free Press, 1985), p. 33.

CHAPTER 5

The Challenge of Change

As you gaze at the barrels of tea floating in the water, you will have a sense of great satisfaction that you had the courage to throw them overboard. When your leader called you to action, you were there, and you made the personal decision that enough was enough. You weren't going to stand for the way things have been, you would join forces with him and the others, and you would rebel against the previous order. It was great—the energy and excitement of the moment—when all of you pitched the barrels into the sea. Slowly, however, as you stand on the deck of the ship with your comrades in arms, there will be a stark realization that you, like the colonists in Boston some 220 years ago, have committed to a new way and you cannot go back. It is what you have to do. That's the revolution.

It will not be easy advancing ideas that conflict with your organization's paradigms. That means some personal and professional risk, but, as in any revolution, the risk is there although it becomes secondary to the ideal. Revolutionaries understand the risk that they are choosing to accept. They know that they might not survive, but they press on, knowing that what they are fighting for is better than what they have now, confident in their own abilities and actions. They have to have that attitude. They have to play to win. It's a complete commitment to an unknown desired state.

The situation is similar to what happened in the movie *Field of Dreams.* The baseball players, whom only a few could see, asked James Earl Jones, portraying the poet Terrance Mann, to cross the foul line onto the field and thus enter their world from which he could not return. He studied the proposition carefully, understood the consequences, and crossed the line, going to a completely different existence. He knew he would never see his friends Ray and Annie Kinsella again. He knew he would never return to his studio in Boston. It was just something that he had to do. As he went, he was laughing. That's what we should do.

Most of us, however, don't have the courage to cross the foul line on blind faith like Terrance Mann did, especially those of us who are products of the structure and style of most banking companies. There are a few, I will suggest, who have had the foresight and fortitude to do new things such as offering services over the Internet as Wells Fargo and First Union have done, but for the most part sticking to the old ways is the norm for banks.

Remember the boiled frog.

> Most senior managers recognize the need for a radical change in their thinking and behavior. Yet most shy away from making it. Why? "It is more reassuring for all of us to stay as we are, even though we know the result is certain failure," says the CEO of a major U.S. company, "than to jump into a new way of working when we cannot be sure that it will succeed."[1]

That is exactly what has to change. Thus, what we have to do is learn how to change ourselves and our organizations. We will start by developing an understanding of what change is and of how important leadership is to making the required transformation successful. That is the message of this chapter.

THE INTERNET?

At the outset of this book, I introduced the first major threat to the banking industry that began with Merrill Lynch's cash management account and has continued with the advances of the brokerages and mutual funds. I also talked about the power of a Microsoft/Intuit relationship, which was later called off by Bill Gates, the CEO of Microsoft, in response to the challenge of the U.S. Department of Justice. This is the second fundamental shift in banking. It is more serious than the charge of Merrill Lynch and the others because it threatens them as well as the banks. This innovation will completely transform the notions of banking and investment.

> To find worthwhile sources of investment information in the World Wide Web . . . start with one of the various index pages. . . You can now use your on-line brokerage which enables you to send your order to the floor of the exchange.[2]

It is apparent that if we have the time and the inclination, we may not need Merrill Lynch either. We can do our investing from home now and don't have to call our broker to do it.

What the Justice Department may not have understood completely about the Microsoft/Intuit deal is that even if it scuttled this proposed combination, something like it will happen somewhere else. Other entrepreneurs will get together to provide this kind of service. It's only a matter of time. In fact, derivations of it have already occurred.

Remote, electronic banking, like the introduction of the CMA, is another watershed event. It has signaled a rush to a new banking paradigm using the information superhighway as we pay bills and transfer funds with our PCs. Electronic banking will not end there. It has just started. Microsoft will be back. Microsoft was prepared even before the merger with Intuit fell through to offer, by arrangement with the banks, electronic banking services to bank customers.[3]

Microsoft might next find the bank to be a cumbersome distraction and will launch a direct campaign toward bank customers. This kind of change is profound. Electronic banking poses a significant structural problem as well as a competitive one for the banking industry. It will, in all likelihood, eliminate the bank's traditional delivery system. Banking over the Internet means that the branch system is obsolete. Maybe corporate headquarters is, too. If that is the case, what are the implications for you?

Here's a case in point. Rockville, Maryland, is a suburb of Washington, D.C. Rockville is lovely in the spring with large trees coming to life, well-manicured lawns, and very nice homes. Four-lane highways take the residents to work in the capital and bring them home again at speeds of 45 to 55 miles per hour. As I was driving to my destination on one of these highways on a sunny day in April, a modern, attractive branch of Mellon Bank appeared on the right. A duplicate model, with the Citicorp logo on it, was on the left. Neither had any cars in the parking lot. These branches were expensive to build and to maintain, much less staff. They would appear to be in a great location, but in reality, they are logistically deficient.

It is difficult to get to the branch banks, so customers may be looking for other ways to effect their banking. They can either hop in the car, get on the expressway, and drive five miles in speeding traffic to the branch, or they can fire up the PC at home to pay the bills and to transfer money between accounts. Perhaps the Internet and other such technological creativity will eliminate the need for going to the bank at all. If routine and even special transactions can be accomplished from home or the office, that necessity disappears. There are ATMs and cash dispensers everywhere; loans can be arranged over the phone; branch banking as we have come to know it has gone the way of the buggy whip. We just don't need it anymore. If we dare to think about where all of this is going, we may not need the rest of the bank as we know it either.

Let me draw a parallel. On July 6, 1995, the headline in the paper read, "Smith Corona Declares Bankruptcy. Typewriter Maker a Casualty of Technology."[4] With a PC and a laser printer, who needs a typewriter anymore? The same may be true for the bank. Technology has changed the very structure and style of banking. Jackie Gleason's trademark opening was, "And, away we go!" He could have been talking about banking.

> There is a new economy, undergoing a restructuring as rapid and deep as the Industrial Revolution of the last century. The large manufacturing corporation was a product of that earlier transformation. So were the big banks, insurers, transportation companies, retailers, and other nonindustrial companies that grew up to serve the financial and marketing needs of the factories.[5]

Those days are gone as there's been a sudden and dramatic paradigm shift; now there's even more reason for revolution. Money whizzes across telephone lines as bankers trade currencies with one another across the globe. Corporate treasurers at even the smallest companies gaze intently at their CRTs trying to maximize their interest rate spreads and the time value of money. Now, all of the people, not just the treasurers, in Utica, New York; Hazard, Kentucky; Mattoon, Illinois; and Paradise, California, will be able to turn on their computers and to access the same kinds of programs that will let them maximize the earning power of their money.

This technological innovation further disadvantages the competitive position of the banks that have not invested in it. It gives the competition another leg up. They offer better service, often at a lower price, and they, along with other new entrants, have decidedly better delivery systems. That means further customer attrition and another frontal attack on the income statement. It also means a higher cost structure as the branches are still sitting there, serving fewer customers, while marketing expenditures increase as contact officers and staff try to convince potential customers to utilize their service. The dilemma for the banker is what to do.

Change of this magnitude mandates a response and a new behavior if the bank is to survive. Customers are flocking to the new technology and its new capabilities, leaving the organizations that cannot provide it behind. We have studied the prevailing structure and style that limits the banker from responding to this challenge in some detail. It is even more critical that they do so now. This is the change that I am asking you to make. The industry that we used to know as "banking" is in jeopardy. We have to realize this and adapt to take advantage of the change.

ELEMENTS OF CHANGE

The knowledge economy that Drucker predicted has occurred, and it has come to banking. Customers are more knowledgeable, as are markets, employees, and the competition. Deregulation, automation, and the information explosion have seen to that. Think of the speed with which this has happened. "Internet" wasn't even in our vocabularies as we charged into the 1990s. To repeat, technology and competition have fundamentally changed the bankers' environment. To survive, the banks will have to make some very basic shifts as well.

The remainder of this book is devoted to showing what you have to do to effect the required change. We have seen *what* has to be done:

- Focus on the customer.
- Become servant leaders.
- Adopt the long-term view.
- Create a horizontal organization.
- Engage in *kaizen,* a process of continual renewal.

When is a moot point; it has to be now. So is *why.* We saw the reason for it in the discussion of disintermediation of Chapter 1. There is also another reason that we have just seen: the Internet. Now that we all agree that we have no choice but to change, the question is, *Who* can help the bank deal with its lightning-quick pace? There is only one answer:

Management has to lead the revolution!

These are the people who make things happen. They have the power; without them, nothing will change. John Ginnetti, an executive vice president of Hartford Life Insurance says, "Management creates the identity of an organization. It builds reputation by providing focus, direction, and incentive."[6] But most bank managements have been prevented from implementing much substantive change due to the strength of their prevailing cultures and paradigms.

Their organizations feature layer upon layer of people and barriers between organizational units, which makes communication and cooperation between fellow teammates very difficult and substantive change hard. Furthermore, with its boxes and compartments, no one can see "out there," so they assume that everything they do is right and keep doing it even when the environment in which they operate changes. Dissent is discouraged because people always tell the boss what they think he or she wants to hear. Banks all look the same; they do the same things; they establish habits and traditions that never vary.

Board meetings are at noon on the third Thursday of the month, starting with a light lunch and an agenda that never varies. Be there at 11:45 A.M. to check the overhead projector and to meet Mr. Wilson, who is always early. Management committee meetings: Monday morning, 9 A.M., bring your own coffee, an agenda that never varies. Lunch: 12:00–1:30. Get in at 7:30 A.M.; leave at 7:00 P.M. They always did it this way, even when Merrill Lynch was knocking down their customers' doors, as Ed Crutchfield described. Here's the wake-up call: The Internet is here, and it's not going away, even if we bury our heads in the sand and think it will. Start looking "out there" and get rid of ostrich syndrome.

Rosabeth Moss Kanter, of the Harvard Business School, and her colleagues wrote an enlightening book, *The Challenge of Organizational Change,* in which they discuss the decline of maturing industries. From this we can learn a little about ourselves as bankers. Their premise begins that as an organization grows, it adds layers of management and divides labor as we saw in the story about the founder of the bank. That results in increased cost and more bureaucracy. Even so, things stay pretty good for awhile, even several years or decades, as the organization and its competitors have a lock on the market. The increased cost is passed on to customers in terms of higher prices (i.e., fees), but that's OK because everyone else in the industry is charging the same thing. In reality, it's not OK because it decreases value from the customer's perspective. It means that the organization is offering the same service at a higher price with no offsetting gain in utility. That opens the door for a new player to come along with a similar or better service and a lower cost structure.

Remember Deming's lesson: Low cost and high quality will create a market. The new player succeeds in luring customers away, which has a negative impact on the profitability of the older organization. In response, it tries to retaliate by matching the service and price offered by the newcomer, but it can't do so because of its structure and style. So, the older organization starts cost cutting, then thinks it has to diversify into things about which it knows little such as insurance or mutual funds; or it jettisons existing businesses such as credit cards and mortgage processing. Thus, say the authors of *The Challenge of Organizational Change,* the new player gains a foothold and the older one either fails or changes its form dramatically.[7] Perhaps they were thinking about the railroads when they developed this thesis; maybe it was about the American automobile manufacturer. But it certainly applies to banking and should ring a bell of concern. How do we change?

There are only two ways to change: evolution and revolution. In the former, change sort of happens. Nobody realizes it. It's like the water in the pot growing hotter as the frog sits there enjoying the warmth. "Oh sure," we used to say, "if you can prove that a PC will increase your productivity, you can buy one." That was how personal computers crept into the world of the banker. Not with a splash, but slowly and surely, once the initial ones arrived. First, it was the guys in the financial analysis area who discovered that a Mac could do their complex calculations faster and better than they could. Then we all had to have them. The first one took a long time to justify, but then we bought them by the carload.

Let's look at evolution on a little higher plain.

1. John G. McCoy, chief executive of BancOne in the 1960s, 1970s, and early 1980s knew intuitively that the future was very bright for his organization on a grander scale than trying to survive as City National Bank of Columbus. He understood that some day BancOne could be one of the first "national" banks.

2. He understood what the future of banking could be in the United States and helped shape it.

3. He enlisted the support of his team to think through what this future picture meant in terms of customer support and the organizational structure that would be needed to provide it.

4. He then invested in that vision, committed himself and his people to it, and never looked back.

5. They implemented their vision, carefully and slowly, experimenting as they went and learning a great deal about the best ways to acquire and integrate other banking companies.[8]

That's evolution. It is slow and methodical, and as BancOne instructs, requires conviction, consistency, and a sense of direction. With all of the change that is occurring in the industry today, those qualities may be missing in many banks at a time when they are sorely needed. In the old days, though, evolution was sufficient. It's not enough anymore, but what does that mean? Closing the doors and starting over? Although I'd like to answer that in the affirmative, I don't think we can ask bankers to abandon their structures and styles completely. What I am asking for is revolutionary thinking and action that is completely different from what has gone before.

rev-o-lu-tion *n.*
_____
1. a complete or radical change of any kind

This is change like the introduction of the CMA, CNN's coverage of the Gulf War, overnight package delivery, E-mail, Home Shopping Network, the destruction of the Berlin Wall, PCs that you carry in your briefcase, pizzas with cheese in the crust that you eat backwards, Nintendo and Sega Genesis, CDs (not certificates of deposit but compact discs), and thousands of others. One of my favorites is the desktop copy machine which was made possible when a Japanese engineer looked at a beer can and noticed its resemblance to its larger cousin, the drum that rotated inside the big, freestanding copy machines. This is radical stuff, too, like push-button telephones, cars that talk, and space shuttles. Another favorite, the TV remote. How about 3M's Post-it Note Pads? And thank goodness for Windows and WordPerfect 6.1.

All of these innovations probably happened when someone said, "What would happen if . . . ?" a slogan made popular a few years ago by Hewlett-Packard. The difference is that when the question was asked, the answer was encouragement to find out the answer, and if promising, to act on it. That's what the management of the bank has to do. It has to create an environment where innovation is the norm. Management has to be the first on deck, ready to heave the barrels of tea over the side. The revolution starts with the conscious decision to want to change and to do something differently, even though you may not have a clue as to where that decision may lead.

James Kouzes and Barry Posner offer a glimpse of what's required to change in their book *The Leadership Challenge:*

> To change, take risks, accept responsibility, and be accountable for our actions.

> To respect all people, promoting unity, trust, pride, and dedication to our mission.

> To achieve a high quality of work life through involvement of all of our people in an environment of openness and fairness in which everyone is treated with dignity, honesty, and respect.

> To promote good communications among all employees by operating in an open atmosphere with freedom to share ideas and speak one's mind without fear of reprisal.[9]

That is what management must do.

"I'M TOO BUSY!"

So, why don't we change? We saw the answer to that in the last chapter: culture, in terms of structure and style. The bank has fostered and encouraged a bureaucratic behavior based on layers of people and the division of labor that prevents it from doing anything new. People run around the building doing things for the boss that have no bearing on customer satisfaction. "Busy work" was the term we used, but we had to do it. That culture has been maintained by a management that, for the most part, has a short-term view, sees annual earnings as the ticket to personal success and wealth, and really sees no need to change. This is not to place blame because the bank management has inherited this style and structure, but it is to place responsibility since only the management can lead the way out.

Janet Gray, my coauthor of *Quality Value Banking,* and I had the privilege to be on the same agenda with Bob Kriegel, author of *If It Ain't Broke . . . BREAK IT!,* at a leadership forum sponsored by Digital Equipment a couple of years ago. Kriegel put into perspective the lack of ability to change due to "busy work." Within the walls of our compartments, we maintain the same patterns of behavior, being busy at all times, so that we look like we are contributing something. We even invent things that prevent us from changing, using them as the excuse that we don't have time to do anything else. According to Kriegel, "The Gotta's Can Run Your Life":[10]

- I gotta make this deadline.
- I gotta be great in this presentation.
- I gotta finish this paperwork, make three phone calls, and get to this meeting and I'm late already.

- I gotta make a decision.
- I gotta read all this material before tomorrow's meeting.
- I gotta cut costs.
- I gotta make my quota.
- I gotta pick up my kid at child care, do the shopping, make dinner, and finish that report.
- I gotta catch that plane.
- I gotta _____.

You can fill in the last one. In our ever-warming pots of water or with our heads in the sand, we continue to make excuses as we fail to confront our ability and/or want to change. We continue the same behavioral pattern which I like to call the "I'm too busy" syndrome, a task orientation that keeps us from looking at the big picture. When I'm too busy, I am like a pinball bouncing from one task to another. Even the most cerebral event, strategic planning, becomes just another task, something to finish so that the next assignment can be tackled. With all the downsizing of people and no change in the quantity of work, the pressure to get things done becomes even greater. The result is that everyone in the bank becomes too busy.

When that happens, another phenomenon occurs. When the boss is too busy, the people who report to him or her see this as the acceptable model of behavior. They then pattern their own actions after that of the boss because they think the boss will look favorably upon them. So, these people get real busy too, doing all sorts of things that may not add any value to their customers. That's the heritage. If you produce a lot of stuff, that's good, and you will be compensated for it. In all reality, I'm not so sure that either the behavior or the reward was what the bank really needed.

Bob Kriegel showed us the elements of the "I'm too busy" syndrome. We can learn about ourselves from his instruction. I know that I was too busy when I worked in the bank. Everyone was. To make a successful transformation, we have to slow down on the number of things that we do, while creating a different sense of urgency and a dramatically different behavior. Let's try a different list.

- I need to visit with my customers to understand their expectations. A semiannual survey will take care of it.
- I must talk with the team daily about the importance of performance.
- I should also conduct a culture survey within the bank to see what everyone thinks about what's going on.
- We need to think about what our markets will come to expect two or three years from now.

- I need to make sure that reward and recognition ceremonies happen on schedule.
- I must review the educational curriculum for the next group of participants.
- I have to talk with the CEO about the changes that I see coming in my environment.
- Before I do that, I had better see the CFO and find out the cost of quality and the impact of the open Back Door.
- We need to visit with the information systems folks to understand the new technology.
- Then we should think about ways to acquaint our customers with new kinds of services.
- I need to make a personal change. I have to become a "coach."

General? Yes. But my purpose here is to ask you to work a bit by applying these precepts to your own behavior. The requirements of the two lists are remarkably different. The first one is extremely reactive as time controls daily life. "I gotta produce, produce, produce." That is the legacy of the emphasis on productivity that the 1940s, 1950s, and 1960s left us. Pack as much activity into every hour and every day as you possibly can; people with "to do" lists, racing from one thing to the next. Perhaps the best way to describe it was "organized chaos," but that was what the reward system compensated and probably still does.

The second list is indicative of taking control of one's time and activities. It is not task-oriented. It is knowledge-oriented. It includes communication with others, research, "future thought," and consideration for people. Leaders need to consider the different behavior it asks for and to develop their own lists. Based on all of this and on what is to follow, what do you have to do to change your own behavior and that of your team to meet the new competition? Take out a legal pad and start your own list, using these ideas as thought starters. Remember that this is not a "to do" list, but an itemization of the things that you think will help accomplish the revolution.

Also, understand that it is not going to happen if everyone is too busy accomplishing tasks, running from one fire to the next, spilling the water from their buckets as they go. It will take time and, as I have said, I hope that there is enough. We need a change of thinking and a change of focus, from the short to the long term. It is either putting out fires today or guaranteeing prosperity in the future. There is urgency in both, but I am asking you to put your water buckets down, to think about what you are doing, and to use your energy in a different way.

As the process begins, it is important to understand that change starts at the organizational level, not the individual level. To really change what people do and how they do it, there has to be a new organizational model superimposed on the old that changes what is expected of the workforce. The CEO has to state the new direction clearly and then to hold his or her team accountable for communicating and modeling it. Try this: "We will be customer-focused." To succeed, people throughout the bank will have to change their attitudes, beliefs, and behaviors. They will have to find out what their customers want. They will have to work together to build delivery systems to provide what is expected. They'll have to stop the internal focus. They will have to put their buckets down or they may not survive.

Rosabeth Moss Kanter and her colleagues identify three different roles in the change process: strategists, implementors, and recipients.[11] I'm adding one more: scouts. Let's start with them. These are the people with the foresight to understand what their environment is telling them. They are the ones who are always on the lookout for change. To return to the analogy provided by Joel Barker, they are not the pioneers or the settlers. These people are "out there" with the courage and self-confidence to look at the horizon to see what might be coming next. They look for changing customer attitudes, new market opportunities, advancements in technology, changes in regulations, innovative ways to serve clients, better ways to help their people succeed, and the like. They find out what their markets want today and five years from now.

Even if there are potentially dire circumstances, the scout communicates to the strategists who take that information, synthesize it, and plan new competitive tactics. Unfortunately, we have all heard the phrase, "shoot the messenger." Many times, even with the right information and proper analysis of it, scouts get shot when the strategists don't believe them. That's the risk the scout takes, but if the risk is known and accepted, it does not deter the scout from taking action.

You, as the reader of this book, have become a scout. All now depends on what you do with the information. Understanding that there is some risk involved, you somehow, some way, have to convince the organization that there is a problem. The words "urgent" and "crisis" are applicable. Maybe it's not as evident as that herd of buffalo that is stampeding your wagon train, but that is the kind of urgency that's required. As you fly up to the wagons on your lathered horse, waving your stetson to get attention, approach the board, the CEO, and your divisional vice president with words such as "disintermediation," "the Internet," "Microsoft and Intuit," and the like. Create a sense of excitement, substantiating it with data. Calculate the cost of quality, using the workbook at the end of Chapter 2. Find out how much has been lost to the new competition through customers who have walked out the back door. Ask if your bank is ready to market services through the Internet. Ask if the expectations of your customers are known. Ask why different organizational units have conflicting goals. It will be a little dangerous, but show them the contents of this book and other literature that talks about where banking will be in five or ten years. Show them Ed Crutchfield's quote at the end of Chapter 3.

As the scout who sees what's coming, get the attention in whatever way you can of people who can make things happen—the strategists and the implementors—and enlist their support. You can't take much time to build these alliances so you will have to be creative. Eventually, you are going to need the CEO, who may not think there is any need for what you propose.

This poses a problem: the immediacy of corrective action and the banking tendency to delay because nothing seems to be wrong. To bridge that gap, find a trusted lieutenant, if you aren't one, of the CEO who can present the case and the necessity for action. As you do so, be sure not to point fingers at the CEO or the management team because that might jeopardize the effort. Make it as positive as possible by showing the opportunities where the organization can gain an advantage and can prosper. But do it now. Make it fast. Make it a crisis. Make it the vision of what you want the company to be. Tom O'Brien, CEO of PNC Bank, had a great vision for his organization: to be an "exceptional marketing company." That tells it all. If we are an "exceptional marketing company," everyone knows what we're going to do. We're going to become sales oriented and we're going to succeed. There is no doubt.

Second, understand that you can't accomplish an organizational transformation alone. That herd of buffalo is getting near the wagon train and, as an individual, you are going to be trampled. Having the CEO on your side makes it a lot easier to get the necessary help, and there is absolutely no question that you have to have that support. Personal experience has shown me several scouts who understand the threat to the banking industry, but who cannot make change happen in their organizations alone because the CEO doesn't see the herd of buffalo coming. Take the CEO and the rest of the strategists out to see what you see. Show them the cloud of dust coming their way. When they realize what is about to happen, they had better get on board to lead the revolution.

That should ease your burden as the scout who presents the facts that convince the strategists that new approaches are needed for the new circumstances that surround them. It also requires the strategist to adopt a new behavior: *listening* to the scout, something that most leaders have a difficult time doing. By definition, the strategists and the scouts are the leaders of the bank. They must change before anyone else. The new information from the scout must be translated into behavior that assures competitive advantage—maybe not tomorrow, but a few months or even a year from now—by working together with that desired state in mind. The people who are being asked to follow have to see that the commitment is real and that you are going to try. Together you can succeed, apart you will not. Once they have grabbed onto the new behavior, the work of the scout is over . . . for now. Take a short break, you've earned it. Then get up on your horse again and start looking "out there."

With your assignment fulfilled, it is the leadership that must champion and empower the change process. To do it, they will have to upset the organization.

> To facilitate the renewal process, top managers must take on a new role—one that disturbs the organizational equilibrium. We are not suggesting that top managers' job is to create chaos. Their role as shapers of corporate purpose still means that they must provide direction and coherence. But we are saying that top managers must also direct some of their energy into more disruptive pursuits.[12]

With the commander prepared for the change, he or she asks the members of the leadership team to offer their suggestions about what to do; together they decide on the most appropriate course of action. Notice that the CEO listens to the report of the scout, entertains various recommendations from the strategists, listens to pros and cons, assures general consensus, and says, "Let's go," without a lot of numbers being crunched. Quite different from command-and-control. Once the strategy is outlined and everyone has agreed, mobilization occurs. Translate that activity to the bank.

Therefore, the first role is one of strategy. The key players are the scout who sees what's coming and the CEO and his or her staff who listen, evaluate, and plan the appropriate course of action. The second role is one of implementation. Who is going to be responsible for getting the chosen course of action accomplished? Typically, in the cultural change that we are talking about, it will take everyone in the bank. It starts at the top with change in the behavior of the leadership because they cannot command people to adopt the new service philosophy. If they want their people to be servants, they must be servants themselves, persuading them of the benefits of the new way. As they do so, they start to overcome the inertia of resistance that they are bound to encounter. This is the task of implementors. They must understand what the scout and the strategists are telling them and the direction that the leadership has determined. Then, they must translate that into the actions that are necessary to take advantage of the news, communicating effectively as they enlist others to follow.

> "You don't do it by screaming at people. A lot of it you just have to do one-on-one, and you change a few minds here and a few there. It isn't like flipping on a light switch. . . Little by little, people start listening. It gets contagious. They talk to each other. They see where we're going. Someday I think we'll look back and be proud. But you don't think of that at the time. You just try to get through one day and then another day and keep explaining and keep taking the fear out."[13]

The implementors are the facilitators of change who provide the style and structure for accomplishing it. They are the coaches who help everyone else through it. They have a tough, unrelenting job and the strategists need to realize it. It would be easy for those at the top of the house to sit back and say that the new course has been charted and that, therefore, their assignment is complete. But, it's not! The implementors need support and encouragement. They have to know that this is not just another "flavor of the month." They need resources. They need someone to talk to when things don't seem to be going well. The strategists need the implementors, and the implementors need the strategists. Both need the scouts who have seen what's coming and have a pretty good idea of what the impact is going to be. All have to think about the recipients of the change, something that is rarely done.

The recipients are the foot soldiers who will be affected by the change but have little control over it. It is vital that the implementor and the strategist understand that these people are human beings, too, with their own attitudes, opinions, and natural reluctance to change. Most of the resistance comes from these people who perceive that they have the most to lose, and it is typically those without information that have that perception. They are the ones who believe that they are not in control of their own destiny. These recipients of change have an innate resistance to the fear of the unknown, potential loss of their jobs, and possible failure. Therefore, communication and education about the new expectation is essential. Persuade them, indicating why the change is necessary and tell them how they can help.

A distinction needs to be drawn here. Change of a technical nature is understood and fairly well accepted. People see the evolution of technology and get excited about it. What they don't like is social change, which is changing their work habits or their social relationships.[14] They dig their heels in and refuse to move, much like our boiling frog, and create a barrier between themselves and the implementor of change. Anne Fisher writes:

> Even subtle resistance, though, can be a problem. Most dissenters won't stand up and shout at you that they hate what you are doing to them and to their comfortable old ways. Instead they will nod and smile and agree with everything you say—and then behave as they always have.[15]

There will be those who follow willingly, but others will have to be convinced. Give all of them the option to follow or not. The implementor has to show the recipient the new behavior. You have to tell them that "I'm too busy" does not work anymore. It will take coaching and affirmation, but by demonstrating the personal and organizational benefits to be achieved, the message will get across. This change process is made easier if the compensation plan supports what people are being asked to do, so it also has to be revised immediately.

Understand that the change process will never end. Everyone in the bank has to realize that the industry will never be the same. The things they grew up with don't work anymore. Just look at a routine checking account transaction. In 1980, only 15 years ago, a customer would walk into the branch, wait in line, present a check to a teller, and leave with $25. In the next 10 years, automatic teller machines (ATMs) took over. The customer still had to come to the branch, but could get cash from the machine. Today, the customer gets cash at the supermarket. Don't forget the Internet and what electronic banking will mean.

Other companies are also trying to change. GTE Mobilnet is one of them. It wants to have the best customer service in its industry, a terrific objective. They began the process in 1993, but did not realize how long the change would take. In the words of Ben Powell, a former financial manager who now works full time as an implementor:

> It has been so aggravating. Finally in the last six months or so, we have been getting to the point where we're really changing how we do business. But it's taken years. Not weeks. Not months. On a day-to-day basis, it feels like bowling in sand.[16]

But you "gotta" pick up the bowling ball and begin the game, even if your first throw winds up in the gutter. For starters, have a meeting with everyone in your value chain with one agenda item. Ask them, for example, "What will happen to our business when none of our customers use checks anymore?" That's the kind of change with which the bank will have to deal.

When the scout rides up to the captain of the wagon train and vaults to the ground from his exhausted horse, the status quo has been disrupted. That is exactly what we have to have if we are to have an organizational transformation. That's where you come in. Your organization is different from any other. It is in a different place in terms of markets, technology, and culture. That is why there is no cookbook, no detailed recipe, but it is also the reason that you should have the freedom to experiment and to try new things. Take what you read here and apply it creatively to your circumstances. You may not know exactly where you are going or how you are going to get there, but you have to start.

LEADERSHIP THEMES

I hope that it is evident by now that the revolution has to start with the leadership. It is the leadership that has been entrusted by the shareholders to create a prosperous business. It is the leadership to whom the workforce looks for direction. However, it is not the leadership to whom customers look for service. It used to be but not anymore. Think back to the story about the founder of the bank. By adding more people and more layers, the leadership became removed from the customer and, with the preoccupation with earnings, the senior people spent more time with analysts and market makers than they did with their staffs. That, as the preceding section described, has to change. The leadership has to understand that there is a crisis and they are the ones that have to lead the way out.

Whether it is a large bank or a small one, the leadership is responsible for the current situation. Note that I have not used the word "management." There is a big difference between the two. Managers were created to tell people what to do and to make sure that they did it. Leaders, on the other hand, get people to want to carry out their responsibilities to the best of their abilities. It is much harder to lead than it is to manage.

That challenge was captured succinctly in an article by Lieutenant General William G. Pagonis, author of *Moving Mountains: Lessons in Leadership and Logistics from the Gulf War.* He wrote: "Leaders must be motivators, educators, role models, sounding boards, confessors, cheerleaders—they must be accessible, and they must actively pursue contact with colleagues and subordinates."[17] With that definition in mind, we are going to take a look at what leadership is all about.

To start with, the leadership of the bank owns the problem. These people are responsible for carrying out certain economic, organizational, and social strategies. Even if they have inherited them, they are accountable for what happens in the bank, good or bad. Therefore, it may just be that the water in the pot was lukewarm and rather comfortable when they jumped in, but with everything that is going on in their environment, it's starting to heat up. As it does, they don't see anything really wrong and continue to run the bank with its hierarchical organization structure and command-and-control management style. We know those will not work anymore.

One of the hardest things to do as a human being is to admit that the problem is yours, especially if you have not originated a situation that was going downhill. Today's banker has a legacy of 50 years of regulation and the culture of Adam Smith and Frederick Taylor. They are the ones who have watched as Merrill Lynch and Fidelity have swooped in and gobbled up their customers. Still, they are also the ones that must change it. What must they do? They could say, "Oh, woe is me," and wait for AT&T and Microsoft. Or they can act.

The assignment is to make the transition from managers to leaders. Leaders are visionaries who are always asking the scouts about what's "out there." The best leader I ever worked for was Bob Gillespie, now CEO of KeyCorp. Bob has the innate capability to see the big picture, the foresight to keep looking out at the horizon, and invariably listens to his scouts. He may not always agree with them, but he *listens* to what they have to say. He also has an intuitive feel for the industry and where it is going. KeyCorp was lucky. Bob's always been this way.

If they don't have this quality in their role as leaders, many of America's bankers must first make that major change. They have to give up the focus on the short term and start looking "out there"; they also need to realize that *they* may be the problem that has to be rectified above all others. They also have to understand that all of the people of the bank, not only themselves, hold the key to success. This required personal change will be hard for many managers to make but they have to try. To start, a good dose of humility is required. Management must move from the dictatorial style of the past to one of servant leadership. As that transformation occurs, command and control (management) will start to disappear and will be replaced by a people orientation (leadership). It can start tomorrow. Better yet, it can start today.

The concept of servant leadership was introduced by Dr. Robert Greenleaf and has been amplified by Dr. Peter Senge. As we saw in Chapter 4, to be a servant leader, there are three new capacities in which we must act:

- As *designer,* showing the people the big picture and why the transformation is necessary.
- As *steward,* giving the people time to adjust, empowering them within their responsibilities to define their own behavioral patterns.
- As *teacher,* explaining the new behavior as one that is focused on the customer, demonstrating why it is important and serving as the example.

James Belasco and Ralph Stayer, in *Flight of the Buffalo,* suggest a simple way to begin the journey to servant leadership. They gave us some questions to ask of the people who work for us. Take a look at them and tomorrow morning go out and ask each of the people on your team to answer them. They are simple to ask, but be prepared to act on what they tell you.

- What are the biggest problems that you face?
- What prevents you from being a great performer?
- How can I help you be a great performer today?
- How can I help you remove the obstacles that prevent you from being a great performer today?
- How can I help you prepare to be a great performer in the future?[18]

Notice the key word *help.* Many of us in leadership roles may have forgotten what it is like to really help someone. Helping does not mean that we take ownership of their problems or obstacles as we probably did as parents for our children, solving them and making things better. It means that we have true dialogue with our people to find out what is getting in the way of their success, coaching them, providing resources, and making sure that they own both the problem *and* the solution. It's amazing what the people in the bank are putting up with as they try to do their jobs. Go to them and ask the questions. Then together help them find and implement the right solution. Don't tell them what to do and how to do it. That means that you have taken over. That's management. Instead, encourage them to think and to be creative. They will reward you with brilliance. That's leadership.

> Our organizations are constructed so that most of our employees are asked to use only 5% to 10% of their capacity at work. . . It is only when those same individuals go home that they can engage the other 90% to 95%—to run their households, lead a Boy Scout troop, or build a summer home. We have to be able to recognize and employ that untapped ability that each individual brings to work every day.[19]

Leadership means helping the people of the organization to unlock that talent and to put it to use in the service of the bank's customers. A synonym is *growth*. The task of the leadership is to work at helping their people grow. To do that, they will have to become servants themselves. No more John Wayne behavior of seeing a crisis, riding in with guns blazing, and saving the day. Nurture your people to own and to solve their problems themselves. They do that by learning. The first prerequisite, then, is to *design* an organization or a value chain where that happens.

The importance of design cannot be minimized. Companies spend countless hours drawing charts with boxes and lines, like the one produced in the story of the founder of the bank. They call that organizational design. What they need to be concerned about is the design of their value chains and how best to provide service to their customers and a working environment for their people that is conducive to excellence. That is the real job of the leader.

> Circumstances have changed. The paradigm has not. The result: consistent organizational underperformance, as individuals withhold their intellectual capital. Management responses of cost cutting, restructuring, and leveraged buyouts reflect the old paradigm. They are actions that leaders do *to* organizations, and the people, to *fix problems*. We are treating the symptoms of high costs, inefficiencies, poor quality, lousy service, but not the root causes—inappropriate leadership paradigms.[20]

Deming instructed that 85 percent to 90 percent of the problems and errors encountered in organizations are the result of poor design. Therefore, as you go to visit with the people about their obstacles, start thinking about the concept of design. What are the things that are getting in the way of service excellence? I recently heard a story about Karen Kleinhenz, regional president of Society Bank. She had noticed a preponderance of activity that looked a lot like "I'm too busy" and told her staff that if a task or an assignment did not contribute to customer value, to stop doing it. Precisely. The leader, by going out and asking the people about impediments to performance, exemplifies the behavior that everyone should have. She is saying to her customers, "How can I help you?"

The task of the leader is not to draw boxes and lines, but to design an organization where people can learn, grow, and succeed, achieving a greater sense of self-satisfaction and self-esteem. The leader sees the big picture and how all of the pieces fit together to perform as one unit, much like the conductor of the orchestra. The leader may not know all of the intricacies of every job in the value chain and shouldn't have to. He or she has empowered the people within the chain to learn their jobs better than anyone else, given them the resources that they need, and helped them remove the obstacles that preclude great performance. The leader has communicated the vision in words and in deeds, and has enlisted and encouraged the others in the value chains to believe in it, too. In addition, the leader has made sure that everyone in the chain understands how they fit in with the others, ensuring that all "handoff" points are clear and that expectations are known. Notice one more attribute of the leader: action. Not only does the leader believe in what the company stands for, but he or she works at making it a reality. You can't sit on the bench and be a true leader.

Notice that I said the leader gives the people of his or her value chain the resources they need to serve their customers? Providing resources falls under the mantle of *steward*. Leader as steward means responsibility for making sure that the vision is achieved. It means doing whatever is necessary to accomplish it. Designing the processes and teaching others are part of it, but the main essence is helping others to make it happen. The challenge becomes one of maximizing the abilities and the talents of the people within the organization, much like the one presented to a football coach each fall. The steward is the enabler: "How can I help you achieve greatness?" That is quite different from "Have that analysis on my desk at 5 P.M. on Friday."

Here's another paradox. True leadership is enabling others. *Enabling* is defined as giving people what they need to do their jobs well. When that is the case, cost cutting, restructuring, downsizing, and the rest contradict the basic essence of "leadership." That makes the revolution even more relevant. We have to get away from those kinds of behaviors as we begin to change the bank's structure and style. Start it with a change of your own attitude that refocuses on the success of the people of your value chain.

The steward sets the example as he or she demonstrates a passionate commitment to the organization's vision. If the competition has introduced electronic, PC-based transaction processing, the steward figures out how to provide it for the organization, being courageous enough to say potentially unpopular things to his or her colleagues. The steward might have to talk about immediate investment in technology, for which there may be no return for several years.

The steward also might have to suggest the abolition of various fiefdoms, so that cooperation and communication across the organization is improved. The steward's conviction as leader is that the organization itself comes first. That belief must be honest and unwavering. If this commitment is required of the rest of the people, the leader must demonstrate it first.

As such, the leader has moved into the third role, that of *teacher.* By virtue of his or her leadership position, the teacher has qualities that make others want to follow. Whether it is vision, courage, expertise, and so forth, the teacher has something that we, as followers, aspire to. We want the teacher to instruct us in it, but many managers are reluctant to assume this role. If we remember the command-and-control style, we can see why. The hierarchy and its chain of command was based on the military model. Orders went down the chain, progress reports went up. Further, we were "too busy" to take time out to show subordinates new things. The real leader, as General Pagonis instructed, takes time to be with the troops and helps them understand what's going on and what they will have to do to learn and grow.

The teacher explains the need for change and what it will mean. He or she must show people the root causes that call for organizational and personal paradigm shifts. As such, the teacher not only has to keep in mind the big picture, but also has to be completely aware of what is happening each day, relating those events and activities to the environment in which the bank is operating. Where the steward embodies the vision, the teacher guides it, helping people to overcome their natural resistance to change. The teacher stirs the pot, showing the people new things and giving them a chance to experiment with them.

It has to be for everyone. If the people of the bank are not given the chance to learn and grow, the status quo will be maintained, which creates a huge opportunity for the competition. As such, the teacher must make learning a priority. Learning challenges people and keeps them from getting stale or burned out. It gives them a sense of accomplishment. It should also put additional dollars in their pockets, presuming of course that the incentive compensation system has been modified to include rewards for skill development. Everyone at Motorola attends formal classes every year. They learn new skills and concepts that they take back to their jobs, improving themselves and their company—the Japanese as we have learned, call it *kaizen.*

As managers begin to make this transition to leadership, I offer some guidelines as reference points. The most important guideline concerns their own behavior. As the change process is under way and the organization has defined what it wants to be in terms of its vision and values, the true leader lives them every day to the best he or she can. If, as Tom O'Brien of PNC has stated, the bank is to be "an exceptional marketing company," the leadership must live it and breathe it. If not, nobody will really believe them, and the endeavor for change will be for naught.

In that role, leaders should neither expect nor want to solve all of the problems within their organizations. The people who work there can be creative and innovative. All they need is a chance to express themselves. That is why I suggested a visit with each one, asking them, "How can I help you achieve great performance?" When the answer comes in, work with them in an environment of innovation and trust to accomplish that goal. Ask the question regularly because new issues will often crop up. Soon, the people of the value chain will get the idea that they should create their own solutions, bragging to you as they do. You can help them by facilitating the communication and cooperation between them and other teams, but let them tell you about what they do.

That means that leaders consciously empower the people in their value chains to serve their customers in the best way possible. "Empowerment" is an overused word, but it is a good word. Show the people the boundaries of their responsibilities; empowerment without some limits looks a lot like anarchy. Once those boundaries are established, abandon the command-and-control management style and let them go. When that happens, you will have more fun because you are doing something creative instead of looking over someone's shoulder, making sure that whatever is being done is done right. There is so much happening out there in the external environment that you're going to have to keep an eye on it. Make the transition from manager to scout and help the organization adapt. Take a few minutes tomorrow when you get back from your "obstacle meetings" to play with the Internet. You'll be amazed at what you can do.

The workforce will reward that behavior, especially if they have pledged themselves to the vision and values and have become passionate about performance. Develop them and help them grow, systematically and steadily. This, as noted, is the teaching role that requires some sensitivity concerning the ability for and timing of learning. People like to achieve success and they like to learn new things. When they do, their confidence level improves, their commitment to the bank is strengthened, and their performance in the service of their customers gets better. It is quite different from the present paradigm.

The last guideline concerns trust. Companies that succeed realize that trust among the people who walk in the front door every day is essential to success and prosperity. Look at MBNA America. Look at Motorola. Trust has to be earned, and people today are very skeptical. They hear that loyalty to the organization is a thing of the past. They announce proudly that they are out for themselves. The greed and downsizing of the 1980s taught them that. But each of us performs better when we know that the team is depending on us and when we can trust the team members to do the jobs they were hired to do. A significant opportunity in the building of trust is here, but the leadership will have to earn it.

The officers of a bank that we know were surveyed about trust. When asked if they had filled out a confidential survey honestly, all of them indicated that they had. When asked if they thought their colleagues had completed the survey with integrity, less than half believed that they did. The trust factor was very low and prohibited greatness.

Getting people to trust may be the hardest part of the change process. Here's what it means:

> Trust makes colleagues willing to spend time together and make sacrifices for one another. Trust is an expression of faith that makes it easy for colleagues to have confidence in one another's ability to perform well and to know that they will be there if needed. Trust means that promises will be kept, and it also means that when a promise is not kept, it was probably for a good cause. And, finally, trust means that a relationship will not last because it is good business, but because the relationship itself is valued.[21]

VISION

The crisis in the American banking system is so severe that the leadership has to direct itself to reestablishing trust and working hard to be designers, stewards, and teachers. I hope that by now they realize they do not have anything more important to do. They have to work together to chart the course that will assure their survival. The first thing to do is to figure out what they want their organization to be. That's called vision. Vision clarifies things for you and for the people of the bank. It provides a focal point.

There's been a lot written and said about vision recently. To avoid any confusion about it, the vision defines, as Tom O'Brien has, the business in which the company is engaged, and perhaps more important, the business in which it is not involved. It tells people what the organization stands for and what it wants to be. What is the vision of your organization? And, please don't just recite what is typically displayed on the walls of most banks: "to maximize shareholder wealth by providing high quality financial services to our customers." That's a goal, but it is not a great vision. It does not speak to what makes your organization different and great. Vision answers the following questions:[22]

- What is our business?
- Who is our customer? Who is our potential customer?
- Where are our customers and how can they be reached?
- In all reality, what does the customer buy from us?
- What does the customer consider value?

- What do we want to be an organization?
- What should we be?

In five words or less, write down your vision.

Vision

It goes back to what we learned from Peter Drucker in the last chapter. What do your clients expect from you? Financial services? Yes. Safety and soundness? Yes. Convenience? Yes. Understand as well that you may be selling different things to different customers.

As a case in point, I was honored to be asked in early 1995 to teach a course in asset-liability management and strategic planning at the Institute of Banking in Vladivostok, Russia. Delta Air Lines took me to the Russian Far East. As I rode along at 36,000 feet, I wondered if Delta understood its different customer constituencies. The people riding first class were buying luxury and comfort; they took the transportation part of it for granted. Those of us in business class bought convenience and expediency because we wanted to get to our destinations as fast as we could. The people in the economy section were buying basic transportation, much like I do when I am flying to Washington on Southwest. It is much like Mercedes and Lexus. Their main product is elegance. Anybody can make a car. What are you really delivering? What exactly are you selling to your customers?

As the leadership wrestles about the vision, each person must make input to it. It is the long-term statement about what the bank will be and the foundation from which all other decisions will be made from then on. When the vision process is made final, the change process can begin in earnest. Communicate it to the rest of the organization as creatively and as often as possible. Be aware, though, that the recipients may not be getting the idea. "It is important for the messages to be consistent, clear, and endlessly repeated. If there is a single rule of communication, it is this: when you are so sick of talking about something that you can hardly stand it, your message is starting to get through."[23]

As you describe the necessary change to the staff, use the vision to help them understand it. Teach them why it is so important, showing them what will happen if the organization doesn't take a new, revolutionary course of action. But don't let them stick their heads in the sand. Don't let them commit "ideacide"; that is, killing your good idea intellectually before it is completely explained and understood. The key word here is *persuasion;* you need to convince people that the new way is the best way. They have to buy in. Persuade them as best you can, but the most effective way to get the message across is to live it.

As you are marching down the new road, don't stand for phrases like, "Oh, that'll never work," as people walk away. Don't let them say, "Well, we've never done that before so we can't do it now." Don't let them sit there while the temperature in the pot is getting uncomfortably warm to the outside touch. Stir it and make them move. Even with the CEO championing the cause as the primary change agent, you're going to have to show staff how they will win; otherwise, they probably won't support you. Show them that the new course will be advantageous while the old one might be costly.

Tell them about the behavior the organization wants and what will happen when they subscribe to it. Show them what will happen if they don't. Somebody took the time to explain it to you; you got the message. Now it's their turn. Teach them well. It will be difficult, but nobody ever said undertaking a revolution was going to be easy.

This is the new turf. This is where the leader says, "OK, here we go. I'm not sure exactly where we are going, but I know the direction. Follow me." The true leader says it to the entire organization because it is imperative to share the change in direction to everyone in the bank, from the scouts, to the strategists, to the implementors, to the recipients. Let the people see you. Let them interact with you. Their lives are being affected, too. In a great analogy, "Washington D.C. consultant Andrew Lebby . . . likens the leader of the transformation to the catcher in a trapeze act, hanging by his knees and calling: 'Yo! Jump! Trust me! I never did this before either.'"[24]

It is critical to make sure that people understand that this change in direction is not a "quick fix" or a "fad of the month." It is a long-term strategy based on serving customers and creating the organization that will be able to do it better than anyone else. This initial communication starts to suggest to the recipients that maybe there can be a partnership and a sense of teamwork as the entire organization contributes to the formation of the new culture and new behavioral norms.

> People in the organization may need to hear a message over and over before they believe that this time the call for change is not just a whim or a passing fancy. It takes time for people to hear, understand, and believe the message. And, if they don't particularly like what they are hearing, then it takes even more time for them to come to terms with the concept of the change.[25]

Communicating with the workforce will be a challenge because they may not be buying it. They have been through a lot of these things and may be numb to the whole idea. What was promised before did not happen, and they may be quite skeptical that this initiative for change will produce anything either. The leadership cannot simply communicate once or twice and be done with it, reverting back to the old ways.

Change cannot be mandated. There has to be good reason for it before people will adopt new ways of conducting themselves at the bank. Leaders

throughout the institution are the "change-masters . . . adept at the art of antic-
ipating the need for, and of leading, productive change."[26] Nevertheless, it really helps if everyone can see the herd of buffalo bearing down on the wagon
train and a leadership team that has an action plan that will divert them. That's
when they will realize that change indeed is good.

That kind of foresight and action inspires people to believe in their leaders. It shows them that they care more for the organization than they do for
themselves. It is precisely what the bank needs to do to survive and prosper. Always understand that the recipients and the implementors are looking for it. For
organizations to be truly successful, the leadership in its role as servant must
establish that type of bond. If it does not, you can imagine what the response
might be as the leader swings upside down on the trapeze and yells, "Yo!
Jump!"—"Not me, baybee!"

That is why vision is so significant and why communicating it honestly
and consistently is so important. The workforce looks to the leadership and has
to be convinced that it knows where it is going and what it is doing. Otherwise,
the leadership will not be clear about the purpose of the jobs.

MISSION

With the vision clear, the leadership can begin to really define the organization.
That means mission. The mission is a little more concrete than the vision. It begins to quantify the elements of the vision and to prescribe the behavior that
will be required to achieve it. Try this for a mission:

> It is the mission of ABC National Bank to serve the needs of our customers
> and our community. We will adhere to the high ethical and performance stan-
> dards that we have set for ourselves. We will not waiver from these principles
> as we strive to meet the expectations of our stakeholders.

As this mission is developed, the leadership, scouts, and strategists must
commit to excellence right here, if they haven't done so already. This is where
my friend the Reverend Ernie DuRoss said that "the rubber hits the runway."
The goals that they establish will guide their thinking and their action since
their performance will be measured against them. If they can't believe in and
commit to the goals, it is unlikely that their performance will be one of excellence. The goal of Motorola is Six Sigma, 99.9999998 percent defect free.

How exacting is six sigma? At five sigma, only 99.9 percent defect free,
there would be:

- Approximately 20,000 wrong medicine prescriptions annually.
- Some 25,000 babies dropped accidentally every year by doctors or
  nurses.

- No electricity, heat, or water for about nine hours annually.
- About 500 wrong surgical procedures a week.[27]

Six sigma is three defects in one million. Hard to achieve? You bet. But it is out there as a target. The bank's quality goals quantify the question, "Just how good does your organization want to be?" That's what mission tells you.

The mission also starts to prescribe the horizontal organization. It says that the bank will develop the processes by which to meet the goals. That means efficient and effective value chains of people who are not encumbered by style and structure (i.e., horizontal organization) as they endeavor to serve their customers better than any other financial institution in town. It also means that at the top of the house, the leadership is committed to dismantling the old hierarchy and grouping people instead by the work they do and the customers they serve, even if that means abandoning the title of executive vice president.

There is some safety here, for if only one person were being asked to lead a value chain of people, the reaction would be, "Well, why me?" But if all of the senior people are committed to new and better ways to serve, and that includes doing away with the pyramid, there is some comfort knowing that everyone else is doing it, too. Not so subtly, the leadership has started to change the bank's structure and style with this definition. It says that the bank is committed to excellence, has established goals based on customer expectations, and is designing the processes by which to achieve the goals.

As such, the entire organization must understand its mission: to work within the mental and physical processes that have been designed to provide high-quality service each and every day. The leadership has set the tone. Now, the mission of the people is to live up to it. To do so, each value chain should develop a mission statement which supports the bankwide one. These formal statements contain their own specific goals and objectives, the attainment of which will assist in reaching the vision. The people should include a commitment to excellence, to meeting customer expectations, and to the values upon which the company rests. This is the document to which the workforce looks when there is confusion about direction as it makes the company's principles very clear.

VALUES AND PHILOSOPHY

How many banks consciously talk about and study their values? What do they stand for? What is the overriding philosophy that shapes the thinking and actions of the people?

When you are communicating with the people of your value chain, give them a good dose of philosophy that is evident in the vision and the mission. Just what do we stand for? Just what do we believe? Values are the personal and organizational codes that prescribe the desired behavior and are the very foundation upon which the company rests: honesty and truthfulness, pride in performance, doing the right thing, not taking shortcuts, and putting others first. Service excellence thus becomes one of the most highly prized values as the workforce begins to see that the commitment to it and to serving others is the organizational expectation. Values guide thinking and action, which is needed as the hierarchy tumbles down in favor of a horizontal organization.

Make sure that everyone in the bank knows that he or she is expected to live by those codes every day. That's how you change the behavior of individuals. This mission supports the vision, the values support the mission, and the philosophy guides action. In a cascading effect, excellence can permeate the entire organization and should manifest itself in individual behavior, including such things as:

- Resisting the temptation to shave some quality from a process by not disclosing everything about a particular loan opportunity.
- Shoveling the snow from the parking lot and making sure that there is no ice on the steps, even if it means getting up at 5 A.M.
- Being truthful in a meeting, even when it hurts.

Values beget the organization's philosophy. Many banks either pay no attention to or think very little about their philosophy. Its importance, however, is seen by all who come in contact with it. It is the spirit for which the organization becomes known. At MBNA America, the philosophy is one of putting other people first—golden rule management—and you can feel it the first time you walk into its headquarters in Newark, Delaware.

As leaders, spend considerable time in individual thought and in group dialogue about your philosophy. Go away someplace where you can elude the telephone or the pressure of a three o'clock meeting. Think about what guides the decision making of the organization. This is another of those areas where you will have to do it on your own. Ponder and debate the bank's vision as defined here. Reduce it to five words or less. Examine and evaluate the statement of mission. Does it support and reinforce the vision? If it doesn't, ask why. There can be no inconsistency between them. Then study your values. What do your customers, employees, and shareholders think about the bank? Helpful, caring, considerate, state of the art, on top of things, honest?

These are the most critical tasks for the leadership instead of racing to another fire three floors away, with water slopping onto the stairs as you go. When everyone has agreed to the vision and values, they will become the basis for an exciting and focused strategic direction, a statement of personal and organizational belief, and a guideline for the behavior of the people of the bank. The bank's vision and values will manifest themselves in the way in which customers are treated and how members of the workforce treat each other. That means culture, and hopefully, by now I have convinced you that it should be one of service.

The problem occurs when the daily philosophy does not match the lofty, well-crafted statements of vision and mission that are emblazoned on plaques throughout the building. The bank's customers and employees know and understand the guiding philosophy, especially when it differs from what they are told by the leadership. Because honesty is the most important attribute for a banker, any inconsistencies give rise to skepticism and doubt, even before the transaction is processed. The classic example: a vision and a mission that is correctly concentrated on serving the needs of customers with a philosophy that is centered on the efficiency ratio. If your bank is going to focus on cost, let your stakeholders know it, but if it is really going to be devoted to serving others, brag about it and make sure that it happens.

One more word of caution: There is some risk involved in asking your colleagues to think about things such as vision, mission, values, and philosophy. Even though we all know what each other stands for, it can be difficult to talk about the personal side in a professional setting. Further, there is the risk that the leadership can adopt a philosophy and a set of values with which you disagree. In these cases, you can continue the fight, trying to persuade others to see and adopt your views; you can acquiesce and adapt to what the others espouse; or you can stand firm, realizing that the organization has principles different from yours, and attempt to find an organization that is more in agreement with yours.

CRITICAL SUCCESS FACTORS

One would hope that the examination and definition of vision, mission, values, and philosophy is one of clarification, not divisiveness, because the bank needs to be very clear about its purpose and principles. It also needs to have a way to ensure that actions are taken to support them. Critical success factors (CSFs) are used to keep everyone in the bank focused. CSFs were first brought to my attention by John Rockhart of MIT's Sloan School of Management. Critical success factors are those things that have to be achieved every day for the bank to realize its vision and mission. Five or six will do for the entire organization. The leadership team must clearly identify these fundamental contributors to success and may include the following prerequisites:

- Systematic identification of customer expectations in the bank's various markets and providing the service by which to meet or exceed them, thus increasing market share.

E X H I B I T   5-1

Critical Success Factors

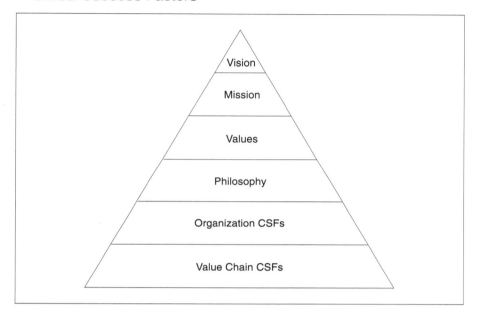

- Hiring only the most qualified people, educating them, giving them the tools by which to serve customers, and rewarding their efforts.
- A continuous process of renewal, based on changing markets, technologies, regulations, and so forth.

These are clear statements of what the bank has to do and are governed by and embody the guiding philosophy. In a comparatively short period of time, the bank starts with a five-word vision, then the statement of mission takes shape, values and philosophy become subjects of dialogue and debate, and finally CSFs are identified. If done correctly and with discipline, everyone in the bank will understand what the company stands for, the spirit that drives it, and the things that have to be done for it to succeed. At that point, they are all headed in the same direction and should be clear about what is expected of them. This is made possible by the CSF process as shown in Exhibit 5–1, the only time that a pyramid is still accepted. Once the bankwide CSFs have been formulated, it is the responsibility of the people within each value chain to figure out what they have to do to achieve them. They develop their own CSFs, which, when viewed in the context of the bankwide ones, enable the

leadership to see where any inconsistencies might lie. Using the CSFs identified above, the commercial loan value chain might come up with:

- In coordination with the information systems specialists, leverage the
  latest technological advances, including E-mail, executive support
  systems, and remote processing.
- Develop a marketing plan based on customer surveys to document their
  expectations of us and to detail how we will meet them.
- With the aid of the education staff, implement a learning initiative for
  the staff about the importance of customer service.
- Revise, in accordance with quality council request, compensation
  schedules to be based on customer satisfaction levels.

Once CSFs are developed, it is critical to ensure consistency throughout
the bank. Accordingly, in a leadership forum, they are presented, reviewed, and
subjected to respectful questioning as to how the commercial loan value chain
supports the overall CSFs. Each presenter is then asked two basic questions:

1. What do you need from the others to be successful?
2. How can you help the others be successful?

When that exercise is complete, each member of the leadership team
knows what is expected of him or her and is prepared to develop the detailed action plans that will result in success. It becomes the leadership's job to monitor
progress on those plans, providing whatever assistance and support is needed to
accomplish them. Exhibit 5–2 shows how that works in a horizontal organization. We call it the "pizza" structure, with value chains and specialists operating
on the same plane as the leadership team. It is not an inverted hierarchy as some
would have us construct, but flat and horizontal like a pepperoni pizza.

> This [new universal] model . . . describes more flexible organizations,
> adaptable to change, with relatively few levels of formal hierarchy and loose
> boundaries among functions and units, sensitive and responsive to the envi-
> ronment; concerned with stakeholders of all sorts—employees, communities,
> customers, suppliers, and shareholders. These organizations empower people
> to take action and be entrepreneurial, reward them for contributions, and help
> them gain in skill and "employability."[28]

When this process is under way, the people of the institution will recognize
that change is occurring. As such, it is vital to make sure that the leadership
group communicates regularly about what is going on. They need to explain

E X H I B I T   5–2

The Pizza Structure

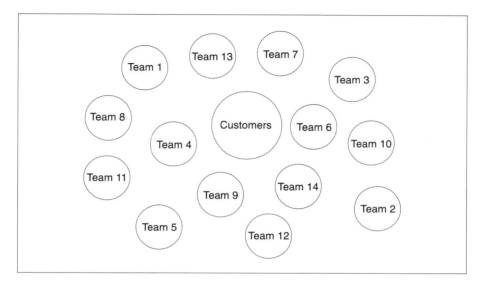

why, for example, people in all corners of the bank are being asked for input about the state of the bank or how their customers like the treatment they receive. They need to outline the vision, mission, philosophy, and values every chance they get and through every medium possible. I do not have to describe the ways to do that; rather, I hope that you are creative in the way it is done. But there is one more behavioral trap.

Like the potential inconsistency between philosophy and vision, be on the lookout for inconsistencies between what is being communicated and the behavior of the communicator. People will see through the words if they are not genuine, and when they do, the trust and commitment that is so necessary for success vanishes.

> The new breed of employee wants to work for an organization that has values and viewpoints compatible with their own: an organization that is oriented toward the long haul, working toward the prevention of ills, rather than only curing symptoms; an organization that cares about morals and ethics, doing what is in the best interests of its clients; and one that cares about the impact it has on the environment.[29]

This new breed places a demand on the leadership to create an organization that meets with this kind of expectation. It almost forces servant leadership, but it is much better if it can be voluntary.

THE TASK

The challenge is daunting, of that there is no doubt. There is also no question that America's banks have to change. They are changing, technologically, but they also need to change behaviorally. That has been the entire focus of *The Banking Revolution.* The task for management is to decide, as Ed Crutchfield did, that he and the organization had to change. Otherwise, someone or some institution will implement the change for him.

With that understanding, start the change process. It starts at the top of the organization with a scout seeing a change on the horizon and the commitment of the leadership to take advantage of it. It is guided by the establishment of and commitment to a vision of the future. The leaders then must filter it down through the rest of the bank, showing the people what that new direction and concentration is to be. All the while, remember that customers have to be served while the cultural change is taking place, so incorporate that into your style.

In *Flight of the Buffalo,* the authors give some sound advice as the change process begins. Transfer ownership of the work to the people who execute it. Don't own their problems and try to fix them. That negates accountability and pride. Next, create an environment where accountability is expected, where people want to be responsible for their own results. Let them define what great performance is, let them concentrate on their personal critical success factors, give them a stake in the business, and show them how they and the company can succeed. Then coach the people in your value chain, helping them improve their skills and competencies. Finally, develop an environment of continuous learning. Keep looking "out there" for change. Anticipate it, learn about it, experiment with it. And don't just stick your head in the sand, thinking that it will go away.

The banking revolution is in the hands of the leaders of the nation's banks. It is up to them to grasp these new concepts and to run with them, keeping ever aware of the changing expectations of their customers. As we have seen, nothing else but the relationship with clients matters. It will not be easy to change the focus to one of customer delight, but it has to happen. Coach the people in your value chain. Help them remove any obstacles to excellence. Teach them about the importance of meeting customer expectations. Then call your customers and tell them that you have thrown the tea into the harbor and that a transformation is happening in your bank. They will be glad to hear from you.

ENDNOTES

1. Sumantra Ghoshal and Christopher A. Bartlett, "Changing the Role of Top Management: Beyond Structure to Processes," *Harvard Business Review,* Jan.–Feb. 1995, p. 96.
2. Gary Weiss, "Online Investing," *Business Week,* June 5, 1995, pp. 66–67.
3. Philip Elmer-DeWitt, "Mine, All Mine," *Time,* June 5, 1995, p. 48.
4. "Smith Corona Declares Bankruptcy," *The Plain Dealer,* July 6, 1995, p. 1C.
5. Thomas A. Stewart, "A New 500 for the New Economy," *Fortune,* May 15, 1995, p. 166.
6. Rahul Jacob, "Corporate Reputations," *Fortune,* March 6, 1995, p. 54.
7. Rosabeth Moss Kanter et al., *The Challenge of Organizational Change* (New York: Free Press, 1992), pp. 55–56.
8. Ibid., p. 66.
9. James M. Kouzes and Barry Z. Posner, *The Leadership Challenge* (San Francisco: Jossey-Bass, 1991), p. 36.
10. Robert L. Kriegel, *If It Ain't Broke . . . BREAK IT!* (New York: Warner Books, 1991), p. 13.
11. Kanter, *The Challenge of Organizational Changes,* pp. 377–81.
12. Ghoshal and Bartlett, "Changing the Role of Top Management," p. 94.
13. Anne B. Fisher, "Making Change Stick," *Fortune,* April 17, 1995, p. 131.
14. Paul R. Lawrence, "How to Deal with Resistance to Change," in *People: Managing Your Most Important Asset* (Boston: Harvard Business Review, 1988), p. 36.
15. Fisher, *"Making Change Stick,"* p. 124.
16. Ibid., p. 121.
17. William G. Pagonis, "The Work of the Leader," *Harvard Business Review,* Nov.–Dec. 1992, p. 126.
18. James A. Belasco and Ralph C. Stayer, *Flight of the Buffalo* (New York: Warner Books, 1993), pp. 120–21.
19. Christopher A. Bartlett and Sumantra Ghoshal, "Changing the Role of Top Management: Beyond Systems to People," *Harvard Business Review,* May–June 1995, p. 135.
20. Belasco and Stayer, *Flight of the Buffalo,* p. 51.
21. Frank K. Sonnenberg, *Managing with a Conscience* (New York: McGraw-Hill, 1994), p. 191.
22. Peter F. Drucker, *The Practice of Management* (New York: Harper & Row, 1954), pp. 50–58.
23. Jeanie Daniel Duck, "Managing Change: The Art of Balancing," *Harvard Business Review,* Nov.–Dec. 1993, p. 111.
24. Thomas A. Stewart, "How to Lead a Revolution," *Fortune,* Nov. 28, 1994, p. 50.
25. Duck, *"Managing Change,"* p. 111.
26. Rosabeth Moss Kanter, *The Change Masters* (New York: Simon and Schuster, 1983), p. 13.
27. Suzanee de Treville et al., "Getting Six Sigma Back to Basics," *Quality Digest,* May 1995, p. 43.
28. Kanter, *The Challenge of Organizational Change,* p. 3.
29. Sonnenberg, *Managing with a Conscience,* pp. 11–12.

CHAPTER 6

It's Gonna Take Work!

By now, I hope there is ample evidence that the banking system in this country is under siege and that substantial attitudinal and structural change is necessary for its survival and success. I also hope that it is apparent that the most senior people have to lead the charge; without them, the troops won't change.

In that regard, there are two books that I recommend that you read after finishing *The Banking Revolution.* Both of them will provide some sage advice about the issue of leadership in the 1990s. The first one, *Flight of the Buffalo,* I have referenced before. The authors, Jim Belasco and Ralph Stayer, speak directly to the dilemma that you face. Their principal point is this: Buffalo travel in herds and wait for the leader to move before they do. If there is no leadership, the herd just stands around and is easy prey for hunters.

Belasco and Stayer want leaders to become geese, not buffalo. Geese travel great distances in the air, flying free and clear. When the leader of the "V" tires, it turns over the point to another who can continue the journey. As the formation flies along, the original leader drops to the back and drafts off the others, resting and gaining strength. It is a neat concept. Teamwork at its best.

The other book is *The Mind of the Strategist: The Art of Japanese Business* by Kenichi Ohmae. It provides valuable insight into strategic thinking, one of the main themes of this chapter. Ohmae differentiates strategic thinking from strategic planning and demonstrates how it can be translated into a cultural and competitive advantage. As a former CFO who spent a lot of time in the planning process, *The Mind of the Strategist* enabled me to recognize that we need to spend more time on the thought and less on the exercise.

Both books are very clear on one point: If the organization is to succeed, it is up to the people in charge to determine the overall goal and to enlist the support of their people to achieve it, motivating and helping as they go. It is a personal as well as an organizational journey that they have to lead.

BOWLING IN SAND

A friend of mine is vice president in charge of retail banking in one of the regions of a rather large commercial bank holding company. We have discussed the issues and concepts that are central to *The Banking Revolution* for some time. My friend teaches a class for his people which he concludes with a question from Joel Barker's *Paradigms.*

> What is impossible to do in our business today, but if it could be done, would fundamentally change it?[1]

His students say things like, "checkless society," "no more branches," "loans by phone," "cashless society," "remote banking," "virtual banking," and the like. When hearing that, he tells them that those kinds of things are already present in the bank's markets and, because they are, the fundamental business of banking has changed. Their response? "Oh, wow!" That's as far as it goes. They can't translate the knowledge to action.

Some bankers are making substantial progress toward doing the impossible, but most are like these bankers and can't. They continue doing the same old things. Even my friend, a vice president, can't change what his bank does. The prevailing paradigms prevent it. He wishes that the CEO would take charge of the transformation to a fast-paced, unencumbered financial provider. Unless that happens, nothing will be different at a time when it is very much needed. The changes that are necessary need the support of the most senior people in the bank. Even then, it will take a great deal of hard, conscious effort.

To get started, there has to be a goal, a plan, and a significant reserve of energy. Above all, there has to be commitment to the vision, the kind of dedication that shines through even when the whole thing looks like it is doomed to fail. It is up to the leadership to determine what the bank will be in the future and to figure out how to get there.

> Why do we live? Most of us need the very thing we never ask for. We talk about revolution as if it were peanuts. What we need is some frank thinking and a few revolutions in our own guts; to hell with most of the sons of bitches that I know and *myself along with them* [italics added] if I don't take hold of myself and turn about when I need to—or to go ahead further if that's the game.
>
> *William Carlos Williams*
> Selected Letters of William Carlos Williams[2]

William Carlos Williams is right. Each of us is responsible for the situation in which we find ourselves. There is nobody else to blame. It is our responsibility to "turn about" when things are not going right. That is exactly what the banking industry in the country needs to do. It must concentrate on service and not on the quarterly results. It must pursue excellence.

What do I mean by excellence? In their book, *Service Quality,* Len Berry, David Bennett, and Carter Brown, defined it this way:

> Service excellence comes from a "chemistry" of leadership, solid information, organizational infrastructure, good people who are free to serve, technology that supports their efforts. . . Service excellence is "heart" not just "things," execution not just strategy, little ideas not just big ideas. It is the marshaling of resources—human and otherwise—in a well-designed service system.[3]

Harvard professors James Heskett and W. Earl Sasser, Jr., along with their collaborator, Christopher W. L. Hart, add some further insight to the definition:

> Service excellence is built first around an understanding that:
>
> 1. The value associated with the results a service provides and the quality of the way it is delivered depends on the extent to which a provider can reduce a customer's perceived risks.
> 2. Increased value in relation to the costs of acquiring a service leads to a higher probability that a customer will become a repeater.
> 3. Repeat customers, because they have established expectations, growing respect for the provider, and greater knowledge of what is expected of them in the service delivery process, are less expensive, and therefore more profitable to serve, than new customers.
> 4. The value of service to a repeat customer grows with the reliability of the way it is delivered and the results it achieves.[4]

I have a little different spin for you. Think about this: *We like to give our hard-earned money to great companies.* The most amazing one, to me anyway, is Disney. This struck me about two years ago as I pulled into the parking lot at Disney World in Orlando for the third or fourth time. Other cars streamed into the lot. Their passengers parked them as they were told, jumped out, and ran for the trams. It occurred to me that this doesn't happen only when I'm there. It's standard. It happens every day. People line up by the thousands to pay $30 apiece for a day at Disney World. Once inside the park, we buy Mickey and Donald T-shirts, note cards with Minnie's likeness, and all sorts of other paraphernalia with Goofy, Chip and Dale, and the rest of the gang emblazoned on it. When we get home, we gather up the family to go see *Snow White, Aladdin,*

T A B L E   6-1

Cost Cutting Effects
The Aftereffects on Big Companies That Downsized between
1989 and 1994

	Increased (Percent)	Remained Constant (Percent)	Decreased (Percent)
Operating profits	50.6%	29.1%	20.4%
Worker productivity	34.4	35.5	30.1
Employee morale	1.9	12.1	86.0

Source: The Wall Street Journal, July 5, 1995.

and *Pocahontas,* sometimes several times, and even the teenagers get into the act by buying Elton John's CD that featured "Can You Feel the Love Tonight," the title song from *The Lion King.* It was all we heard during the summer of 1994 as it was number one on Casey's Top 20 for three months.

Consider this: Wouldn't it be great if the banks had people lining up to buy their financial services like the guests do at Disney World and Disneyland? There wouldn't be enough tellers and ATMs to handle the volume. Can that happen? Yes, I think so, but it will take a new, strategic vision; a reformulated set of organizational values, based on the concept of service; an unwavering commitment, even when it looks grim; and a lot of hard work. It is a different way of looking at the conduct of the business, but it is the only, and the basic, way out. It provides value to customers so that they "buy from you," which is a lot different from "selling to them." A basic premise of business is doing what customers want, which is quite the opposite of the downsizing we have been seeing for the last 10 years or so and which, we are finding out, has failed.

I have been skeptical and cynical about downsizing and other forms of cost cutting. There really wasn't much proof that they did not work, but that is starting to change. On July 5, 1995, *The Wall Street Journal* carried an article headlined "Lean—and Frail: Some Companies Cut Costs Too Far, Suffer 'Corporate Anorexia'" (see Table 6–1). Only one-half of the companies in this American Management Association study showed increases in operating profits, which means that the other half saw *no improvement at all and some even saw deterioration.* The most telling stat, however, is in the segment at the bottom right of Table 6–1: 86% of the companies saw morale decline. It is hard to deliver excellence that way. That's why we need the revolution. This latest fad that we have pursued diligently for a decade hasn't worked. It had the wrong

focus. Throughout this book, I have argued that it is not these artificial or con-
trived strategies that ensure success. Rather, it is the way that companies are organized to serve the needs of their stakeholders. They consciously look at what
they are doing and how they are going at it as they seek to provide something
of value. Just like Disney.

> What makes top performing companies different . . . is their organizational
> arrangements. Specifically:
> - They are better organized to meet the needs of their *people,* so that they
>   attract better people than their competitors do and their people are more
>   greatly motivated to do a superior job, whatever it is they do.
> - They are better organized to meet the needs of their *customers,* so that
>   they are more innovative in anticipating customer needs, more reliable
>   in meeting customer expectations, better able to deliver their product or
>   service more cheaply, or some combination of the above.[5]

Think about what this says. Top performance is a matter of better organization
(structure) and meeting the needs of people (style). We start to make the
change now.

CROSBY'S GRID

In his book, *Quality Is Free,* Philip Crosby included a matrix called the Quality
Management Maturity Grid, which is reproduced in Table 6–2. The grid contains the various stages that organizations must go through to achieve excellence and is designed to let you see where your bank is on this journey. As a
road map, it moves from left to right, from top to bottom. Across the top are the
five stages of the progression to excellence: uncertainty, awakening, enlightenment, wisdom, and certainty.

   Down the left side are six categories by which to measure how well the
bank is doing: management understanding and attitude, quality organizational
status, problem handling, cost of quality as percent of sales, quality improvement actions, and summation of company quality posture. In the worst-case
scenario at the upper left of the grid, the bank is in the stage of uncertainty in
the most important category, management understanding and attitude. In this
phase, the leadership of the organization has no clue about how effective the
commitment to excellence can be. They may say the right words, but they really do not understand what they mean, nor do they behave in a way to inspire
the best in those who follow. There may be a quality department but in typical
bureaucratic fashion, command and control prevails as management blames it
for service quality problems. In this stage, they have no idea why customers are
complaining.

T A B L E 6-2

Quality Management Maturity Grid

Measurement Categories	Stage I: Uncertainty	Stage II: Awakening	Stage III: Enlightenment	Stage IV: Wisdom	Stage V: Certainty
Management understanding and attitude	No comprehension of quality as a management tool. Tend to blame the quality department for "quality" problems.	Recognizing that quality management may be of value but not willing to provide the money and time to make it happen.	While going through quality improvement process, learn about quality management; becoming supportive and helpful.	Participating; understand absolutes of quality management. Recognize their role in continuing emphasis.	Consider quality management essential part of company system.
Quality organizational status	Quality hidden in production departments; inspection probably not part of organization. Emphasis on appraisal and sorting.	Stronger quality leader is appointed, but main emphasis is still on appraisal and moving the product. Still part of production.	Quality department reports to top management; all appraisal is incorporated and manager has role in management of company.	Quality manager is officer of company; effective status reporting and preventive action. Involved with consumer affairs and special assignments.	Quality manager is on board of directors. Prevention is main concern. Quality is thought leader.

T A B L E 6-2 CONTINUED

Quality Management Maturity Grid

Measurement Categories	Stage I: Uncertainty	Stage II: Awakening	Stage III: Enlightenment	Stage IV: Wisdom	Stage V: Certainty
Problem handling	Problems are fought as they occur; no resolution; inadequate definition; lots of accusations.	Teams are set up to attack major problems. Long range solutions not solicited.	Corrective action communication established. Problems faced openly; resolved in orderly way.	Problems identified early in their development. All functions open to improvement.	Except in the most unusual cases, problems are prevented.
Cost of quality as percent of sales	Reported: Unknown Actual: 20%	Reported: 3% Actual: 18%	Reported: 8% Actual: 12%	Reported: 6.5% Actual: 8%	Reported: 2.5% Actual: 2.5%
Quality improvement actions	No organized activities. No understanding of such activities.	Trying obvious motivational short-term efforts.	Installation of disciplined process with understanding of each step.	Continuing improvement process and starting to "make certain."	Quality improvement is normal and continued activity.
Summation of company quality posture	"We don't know why we have quality problems."	"Is it absolutely necessary to have problems with quality?"	"With management commitment and quality improvement, we identify and resolve our problems."	"Defect prevention is a routine part of our operation."	"We know why we do not have problems with quality."

Source: Philip B. Crosby, *Quality Is Free* (New York: Penguin Books, 1980), pp. 32–33.

193

With a culture like that, there are a lot of problems, represented by Crosby's worst estimate of the cost of quality: 20 percent of sales. Fire fighting prevails, blame for errors and mistakes is leveled at everyone else, and no one has any idea why customers think there are problems and are talking with their feet, walking out the back door.

In the best-case stage, certainty, there are minimal problems with customer satisfaction, 2.5 percent of sales, which the leaders want to reduce even more. They know and understand the relationship of culture and excellence as they subscribe to *kaizen,* whereby improvement to meet the needs and expectations of customers is the norm. The culture, and the company, has elevated *kaizen* to the centerpiece of its structure and style, the driver of management and organizational behavior. This is the desired state and should be the goal of every bank in the United States. "We know why we do not have problems with quality."

Whether we call it "quality" or "service excellence" makes no difference. The behavior and organizational commitment to serving others flawlessly is the key issue. In between uncertainty and certainty are the stages that your bank will have to go through to get to the goal.

First, there will be awakening, which I hope that this book is doing. In this stage the leadership says, "Yes, I think having excellent service is a great idea, but we have to watch the overhead ratio; the analysts are being sensitive." The emphasis is still on production. Get as much of the product out of the plant as possible. There is some understanding of the sources and seriousness of customer dissatisfaction, but they really don't know the full extent. In this stage, they attack symptoms of the problems, not the root causes. It is characterized by a short-term view in which people are just starting to become a little curious about sustainable improvement. Some of them are beginning to wonder if they can achieve excellence because they are getting a little tired of making and correcting errors. The cost of quality stands at 18 percent of sales, but it is reported as 3 percent. There is still a long way to go.

The notion of service excellence really starts to catch on in the stage of enlightenment, in which the leadership understands how powerful a competitive weapon it can be, but doesn't understand yet what to do. They are committed to *kaizen,* but are only functioning in a supportive role. They want to help, but let others take the lead; however, some progress is being made. The manager of the quality department sits on the management committee and delivers regular reports. Some standards have been set—in accordance with customer expectations, it is hoped—and corresponding measurement is starting to take place. There is no finger-pointing, problems are resolved at the root-cause level, and people of the bank's various value chains work together in the service of their customers. The cost of quality is starting to come down, but there is still a discrepancy between the reported amount, 8 percent, and the actual percentage, 12 percent.

The next stage is called wisdom, in which service to others has become paramount. All over the bank, people try to prevent errors from happening in the first place. Management understands how vital this new attitude is to the improvement process and how they can improve themselves and the areas for which they are responsible. Service has not quite become the essence of the bank's culture yet, but it's very close in the wisdom category. *Prevention* is the watchword as managerial defensiveness gives way to a spirit of cooperation and teamwork in the service of the bank's customers. The cost of quality has been reduced even more, and the gap between what is reported and the actual cost has also narrowed. Presumably, customers are experiencing better service while at the same time market share is starting to increase.

Which brings the bank to the stage of certainty, the kind of culture and production that characterizes Motorola, Levi Strauss, Disney, and others whose reputations are based on continuous improvement of products and services. These companies know that customer loyalty is the most profitable business possible. Service excellence is on everyone's mind. The entire workforce understands the power it wields in the marketplace as they seek to make sure that errors and mistakes come nowhere near their customers. These companies have embraced the idea of continual improvement of processes and people every day. They know what they are doing, have set a standard like six sigma as a goal, and are trying hard to achieve it. They know that to get your business, they have to be the best. There are too many other options. The bank is in the same spot. It has a lot of competition that is giving value to the consumer of financial services.

As you study Crosby's Quality Management Maturity Grid in Table 6–2, think about where your bank is in each of the stages and categories. Take a red pen, the one you used to eliminate the structure developed by the founder of the bank, and circle the boxes where you think your bank is on this journey. Do a little survey and ask others to give an honest assessment. The results become your stake in the ground. Share them with the rest of the leadership. This is where you think you are. Presumably, you know where you want to be, bottom right on the grid. The challenge is getting there. It starts with a change in thinking for both organizational and personal growth.

"OK, BAYBEE, HERE GOES!"

Service excellence and quality are delivered by the bank's people. These people look to those in leadership positions in their value chains for the accepted mode of behavior. In his book, *The Genius of Sitting Bull,* Emmett Murphy puts forth a series of qualities that characterized this great leader of the Sioux nation as he sought to maintain their heritage and way of life.[6] Ultimately, forces superior to those of Sitting Bull would change the lifestyle of the Sioux forever, but without his leadership, it would have happened a lot sooner.

These personal attributes enabled him and others like him to help their people become successful. I have talked about the roles that the servant leader plays—designer, teacher, and steward—but now I'm talking about the behavioral characteristics that are instrumental in making the change. It's a reality check and an agenda for personal learning and growth.

As you are working on your plans and implementing your change strategies, think about how incorporating, or improving on, these traits could help your people accomplish their goals. You have learned about what servant leadership is; now I will show you why it is important and how you can achieve it. For your organization to change its culture, the behavior of the people must undergo some modification as well. And it starts with the top guys.

As you read the next several paragraphs, think about people you admire who have helped their organizations improve. They don't have to be presidents although there are some pretty good models. They don't have to be public figures at all. They may have quietly helped the United Way, coached your kid's basketball team, agreed to lead the fund-raising campaign for the library, or provided exactly what you needed to get a project done at work. These are the people who, when they holler, "Yo! Jump!" you answer, "OK, baybee, here goes!" as you leap off the platform toward the swinging trapeze.

COMMITMENT

My synonym for commitment is "passion." Be passionate about what your organization is trying to accomplish. If it is worth doing at all, it is worth doing the very best you can, and this is what the others in the bank watch. If you, as leader, are not fully committed to the overall goal, the direction, and the task at hand, it is unlikely that the people that you are asking to follow will show any more passion than you do. Ask for mediocracy and that's what you will get, even as the water in the pot is getting warmer and warmer. If I were the CEO of the bank right now, I'd be really vocal about what's happening out there. The status quo won't be good enough.

Commitment is a personal decision that each individual in the value chain has to make. "Am I committed to this or not?" "Do I believe in it or not?" The answer can be yes or no. If it is positive, then give it everything you have. If it is negative, you might want to find something else to do. Whatever you do, don't just drift along. Life's too short.

EMPOWERMENT

Empowerment is an overused word, but it is the key to success. Sitting Bull made sure that each of his leaders knew what the objective was, understood the role that he was supposed to play, and had the authority to carry it out. If they had not been so empowered and had waited for the chief to tell them exactly what to do as the bullets started flying, the chances for success in battle would have been fairly small. Doing only what you are ordered to do without the ability to think and reason about possible outcomes can lead to disastrous consequences. Think about the thousands of Confederate soldiers who heard the command to cross that wide-open field at Gettysburg, now and forever known as "Pickett's Charge."

The key to empowerment is the boundary that we put around it. A client once said, "Empowerment without boundaries is anarchy." That's very true. Therefore, we must channel it, which is what most people want anyway. They want to know the goal, they want some idea of the direction, and they want to get going. What it means for the leader is putting the organization's needs first and subordinating personal advancement to action for the good of the team.

Leadership is like raising kids. You want the best for them, you set some limits for them, and you let them make mistakes, knowing that they will learn from them and thus will grow in ability and stature. That's empowerment.

HEALING

People cannot succeed if they are hurting. That's why the statistics in Table 6–1 are so disturbing: 86 percent of the companies that have undergone downsizing report lower morale. The leader's job is to help them. Perhaps those numbers indicate that we have a leadership crisis. In the bank, I doubt whether the hurt is of a physical nature; I suspect it consists of "survivor syndrome" and other such maladies. That's why it is important for the leadership at all levels to be out and about, talking with the folks in their value chains not only about what's going well, but about what's wrong.

The late J. P. McCarthy, on his morning radio program on WJR in Detroit, used to do a segment called, "What's Bothering You?" It was a chance for individuals to call up and express themselves. People need to do that from time to time. It doesn't have to be formal. It can be something as simple as having an open door where a member of the team can walk in, slump down, and say, "Chief, we have a problem."

It is the responsibility of the leader to create a comfortable environment where that can happen. By really listening and applying the proper resources, healing occurs. It also provides input for future strategies because the people can feel free to talk to you about what is of most importance to them.

STRATEGIC VISION

I have talked at some length about vision, but true leaders do something with it. They internalize it, they believe in it as a worthwhile personal matter, and they encourage everyone to think and plan for the future. It is quite the opposite of all the people in the story about the founder of the bank, where there are so many compartments and levels and so much is going on that nobody can think past noon or, at the latest, 5:00 P.M. It goes with empowerment, asking those people who are closest to their customers and their value chains about the things that they will have to do in the future to prosper.

Henry Mintzberg calls this talent "synthesis."[7] The strategist is able to take what the scouts and others are saying about the environment, to ask the right questions, to evaluate the pros and cons, and to come up with an idea of the vision. He or she is also able to develop some impression about what to do. This is the attribute that you need to assess your position on Crosby's grid (see Table 6–2). Not only do you have to have a keen understanding of where you are, but also you need to know the actions that will allow demonstrable progress to be made.

You have to look at the many small pictures honestly and objectively, and then create a big picture that will inspire the others. Be sure of your logic and be persuasive with the boss. Show him the dust cloud that the herd of buffalo have raised as they have come ever closer to the wagon train.

COURAGE

It takes some courage to walk into the CEO's office with an invitation to view the onrushing stampede, to give your assessment of the situation, and to provide your innovative solution for it. But if you have done your homework and are prepared, it will be easier. This is the ultimate challenge for the servant leader, to take a position and to defend it in spite of odds that may be unfavorable. It means enlisting the support of others who may not have as much gumption as you do and it means riding at the front of the column, knowing that you may be the target of a few shots.

There is also a matter of instinct and intuition involved with courage. Sometimes that little voice inside tells you that something is wrong and that you should proceed in spite of what the numbers might indicate. Courage also means knowing when it is time to withdraw when the odds really favor the opposition.

> During the Civil War, General Robert H. Milroy was in charge of the Union garrison at Winchester, Virginia, during the winter of 1862–1863. There were about 6,900 Federal troops encamped there, guarding the entrance to the Shenandoah Valley. Among them was Lt. Tom Armstrong, my great-grandfather on my father's side. When spring came . . . Robert E. Lee and 100,000 men of the Army of Northern Virginia were on the move toward Pennsylvania, a march that would take them right through Winchester.

General Milroy engaged the Second Corps of Lee's Army, convinced that he could defend his position. He was wrong. Even with orders from President Abraham Lincoln, he refused to withdraw to Harpers Ferry. The Union lost Winchester; approximately 400 Federal soldiers were killed or wounded; and 4,443 were taken prisoner.[8]

There are times when the courageous thing to do is think of a new strategy. General Milroy ignored the data and showed terribly poor judgment. He was rewarded accordingly. At the bank, based on the data and your good instinct, marshal all the resources possible to win the competitive battle and to provide value for your customers.

RESPECT

Respect everyone until they prove undeserving of it. Primarily, leaders have to have respect for each member of the value chains; that goes without saying. They honor the contribution of each person because they know that the success of the entire team depends on them. There's also another group that demands your respect: the competition. Your competitors are doing something better or different than you are. If they weren't, you would have their customers right away, but those people are satisfied to stay with First National from Across-the-Street and Dean Witter. You have to respect that, but you can also take advantage of it.

The first step is to benchmark your bank; use Crosby's grid as a starting point in Table 6–2. Later, I will provide some other tools that you can use. Next, assess what the competition is doing. As you do so, learn how they have been able to achieve their position. There is an old adage in sports that you "tend to play to the level of the competition." Presuming that Merrill Lynch and Charles Schwab are delivering excellence, that's what your bank has to do as well.

LEARNING

The first assignment? Learn the rules of the game that your bank is playing. Answer the following questions:

- What services are we offering that we did not offer five years ago?
- What technological advancements have been made in the last 5 years?
- Where will technology take us in the next 10 years?
- Was your bank a merger target then?
- Is it now?

- Who's the competition (see above)? What services are they offering?
- How can we do that better?
- What do we have to learn?

Learning is essential; we have talked about that before. In these days of speed and innovation, the bank needs everyone possible up to speed on the latest advancements in how to serve customers better. Whether there is a formal education about behavioral modification or a review of a series of customer surveys, all the people of the bank must keep pace with the changing environment. Not all will be the "scouts" who have a natural curiosity. There will be the "recipients" who will require some encouragement. That's where you, as leader, come in. Show them why improvement is important. Help them achieve it.

JUDGMENT

Judgment concerns the people of your value chain. It means having the right number of people, properly educated and with the right technology to provide service excellence. Therefore, you have to know what is expected of them in terms of volumes of transactions and the quality levels that your customers want. You have to know the elements of every job in the value chain. You have to know whether the people have been adequately prepared to serve and whether there are enough of them.

Based on that kind of information, you can begin to manage the human side of your business. Suppose that you are in charge of retail banking and see and understand the service capabilities of the new delivery systems of Fidelity and others. You also know what your customers expect from your delivery system and can see a gap between yours and the competition. With that information, you can design a delivery system that will provide your clients with value and will keep them from walking out the back door. It takes educated judgment to do that.

GUARDIANSHIP

Leaders must also protect what has been entrusted to them. The guardian makes sure that the fort is sound, that the wide double doors of the entrance work, and that the troops have what they need to live. Having asked the high command—the board of directors—for these resources, the guardian is accountable for them and responsible for putting them to good use.

The guardian also watches the commitment of the people, making sure that the vision remains intact and fully supported by them. He is a trusted ally of those on the front lines, one who will vigorously and in good faith represent their position with the higher-ups. There is a great deal of trust here, because

the people making the resource allocation decisions look to the guardian to ensure that what is being provided is used well. Tough job, that of guardian. The
line being walked can be a narrow one.

SUCCESS

Success means giving it your best every day in pursuit of the vision that the organization has chosen for itself. It means never settling for being number two
unless there are overwhelming odds like those General Milroy faced at Winchester. But it also means encouraging the people of your value chain to adopt this
same attitude in the service of their customers, whether they are internal or external ones. It is providing your customers with services of value that results in
your bank being successful. The alternative, it seems quite clear, is not pleasant.

Success also means sharing the victory, not only with the other leaders
and coaches, but also with the whole team. Whether that means distributing the
proceeds of a profit-sharing program equally or inviting all members of the
team to come up on the stage and receive the applause that some might have
thought was only for you, it has to be understood that the leader is only as good
as the team. All teams win because of talent and coaching, and all should share
equally in the success.

"LOOK OUT! HERE THEY COME!"

Riding toward the column of covered wagons, you know that you must get the
rest of the bank's leaders focused on the stampeding buffalo which are getting
pretty close. Ideally, it would have been better to have had the foresight that the
buffalo might charge and to have come up with a way to keep them from charging, but that's 20/20 hindsight. As you dismount, tell the senior people and anyone else who will listen about the pending crisis. If they don't believe it, you can
get their attention by asking them to ride toward the stampede, in essence, looking "out there." When they do and see the cloud of dust headed their way, there
should be a heightened sense of urgency. That is the time when I hope they realize that the water in the pot is getting pretty darn hot. While they, and the bank,
understand that they are going to have to move fast, there will have to be some
structure for the initiative, one that will facilitate its implementation because service excellence and a focus on the customer do not happen by accident.

The organizations that have demonstrated first-rate products and services
work at it by:

- Creating a behavioral expectation of servitude.
- Expending the energy to understand the expectations of their
  customers.

- Spending time and thought to design their delivery systems according to those expectations.
- Working together to develop measuring techniques by which to judge their performance against ever-increasing service standards.
- Giving a great deal of time to their reward systems in order to provide an incentive for the behavior that they want.

Additionally, they plan for excellence, but in a very different way. Then they create their organizations to achieve it. Planning, however, is an ongoing, strategic exercise for the whole bank, which is defined as "the process of concentrating thoughts and actions on those unique factors that enable the organization to gain and sustain competitive advantage in the markets it chooses to serve."[9]

J. M. Juran simplifies it as "the activity of developing the products and processes required to meet customer needs."[10] However, it is not the typical planning grind that most bankers put themselves through every year. It is not a three-day retreat where management goes off to study reams of data and tries to predict the future. Rather, it is *continuous* attention paid to the environment, the result of which is translated into ways to achieve advantage.

> Real strategists get their hands dirty digging for ideas, and real strategies are built from the occasional nuggets they uncover. These are not the people who abstract themselves from the daily details; they are the ones who immerse themselves in them while being able to abstract the strategic messages from them. The big picture is painted with little strokes.[11]

Strategic thinking about excellence is a new role for the leadership, which requires a different kind of understanding of the bank's position in its environment and how the activities that are undertaken every day impact it. It is a willingness to incorporate the short-term view with a concentration on creating value for the bank's stakeholders in the long term. It asks the question, "How can we serve our customers better every day?" It is comprehension of the Big Q of Juran which, as a refresher:

- Focuses on all products, good, and services, whether or not for sale to external customers.
- Addresses all processes within the organization: production, support, business.
- Views quality as a business problem, not a technical problem.
- Includes internal and external customers.
- Incorporates quality goals in the business plan.
- Defines the cost of quality as all expenses that would disappear if everything were perfect.

T A B L E   6–3

The Quality Council

Chief executive officer	Human resources
Administration	Finance
Loans	Marketing
Deposits	Operations
Trust	Quality
Fee-based services	Information systems

- Directs improvement at the entire organization, not just departments.
- Evaluates excellence on the basis of customer perception.
- Institutes bankwide education in managing and producing excellence.
- Establishes a quality council of senior leaders to coordinate the improvement effort.[12]

The companies that have chosen this direction, and most importantly their CEOs, understand that service excellence is everyone's responsibility. They encourage everyone to think about improvement every day, and they integrate their suggestions and recommendations wherever they are appropriate in support of the bank's vision. The strategic quality plan then becomes a vibrant, dynamic, long-term guide, which is changed as circumstances warrant, for the people of the bank. It is not simply a 200-page document in a loose-leaf notebook that is filled with numbers and ends up gathering dust on a bookshelf. It is used daily to help everyone to know that they are on the right path, and it is subject to constant challenge and revision.

The ultimate responsibility for the development and implementation of the bank's strategic quality plan rests with the senior leaders who represent all areas of the bank; typically, it is the management committee that can ensure that the plans and directions of each of the various value chains are consistent with, and support, one another. This group can be called the quality council, the service council, the excellence council, and so on. Whatever name you choose, this group must differentiate itself from any other existing committee and the name must indicate that significance. But watch out. If the senior leadership group is named the "quality council," its members have to demonstrate their commitment to the concept all the time. The rest of the bank is watching.

The quality council consists of the scouts and the strategists with a membership typical of that shown in Table 6–3. These are the people who should be spending the major part of their time thinking about the future of the bank and be constantly attentive to changes in the internal and external environment. As their people tell them of the hint of change that is occurring, with some fore-sight the quality council can anticipate the end result and can position the orga-nization to take advantage of it. You say, that's not been their job in the past when they were supposed to keep track of what happens on a daily basis. You're right. This is a new way of thinking. These are probably the people you had to force to look out at the onrushing stampede, but when empowered and dedicated to the bank's vision, they are the people who, with the help of their teams, can save the wagon train .

Their most important task? The people on the quality council must be the first ones to embrace the new expectation. Even before they work on the bank's vision, mission, values, philosophy, and critical success factors, the CEO has to involve them in setting the new direction. They must under-stand that:

- The ways in which they manage will have to change.
- They will have to act as coaches, helping their people succeed.
- The old hierarchy will give way to a new, flat one.
- It is the long term that counts.
- It is the customer who is important.
- Continuous improvement is the order of the day.

This cannot be overemphasized. For the change that is necessary to occur, this group of leaders has to be convinced that it is the only way out.

Once they have made the commitment, the thought process can start, but it too has a different focus. They must encourage the people of their value chains to think about better ways to serve their stakeholders. That means the bank's strategic quality plan is based on an external view of customers, technol-ogy, what the markets are doing, government involvement, current economic conditions, and the advances of the competition, as it should be. Why is that important? There are four reasons.

1. It demonstrates to the people of the bank that the leadership is willing to embrace change and continuous improvement proactively instead of as a reaction.

2. It creates goals and performance metrics that mean something because they are based on the expectations of customers, both inside and outside the bank.

3. It shows everyone in the bank that there are areas where improvement is necessary as exemplified by inroads of the competition.

4. It allows people within the same value chain to come together to work on satisfying their customers, based on data and measurement, rather than on hunches or the best guess.[13]

It is very different from the ways in which most organizations have thought about it. The typical planning effort is more concerned with financial goals, which are merely the measures of behavior that contribute to the internal focus, but do not consider the external changes that forge the future of the bank. This does not mean, however, that finance is not important, but it should not be the driving force behind the plan. Service excellence and quality start and end with the bank's markets, so that is where the planning effort must begin and end as well.

Every one of the bank's value chains has to have a plan. That means that planning teams have to be assembled for deposit products, credit products, trust services, and fee-based services, each of which follows the same discipline. Team members coordinate the development of the external view of their situation. Armed with what they have seen and given the bank's overall vision and values, they too can formulate strategy, communicating constantly with the quality council about their goals and direction. The council acts as a sounding board and ensures consistency of direction.

The planning process is continual and is neither top-down nor bottom-up. If we remember the "pizza" structure, it has to be participatory and spherical in nature, not hierarchal. People simply have to have the freedom and responsibility to communicate wherever required within the organization. Those representing the credit side should talk with those in deposits, fee-based, and trust about what their markets are doing, what customers think, and the like to leverage the bank's position. Strategic thinking, therefore, is never ending and comprehensive because it has to include all areas of the bank in support of its overall vision.

> Such strategies often cannot be developed on schedule and immaculately conceived. They must be free to appear at any time and at any place in the organization, typically through the messy process of informal learning [about the external and internal environment] that must necessarily be carried out by people at various levels who are deeply involved with the specific issues at hand.[14]

This is the essence of strategy. At the outset of this chapter, I mentioned *The Mind of the Strategist* by Kenichi Ohmae. In it, the author sets forth a great definition of strategy: "The object of strategy is to bring about the conditions most favorable to one's own side, judging precisely the right moment to attack or withdraw and always assessing the limits of compromise correctly."[15] The key words are "judging" and "assessing." They mean thought, which is what differentiates strategic thinking from strategic planning.

WATCH OUT, THOUGH . . .

For our purposes, strategic planning is only the structure that enables strategic thinking to take place. Most organizations get hung up on it, instead of concentrating on the thought process. There has to be some order as the strategies are defined, documented, implemented, and measured, but that should not be the focus. It's the thought process that counts. As it begins, however, be on the lookout for some danger signals. These were first identified by George Steiner, author of *Strategic Planning,* but discussed in some detail by Henry Mintzberg in *The Rise and Fall of Strategic Planning.*

The first of these traps is the assumption that the leadership can delegate the planning function to a planner or a planning department. Such action only adds to the bureaucracy. The process has to involve the leadership and all of the people in the bank's various value chains who might have some notion about what's going on "out there," whether they are in staff, line, or operational areas. A planning department institutionalizes the process and makes the result of the effort "theirs," not "ours." It's more form than substance. The outcome of processes like this usually is a notebook that is seldom read, not behavior.

Then there is the short-term view in which the senior people become so caught up in the day-to-day operation of the bank that they don't think about how to keep the stampede far away from the wagon train. This near-term outlook of fighting fires fosters a culture that mirrors it and leaves some people wondering about the prospects for the future as they realize no one is thinking about it. One of the greatest lessons I ever learned was from a colleague who told me always to hire people smarter than I was. That way, I could stay out of their way as they fulfilled their responsibilities and could concentrate on other matters, notably ways to improve the bank's performance a couple of years out.

Another of these problem areas concerns goal setting. If the goals of the bank are improved profitability from quarter-to-quarter, they don't lend themselves to strategic thinking. Those kinds of targets generate tactical actions designed to produce instantaneous results. That is why setting the vision is so important. It asks the leadership to be lofty and forces thinking about the future which is, it is hoped, concentrated on stakeholder enrichment.

There also is the question of why the plans that have consumed so much time and so many dollars are not used. They end up on the shelf and are hardly ever utilized when they should be the standard for measurement. If they are going to end up as a bookend, why go through the process at all? That is the reason for establishing plans and making sure that they are in sync with the vision and with the plans of the rest of the bank's leaders. Plans can and should be used to measure performance every month. It is a different way of managing, but that is the way to get people to make the required behavioral change.

The process of thinking about and planning for the future has to be a vital part of the bank's culture and it must contain the standards that guide daily activity.

Most institutions have formalized the planning process into a series of tasks and assignments that become items on a "to do" list, rather than something to be contemplated carefully. They limit creativity and innovation, are much too complicated, and ask for too many numbers. As such, they do a triple disservice. First, they are limited to the people who have the corner offices and typically do not include those closest to the action. That quite possibly can raise the issue of relevancy because the plans that are developed may not address current circumstances. Second, the "to do" list does not encourage strategic thinking about where the bank could be five years from now. By asking for so many details, it narrows the focus to the individual's particular responsibility, represented by the metrics and not by the behavior. And that causes the third problem. In the grand scheme of things, even putting out fires is a better way to spend the day than to developing pages and pages of facts and figures that nobody will ever seriously use. I would rather be solving problems and correcting failures than be gathering reams of data for no purpose. The first action at least is productive; the second isn't. That gives rise to the last danger signal: complete rejection of the plan.

This may have been implied before but it deserves specific mention. When management has criteria for making decisions, other than the plan, the document is of little value and invalidates the entire process. After all of the hoopla about the long-range plan that is supposed to guarantee success and prosperity, the book that contains it just ends up on your credenza where everyone can see it. They can also see the inconsistency between what it says and what they are being asked to do. If the bank is to be managed differently from what is described in the book, there is no need for a plan nor is there much evidence of thinking strategically about the five organizational imperatives:

- Customer focus
- Servant leadership
- Long-term view
- Horizontal organization
- *Kaizen*

TURNING THE STAMPEDE

Herds of buffalo, ocean liners, and bureaucratic organizations are a lot alike. Once they start moving in a given direction, they are hard to slow down. It is said that if you want to stop an oceangoing freighter, you must give the order to do so several hours in advance. Likewise, each of the three are hard to get started. It's the law of inertia. Typically, there needs to be a substantial and sudden change in the environment that prompts them to want to move.

> Buffalo are loyal to one leader; they stand around and wait for the leader to show them what to do. When the leader isn't around they wait for him to show up. That's why the early settlers could decimate the buffalo herds so easily by killing the lead buffalo. The rest of the herd stood around, waiting for their leader to lead them, and were slaughtered.[16]

They do exactly what the leader instructs, following obediently. Knowing that, it should be easy to turn the stampede. It is the same with the bank. It is the leader that has to start things moving in response to change, and it is the leader who influences the actions of everyone else.

As the scout was telling the strategists and other leaders about what he had seen, they could hear the rumble as the herd neared the wagon train. Most of them were in a quandary as to what to do. "Quite simple," one of the outriders suggested quietly. "All we have to do is make the leader turn away." What a novel idea, but with our hierarchical, divisionalized organization, we can all imagine what was said next.

> "Oh, that'll never work."
> "Who thought of that?"
> "Yeah? Who's going out there to turn them?"
> "We've never done that before."
> "Can we get some data to support that?"
> "What procedure number is that?"
> "Maybe they'll miss us."
> "The regulators won't let us."
> "Look, my guys have been over that a hundred times. . ."
> "Can we visit another wagon train to see how they did it?"
> "I'll have one of my guys call a friend who's been through it."

This committee certainly wasn't enlightened. The water in the pot was getting real warm as the herd thundered toward the wagons. They didn't have time to call anyone, to visit with those who had experienced the same problem, or to study it anymore. They had to act, but their paradigm wouldn't let them. Then, suddenly, two of the scouts, riding hard, charged toward the stampeding herd, shooting their guns in the air and hollering like crazy. A couple more followed and soon there were six of them, bearing down on the lead buffalo and forcing him to change direction. As the lead buffalo did, the rest of the herd went after him. A simple analogy, perhaps, but applicable.

As the horsemen ride slowly back toward the wagons, they decide that maybe such desperate action shouldn't have been necessary. They might not have enough time if it ever happens again. They will need to consider all the possibilities and alternatives that will ensure that their caravan reaches its destination safely. I am not sure how they will go about the business of preventing another stampede, but they are the experts on buffalo and other such matters. Working together and with the leadership, they'll think of something.

Thinking strategically within the planning process means being curious. It is an opportunity to ask some fairly profound questions. It starts with a goal. What does your bank want to be? How will you know when you have achieved it? How will you know how you are progressing? In other words, you need a quality target that is quantifiable with a deadline. "We will achieve 100 percent accuracy in statement rendering by year end." Simple, yes. Descriptive, yes. Measurable, you bet. When January rolls around, it will be easy to see whether or not the goal was achieved. "Start with a goal, assemble an organization, raise the money, tap the best technology the world has to offer, test and try out seemingly crazy ideas—all with a crystal clear focus."[17]

Goal setting starts at ground zero. As the leadership ponders the future, it must answer some questions. We looked at some in the last chapter as I wrote about vision, so the ones that follow are a little less grand in scope. We already know the business that we are in and who our customers are. Let's be more specific.

- How do our markets view our company?
- How do we want our markets to view our company?
- If there is a difference, what can we do to change the perception of our markets about us?
- Why do our customers buy from us and not the competition?
- Why do our competitors' customers buy from them and not from us?
- Is the service we offer notably better than our competitors' service? How do we know that?
- Are we giving our markets value, that is, high quality at a low cost?
- Are the bank's value chains functioning efficiently to keep cost in line?
- Is there anything that our markets and customers want that we could provide but are not?
- Do we know what the competition is doing?
- What do we think they will do if we do _____?
- Is what we do needed in other markets?
- Should we think about expanding into those markets?

- What will give us an advantage in those markets and in the ones we currently serve?
- Do we have the capabilities to maintain an advantage?
- Are we doing things that our customers and markets don't want?

The bank cannot afford to make strategic decisions based on assumptions and hunches. It has to have data on lots of data, but it can not result in analysis-paralysis because, like the soldiers guarding the wagon train, the bank does not have time. It is a process that is continually updated. How often you revisit it is up to you. We start with the quality council, but the methodology that follows also applies to the strategists of all of the bank's value chains.

The data that are to be developed are different than most planning people are used to seeing, and they come from a variety of sources. The quality council's first priority is for each member to complete the Strategic Thinking Grid shown in Table 6–4. At the inaugural meeting, pass out blank copies of the grid and have the members spend two or three days thinking seriously, and working with their teams, about the answers for each member's value chain. What each one comes up with will become subject for comparison and debate, so they should take the grid very seriously.

When the council reconvenes, have a facilitator draw a large Strategic Thinking Grid on the whiteboard or flip chart. As each member of the council supplies answers to the questions, record them in the appropriate place. Give smaller copies of the blank grid to the participants so that they can takes notes as the meeting progresses. Like the critical success factors, the grid will graphically point out places where there are inconsistencies among team members. Differences are OK as long as everyone agrees that they are, but for the most part the answers have to look pretty much the same.

In Table 6–4, the column headings stand for the bank's value chains:

- I/L—Installment lending
- M/L—Mortgage lending
- C/L—Commercial lending
- Invest—Investment products
- DDA—Demand deposit products
- Time—Time deposit products
- MMA—Money market accounts
- Trust—Trust products
- CM—Cash management products

These are a few examples of the areas that need to have input. If they don't fit your bank, substitute ones that do. It is the answers to the questions

TABLE 6-4

Strategic Thinking Grid

	I/L	M/L	C/L	Invest	DDA	Time	MMA	Trust	CM
What is our business?									
Who are our customers?									
Potential customers?									
Customer locations?									
Reach customers by?									
What do customers buy from us?									
Customers value?									
What do we want to be as an organization?									
What should we be?									
How markets see us?									
How do we want markets to see us?									
How to change customers' perceptions?									

T A B L E 6-4 *CONTINUED*

Strategic Thinking Grid

	I/L	M/L	C/L	Invest	DDA	Time	MMA	Trust	CM
Why do customers buy from us, not others?									
Why do customers buy from others, not us?									
Who serves better?									
Do we give value?									
Are we efficient?									
Other opportunities?									
Competitors' actions?									
Competitors' strategies?									
Other markets?									
Market expansion?									
What gives advantage?									
Can we maintain it?									
Doing wrong things?									

that hold the key, but make sure that you have all of the service lines filled. The questions may be changed to fit individual circumstances, but the ones on the grid provide a good basis from which to start. Each person completing it should make sure to document, where possible, how his or her conclusions were reached. With each answer, the question has to be, "On what basis did you decide that?"

> The strategy-making process should be: capturing what the manager learns from all sources [both the soft insights from his or her personal experiences and the experiences of others throughout the organization and hard data from market research and the like] and then synthesizing that learning into a vision that the business should pursue.[18]

BENCHMARKS: MOURNING OR LEARNING?

Now that the leadership is thinking about the bank strategically and has an understanding of where it thinks the bank is, the next step is to find out what its other stakeholders are thinking. In other words, after developing the initial bank benchmark that is in the Strategic Thinking Grid, we need to add more input, so that we can find the actual starting place for the improvement process. This benchmarking process is defined as "an external focus on internal activities, functions, or operations in order to achieve continuous improvement."[19] Quite simply, the bank has to take an objective look at itself first and cannot solely rely upon what management thinks.

In research that I have seen about organizations, customers typically have one view of service levels: The people who work within them have a slightly worse opinion, and management usually thinks that everything is just fine. Why wouldn't they? They are running the show, but because they are isolated by the pyramid, they may not know everything that is going on. Style and structure make it so. I am reminded of the CFO whose office was on the fifth floor of the building with the majority of the finance department on the third floor. The folks who worked two floors below the boss said that he had never been down to see them, even to visit briefly. They always had to go up to "five." I can only wonder what he did not know, and if memory serves, he was responsible for the strategic plan.

As the leadership begins this self-assessment process, two points need to be made. First, in the absence of facts, the organization can make serious mistakes if its decision making is based on things generally thought to be true. What happens if they aren't? The choices that are made will be the wrong ones and will hurt instead of help. Second, in the definition of the word *benchmark,* the word *external* is crucial. The leadership needs to examine the organization from the perspective of the people who know it best: customers and employees.

When additional data from the outside are brought to light, the Strategic Thinking Grid can be validated. It is a way to synthesize several different inputs to get an accurate picture of the bank.

Acting as servants, the leadership can learn a great deal about their organizations from their customers and their employees; hence, the reason for the continuing self-assessment. They had better be prepared to hear some things that they might not like, but they have to understand that criticism only represents areas where major stakeholders think that things can get better.

This initial benchmarking activity does not take very long, but it has to provide accurate information. It is best to have a totally independent party conduct it to avoid any bias in covering of bad news. The leadership simply has to have an objective view of the organization. They have to know things such as what happened the other day. I went up to my favorite ATM—the one that is never out of cash—and tried to deposit a check after keying in my PIN. The screen told me that the machine was not going to let me do that. Not allowing me to take money out is one thing, but not permitting me to make a deposit? It is a "user-unfriendly" delivery system like this that they need to know about.

By surveying a sample of the bank's customer base and the workforce with some open-ended questions about service levels, the leadership can quickly see how their organization, the one for which they are responsible, is perceived by these major stakeholders. Their perceptions of the bank are reality and cannot be dismissed lightly. They are, if you think about it, all that matters.

The quality assessment is an organizational self-diagnostic that has some very specific goals:

- To determine what is working well.
- To identify quality initiatives already in place.
- To solicit suggestions for improvement opportunities.
- To gauge the readiness of the culture to engage in an improvement initiative.
- To provide background by which to develop a customized process for the institution that wants to improve, taking all of these factors into account.

The questions for customers and staff invite dialogue, and although there should be sufficient standardization for analysis, the interviewer should provide room and time for follow-up questions. What we want to determine is:

- The extent of management commitment, as evidenced by perceptions about bank policies, procedures, structure, and style.
- Attitudes of customers and workforce about service excellence.
- The perceived strengths and weaknesses of, opportunities for, and threats to the bank.

The assessment is a high-level effort designed to start the bank in the direction of the root causes of service quality problems. This is a "drill-down" technique aimed at finding the most serious issues first, so that the bank can deal with them in the most productive manner and not waste time, energy, and dollars on matters that are not as important to customers. Appendix 6–1 at the end of this chapter provides a sample of the assessment report. It is general in nature, designed to give you an idea of the kinds of issues that it covers and some thoughts concerning the actions that should be taken. The assessment report can be as detailed as the leadership wants it to be, but the most important aspect of the assessment is to conduct it. It shows your customers and the workforce that you are serious about improvement and believe that they have valuable input into that process.

The point of the assessment is to develop a clear picture of where the bank stands in order to develop the steps that should be taken next, presuming that the bank wants to improve. Simultaneously, other data are being gathered about the external environment. This is the purview of the bank's scouts who are constantly looking out there within their areas of expertise. I don't know who the scouts are in your bank, but there is enough happening in banking these days that someone should be looking at them all the time. Periodically or when considered necessary, each of the scouts gets an opportunity to talk to the quality council about what they have seen concerning the following:

- Local and national economy
- Regulatory issues
- Local and national competition
- Demographic, sociological, and psychographic trends
- Market share gains and losses
- Technological position
- Technological opportunities
- Pricing and quality issues
- Market strengths and weaknesses

Even though all of these data result in identification of areas where the bank can improve, that isn't always the response from the leadership. Some will latch onto the scouts' reports right away and get to work. Others will choose to ignore the results, especially if they are unfavorable. Some choose to discredit them, especially if their own subunits have been singled out. Still others actually read them and find a convenient place for them on the shelf and continue business as usual. *Information from your customers and employees is the best you can get. They are telling you where you can get better.* If you don't choose to change to meet those expectations, you might not have either one very long. Most companies do not last if they lose their customers or their talented and experienced employees.

It is perfectly normal to be defensive about results that are not as good as we would want them. In *Benchmarking: A Tool for Continuous Improvement,* Kathleen Leibfried and C. J. McNair devote some time to the "five stages of mourning" that occur when the members of the council receive their first benchmarking report that specifies some areas that could use some help.[20]

Denial

Management has worked hard to improve things and to stay competitive for years. Profits are up, even though that was due to an aberration in the financial markets. Customers, however, are saying that the bank really has some problems. The delivery system is unfriendly and there are inconsistencies between the service the bank is providing and what the ads on the television are asking them to believe. The "back door" calculation suggests that they are talking with their feet, and the assessment confirms it. It's frustrating and depressing, but guys, you've fallen behind. To the leader responsible, it means failure—and there goes the bonus check and the vacation in Australia. How are you going to tell your spouse about that? Obviously, something is wrong with the data. It has to be. Denial happens first.

Anger

Pity the poor person who delivered the report. That's why it is best to have an independent party conduct the benchmarking. The leadership has denied the results and this develops into anger very quickly. This is natural. After all, your customers, employees, and the competition have indicated that the bank is not as good as you think it is. How could they possibly not see it as we do? Of course, you're going to be angry. Just think about all the time and effort that have apparently been wasted. Go ahead, get mad. It's OK, but direct the emotion at the right place. Don't shoot the messenger; take time to understand what the problem really is. The bank's not going out of business tomorrow, but get to work.

Bargaining

Be careful, though, don't try to bargain your way out. In this stage, management questions the method and takes its eye off what the data are saying. They are trying to find different outcomes or to determine that the published results are wrong. When they learn that the information is accurate, they try to rationalize it. "Oh, the Fed won't let us do what Merrill Lynch can do." "Well, we could have that kind of result if we could only. . ." How the bank treats this phase determines success or failure. If the leadership buys these rationalizations, they are accepting a tainted view of their world that will come back at some point to haunt them.

Depression

"Maybe we do have problems, but what can we do about them?" The CEO has made sure that there is no bargaining or rationalizing as the quality council meets again. It's a somber group that sits around the table. They have two choices. They can sink into a sense of self-defeat, giving up hope and believing that nothing can be done about it. That is probably easier than the alternative, but it signals even bigger problems for the bank. As soon as defeat is admitted, the prospect for the bank's survival is bleak. The other, harder, option is to face the problems, knowing that there is a lot of work ahead.

Acceptance

> The man who gives up accomplishes nothing and is only a hindrance. The man who does *not* give up can move mountains.
>
> *Ernest Hello*
> Life, Science, and Art[21]

"OK, the report is accurate. What are we going to do about it? We want to succeed and serve our customers and markets. What are they telling us that we have to do?" Even if it is bad news, for the bank to survive and prosper you must grab hold of the data and get creative. Learn from what the data are telling you. Learn what customers want from you. Learn what will motivate employees. Look at the competition and see what they are doing. Go back to the question: What is the competition doing that we're not?

With the answers to questions like these and with the information that the benchmark has provided, you will be able to see those areas where the organization can improve. Goals can be set. Resources can be allocated. People can be energized. And a spirit of achievement can start to take over. This is how the place gets revitalized. This is how the revolution spreads.

STARTING TO PERK

There is significant room for growth as you start to turn the bank around. The prevailing thinking is probably, "I don't have time for all this. I have too much to do." Let me counter this view. I really don't think you can afford to do anything else. If you want the bank to survive and prosper, there is no choice. In

Table 6–1, we saw the statistics from the American Management Association, which show that downsizing, restructuring, and cost cutting have not worked. The survey showed us that:

- 50 percent of the companies in the survey reported profits had remained the same or had declined.
- 86 percent of them indicated that the morale of the people suffered.

What the survey did not tell us was how much market share has been lost to companies like Procter & Gamble and Motorola, which emphasize continuous improvement. Nor did it indicate how hard it is to rekindle the spirit of the people and how costly that will be.

The improvement process requires change. We have seen that and we understand how hard that may be, given the inertia that plagues the cultures of most of America's banks. We also know that it is the leadership that is responsible for leading the change and improvement effort. Without the CEO and the rest of the senior management of the bank, the effort will not be successful no matter how hard you may try.

The change starts with them, period. Fundamentally, it means opening up communication lines with the people who know what is going on: the tellers and CSRs in the branch, the calling officers from the commercial department, the administrative assistants in trust. These folks are working with customers every day. They need the freedom to call the operations department about ways to improve processes.

The walls and barriers have to come down. People who are involved with the delivery of service to customers have to talk with one another. They need to plan. They need to say, "What if?" Above all, they need leaders who will support them and what they are trying to do. Making this personal transition to servant leadership is a grand journey that is a rewarding experience. So is having the people of the bank think strategically. So is looking at the bank through the eyes of your customers and the workforce. You may not like what they are saying, but it is what you have to hear. It is the only way to improve.

Kaizen, continual improvement of people and processes, starts with an understanding of strategic thinking and an ongoing assessment of the organization as it presently serves its stakeholders. It is a spirit, not a cookbook. I hope you have realized by now that I am not going to give you a rigid series of tasks and assignments that hold the promise of success. There are other books that prescribe it, "A," "B," and "C." My purpose is to help you think and to ask you to apply what you are learning to your organization and to your own style. There is no single "right way" as some would have us believe. Because you and your organization are different from any others, the process of growth and improvement has to be personalized.

As you go, it will take vision, direction, passion, empowerment, healing, and helping. Even if the scout doesn't ask, get up on your horse and take a ride with him. Take a good look at what's "out there." And then work closely with those who have the knowledge to plan and execute an appropriate strategy that works for you.

Ride toward the herd of buffalo together and turn it away. Once it has taken a different direction, you still must always be on the lookout for another stampede. You never know where it will come from.

Assessment Report

THE ABC NATIONAL BANK

Service Quality Assessment Results

METHODOLOGY

We interviewed 10 percent of the bank's employees and a representative sample of customers using the questionnaire previously designed and approved by the quality council. The answers to the questions have been classified and summarized into six categories:

1. Knowledge of Organizational Role and Fit
2. Customer Knowledge
3. Strengths
4. Weaknesses
5. Quality
6. Improvement Opportunities

They address the objectives established for the study:

- The extent of management commitment and employee attitudes toward quality.
- To assess organizational strengths and weaknesses.
- To solicit improvement ideas.
- To determine the progress of various improvement initiatives.
- To design, if appropriate, an "umbrella" quality improvement process for the bank.

KNOWLEDGE OF ORGANIZATIONAL ROLE AND FIT

There is a fairly good knowledge of who customers are, but there is less immediate understanding of the concept of "internal customers," especially in the areas of mortgage lending and cash management services. A better understanding of the origination of work and its ultimate destination is needed.

Likewise, there is a fairly good understanding of the bank's mission, but less recognition of the meaning of the corporate vision. There are also inconsistencies between the missions of areas within the same value chains, notably in commercial lending, and how they relate and support the bank.

Overall, there is an organizational "murkiness," which indicates a need for clarification of mission, fit, and work flow.

CUSTOMER KNOWLEDGE

Most of those persons interviewed think that they know the expectations of their customers but cannot provide data to support that contention. Feedback mechanisms are informal, the branches being the exception. Due to the ad hoc nature of obtaining feedback, it tends to be more negative than positive.

Customers are relatively satisfied, but there are opportunities to expand the service offering because most only utilize one or two services.

Customer service is a source of both pride and frustration. To improve it, three needs are identified: active solicitation of service requirements, resource analysis, and a service quality policy.

STRENGTHS

Basically, the people like their work and the people with whom they work. Customer service is clearly its strength, followed by their individual skills, teamwork, personal satisfaction, and technological curiosity. These are solid blocks upon which to build for the future.

WEAKNESSES

Lack of resources—time, staffing, information systems—is cited most frequently, 45 percent of the time, as the biggest weakness. Internal weaknesses include communication, leadership, and skill levels of other employees, especially in operations. Seventeen percent of the answers address cultural weaknesses such as focus and boundaries. Four factors were cited both as strengths and weaknesses, leading to the conclusion of "organizational murkiness." There also appear to be questions of prioritization, definition, and empowerment.

QUALITY

There is good knowledge of the programs that are under way although there is general confusion about how they fit together. There is no overall understanding of the cost of quality or the "back door," which suggests a lack of comprehension of how it all fits together. There is also concern that quality is the latest fad of the month.

IMPROVEMENT OPPORTUNITIES

The answers are consistent: more resources—time, space, people, training—and better communication. The issue of boundaries surfaces many times in different guises; it is often stated explicitly but also mentioned in related concerns about communication, worker/officer gaps, politics, and cross-training. There is also some dissatisfaction with management: too many managers with insufficient knowledge and nonexistent strategic focus.

A complete list is included in the appendix.

RECOMMENDATIONS

The bank should conduct surveys of both customers and employees to determine the undermining cultural issues, service expectations and perceptions, and resource utilization. Planning and a formal educational program for all employees is also suggested.

ENDNOTES

1. Joel Arthur Barker, *Paradigms: The Business of Discovering the Future* (New York: HarperBusiness, 1992), p. 147.
2. Quoted in Kathleen H. J. Leibfried and C. J. McNair, *Benchmarking: A Tool for Continuous Improvement* (New York: HarperBusiness, 1992), p. 204.
3. Leonard L. Berry et al., *Service Quality* (Homewood, IL: Dow Jones-Irwin, 1989), p. 144.
4. James L. Heskett et al., *Service Breakthroughs* (New York: Free Press, 1990), p. 11.
5. Robert H. Waterman, Jr., *What America Does Right* (New York: Penguin Books USA, 1994), p. 17.
6. Emmett C. Murphy, *The Genius of Sitting Bull* (Englewood Cliffs, NJ: Prentice Hall, 1993), p. xxvii.
7. Henry Mintzberg, "The Rise and Fall of Strategic Planning," *Harvard Business Review,* Jan.–Feb. 1994, p. 107.
8. Charles S. Grunder and Brandon H. Beck, *The Second Battle of Winchester* (Lynchburg, VA: H. E. Howard, 1989), p. 63.
9. Stephen C. Tweed, *Strategic Focus* (Hollywood, FL: Fell Publishers, 1990), p. 2.
10. J. M. Juran, *Juran on Quality by Design* (New York: Free Press, 1992), p. 14.
11. Mintzberg, "The Rise and Fall," p. 111.
12. Juran, *Juran on Quality by Design,* p. 12.
13. Leibfried and McNair, *Benchmarking,* p. 28.
14. Mintzberg, "The Rise and Fall," p. 108.
15. Kenichi Ohmae, *The Mind of the Strategist: The Art of Japanese Business* (New York: McGraw-Hill, 1982), p. 13.
16. James A. Belasco and Ralph C. Stayer, *Flight of the Buffalo* (New York: Warner Books, 1993), p. 17.
17. Tweed, *Strategic Focus,* p. 15.
18. Mintzberg, "The Rise and Fall," p. 107.
19. Leibfried and McNair, *Benchmarking,* p. 1.
20. Ibid., pp. 204–209.
21. Ibid., pp. 208–209.

CHAPTER 7

The Challenge of Customers

The world is a faster place than it was 10 years ago, even 5 years ago, which has created a new and increased expectation in the minds of most American consumers. The reasons: technology and new forms of competition, which have shaken the way we live.

Many of us can flip on the tube and use the remote to surf the 200 channels that our mini-satellite dish provides. That development will certainly pose a threat to the cable TV industry, which is a relatively new one itself. We can also shop at well-known national stores with our computers, which is becoming a real hazard to the recently successful Home Shopping Network. Whether we like it or not, things don't take as long anymore in our search for value. Photos developed in one hour; laundry into Ajax Cleaners by nine o'clock, out by noon. Red Baron pizzas are ready in minutes after being nuked in the microwave. The technologies and companies that have given us these advancements have raised the bar for all service providers. We consumers of the waning days of the 20th century simply have higher expectations of the organizations from which we buy. The speed and accuracy at McDonald's has created an expectancy of speed and accuracy at the drugstore, the bookstore, the brokerage, and the bank.

As a good customer of a commercial bank, I have come to expect fast, unerring treatment at the branch and the ATM or with my PC. I want my telephone calls returned promptly (they are not) and my statement to reflect all of my transactions accurately (they do). I don't want to visit with a teller anymore, nor do I want to spend a lot of time with a loan officer. Banking should be easy for me to accomplish, but many times it isn't. Has my bank asked me what I want? No! Has my banker heard about what I would like? Yes. Can he or she do anything substantive about it? No, not really.

Let's return for a moment to my favorite ATM, which is never out of cash. At 2:00 P.M. yesterday, as I was on my way to the airport, I drove to the bank and, to my surprise, no one was parked in front of the machine. I breezed in, took out my card, put it in the machine, and got the following message:

> SORRY FOR THE INCONVENIENCE. THIS MACHINE IS TEMPORARILY OUT OF ORDER. IT IS
> BEING SERVICED. PLEASE FIND ANOTHER ABC BANK MACHINE. THANK YOU FOR STOP-
> PING. HAVE A NICE DAY!

Have a nice day? I was having one until now. Here it was, the middle of the afternoon, I have an airplane to catch, and the machine's out of money. Now, my decision was either to go to the airport directly or try to find another machine that would give me the cash I needed for the trip. I should have realized that the ATM was down. While the parking spaces in front of it were empty, four cars were in each of the two drive-up lanes, which was unusual for that time of day. Those customers had discovered that the ATM was down and had decided to wait it out.

I will grant you that severing my relationship with my bank would be a hassle, but I am thinking about it. It won't let me put my money in; it won't let me try to take it out. There seems to be little concern for the customer at ABC, but there is on the part of the competition.

That's what the disintermediation is all about. That's the stampede that you just avoided. It's also the next one for which to keep your eyes peeled. As I have reminded you before, you have to constantly look "out there" at what's happening in the external environment. At the same time, you have to examine what's going on inside the bank. Every member of the workforce should be looking at the "customer-unfriendly" practices that occur and question them. As they say at MBNA America, "Think of yourself as a customer." Then look at what is going on in the bank. I know that the ATMs have to come down to be balanced, but why at 2:30 in the afternoon? Keep asking the question, "Why?"

"TREAT 'EM LIKE GOLD!"

Remember the teaching of Peter Drucker: Customers are the reason for the bank to exist and to be in business. As such, they should be treated like gold. The people of the bank ought to be thankful that customers have chosen to drive into the parking lot, walk in the front door, or call on the phone. They should do everything possible to give them value, providing exactly what they want, and not do things such as denying them access to their own accounts while wishing them a nice day. Customers have a wide choice of firms that provide financial services, and those alternatives are increasing. Therefore, the bank leadership must understand why the people of its markets have chosen the institutions that they have. What makes one bank in your market more attractive than another?

That is the next question to be answered. In addition to the information gathered in the assessment, the bank should devote time and effort to the identification of the companies, banks or otherwise, that are marketing the same or similar services to its customers. In a brutally honest self-assessment, ask: "What are the features, functions, and benefits that the competition is offering?" And then, "How do they differ from what we are doing?" Finally, "Which one appears to be more accepted in the market?"

Make a grid—patterned after the Strategic Thinking Grid—by value chain, and chart exactly who your competitors are, what they are doing, and how well they are being received. This exercise will take considerable creativity because you have to consider all competitors, even if they have absolutely no resemblance to the bank. They include stores like OfficeMax, which offer their own credit cards; Safeway Supermarkets where you can get cash; and the new trust company that just opened. Brainstorm every possible organization that is or could be providing what you are and understand the various differences that appear. There will be local and regional differences, and those with a national presence; regardless of where they are, it is important to determine who they are and what they do, so that the bank can determine its competitive strategy.

After the list is compiled and you know who the competition is and exactly what it is offering, ask the hard question: "Why do some consumers of banking services go with the competition and not with us?" In the Strategic Thinking Grid, you were asked to put down your opinion about why they behave that way. Now it is time to find out. Again, being creative, identify the customers of other service providers and find out why they bank at Mercantile, Barnett, or UJB. Or why they use Merrill Lynch's CMA, GM's credit card, or General Electric Credit Corporation? Maybe it is Huntington's idea of "virtual banking" or the ability to use the World Wide Web.

It is important for you to know what the competition is doing for three reasons. First, there can be a marketing advantage in the pursuit of new customers. With this information, it is entirely possible that you will be able to replicate or improve on a service offered by a competitor that is well-received in markets where you have not been very successful. Second, you will be able to protect your existing clients from the onslaught of the competition because you have everything they do, and more.

Understanding the competition also enables the leadership to make a choice: whether or not it has the capability and the desire to compete with other service providers in its markets. It's niche strategy. The time when the bank could be all things to all people is long gone. Understand who the competition is and why it is successful in terms of the strengths of your institution. Given that, identifying a strategy is made simpler. Then, regardless of the chosen strategy, it is imperative that the people in each of the bank's value chains devote themselves to being the very best they can in the service of the bank's customers.

That's your advantage and it can't be shared. That is what the revolution is all about. Bankers can no longer sit in their offices and think that just because they have been around for 100 years that customers will continue to walk in the front door. It doesn't happen that way.

> According to the American Marketing Federation 1992 study, 47 percent of consumers surveyed believe that all banks are the same. They are sufficiently dissatisfied that over 25 percent change banks during an average year, according to a Retail Advertising Bureau 1991 Study. They expect banks to deliver service, products, and convenience . . . They want additional benefits.[1]

The problem is the advance of the innovative competition while the banks have, for the most part, kept on doing the same old things, not differentiating themselves at all. The issue becomes one of finding a niche. What services do your customers want from you? What business do they want you to be in? How do you provide value and thus demonstrate your uniqueness to them?

Consumers of financial services are looking for value, like they do in all of their purchases. Most of them do not care where they find it. It is a buyer's market now, which necessitates an understanding of what your own customers expect, what your competitors' customers consider to be of value, the way your bank is providing service, the services that your competition is delivering, and a choice of whether you want to challenge them or not.

Gary Hamel and C. K. Prahalad, captured the essence of this thinking in a recent article in the *Harvard Business Review.* They ask you to think about and to answer the following questions.[2]

Today	Tomorrow
Which customers do you serve today?	Which customers will you serve in the future?
Through what channels do you reach customers today?	Through which channels will you reach customers tomorrow?
Who are your competitors today?	Who will be your competitors in the future?
What is the basis for your competitive advantage today?	What will be the basis for your competitive advantage tomorrow?
Where do your margins come from today?	Where will your margins come from in the future?
What skills or capabilities make you unique today?	What skills or capabilities will make you unique in the future?

TIME TO DECIDE

The last question is the most puzzling and should be considered carefully. However, I doubt that many bankers have slowed down for long enough to give it any thought. The task? To honestly determine the bank's primary concentration of expertise and competence. What does your bank do best? The information gathered in the assessment and the research about customers and competition is critical for determining future strategies, but there must be an understanding of what your bank does well for you to take advantage of it. A strategy based on a perception of strengths and competencies that is not real will lead to some serious problems. Therefore, we must consider the bank's real expertise as the revolution gains in strength and momentum.

A colleague of mine, Tanja Lian, editor of *Bank Marketing,* had an article published which was titled "The Threat of the Piper: Losing Customers to High-Tech Competitors." In it, she introduced some concepts that are most relevant to banking today that were fully explored in Michael Treacy and Fred Wiersema's best-selling book, *The Discipline of Market Leaders,* which it provides guidelines to help you understand what you do best. Consider what they may mean for your bank.

> Customers today want more of those things they value. If they value low cost, they want it lower. If they value convenience or speed when they buy, they want it easier and faster. If they look for state-of-the-art design, they want to see the art pushed forward. If they need expert advice, they want companies to give them more depth, more time, and more of a feeling that they are the only customer.
>
> Whatever customers want today, they want more of it. That's precisely why companies like Kellogg, Kmart, Hilton, Aetna, American, United, Delta, Rolex, General Foods, Lotus, General Motors, and IBM are on a slippery slope. One or more companies in their markets have increased the value offered to customers by improving products, cutting prices, or enhancing service. By raising the level of value that customers expect from everyone, leading companies are driving the market, and driving competitors downhill. Companies that can't hold their own will slip off a cliff.[3]

With that background, here's the issue. Treacy and Wiersema suggest that there are only three ways to differentiate an organization:

- Operational excellence
- Product leadership
- Customer intimacy

These are the core competencies that attract customers because they satisfy a basic need. By definition, no company can emphasize and feature all three equally because they are incompatible with one another. The company has to decide which one of the three it should work through to provide excellence, and thus gain the advantage, but it cannot completely forget the other two. To demonstrate the concept, let's think about some companies outside of banking.

Operational Excellence

Operational excellence means being able to process thousands of customer transactions accurately and promptly every day. It means handling a huge volume with few or no defects with the lowest unit cost as the objective. Companies known for operational excellence "make it up on volume and quality." Their margins are narrow by design, and their systems and processes do not allow errors and mistakes to happen. They have broken down tasks into their simplest form, trained people to accomplish them, flattened the organizational pyramid by emphasizing teamwork, and have come to expect the team to function according to procedure on every transaction.

McDonald's is a prototype of companies that feature "operational excellence." The fast-food franchise charges $2.39 for a Quarter Pounder with cheese and a large Diet Coke, whether it's at the corner of Sepulveda and Manhattan Beach Boulevard on the way to downtown Los Angeles or off I-90 at Ohio Route 534 near Ashtabula. It is the same in every McDonald's as customers seldom wait long for service while knowing exactly what they will get when they pull into the parking lot. That's operational excellence. The same product, the same service, no errors, at a high rate of speed. The people it hires are ready for the regimen day after day. Duties are simple: take the order, fill the bag, make change, and "Come back again, soon!"

Labor costs are minimized, but employees know that up front. They also know that McDonald's has opportunities for significant advancement because people get promoted from within. There is a great sense of teamwork because employees know they are dependent upon one another. It would be tough to fill the bag if the guys in the back weren't flipping burgers, making fries, and ensuring that there were enough cups in the dispensers. It's not lavish, but that's the way customers and the employees like it.

In what is an industry generalization, the data supports the contention that banks are not operationally excellent. As we saw earlier, 30 percent of what banks do is related to doing things wrong or to things that customers do not value. That suggests that operational excellence may be more of a goal than a reality in the banking industry. The error rate at McDonald's would be nowhere near 30 percent. An operationally excellent company does not incur the additional cost of correction, which means that it can keep prices low. High error rates in the banks keep costs high, which is the fundamental cause, we are told, for the fees that bank customers are forced to pay.

The legacy of the 1950s has led bank customers to expect some kind of personal service. To continue it, we are told in the advertising that the banks want to have a relationship with us. If operational excellence is the goal, that's not really possible. At places like McDonald's, there just isn't time for extra service. Move the customer through the restaurant as fast as possible. That doesn't happen at the bank. Most customers of U.S. banks would not tell you that speed is an attribute of their institution. It takes a long time to have a loan approved, to obtain checks, or to get through the drive-up station. Cost cutting has seen to that, so there aren't enough people around to take care of customer needs. If relationships are the goal, people have to be around to take care of even the most complicated customer request.

Furthermore, it would be inconceivable for McDonald's to be "down" at 2:00 P.M. like my ATM. Operational excellence is devoted to accuracy and speed, to serving as many customers as possible, and to meeting their expectations at a low cost. Some customers want that from the bank, so here is a niche for the one that can develop processes and technologies to guarantee it. To do so, however, it will have to abandon the idea of relationship banking and have to reduce the error rate to zero.

Product Leadership

The second possible attribute is product leadership. It is typified by those innovative companies that keep stretching the limits of the products and services they provide. These are high-tech organizations like Microsoft and Canon which know that the products they are putting in the marketplace will be obsolete in a very short time. While Windows 95 was introduced in the summer of 1995, it is a pretty sure bet that the software engineers at Microsoft are already working on something to replace it. They acknowledge it outwardly; that is their public strategy.

Companies such as 3M allocate a certain portion of their budgets to unspecified innovations that result in products like Post-it Notes. They also want their existing products to be cannibalized as happened with the handheld camcorder that replaced the cumbersome 20-pound machine that we used to lug around. These companies are fast to bring products to market because they see a need and exploit it right away, even if the buying public isn't quite sure that the need is actually there.

Speed of development necessitates an organization that has a very relaxed structure and style. People from all areas have access to one another in the development of new products aimed at further increasing market share.

These organizations also have flattened their structures, and titles don't matter. Innovation and getting the product to the market, even with a bug or two, is the goal.

These companies also allow mistakes to happen as teams of people experiment and try different approaches. With a culture like that, they learn from their errors and mistakes—even though they have to pay for the cost of correction—but they consider that expense as an investment in the pursuit of future market share. Operational excellence? No, not really. These companies whet the appetite of the consumer with new capabilities, even if they don't always work right. But once they get the problems ironed out, they've got you in a relationship.

> Frustrated customers found little help from computer manufacturers whose help lines referred Windows 95 questions to Microsoft unless the software had come preinstalled on the PC. Microsoft, in turn, appeared to be understaffed despite months of elaborate launch plans. The software giant added capacity to handle 20,000 Windows 95 calls a day, nearly doubling its usual load. But, with more than 300,000 copies sold in the U.S. the first day, capacity was overwhelmed.[4]

Microsoft will get it right. Users will be happy, eventually, and they will have greater PC literacy than ever before.

The attributes of product leaders do not seem to characterize most banks. Financial institutions are followers instead of product innovators. We may hear about financial services that are new and different from time to time, but it's hard to get very creative with a checking account or with an installment loan. Organizationally, the bank's style and structure prevent close cooperation between people in the same value chains on product development and service delivery. As we have seen, there are too many "silos" and blocks as we saw in the story about the founder of the bank. That is why the "pizza" structure, the horizontal design, is so necessary.

That's also why the prevailing management style has to change. Command-and-control prohibits freedom of expression, thus stifling innovation and creativity. It also reinforces the concentration on the numbers and an internal focus when the bank has to be centered on its customers.

Let's drive back through McDonald's for a cup of coffee. There's not a great deal of creativity present as the Big Mac has been made the same way for years. It is the same thing with the fries and the shakes. Most important, it is the same thing with the service that the counter personnel deliver. Any innovation that has occurred was aimed at driving unit cost down. This is an operationally excellent company, but it has not ignored suggestions by which to simplify and quicken the tasks of the staff. That is why they use a cash register with the buttons that have the names of the various food items on them. It is faster and more efficient to let the computer calculate the price of the meal that's ordered than to have the person behind the counter do it. If the objective is to move customers through the store, McDonald's wants that smiling person behind the counter to be fast and accurate, not to spend time in the unproductive task of totaling the bill and computing the right amount of change.

With this operational culture of wanting to drive unit cost down as low as possible, McDonald's created the drive-through window as another way to serve more Happy Meals. We also can have breakfast there, which makes use of the equipment for a few more hours besides lunch and dinner. There are probably other, subtler, innovations that you and I never see, but all of them are done to enhance the speed of the delivery of value to the customer. McDonald's puts operational excellence first, but it maintains a place for creativity and innovation without featuring it like Microsoft does. It does not change the basic product very often. There is no Big Mac 95. Rather, McDonald's changes the way it is delivered, looking for every possible efficiency. Microsoft, on the other hand, would have a Big Mac 97 in production and a Big Mac 2000 in design.

Customer Intimacy

The third potential competency is customer intimacy, or establishing solid client relationships. All over the country, I hear bankers talking about wanting to have relationships with their customers. That is a challenging assignment because cost cutting has reduced the banks' ability to provide service. In addition, banks get a bad press when newspapers carry stories that contain statements like this: "A bank is a place where they can charge you a fee to stand in line so you can give them your money, and then they charge you another fee when you want to take it out. Talk about a license to steal . . ."[5] The banks want relationships, but their behavior prevents it. We need a lesson from Gerry Koprowski.

Gerry runs a small catering company. She can make any party a hit for her clients simply by choosing the right combination of appetizers, entrees, breads, vegetables, and desserts. She brings the napkins and will, if need be, provide the flatware and the dishes to complement the meal that she has planned. Her people bring it all in and arrange the tables; when the party is over, they clean it up. She sends a bill and her clients pay it gladly, for she has given them value. It's a no-brainer. Whenever the word "party" is mentioned, they call Gerry. They know that she will take care of their needs with excellence, and they don't have to worry about it.

What differentiates customer intimacy? Companies that specialize in it solve specific problems and take time to gain your trust. It is not a one-shot deal that counts with them, but the value of a long-term relationship. They realize the value of customer retention and, because they give you personal service, you will pay a little more. These companies are good and reliable and that means value.

Bankers say that they want relationships, but they do things that sabotage them. They change loan officers and branch managers at will. With the advent of Merger Mania II, it is likely that additional personnel changes are on the horizon. Not really knowing our banker causes some anxiety because it is hard to trust someone that you haven't worked with before. Relationships are built on the confidence that we have in others. If we don't know our bankers and they don't know us, what will be the cooperation level when we need something, or even worse, when something happens to go wrong?

In relationship banking, it is the need of the customer that comes first. It is charging a fair price for the service rendered; providing extra and excellent service in the branch, in loan operations, and in the bookkeeping department; and taking the time to understand the customer's business. Relationships are built on individuals working with each other, and that means doing whatever it takes to handle even the most complex transactions.

Here's a personal story about customer intimacy:

> Some good friends of mine were building a house in southeastern Florida. There is no doubt that they could afford it, and negotiations were begun with one of the area's largest banks. As time rolled on, there were papers to sign and construction plans to look at, but there was no decision from the bank about the financing. Finally, the loan was due to close on this particular Friday afternoon when someone from the bank called and said that they needed one last piece of paper to be signed. My friends were asked to come over to the bank on Monday to sign it.
>
> Because the bank had said that everything would be done by that Friday, construction was set to start on Monday. That's what the bank had promised, so that's what they told the builder. There was an earthmover already sitting on the vacant lot.
>
> My friends, needless to say, were undone that the process was to be delayed even longer. At dinner that night, they chanced to see a longtime friend who ran a community bank in a nearby town. Talk turned to the ill-fated closing.
>
> "Bob," the banker said, "I'll guarantee the loan right now. It's done. I'll come over to your place in the morning, and we can take care of the details."

That's relationship banking. Product innovation occurs only when customers demand it. Operational excellence comes in third. Doing whatever it takes to make customers happy is the goal. When there is a financial question in their minds, there should be no question about whom they call.

One more trip to McDonald's. I recognize the faces of the counter personnel, but I don't know their names. They all wear the same uniform, say the same words, and execute the same procedures. Perhaps I don't have a relationship with a particular individual, but it could be said that I have developed one with McDonald's as a whole, even though it is not the company's primary emphasis. If I want this kind of relationship, I will go to Friendly's and Appleby's, as will most people, but McDonald's knows and understands that. From Microsoft, I have the software and a phone number. It's a relationship, but not like the ones that Gerry Koprowski has with her clients. These companies know their competencies and they are excellent in delivering on them.

Here's the dilemma: Most banks do not appear to fit very well in any one of these "value disciplines," while the competition does. Just look at Charles Schwab and the way it processes customer transactions fast and well. Merrill Lynch and some of the others are innovative, but they may be surprised by other financial service providers who are even more creative. Some of the brokerages, mutual funds, and trust companies are establishing solid, long-term relationships. The banks have to decide which one of the three core competencies they want to emphasize. They have to realize they cannot be all three. *The Banking Revolution* is about changing the way bankers think and act. Check out the environment. Who's doing what in the service of your markets' customers? Determine just what is your "value discipline." Is there a gap between what your customers want your bank to be and your ability to serve them better than anyone else? That's the kind of thinking that we need because the bar has been raised again, this time by a company that most would not have suspected.

UP IT GOES!

The headline in *The Wall Street Journal* read, "Intuit to Unveil On-Line Pact with 20 Firms."

> Intuit Corp. plans to announce today that it has signed up 20 companies, including such large firms as Chase Manhattan Corp., American Express Co., and Smith Barney, Inc., to use its software products for on-line banking services . . . Such services allow users to check their bank deposits and credit card balances by computer, transfer funds and pay bills electronically, and manage their personal finances . . . So far, many consumers have been reluctant to use home banking services, in part because of the unfamiliarity of such products. But as more banks announce partnerships with software companies and the software itself becomes easier to use, banks hope that consumer usage will increase. Banks see home banking as a way not only to cut costs but to increase their customer base nationwide.[6]

T A B L E   7–1

Banking on Quicken

Credit Card Company	Brokerage Firm	Banks
American Express	Smith Barney	Chemical
		Chase Manhattan
		First Chicago NBD
		Wells Fargo
		Bank of Boston
		First Interstate
		Corestates

Source: *The Wall Street Journal.*

It was Friday, July 14, 1995. The story ran alongside another one that predicted "In Latest Round of Banking Mergers, Even Big Institutions Become Targets." The two most profound issues in banking today were the subjects of articles on the same day and on the same page. What they told us will shake banking again. Big time.

For consumers of banking services, it means significant and fundamental change as we are witnessing another paradigm shift. The Intuit article included the chart shown in Table 7–1. At least 3 of the 10 biggest banks in the United States were among those to ally with Intuit, ready to offer remote banking to customers across the country beginning in the fourth quarter of 1995. Now, that is some great and needed innovation. Looks like some definite product leadership, but what does it mean for the consumer of banking services?

If done right, a whole new world has opened up to them. The key word in the article was "nationwide," so whether your bank is in Horseheads, New York; Berlin, Wisconsin; Clarksburg, West Virginia; or Yakima, Washington, it has a lot of new competition.

> Bank of America's reason for entering the on-line arena is summed up in one key word, according to Harvey Raydin, vice president of corporate communications. That word is "choice." "What we're really looking at here is product delivery," he says. "We made the decision [to get on the Internet] based on what customers have told us, so that they can bank with us at their convenience.[7]

Imagine, First National from Across-the-Street, a $100 million bank, having to go head-to-head with B of A. That's the new reality. Anyone with a computer, anywhere in the country, will be able to sign up with one of these providers.

Intuit and the Internet have really opened the back door at what appears to be an opportune time. Computer literacy is at its highest level ever and will continue to grow.

Not only are the customers of today fairly adept at using their PCs, but think about tomorrow. The future customers of the banks are not the retirees who continue to come into the branch or those of us in middle age who might experiment a little with computer banking. The clients of tomorrow are the kids, the young people who are very skilled at using their computers like my 19-year-old son, Doug, who has had a PC in the house since he can remember. These will be the consumers of financial services in the future.

Most bankers haven't thought about that as the results of a survey of bank executives conducted by Towers Perrin demonstrated. The respondents recounted that competition is fierce, especially on the liability side, but, sadly, they missed the key finding in the research. They did not see how their markets are changing. It was very apparent to John W. Milligan, editor-in-chief of *USBanker* who wrote:

> To me, the survey's most troubling finding was the industry's tenuous grip on future customers. The respondents felt that they were well-positioned with the so-called comfortably retired, one of the wealthiest segments. But in lower age categories—pre-retiree, serious career/serious parenting, early nesters, and finally to young spenders—the executives judge themselves to be progressively less entrenched. The comfortably retired still use bank branches. Many young Americans don't use banks, *period.* It's crucial that the industry begin converting them into customers . . . Gaining investment banking powers won't matter much if banks don't start winning over the younger crowd. The industry may not be dying, but its prospect for enriching the future is not a sure thing.[8]

Even now, the new generation sees no need to go to the bank, and it will continue to get more sophisticated. Institutions that allied themselves with Intuit, Meca Software, Microsoft, and other software firms looked "out there," saw the stampede, and sped out to turn it away. Those who have not might find themselves listening to a rumble, not terribly far from the wagon train, and wondering what it is.

Here's some statistical evidence. By 1997, an estimated 26 percent of U.S. households will be using remote banking services. That number is expected to grow by half again, to 40 percent, by 1999.[9] Who knows where it will go after that. Furthermore, customers are expected to avail themselves of the benefits of electronics in other ways:

> Ernst & Young, a leading financial analyst in the U.S., has carried out a survey of technology in banking. It projects that bank transactions at traditional

Total Number of ATMs

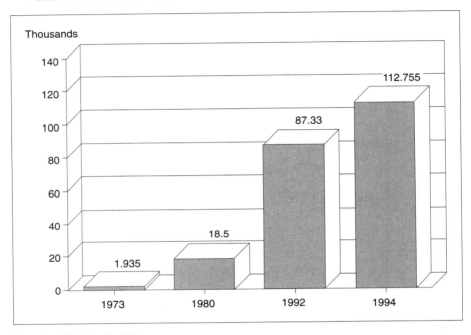

Source: *Bank Marketing*, May 1995.

"brick-and-mortar" branches will drop from 61% to 44% by 1997, replaced by non-branch transactions conducted over a digital media network. The number of ATMs is expected to more than double by 1997, with more than 40% in non-branch transactions. Personal computer and smart-phone use for banking will increase six-fold within the same time span.[10]

Whew! Talk about fundamental change in customer behavior. Exhibit 7–1 shows how that's happening. In 1973, there were 1,935 ATMs in the United States; in 1994, there were 112,755.[11] Yet, many bankers out there see no reason to change as they cling to their branch networks.

This kind of data is important as you think strategically about your bank and where it will be five years from now. Who will your customers be then? How will they be different from those you now have? How will they want you to deliver your service to them? What does that mean for your branch system? Think long and hard about the behavior of your customers and what it represents. Then think about the future and the possibilities that it brings. To do that, you have to start with a complete understanding of who your customers are today, what they want from you, and how you can get it to them better than any other financial organization. Based on that, you have to look into the tea leaves and figure out what it is going to be like 10 to 20 years from now. Intuit and its clients just fired a shot to get the herd moving toward your wagons. If there weren't reason for a revolution before, there certainly is now.

INTERNALLY, TOO!

I was teaching a workshop for a group of bankers a few years ago. The subject was the "back door." We spoke about customers and meeting their expectations, which I said is what the bank needs inside as well. I then posed the following question; it wasn't profound, but I was curious.

> "Everybody knows the difference between internal and external customers, right?"
>
> "Oh, sure," came a response, "the external customer uses the ATM and the drive-up while the internal customer comes into the branch or the main office."

Hmm . . .

For the bank to function efficiently, all of the people in its various value chains must know what is expected of them by the people they serve. In bureaucracies such as banks, that is an exception because the people practice "throw it over the wall." Because of the prevailing style and structure, the "I'm too busy" syndrome is present. When we finish a task, we send the results to the next person in the chain who has to do something else to it, effectively throwing the work over the wall to some place where it will never be seen again. The problem is that we usually don't know whether it is what the person on the other side needs or wants; we have been too busy to find out. We keep on producing, never communicating about the service or the product, except to say, "Whoomp, here it is."

> Another friend was promoted to CFO of a large financial institution. One of his responsibilities was internal reporting, that is, providing the financial results to management every month. The report that his people sent out was about 100 pages long; took a lot of time and effort to prepare, in both the computer room and finance; and contained every possible number that one could imagine. After several months on the job, he thought it was curious that no one ever called him with a question about the report. It couldn't be that good.
>
> His curiosity got the best of him, so one month he included a note with the report, asking people to call if they had read it. One call came in, from the person assigned to proofread it. None of his customers called. None of his customers had read it.

That is an expensive way of doing business. If we do not know what the next person in our value chains needs from us, the chances of getting things right are slim at best. That means unnecessary effort has to be spent in correcting, changing, or revising the original work and, as we have seen, that's expensive. The recipient can take the time and spend the energy to do it. Or he or she can send it back, which delays the process and really doesn't make you happy since it just becomes another task on the pile of things to do. Even inside the bank, "The customer perceives service in his [or her] own terms. The customer alone pays the freight (or doesn't) for whatever reason or collection of reasons he or she chooses. Period. No debate. No contest."[12]

Pity the poor people who can't get what they need from another department to satisfy their own customers. At least external customers have an option: They can choose to buy their goods and services from the competition. On the inside, we're stuck. We have to use the services of the accounting department, marketing department, systems department, loan operations, credit, and data processing. The bureaucracy says so.

The bank should be organized so that each department helps the front line work with customers. Apparently that is not happening because 25 percent of them regularly change banks. Think about what that means. If one-quarter of us change banks every year, in four years we will change again; a back door is indeed open because we don't know what our internal or external customers want.

If everyone in a particular value chain would take the time to find out exactly what the next person needs and would design his or her own work process to provide it, chances are very good that errors would be prevented. When that happens, as we have seen, cost is reduced, customers are happier, and the bank has a good start on improving market share. However, without knowing what your internal customers want, the odds of that happening are reduced.

Here's another example.

When I was responsible for the payroll department, every two weeks or so I would get a call from a senior exec who would complain that one of his people had been paid incorrectly. The complaint had gone up his "silo" and was coming down mine. I would have to stop what I was doing, go to the payroll department, and visit with the folks there about the problem. Invariably, the answer would be found in inadequate documentation from the person who was paid incorrectly, wrong instructions from human resources, or incorrect data entry forms that we had sent to the computer room.

When the errors were discovered, we had to work back through the process to find out what happened. The next course of action was to correct it. That meant walking the documentation back through the chain to make sure it was right and obtaining the proper approvals as we went. That took time away from other duties and ultimately made the cost of running the payroll department higher than it had to be. The same thing happened in accounts payable when people would send their expense reimbursement forms in with columns of numbers that didn't balance with the row totals, weren't signed properly, or didn't have the appropriate receipts attached. Back they would go at considerable expense to the bank.

After a while, we realized that there was more to paying the bank's people than simply taking the HR forms and preparing them for processing. There were more people involved than those of us in finance. So, we convened some sessions with people from around the bank who were involved with it to see how we could smooth things out. It was remarkable what happened when people talked to each other about problems and how to prevent them from happening in the first place.

That is why it is so important for the bank to be organized horizontally. The people of the same value chain have to realize that they are in the business of serving the bank's customers with excellence, that errors within the chain are costly in terms of customer attitude and operating expenses, and that the back door is very expensive. They have to understand that when they shut the back door, good things happen, socially and financially. It's a great motivator. The people in the value chains need to see that they are dependent upon one another to provide the customer with value, and that whatever they can do to prevent problems, they should and must do.

Remember the Saturn commercial where the worker on the production line notices something that is not quite right with one of the cars. He debates mentally whether to pull the cord that will stop the line, appears to fill with self-confidence, and pulls it. The line stops, the repair is made, and the worker is a hero. As long as he communicates to the people responsible for the defect about it, this makes a great story. If the problem continues, they had better get together to determine why it is happening. Stopping the line is expensive, but it is not as bad as putting a "lemon" on the dealership floor. The closer the error gets to the customer, the higher the cost to the bank.

There's another reason, too. Working together to provide value to customers is more fun. When you give the people who are dependent on you exactly what they need to do their job, there is a sense of satisfaction. You know that you have contributed to a team effort that will result in something great. When I talk about this side of the internal customer equation, I liken it to baseball.

Let's say you're playing shortstop, and there's a runner on second base. The batter smashes a line drive over your head. You turn around and charge toward the left fielder who has chased the ball down and is throwing it to you. As you catch it and whirl toward the infield, you see that the runner has rounded third and is headed for home. You throw the ball to the plate, one bounce; the catcher grabs it and tags the runner. Left fielder to shortstop to catcher. You'rrre out!!!

The left fielder feels good, you feel good, the catcher feels good, and so does everybody else, especially the pitcher, the manager, and the fans. But what would have happened if you dropped the throw from the left fielder? Or threw the ball over the catcher's head into the stands? The run would have scored, and maybe your team would have lost the game. Nobody would have been happy, except the other team, that is, the competition.

Thus, when the bank drops the ball internally, the customer is not happy, but the competition is. Unless the needs of your internal customers are considered and met, that is likely to occur. The problem is that the banks have chopped their expenses in terms of the people necessary to provide that kind of service to customers. Those who are left don't have the time to find out what their internal customers want. There's the issue. "Because today's customers are looking for the best deal, they're shopping around more. But, at the same time, banks have cut costs in the wrong areas. They have lowered the level of service . . ."[13]

In the attempt to improve the bottom line, service for customers has suffered. It is as if the banks don't realize, as Tom Peters instructs, that the customer is the one that pays the freight.

PAYING THE FREIGHT

We have seen the impact of an open back door. We know that if banks can close it halfway, there will be substantial increases in ROA and ROE, simply because they are more able to retain their current customers. That's why it is so important to understand what they value and then do everything to provide it. "Every 1 percent improvement you make and sustain over five years of your current customer retention rate will improve your operating earnings by up to 20 percent."[14]

With that kind of opportunity, one would think that all banks would be calculating the impact of the back door—what it could mean to their ratios and how favorably the analysts would look at them. Sadly, that's not the case. The Advisory Board Company developed a database on customer retention, the results of which were presented at the 1994 Bank Marketing Association National Conference and Exposition. The database was characterized by:

- Analysis of retention patterns over time on both the account and household level.
- Retail portfolio data for 38 of its member banks, which ranged in size from $1 billion to more than $60 billion in assets.
- More than 12 million households that do business with both domestic and international financial institutions.[15]

EXHIBIT 7–2

Do You Know the Lifetime Value of Your Customers?

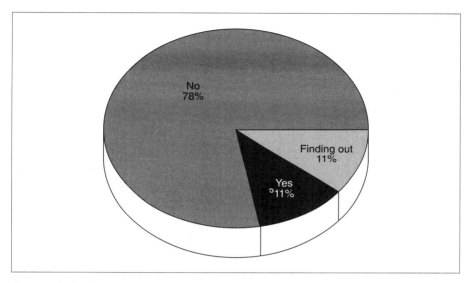

Source: The Advisory Board Company.

The statistics that follow come from that database (see Exhibit 7–2). Please do not dwell on the exact percentages. I would like you to see more than that. Take a hard look at what they mean and the opportunity they present. Then, if you didn't complete the workbook at the end of Chapter 2, go back and do the calculations. They are not hard, but they are most profound.

Let's take a look at Exhibit 7–2. The Advisory Board reports that almost 90 percent of the institutions in its database do not know the value of a lifetime relationship with a customer. That is an astonishing number, especially when we consider that the members of the Advisory Board Company tend to be some of the more sophisticated banks in the world. However, they don't know what their customers are giving them over time. The people at other retailers know. "Phil Bressler, the co-owner of five Domino's Pizza stores in Montgomery County, Maryland, calculated that regular customers were worth more than $5,000 over the life of a 10-year franchise contract."[16] According to the Advisory Board, most bankers don't make this kind of calculation.

> Exactly how much can lousy service cost a company, or even an industry? In the case of retail banks, surveys by Raddon Financial Group . . . indicated that in 1987, 42 percent of consumers who switched banks did so because of service problems. The switchers, on average, had used three bank

"products"—checking accounts, savings accounts, and so forth—and had total deposit balances of more than $23,000 apiece. In total, Raddon estimates, banks that lost customers because of service problems saw earnings worth hundreds of millions of dollars walk out of their vaults.[17]

There are two lessons here. First, the study was done almost 10 years ago. That shows that this kind of thinking has been out there from the mid- to the late 1980s, yet very few bankers have taken advantage of it. Second, whether it is $23,000 or $50,000 or $100,000, there is a number out there for your bank. The organizational imperative is to find out what it is.

It is easy to blame the lack of good cost accounting systems for this phenomenon. The inability to compute customer profitability is a prime contributor, but there is an even more powerful one. Quite simply, bankers aren't being paid to retain customers. For a variety of reasons, I suspect, not only do they not know the lifetime value of a customer relationship, but also they apparently don't concern themselves with it. Just look at Exhibit 7–3.

Of the Advisory Board Company's clients in the database, 85 percent have some kind of incentive compensation program. One bank that we know had 66 different ones, which surely caused some competing behaviors. However, the telling number in Exhibit 7–3 is that only 4 percent of the banks provide their people with some incentive for retaining their current customers. If we understand the premise that people do what they are paid to do, retention is not a big issue for these banks. There are too many fires to put out.

There are bonuses for productivity and asset growth, among other things, but not for retention. But think how an incentive program based on closing the back door would contribute to all three and would be much less expensive for the bank. An estimated 5 to 10 times as much expense is incurred in signing up a new customer as is expended in maintaining one who is already relatively happy. The leadership has to realize this and must start a campaign directed at maintaining and improving their relationships with their current customer base, quite a few of whom are getting ready to move their accounts. "MBNA America has found that a 5 percent improvement in [customer] defection rates increases its average customer value by 124 percent."[18]

After incurring the initial cost to acquire customers, the longer they stay with the bank, the more that cost of acquisition is repaid. First, the profit generated by the service that was initially sold continues to come in, much like the premium from an insurance policy. Without doing anything but providing the service that customers want, the revenue stream remains constant over the time that they stay with the bank and more than offsets the original cost-to-acquire.

E X H I B I T   7-3

Retention and Compensation

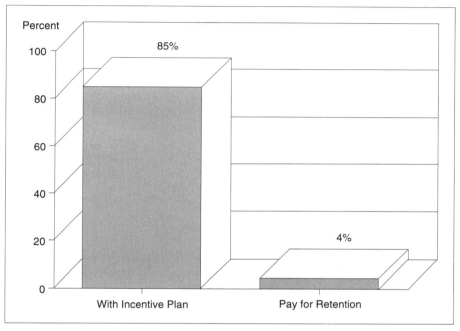

Source: The Advisory Board Company.

Then, as time progresses, there is the opportunity to sell additional services, presuming of course that what has been provided before has met customer expectations. The more that are sold, the more income the bank accrues. That, in turn, lowers fixed costs which, as we have seen, contributes even more earnings to the bottom line. And, we have also seen that people will talk about the service they are getting, more so about bad service, but nevertheless some about good service. These referrals start the revenue-producing process all over again, but they are even more profitable since the original cost of acquisition was not incurred.[19]

Experience has shown that companies in many different industries should be able to achieve results like this, regardless of the service they provide. Loyal customers simply provide increased revenues over time. As long as the bank knows and understands their expectations and does everything possible to meet or exceed them, they have a good chance to reap greater profits.

However, when customers leave, profitability falls. A lot of bankers just accept it. "Culturally, retention efforts are difficult for management to grasp because they are more focused on market share and customer acquisition. Many managers feel that losing customers is simply part of the game."[20] Even if that is true, it does not have to be. The leadership and the people of the bank must understand the financial ramifications of customer attrition. They must understand the organizational side of it because, if you lose more customers than you gain, the outcome is obvious.

> The quality council of a major bank holding company was meeting. The members were talking about their accomplishments. The leader of the retail side of the bank proudly announced that 200,000 new accounts had opened the previous year. Everyone in the room applauded, save one.
> "How many were closed?" was the question from the unimpressed member.
> "Well, gee, I don't know," came the response.
> The chairman asked that the number of accounts closed be presented at the next meeting.
> "210,000."

Another hmm . . .

Quality Digest is a journal dedicated to the study of product and service quality in the United States. It is fascinating for those of us in the services sector because it always contains articles and features about current thinking and events in the manufacturing sector. The June 1995 issue reported the results of a survey about customer retention at Fortune 500 companies.

> Only one-sixth of the companies report using customer retention as a measure to increase profitability. This figure is particularly interesting given that 62 percent of the respondents say that three-quarters of their business comes from existing customers.[21]

If the bank does not consciously attempt to retain customers, share will decrease and cost will increase. Retention is a gold mine. Here's what not to do.

> Another bank instituted an incentive program that paid the tellers $5 every time they could keep a customer from closing his or her account. So, the tellers, being incented and wanting to do their jobs very well, became quite good at convincing their unhappy customers to stay. They earned $5 every time they did and provided what branch management thought was quality service. The problem was that instead of finding out what was causing customers to want to close their accounts, management put the burden of saving the relationship on the teller, effectively treating the symptom, not the real illness . . . It was quite logical: the more accounts customers threatened to close, the better the chance to earn $5.[22]

As you think about your vision, mission, values, and philosophy, take a hard look at how your organization perceives and treats customers. Think about what the behavior of the people of the bank is telling them. As you do, consider the concept of "moments-of-truth."

Every time the customer comes in contact with the bank is a moment-of-truth. By definition, that is when mistakes cannot be made. As you assess your organization from the perspective of customers, think about moments-of-truth and about what the customer might be thinking. It will be more fodder for the cannon of the revolution.

MOMENTS-OF-TRUTH

Excellence has to occur with moments-of-truth. They are times when you have to delight your customers—at the teller window, in the customer service department, or with a statement, loan approvals, or the fees being charged. They are the instances when the bank and the customer meet. Take a minute to think about your personal moments-of-truth.

- When you go to the dentist and it doesn't hurt: There's delight.
- When the young person at the store says that they have "one last pair of jeans" in your size: That's value.
- When the credit card company suspends interest charges for a month because you've been a good customer.
- When the bill for a great meal at a local restaurant turns out to be less than you thought it would.
- When you wanted to check out the scores of last night's game before heading off to an early airplane and saw the paper lying in the driveway, a half hour earlier than usual.
- When you walk up to a customer service desk, expecting a hassle, and you hear, "I'm sorry you had a problem. Please go pick out another item."

That's excellence, but what makes it so? Your perception.

A lot of people, your customers included, have a perception that it is difficult to do business with the bank. Maybe your strategy has been based on it, knowing that others do not have very good service either. Maybe there is some denial going on wherein the leadership believes that service levels aren't as poor as some people think they are. But, regardless of the explanation, bank patrons do not believe that service is very good. This is confirmed by what they see and read in the newspaper. Consider the following:

Since my bank was purchased by a large multiregional this fall, I've found a number of little changes in operating procedures that I don't like. For example, the new bank has taken away (without warning me) some of the payment screens on the ATM that I used to count on. That seems like poor planning on their part . . . Now I have two unsatisfying alternatives: to go into the branch to make a payment (which has become a great deal more crowded since the acquisition) on my lunch hour (which is everyone else's lunch hour, too) and stand in line for 15 minutes (a very precious 15 minutes indeed); or to pay by mail. To avoid the full finance charge incurred when paying by mail, I must wait in line and take up teller time.

It frustrates me to have to spend so much time handling a simple transaction in person and I feel "ripped off" having to pay a full month's finance charge by mail. I don't understand why the payment screens were taken away, and neither do any of the bank employees I've asked. They think it's a bad move, too.[23]

This bank went from one pleasant moment-of-truth (the payment screen that the customer counted on) to two unpleasant ones (having to stand in line and paying a service fee). It is as if the bank doesn't think about things like that, but people are starting to talk and write about it. For those who also feel "ripped off," it confirms their belief and makes them angrier. I guess the question is, When the customer "pays the freight," why do banks make it so difficult for them?

I have mentioned Len Berry before. He and his colleagues, Valarie Zeithaml and A. Parasuraman, are pioneers in the determination of the impediments to excellence. In their book, *Delivering Quality Service,* they provide insightful instruction about the reasons for shortfalls in serving the customer at the moment-of-truth.

First, they suggest that there may be differences between what customers want and what the leadership of the bank thinks they want. With a dearth of information about a particular service, we bankers are very good at deciding that our customers want it. For some reason, we don't take the time to ask our customers what they want. For example, back in the 1970s, the banks introduced automated teller machines, or ATMs. Customers didn't know what they were, they did not trust them, the bank did not provide any training or incentive for customers to use them, and those customers saw no reason to change their banking habits. They liked seeing a teller and visiting with the other people in the branch. That was the way it always had been. Nevertheless, the banks spent a lot of money on the ATMs because the leadership thought that they could reduce the cost of operations by decreasing the number of tellers, the very people who were making the bank a success. The drive for the bottom line dictated a behavior that customers did not want. That is only one example. Think about the services and products that your bank has come up with based on little real research into customer needs.

Product and service development starts with customers. They may tell you what they want, or they may react positively to a suggestion that you have about a potential service. Instead of investing in capabilities just because you think customers will like them, find out first what they really want. That will make your investment decision easier and more cost-effective. Admittedly, our fast-paced society now loves its ATMs and cash dispensers, but their acceptance took a long time.

Second, there is the difference between what the leadership thinks its customers want and what it asks the bank to deliver. This gets back to the "value disciplines" introduced earlier in this chapter. Your bank's customers may want you to be operationally excellent while the leadership insists on having relationship banking but then cuts costs which precludes both. While you continue to think in the traditional manner, your customers may not be doing so and don't care whether they see a loan officer in person. They might prefer to apply for the loan from their PC at home. They would not have to go to the branch, documentation could be done by fax or FedEx, and disbursement could be made electronically, all of which is happening while your loan officers wait for their phones to ring.

The comparison of core competencies and the expectations of your customers will be revealing. It will help you understand the business that your customers want you to be in, where your bank is headed, and the direction in which your opportunities lie. As with the first shortfall, however, the answer to this dilemma lies in the mind of the client, which has to be unlocked for you to bridge the gap.

Third, there may be a difference between the service levels that you want and those that are delivered. Every banker in the country would like to have zero defects. We have seen the reason: low costs and high market share. As such, you might establish service standards that are far in excess of the bank's ability to provide. Let's go back to my friends from Florida. The bank that they originally visited very likely had a standard time within which to grant the loan approval, and the loan officer most likely advised them of this. However, there are so many things that have to be done in the bank's bureaucratic environment that it is frequently impossible to meet the goal. Therefore, loan officers can't keep their promises to their customers, which prompts actions like my friends took: Go to someone who can deliver what is needed when promised.

Standards for performance have to be realistic. Only tell the customer what you can do. Don't promise any more. Engage in *kaizen* and raise the standards whenever possible, but not to guarantee failure. Performing at ever-higher levels puts more and more pressure on you as well as on the competition. The first step in that process is to measure the output of every value chain to see how you are doing. Regardless of where you are, the way the bank is performing becomes the initial benchmark. Next, find out what levels of service your customers want. That becomes the standard. The task is to figure out how to bridge the gap between where you are and what your customers want.

Fourth, there is an insidious shortfall that I doubt many people consider, especially if they are "too busy." This difference is the one between the service that customers are receiving and what the bank is telling the world about it. The marketing department and the advertising agency come up with some slick slogans and campaigns to promote the virtue of the bank's service which, in my experience, has often been overstated or has given a false impression. The bank's customers see the ads and realize this discrepancy, which they talk about with their friends and neighbors.

For some reason, we human beings love to talk about things gone wrong while we don't spend much time on what is right. Therefore, advertise your bank's strengths and competencies, and be completely honest about them. Tell the market what you can do and then deliver on the promise. If you can do more than you say you can, you will be rewarded. Admittedly, some people will be swayed by the fancy new campaigns, but their loyalty is temporary at best. They will probably switch to another institution when it starts its own new campaign. If relationships are really what the bank wants, spend the advertising dollars on the people who can establish and strengthen them. The best advertisement is to give your customers more than they expect.

These four shortfalls contribute to the big one, where the perceptions of customers about the service promised do not meet their expectations. That is the gap that must be closed. The first step in that process is to initiate continuous research aimed at discovering the expectations of your markets. Just what do they want from your bank? Ask those with whom you are doing business and those who are not, using a variety of techniques and methods, about what they want. Once those expectations are known, the bank has a terrific advantage and obligation.

The advantage: You will know the critical information for success, that being customer needs and expectations. With that information, you can design delivery systems to meet them. The obligation is to take the appropriate action. By asking the questions, the bank has heightened customer awareness about service. Customers will now anticipate that any shortfalls they have identified will be eliminated. It is up to the people of the bank to make sure that happens.

More than ten years after the quality movement gained acceptance in the U.S., the concept can be credited with underlining the importance of customers and employees, and emphasizing the primacy of the processes that link the two. Observes Jeffrey Pfeffer, a Stanford business school professor, in his recent *Competitive Advantage Through People:* "The language of quality—'customer' is one term often seen in quality programs—and the orientation of providing service to customers, both internal and external, shifts measurement and attention in important ways."[24]

It is the moment-of-truth that counts the most, both for internal customers and the ultimate consumer of the bank's service. If it can be delivered to the outside the right way, even if internal breakdowns have occurred, there is a much better chance to enhance the relationship. But defining the right way, that's the crucial question. And there's only one way to find out.

ASK THEM!

There has been a great deal of dialogue about meeting or exceeding customer expectations and thus providing value to your customers. To do that, we have to ask what those expectations are. There are a variety of ways to conduct customer research, some of which are straightforward and some of which are more sophisticated. All are useful and have their place. Whichever you choose, it is important to make sure that all of the research is centralized, so that you can obtain a clear and complete understanding of what your markets are saying. As you read the following sections, think about how each one of these techniques would apply at your bank.

Customer Comment Cards

Comment cards are easy to use. They can be placed on the top of the teller window where customers can easily reach them. They provide a direct link with the customer, but if we think carefully about them, the concept is somewhat flawed. First, they are seldom used. Because I travel a lot, I see them in every hotel and restaurant I visit. Unless something is very, very good or very, very bad, I usually do not fill them out. The same is true with the bank's customers. The same cards are on the counter that were there six months ago. Because service isn't *that* bad, they aren't filled out.

Second, comment cards don't reveal anything about the differences between expectation and perception, except to imply that the expectation is perfection when, in fact, that might not be the case. Customers might not need a statement to be delivered within "x" number of business days. Thus, comparing their answers to misunderstood expectations might produce some unrealistic conclusions.

Nor do the cards provide any hint about where the root causes of the problems are. They may tell you that there has been a breakdown, but unless this breakdown is categorized and summarized, the bank will not know whether it is an isolated instance or a recurring symptom of a greater illness. Furthermore, since the cards are random and anonymous, there is no way to tell if the matter raised is real or not. It could be that employees, posing as customers, are stuffing the ballot box. These employees might think that favorable comments will result in greater benefits for them. Despite their limitations, the customer comment cards are a fast feedback technique that gives some customers a feeling that they are contributing to the efficiency and effectiveness of the bank, but you should not rely on them alone. There are other things that should be done.

Mystery Shoppers

Mystery shoppers are people hired by the bank who rate the service it provides. Mystery shoppers can be helpful in looking for trends and patterns across a branch system, but that may be about as far as they can go. I find it hard to fathom a mystery shop on a complex construction loan or a foreign exchange transaction, so their use is limited.

In a perfect world, the concept of the mystery shopper is a good one, but the world isn't perfect. Mystery shoppers are not like other bank customers. Even if they try real hard to hide themselves, it is difficult to avoid showing some bias based on how they have been treated in the past. In other words, they create their own expectation of the service, based on the reason that they are there, which is to view and to judge how the people of the bank perform. That's not the reason that most real customers are there.

Furthermore, the people in the branch learn to recognize mystery shoppers; therefore, service levels increase when they walk in the front door. That is a natural reaction because the employees know that there will be a report forthcoming about the way the customer was treated, which might have a bearing on changes in their compensation levels.

From a little different perspective, I don't think I would like my behavior to be monitored by mystery shoppers, the result of which would influence my paycheck. If I am told that it will be viewed at various times by my superiors at the bank, that's one thing, but where someone is spying on how I behave is quite another. That kind of management action would cause me to have some feelings of distrust about the leadership of the bank, which could very well be manifested in the way I treat the bank's customers.

Customer Interviews

As in the assessment, sitting down with customers and asking them about the service the bank provides is another quick way to obtain some feedback. Typically, because the persons interviewed have never been asked before and have not had the chance to have their say, their response may be more animated and emotional than the situation warrants. They may exaggerate it as the interviewer might strike an emotional cord that has been wound too tight for a long period of time. Any response like that would have to be discounted.

As with the customer comment cards, there is a great temptation to try to solve whatever the customer perceives as a problem right then and there. This is not what we want. Interviews where potential problems are identified do nothing to help the bank solve them at their source. If you can work through the emotion and can talk about things logically, the interview process is very helpful because it points you toward places where improvement is needed. If not, the results may turn out to be invalid and of little help.

A more natural way is to have the bank's calling officers and staff, those who are on the front line, conduct informal interviews every day, visiting with customers in their offices, factories, stores, and farms. Using a customer management system such as Institutional Memory, they can record what customers are saying, which can then be summarized and classified for action if need be. That part of the equation is essential. There must be a way to aggregate the data gathered from all sources, so that extremes are mitigated and an accurate picture of the situation is developed. Truly listening to the customer and communicating what has been said should be everyone's job. That communication is vital, especially when it is what the leadership may not want to hear.

Industry Statistics

Bankers love their numbers, and they love to compare themselves to their peer groups. If there were such a thing as a true peer group, the comparison would be very helpful, but differences in market emphasis, culture, technological advancement, and the like make a good comparison very difficult. Can Mercantile really compare itself to Boatmen's? Can Bank of America and Wells Fargo be compared? They can, but they had better realize exactly what the comparison means.

At Society Corp., we used to compare ourselves with our neighbor, National City, but the only thing that we had in common was the same zip code. Customer bases, operational styles, merger philosophies, and so forth were different. But compare we did, and I am still not sure what it told us. Further, even if we understood it, I'm not sure we could have done anything about it. If the analysts insist on peer group contrasts, make sure that the analysis is meaningful.

It is more useful to look at industry statistics to see the bigger picture. We have seen that the Advisory Board conducts statistically valid surveys and reports on their outcomes. The American Bankers Association and the Bank Marketing Association do the same thing; and there is always the data compiled by the Fed, FDIC, and Office of the Comptroller of the Currency.

The media also provides information on the banks, but care has to be urged there as well. Despite their best intentions, and with all due respect, the reports in the newspaper may not accurately reflect what is really going on. Some of the business shows on television are more helpful, but again there can be some bias.

Focus Groups

The outcome of focus groups sessions can be most revealing. These gatherings bring a cross-section of customers together to provide feedback on how the bank is delivering its service. They can lead to some interesting observations, especially if there is a skilled facilitator leading the participants. As with the other methods, there is a limitation. If the facilitator is not strong and well versed, things can get out of hand as tangent after tangent is visited. If the goal and the scope of the focus group is clearly defined and understood, chances for success are much better.

Focus groups function best when they are transformed into advisory boards that meet regularly to assess the service being provided and to suggest ways to improve it. That avoids the emotion and exaggeration of intermittent interviews. In doing do, the participants develop a vested interest in the service delivery process and tend to be more constructive. These kinds of councils are effective and strengthen the bank's relationship with them.

Customer Complaints

"You should love complaints more than compliments. A complaint is letting someone know that you haven't satisfied them yet. They have gold written all over them."[25] If the bank is not collecting and summarizing customer complaints today, it must start doing so tomorrow. The reason: The complaint of one represents those of a whole lot more. Technical Assistant Research Program, Inc. (TARP) estimates that just 4 percent of your unhappy customers complain to you. But they do talk to others; a dissatisfied customer will tell about 10 other people. About three-fourths of those who don't complain will never buy again from the company that has served them poorly.

Whatever the bank has to do to put a complaint monitoring system in place it should do, but more than that, it has to listen actively for them. Ask why customers are calling the customer service department. Why are they unhappy? When the CEO gets a phone call from a disgruntled customer, don't just put out the fire, register what it was about because it represents a great deal more than what only one customer thought.

Other Techniques

The bank can engage in a variety of other techniques for gathering and collecting information from customers, but they are only effective if the information is funneled to the customer feedback database from which action is taken. Isolated, individual reports of displeasure are one thing, but if they become repetitive and numerous, that is quite another.

Written Surveys

All of the techniques described so far will help, but they won't get to the real issue: the difference between the expectations and perceptions of the bank's customers. Berry, Parasuraman, and Zeithaml were the first to understand and publish the importance of measuring those shortfalls. They reasoned, correctly, that the way in which people want service to be delivered shapes their perceptions of what actually happens. They began measuring levels of service this way, based on the concept of "perceived quality." That's the critical piece. We have to know what our customers expect or want from us; otherwise how can we give it to them?

Other books have cited their work, but I am not sure that the authors comprehend its revolutionary nature and relevance. It is the gap between what customers want and what they think they are getting that's important, not just their perception. If the perception was the critical matter alone, the bank could save a lot of money. It could simply stop surveying its existing customers about what they think because those customers demonstrate relative satisfaction simply by staying with the bank. In order to improve and to outdistance the competition, the bank has to know what consumers of financial services want. The only way to find out is to ask them.

Remember the five dimensions of service quality:

- Reliability—providing the service that was promised accurately and dependably.
- Responsiveness—willing to help customers and being prompt.
- Assurance—knowledge and courtesy, conveying trust and confidence.
- Tangibles—physical facilities, appearance of personnel.
- Empathy—caring for the customer, paying attention.

What differentiates the written survey technique is that it not only enables the bank to measure expectations but it also segregates that which is important to customers into these five dimensions. When customers respond, they are telling the bank the areas in which improvement is needed, which allows the bank to prioritize its actions. That saves time and money and results in better service being provided for the customer sooner.

The survey document to be used contains two major sections, one to measure expectations and the other to measure perceptions. There are about 30 statements in each section, with approximately 6 that address each of the service quality dimensions. Respondents are asked to rate them from 1 to 7, "strongly disagree" to "strongly agree." They are designed for each specific service that the bank offers. Each expectation statement is matched with a perception statement to establish a valid correlation between them. The statements should be crafted in such a way that they are meaningful to the leadership of the bank's various value chains, should relate directly to the service being offered, and should be specific in nature. Table 7–2 contains examples of some general statements from which to start the modification process and shows the relationships between expectation statements and perception statements. The sample report at the end of the chapter (see Appendix 7–1) shows the detail into which the statements go.

A third section of the survey document is devoted to prioritization as respondents are asked to rank the five service quality dimensions in order of their perceived importance. The results of this process are helpful to the bank because they reveal how customers think about them and thus provide insight into where the first improvement should be made.

Survey documents should be given to a sample of customers in each of the bank's value chains. They can be mailed, distributed in a focus group, or administered in a one-on-one environment. How the bank conducts the process depends on the culture and the technique that has yielded success in the past. If something like this has not been done before, the bank can try a combination of methods to determine which one provides the most information. Regardless of the one(s) chosen, it is imperative to show the customers who have participated that you appreciate their taking the time to tell you what they think. Like you, they are busy people and should be rewarded in some way for giving of themselves. Whether it is a monetary gift or a T-shirt or a coffee mug makes little difference as long as you show the customer that you care and are thankful for the input.

After they have been completed, the surveys are scored. The differences between the pairs of statements are calculated and summarized, using any one of a variety of commercially available software programs. The first step is to match the corresponding expectation and perception statements because their correlation has been disguised in the survey process. Those that relate to each service quality dimension are relinked as they, too, have been disguised. Table 7–3 provides an example of how the correlations between questions can be masked.

To calculate the results, subtract the expectation scores from the perception scores across the entire population. The differences between expectations

TABLE 7-2

Service Quality Survey

	Strongly Agree						Strongly Disagree
Examples of **Expectation** *Statements*							
The bank's forms and statements should be easy to read and understand.	7	6	5	4	3	2	1
When the customer has a question, it should be answered in a timely manner.	7	6	5	4	3	2	1
When the bank promises to complete a transaction on a specific day, it should do so.	7	6	5	4	3	2	1
When customers have problems, the employees of the bank should try to understand and help.	7	6	5	4	3	2	1
The bank should undertake research to determine what their customers need.	7	6	5	4	3	2	1
	Strongly Agree						**Strongly Disagree**
Examples of **Perception** *Statements*							
ABC Bank's forms and statements are easy to read and understand.	7	6	5	4	3	2	1
When I call ABC Bank, my questions are answered promptly.	7	6	5	4	3	2	1
Transactions are processed by ABC Bank when promised.	7	6	5	4	3	2	1
The employees of ABC Bank do their best to understand and help whenever I have a problem.	7	6	5	4	3	2	1
ABC Bank continually surveys its customers to determine what they need.	7	6	5	4	3	2	1

and perceptions by dimension should fall in a range of +2.000 to −2.000. Anything outside that lower limit indicates some serious bleeding is occurring and that tourniquets are needed, not *kaizen*. A positive gap means that the service provided exceeds what customers want and that changes can be made to reduce the level of service. Huh? Lessen the service level? Sure.

Let's say that your commercial loan area incurred a lot of overtime and additional computer time to make sure that statements were in customers' hands within three business days of the close of the month. The incremental time

T A B L E   7-3

Service Quality Survey

	Strongly Agree						Strongly Disagree
***Expectation** Statements*							
Reliability #1	7	6	5	4	3	2	1
Tangibles #1	7	6	5	4	3	2	1
Responsiveness #1	7	6	5	4	3	2	1
Reliability #2	7	6	5	4	3	2	1
Assurance #1	7	6	5	4	3	2	1
Responsiveness #2	7	6	5	4	3	2	1
Reliability #3	7	6	5	4	3	2	1
Empathy #1	7	6	5	4	3	2	1
Tangibles #2	7	6	5	4	3	2	1
Empathy #2	7	6	5	4	3	2	1
	Strongly Agree						Strongly Disagree
***Perception** Statements*							
Tangibles #4	7	6	5	4	3	2	1
Reliability #6	7	6	5	4	3	2	1
Responsiveness #1	7	6	5	4	3	2	1
Responsiveness #7	7	6	5	4	3	2	1
Empathy #3	7	6	5	4	3	2	1
Assurance #5	7	6	5	4	3	2	1
Reliability #1	7	6	5	4	3	2	1
Empathy #4	7	6	5	4	3	2	1
Tangibles #2	7	6	5	4	3	2	1
Assurance #2	7	6	5	4	3	2	1

spent is expensive, but that doesn't matter because the folks in commercial loans believe that they have to get the statements out within that time frame. Suppose then that customers, as part of their survey work, indicate that anytime before the 15th of the month is perfectly acceptable. That means elimination of the overtime being incurred and the demands being placed on the computer room to generate the statements so quickly. In this case, the service provided exceeded what was required, and therefore it can be reduced.

A score of −2.000 is a problem. That says customers are real unhappy with what they are receiving from the bank. However, because the survey process shows in which dimension this negative gap is happening, actions can be taken to correct it, *but at the root cause.* We are after the illness here, not only the symptom.

WHAT THEY ARE SAYING

The sample survey report at the end of the chapter reveals a lot of information (see Appendix 7–1). First, we can see the size of the survey: 441 people questioned, with 120 responses or 27.2 percent. Those who replied indicated that they had been customers of the bank for an average of six years or so which, if we remember the statistics from earlier in the chapter, means that they remain quite loyal. That figures. Part of the problem with this type of survey is that your current customers will always tell you that things are at least OK. They may not be delighted, but things are not yet to the point where they are seriously contemplating leaving. That is why it is so important to survey customers of other banks, so that you can determine the overall expectations and perceptions in your markets.

The survey also shows the geographic distribution in a section that asks for this kind of information. Again, don't get hung up thinking that you always have to obtain information by region. Whatever geographic breakdowns are important to you is what your bank should use. Other demographic data include an overall satisfaction rating, which in this case is around 85 percent. That's not bad, but remember Motorola's Six Sigma, 99.9999998 percent defect-free, shows that there is work to be done. We can also see that contact with the area in question is fairly regular with 67.5 percent of the respondents indicating that they have contact at least once a week.

We can identify who the primary contact is, in this case treasurers and controllers of local companies. However, this will be different every time you survey a new customer group. It could be that you want to know an age distribution, occupation, or something else. Whatever you think you need to know about your customers to serve them better is what you should ask. It gets back to the notion of "value disciplines." When the bank knows what it can do best and where it can serve most effectively, it has also determined its target markets. With that, it can identify its customer constituencies, which the survey process can segment even further, to see if there is a match.

In our example, the bank's customers have provided the information as contained in Table 7–4. It includes the gaps between customer expectation and perception as well as the priority they are placing on each of the five dimensions.

The customers of the bank are suggesting that there is work to be done because there are no positive gaps. In each of the five dimensions, as they relate to the delivery of cash management services, there is room for improvement. Because the surveys have been designed this way, the results are more telling

T A B L E 7-4

Service Quality Survey Results

Dimension	Gap	Priority
Reliability	−1.077	32.69%
Responsiveness	−1.200	23.34
Assurance	−0.938	18.43
Empathy	−0.949	13.42
Tangibles	−1.249	11.62

than those of most surveys in that they show where improvement initiatives should be undertaken first. That is the relevance and importance of the "prioritization" question.

In this case, the most serious gap relates to the physical side of service delivery, "tangibles"; for example, statements are perhaps confusing to read, the snow is not removed promptly from the parking lot, or the telephone manner of the people in cash management needs to be improved. This gap is −1.249, but only 11.62 percent of the people responding to the survey think that this is the most important aspect of the service delivery process. Therefore, even though the gap is serious, the priority is not, because the other four dimensions of the survey are more important in the minds of the bank's clients. Thus, as the improvement effort begins, it can be directed elsewhere.

The smallest gap is "assurance," −0.938. Because it is the smallest and only 18.43 percent think that it is the most important, effort should not be expended here. There are more critical things to do. "Empathy" has the next smallest gap, −0.949, and the second smallest prioritization percentage, 13.42 percent, so it too can be relegated to the back burner for the time being.

The results for "reliability" and "responsiveness" provide a bit of a dilemma. The gap for responsiveness is the second highest, −1.200, and is fairly serious at that level. The gap for reliability is a close third, but if we look at their respective priority ratings, reliability is far more important than responsiveness, 32.69 percent versus 23.34 percent. This suggests that customers think that reliability is the most important dimension of service quality and that there is opportunity to improve it. It also says that once those enhancements are made, the bank had better take a look at its responsiveness right away.

Further along in the sample report, there is more information that will help steer the improvement process. The gaps for the individual questions have been calculated so that the people of the bank can see exactly what the customers think about the cash management area at the lowest level. That also starts to point them toward where improvements should be made first.

E X H I B I T   7–4

Cash Management Services Service Quality Analysis

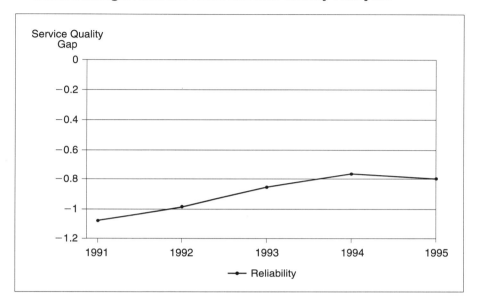

The first time that the bank undertakes this process, it is benchmarking its customers' attitudes and opinions. Each service of the bank should be subject to this kind of scrutiny on a regular basis, at least annually so that the results of improvement efforts can be seen tracked and trended as shown in Exhibit 7–4.

This kind of analysis assists the people of the bank with their behavior because they can see the results of what has been done so far. Combined with profitability information and market share data, it provides a complete overview of their performance within their service delivery systems. When aggregated with the others, the leadership of the bank has a precise and definite understanding of how the efforts of the workforce have contributed to overall customer satisfaction and how that has manifested itself in terms of earnings.

THE CATCH

There's a stipulation that goes with this survey process. Implied in it, and extremely necessary, is the idea that the bank is going to do something with the data it collects from and about its customers. By asking all these questions and trying to synthesize them into a clear picture of where improvement is needed, the expectations of customers have been raised again. They think that the bank will use their input to make things better.

At this point in the survey process, the bank knows where customers think improvement is necessary. The trick is to find out *why* they think that way. In the words of James Unruh, chairman of Unisys, *"Service excellence . . . will be the basis of competition in all industries,* not merely the service sector."[26] The secret lies within your bank. All you have to do is unlock it.

Perception/Expectation Gap Analysis
The ABC National Bank
Cash Management Operations Department
April 1995

Survey Statistics
Cash Management Operations Department
April 1995

	Total number surveyed:	441	
	Total surveys received:	120	
	Response rate:	27.2%	
	Average years with bank:	6.2	
Survey Sector	**Surveys Sent**	**Responses**	**Percent**
North Region	163	55	33.7%
Central Region	229	53	23.1
Southern Region	7	7	100.0
Others	42	5	11.9
Totals	441	120	27.2

External Customer Research
Cash Management Operations Department
April 1995

From the survey conducted with the customers of the Cash Management Operations Department (CMO), the following performance gaps have been identified within each service quality dimension:

Dimension	Average	
	Gap	Priority (percent)
Reliability	−1.077	32.69%
Responsiveness	−1.200	23.34
Assurance	−0.938	18.43
Empathy	−0.949	13.42
Tangibles	−1.249	11.62

Statement Summary
Cash Management Operations Department
External Customer Research
April 1995

Survey Statement	Response (percent)	
How would you rate the overall service provided by the cash management operations department?	Excellent	13.0%
	Above average	51.3
	Average	20.9
	Below average	1.7
	Poor	0.0
	No response	13.0
How often do you call the cash management operations department?	Daily	45.3%
	More than once per week	22.2
	Once per week	12.8
	Monthly	10.3
	Rarely	5.1
	No response	4.3
Your present position is?	Treasurer	31.6%
	Controller	23.1
	President/CEO	18.0
	Other	22.2
	No response	5.1

Gap Identification and Analysis
Cash Management Operations Department
April 1995

Dimension Expectation/Perception Statement	Service Quality Measures		
	Perception	Expectation	Gap
Reliability Overall Gap –			1.077
1. Able to depend on CMO to perform the service right the first time	5.170	6.388	−1.218
2. Accurate deposit, remittances, checks, and wires processing	5.505	6.650	−1.145
3. Accurate reconcilement balancing	5.348	6.573	−1.225
4. Services available during advertised times	5.710	6.513	−0.760
5. Error-free processing	5.280	6.147	−0.867
6. Financial information systems available when needed	5.286	6.181	−0.895
Responsiveness Overall Gap			−1.200
1. Prompt response to inquiry	5.284	6.397	−1.113
2. Timely statements and other information	5.157	6.427	−1.090
3. Phone calls returned promptly	4.712	6.026	−1.314
4. Effective channels for problem resolution	5.362	6.556	−1.194
5. CMO reps always willing to help	4.921	6.095	−1.174
6. Prompt response to phone requests	5.343	6.376	−1.033
Assurance Overall Gap			−0.938
1. CMO reps are knowledgeable	5.481	6.120	−0.639
2. CMO reps answer with name and department	5.486	6.302	−0.816
3. CMO reps are courteous	5.467	6.690	−1.223
4. Feel confident when conducting business with CMO	5.426	6.664	−1.238
Empathy Overall Gap			−0.949
1. State-of-the-art financial services	5.183	5.897	−0.714
2. CMO staff offers personalized attention	5.029	6.342	−1.313
3. Customers addressed by name	4.922	6.034	−1.112
4. Convenient hours	5.583	6.368	−0.785
5. CMO reps understand customer needs	5.275	6.164	0.889
6. Easy to use customer access systems	5.227	6.419	−1.192
Tangibles Overall Gap			−1.249
1. CMO reports easy to read and understand	4.755	6.444	−1.653
2. Staff is adequately trained/supported with information	5.406	6.638	−1.220
3. Monthly statements and reports are neat and professional	5.615	6.496	−0.844

CHAPTER 8

Bureaucracy Bashing!

Give Tom Peters the credit for the title of this chapter. It was the catch phrase of one of his inspirational talks, and it describes what has to happen for the banking revolution to be successful. It is what the revolution is all about: changing the bank's style to be more responsive, creative, and innovative in the service of the bank's customers. It also means adopting an attitude that's based on the long-term view and servant leadership. It also means flattening out the hierarchy and committing to the continuous improvement of the bank's delivery processes.

So far in *The Banking Revolution,* we have learned about servant leadership and the personal changes that the people of the bank have to make to achieve it. We have seen the importance of the long-term view in terms of improved service for customers and the financial rewards that accrue from it. We have also seen how to find out what those customers want the bank to be and what they think about the service that's being provided.

However, none of that is any good and the goal will not be accomplished unless there is a complete and accurate understanding of the organization itself. To increase its effectiveness in the market, we have to turn our attention inward for awhile to develop a profile of the personality of the bank. If we are going to change to meet customer expectations, we have to know where we are now. In other words, we need a very detailed internal benchmark from which to start. The service quality assessment has pointed the way; now it's time to start digging.

The first challenge is to determine exactly what is going on inside the bank and how it relates to and explains the attitudes of your customers, effectively showing why there are gaps between their expectations and perceptions. That means some additional data gathering. But more information does not help unless the bank is committed to act upon what the data reveal, which becomes the second, and most important, challenge: actually changing the way in which the people of the bank behave in order to serve their customers.

In this chapter, we will learn about the information that is needed to enable those changes to take place and the methods by which to capture it. We will also learn about the behaviors that are necessary, notably empowerment, accountability, and teamwork, and one that is to be avoided at all cost, entitlement. As we proceed, think about how each of them applies to your bank and how they relate to the ability to serve your markets.

WHAT DATA?

To start the process, we have to ask the workforce about four things:

- The quality of the service being delivered by their various value chains.
- The effectiveness of other processes within the bank that support delivery of services to customers.
- The prevailing environment and overall state of affairs at the bank.
- What the workforce does on a daily basis.

We saw how to gather information from customers in the last chapter. We have to do the same internally with the workforce. The purpose of this exercise is to learn more about the service that the workforce provides externally. Is there any correlation between what customers and the workforce think about specific services in terms of gaps between expectations and perceptions and in the prioritization of the five dimensions? Whom better to ask than the people involved in delivering the service?

In this particular case, the example is cash management as a whole, but the process is applicable to any service such as wholesale lockbox, controlled disbursements, or the rest of the cash management portfolio. It works for loan and deposit products as well as for trust services, because the method can be applied to any process that has defined starting and ending points, whether or not it ends up in the hands of your external customers.

Everyone who is involved in delivering a particular service is asked to take about 15 minutes to complete the same questionnaire that was used in the external survey. The results are input into the same computer software model to ensure that our research techniques are consistent. The comparison of two data sets can be most enlightening.

Let's start with the results of the survey shown in Table 8–1. By itself, the table does not tell us much except that the people in cash management aren't very happy. "Responsiveness," "tangibles," and "reliability" are perceived as big problems within the walls of the bank because the gaps between expectations and perceptions are huge. By order of priority, "reliability" and "responsiveness"

TABLE 8-1

Cash Management Services
Service Quality Survey Results

Dimension	Gap	Priority (percent)
Reliability	−1.345	29.98%
Responsiveness	−1.612	26.56
Assurance	−0.567	11.99
Empathy	−0.812	15.81
Tangibles	−1.432	15.66

TABLE 8-2

Cash Management Services
Service Quality Survey Results

Dimension	External Customer	Internal Customer
Reliability	−1.077	−1.345
Responsiveness	−1.200	−1.612
Assurance	−0.938	−0.567
Empathy	−0.949	−0.812
Tangibles	−1.249	−1.432

rank highest. Like the external data, it may be an eye-opener, but by itself it doesn't do us much good. In fact, it could steer improvement efforts in the wrong direction. However, compared with the data supplied by customers, we can really start to learn about what is going on. Take a look at Table 8–2, in which the gap comparison is made. Let's see how they match up.

The people of the bank are even more critical about their "reliability," "responsiveness," and "tangibles"' that their external clients. It appears that they do not believe that they are living up to the formal and informal standards they have set for themselves in those three dimensions, which is consistent with the external data and really validates what the bank's customers are saying. Both groups have identified the same areas where they think improvement is needed, albeit with different levels of severity. Where there are differences between what customers and the workforce say, the analysis, diagnosis, and correction is made much more difficult. In this case, "responsiveness" is the most severe problem, and both groups see it well.

TABLE 8-3

Cash Management Services
Service Quality Prioritization Results

Dimension	External Customer (percent)	Internal Customer(percent)
Reliability	32.69	29.98%
Responsiveness	23.34	26.56%
Assurance	18.43	11.99%
Empathy	13.42	15.81%
Tangibles	11.62	15.66%

The dimension of "assurance" is a little curious. The staff gave themselves higher marks for assurance than their customers did. This is somewhat of
a cause for concern because the workforce has a higher opinion about its competency than do their clients. Knowing that, it might be time to step back to see
how well the people really know their jobs. Education appears to be needed,
but that would not be known without the input from the outside.

Now let's look at Table 8–3, which contains a comparison of the priorities.
The external survey revealed that "reliability" was by far the most important dimension, 32.69 percent compared with 23.34 percent for "responsiveness," the
next more important. The numbers from the internal survey are 29.87 percent
and 26.56 percent respectively, which says that customers place more importance on the reliability of the staff to deliver service and to answer questions
than the staff does. In this example, customers would rather wait for an answer
as long as the answer is right. As is the case in most banks, keeping the service
promise is the most important thing to customers. However, without the prioritization data, the conclusion would have been to allocate resources to improving
response time, but that was not what customers thought was most important. It is
both sets of data than enable the bank to pinpoint improvement activities.

This kind of information needs to be developed for all of the bank's services because it helps in the understanding of where improvement is needed
and the emphasis to be placed on it. The results for your bank will in all likelihood be different from what you see here, and they will also be different among
your various services. What this shows is a method to identify those differences. Without it, the chance of identifying the most serious problems would be
pretty slight.

To make it easier to see, try displaying the information graphically. Exhibits 8–1 and 8–2 allow the people of the bank to identify the differences between the opinions and attitudes of the two groups quickly and easily. In Exhibit

E X H I B I T   8-1

Cash Management Services
Service Quality Gap Analysis

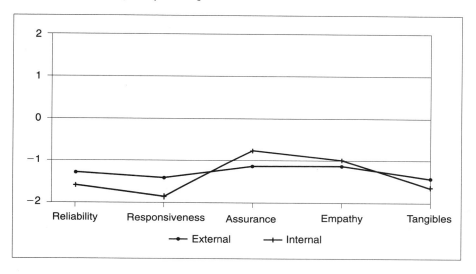

E X H I B I T   8-2

Cash Management Services
Prioritization Analysis

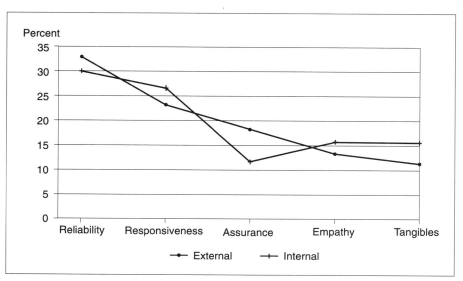

8–1, the staff can see that customers don't think that things are as bad or as good as they do, and the staff can take some satisfaction in that. Beware, there is work to be done. Gaps in the area of –1.200 are serious. By looking at the data this way, the people can see the similarities and the differences between their thinking and that of their customers. Knowing that, they can plan and execute the changes that will bring the two of them more in line with one another.

ANOTHER APPLICATION

At this point, we have a good idea about the attitudes of both customers and employees about the way service is being provided. The next step is to find out what is causing them to think that way. Before we do that, however, we need to understand that this same discipline has another application. Along with the service that the customer sees, there are other things happening in the bank that do not manifest themselves as external moments-of-truth. Using the same survey methodology, we can find out what the people of the bank are thinking about these ancillary, internal processes and how well they are functioning in support of the service to customers. These are the processes that most customers don't think about but which really have a direct impact on them. They are things like hiring, internal communications, planning, training, and so forth, anything that requires people to spend their time and energy in the service of others. The purpose of this research is to provide the quality council with more information about why the bank is operating as it is.

Like the surveys used to question customers and the staff about the bank's products, the steps for designing this kind of survey are the following:

- *Identify the internal processes to be studied.*
  Typically, the leadership has an idea about the processes that might not be functioning as well as possible. Use this feedback or that from the service quality assessment to determine what to survey first. It is the stuff that the staff complain about in their management committee meetings—the mail room, accounts payable, or the telephone system. Until it is quantified, the severity of the problems cannot really be known.
- *Customize the data collection.*
  This is the most difficult part of the data gathering process. Since all processes are different, these questionnaires will not be uniform. Just be sure to address all five dimensions of service quality. As with the customer and staff surveys about external products, include five or six question/statements in each dimension.

- *Match frequent users with services and products.*
  It is productive to have only persons with qualified opinions about the service in question participate in the research. Don't ask people who don't use the purchasing department to give an opinion about it. Make sure that those you ask have enough knowledge to be helpful.

Here's an example of how data gathered in this process can be used.

A service improvement team had been selected to deal with the fact that the hiring process in the bank was ineffective. Surveys distributed to representatives of retail, commercial, trust, and administration revealed some serious gaps in the areas of "reliability" and "responsiveness." The team understood that the negative gaps documented the presence of problems in the bank's talent selection process.

As they were reviewing the data, the facilitator asked the senior member from retail to amplify why the ratings supplied by her people were so low.

"Well," she responded, "I can't speak for all of them, but from my perspective, it seems like there is a problem in responding to my calls. When I call at 8:00 to check on an interview, I always get the voice mail or somebody saying that all of you are tied up. How can we ever hire someone when you guys are never around. We have a lot of open requisitions and you can't seem to fill them."

"What do you mean we're not responsive?" asked the manager of the human resources department, obviously taking some umbrage at the suggestion. "When we get here in the morning, we have a team meeting about the events of the day, and then those involved in the hiring process begin their screenings for you. At 11:30, we break for lunch. When we get back, we start returning telephone calls in the order in which they are received. As far as not being able to fill your open recs, you should check with your people because they don't seem to be able to make a decision."

Oh, boy, was the donnybrook on after that. But does it sound familiar? We had a little problem here in understanding expectations. The manager of human resources thought the group was being efficient and responsive, a position definitely not shared by the head of retail banking. Returning a phone call after lunch just didn't cut it. The problem was that the definition of "responsiveness" differed from one department to another and that caused the communication problem.

This brief episode demonstrates the value of gathering data and spending the time to analyze it, diagnosing the real source of the problem. Instead of fighting on emotion, there was quantified evidence supplied by the customers of the human resources department that there was a problem. Because of some

T A B L E 8–4

Internal Customer Research
Human Resources: Education

Dimension	Retail	Commercial	Executive
Reliability	−1.777	−1.762	−1.646
Responsiveness	−1.412	−1.132	−1.543
Assurance	−0.761	−1.824	−1.460
Empathy	−0.613	−0.679	−0.844
Tangibles	−1.563	−1.846	−1.824

communication blocks and some territorial issues, human resources and retail were having trouble filling open positions. That had a negative impact on the ability of the branch network to serve the bank's customers.

We can only find and deal with issues like this one if we have good feedback from internal customers. The survey documents have the same format as those used for external services. The data from the completed questionnaires entered into the same computer models to ensure the consistency and validity of the output: ratings between the expectations and perceptions within the five service dimensions and a prioritization of their importance.

For reporting purposes, the results should be arrayed to provide the most effective information. If it is a straight ranking of the gaps and the priorities that is most useful, that's fine. But there are other ways to get a handle on precisely where the improvement opportunities reside. The data in Table 8–4 have been ordered to tell the human resources department (HR) how its educational services are received in the three major divisions of the bank: retail, commercial, and executive. Doing so allows them to see any variances between them. In this theoretical example, there is agreement that the people of human resources show genuine concern for the participants of their educational programs. Further, "reliability," "responsiveness," and "tangibles" are certainly problem areas that need to be addressed across the board. However, look at the difference between the gaps identified for "assurance" by the three organizational areas. The people on the commercial banking floor and the executive offices think that the people in HR are significantly lacking in knowledge and competency while the folks over in retail don't see it as quite as bad. Unlike the confrontation in the last story where response time was the issue, in this case it looks like HR is doing well with teller training while it may not be quite as skilled for other educational needs. In any event, having data like these allows the right questions to be asked. When we view it graphically, the difference becomes even more striking. Just

E X H I B I T   8–3

Internal Customer Research
Human Resources: Education

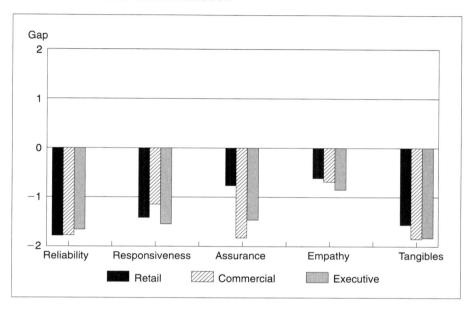

look at Exhibit 8–3, which shows the problem. We can see that the leadership and the commercial bankers are much less satisfied than the people in retail. It is evident that HR is doing something differently when dealing with different people. Instead of worrying about "empathy," there is little question that "assurance" is a problem due to this inconsistency. The director of human resources needs to meet with the leadership of the commercial bank and the senior executive staff to find out why they have rated it so low. When that is known, resources can be applied to improve the knowledge and the competency of the staff. Once that is complete, they can go on to "reliability."

THERE'S MORE . . .

Now that the bank has data from its internal and external customers, it can start the problem-solving process. It has to attack the root causes of those problems, not merely the symptoms. These root causes are found within the bank's culture and subcultures and in the things that people do each and every day. The next step is to find out why the customer results are the way they are. Remember,

T A B L E 8-5

Culture Survey

Examples of Culture Statements	Strongly Agree						Strongly Disagree
1. We spend a lot of time "fighting fires."	7	6	5	4	3	2	1
2. Everyone in the area knows who his or her customers are and understands their expectations.	7	6	5	4	3	2	1
3. The quality of the leadership in my area is very high.	7	6	5	4	3	2	1
4. I have everything I need to do my job well.	7	6	5	4	3	2	1
5. I understand how what I do relates to the output of the entire cash management process.	7	6	5	4	3	2	1
6. Education is available, but we don't always get the chance to take advantage of it.	7	6	5	4	3	2	1
7. We have effective staff meetings where we are expected to talk about process improvements.	7	6	5	4	3	2	1

the objective is to stay focused on meeting or exceeding their expectations, doing little more, doing no less. To achieve that objective, the bank has to identify any behavior that is causing it to fall short.

Everything that happens in the bank is interrelated in one way or another. In essence, it is an "open system" where "everything impacts everything else. Open systems interact with their environment, have interdependent parts, and are very complex . . . Change in one part of an open system begs change in other parts."[1] That explains why there are corresponding relationships between what people do every day, the culture that's in place, the cost of poor quality, and the service gaps. That makes finding the root causes of those gaps, in terms of human behavior, so vital. Just what are the people of the bank, from the top of the house to the bottom, doing to cause these gaps? What policies, procedures, and processes are in place that contribute to them? Those are the key questions that have to be answered. And it starts with culture. We need to find out how the people perceive the quality of life at the bank. Research about culture can be performed for the entire institution, a value chain, or a department, depending on what the bank wants to learn. To determine it, conduct a survey of everybody in the place using the kind of questions found in Table 8–5.

A complete culture survey has about 30 statements. They should be designed with great care and should relate to the attributes of culture such as communication, leadership, teamwork, empowerment, cooperation, and the like. In an annual exercise, questionnaires should be given to the entire workforce, so that both the overall culture and the various subcultures can be identified and examined. The consolidation of the responses begins to show why customers have indicated that there is room for improvement in the service the bank is providing. A few pages of a sample report are shown in Appendix 8–1. Responses have to be analyzed, classified, and summarized into an overall environmental analysis for the bank, but one which can be subdivided to add information that aids in the understanding of the various chains within it. This is a critical piece of the puzzle because it shows why there may be problems in the delivery of a particular service for the bank as a whole.

Individual answers have to be scrutinized carefully as we attempt to identify patterns and not isolated instances of unhappiness. The analysis requires some serious questioning, especially when there are opposing views in any one of the areas being studied; for example, what to do when one group says there is a good sense of mission and another one doesn't.

The results of the culture survey show that we are starting to get somewhere. We know that there are gaps in cash management because the bank's customers and staff have identified them (see Table 8–2). With the information provided in the culture survey, we can begin to see why they exist. We know that both customers and employees have identified "reliability" and "responsiveness": The culture survey revealed that the leadership of the area has not yet abandoned the command-and-control style. Communication is a problem, and the staff wants the officers to back off and let them do their jobs. They do not want to wait to get approval for something that will answer a customer's question. They believe that they are qualified to do it themselves. All they want is a chance to show what they can do.

These kinds of results may come as a surprise to management, but they have to be accepted positively and used as a basis for improvement. A defensive reaction will only serve to make things worse, especially in this example where command-and-control was already a problem. Everyone has to understand that culture correlates to customer service. However, it does not explain the actual reasons why service levels are what they are. We must determine that next.

Culture influences and is influenced by what happens on a daily basis. The bank has to try to explain its culture—to dissect it to see the forces that shape and are shaped by it. To do so, we have to find out exactly how people are spending their time. And what does that cost?

To isolate what happens, workforce activity research may be conducted to find out the activities of the entire staff complement. The goal is to find non–value-adding work, such as excessive support tasks, duplication of effort, fragmented delivery systems, repetitive corrections, and unnecessary effort. The only way that can be done is to survey the workforce. Everyone in the bank completes a detailed questionnaire on which they indicate their activities. To ensure consistency, everyone has to choose theirs from a standardized dictionary that contains all of the bank's tasks and functions whether they are found in multiple places or are unique to a particular one.

The data are entered into another specially designed software system that produces output consisting of:

- Analysis of individual jobs which provides the basis for role clarification dialogue between managers and the staff.
- Workforce distribution by activity which shows all of the people who engage in a specific activity, regardless of their functional area.
- Activity costs, rated from the most expensive to the least expensive, by department, value chain, and for the entire bank.

Table 8–6 is a sample of workforce activity research costs using cash management as our example. An actual report would have much greater detail, but this shows the point. In this case, just under 70 percent of the chain's resources are consumed by the 25 listed activities, and a pattern is really starting to emerge. When we think about adding value to customers, and if we look at the top 10 activities, the leadership of the bank can start to ask questions such as the following:

- Why is almost 10 percent of the budget, or $63,000, spent on "managing"?
- Why is another 7 percent spent handling "customer inquiries"? Further, why are 22 people necessary to take those calls? Unproductive at best.
- Why do "meetings" consume 5 percent? (I'm surprised it isn't more.)
- Why was $17,200 spent to handle "customer complaints"? And worse yet, why are there 12 people taking the calls?

The results of this research can then be related back to the culture survey where they reported that they wanted the officers to back off and to let them do their jobs. It shows that the greatest amount of time is spent "managing," which the people are confident is not needed to that degree. Now we can start to see the specific actions that have to take place to cure the ills in the cash management chain: first and foremost, management must let the troops go. That would give them the freedom to serve their customers and give management additional time to spend in a coaching, nurturing role, helping to improve any obstacles that might be in the way.

The organizational analysis is not complete. One more piece of information will make sure that everyone understands the need for change. The connection that follows is new. It is a totally different way of looking at financial information

TABLE 8-6

Workforce Activity Research Costs: High to Low

Activity	Total Activity (in thousands)	Percent of Budget	Cumulative Percentage	Number of People Reporting
Managing	$63.0	9.6%	9.6%	7
Customer inquiries	46.6	7.1	16.7	22
Collection work	43.8	6.7	23.4	6
Meetings attended	32.5	5.0	28.4	10
Client management	27.2	4.2	32.6	3
Transaction processing	24.9	3.8	36.4	5
Report preparation	20.8	3.2	39.6	9
Research	18.8	2.9	42.5	10
Clerical work	18.5	2.8	45.3	14
Complaints	17.2	2.6	47.9	12
Total activities—10	$313.3			
Inquiries (internal)	$14.5	2.2	50.1	11
Account reconciliation	13.0	2.0	52.1	5
File maintenance	11.3	1.7	53.8	3
Customer inquiries (written)	11.1	1.7	55.5	10
Data entry	11.0	1.7	57.2	2
Account opening	11.0	1.7	58.9	1
Planning	10.9	1.7	60.6	4
Internal consulting	9.6	1.5	62.1	3
Proofing reports	9.5	1.4	63.5	1
Statement rendering	8.0	1.2	64.7	3
Accounts receivable	7.4	1.1	65.8	2
Exception items	7.2	1.1	66.9	1
Application analysis	6.9	1.0	67.9	3
Photocopying	6.7	1.0	68.9	8
Training	6.5	1.0	69.9	6
Total activities—25	$457.9			

because it links behavior to expense. The dimensions of the cost of quality have been introduced before:

- Prevention
- Inspection and detection
- Failure
- Correction

Using the information from the workforce activity research, the bank can assign the activities that have been reported to these four dimensions. Some discretion is allowed here because one bank may classify an activity one way while a second bank selects another. The classification and selection process is to be determined by each individual bank, but once determined it must remain consistent for all departments and divisions. The objective of this research is to show the amount of expense incurred on activities that are either unnecessary or add no value to the customer or the bank.

This is where this improvement process, based on customer satisfaction, differs completely from cost cutting, downsizing, restructuring, and the rest. Instead of simply taking out bunches of people, the bank is able to eliminate the unnecessary work. Only by isolating what people do and challenging its value to customers can the improvement process be done. That is why looking at information in this context is so important. The leadership can see places where excess capacity or unneeded effort is expended and can make the appropriate changes.

The cost classification can be done by individual, department, service delivery system, or for the entire bank, depending on what the leadership wants to see. The sample in Table 8–7 breaks the cost from Table 8–6 into four dimensions for the entire cash management value chain. Let's check it out.

We know that we have accounted for almost 70 percent of the budget. (For your bank, the number to shoot for is 100 percent.) Table 8–7 shows how the budget was being spent. The results are somewhat shocking: Of the dollars spent, $458,000, 31.8 percent of them were incurred in "correction" activities. We need to make a distinction here. Whether the number is 31.8 percent or 25.9 percent makes little difference. What is important is that it is a big number, and it represents things that would not have to be done if everything had been done the right way the first time. Had that been the case in this example, the bank could have saved upwards of $145,000.

"Failure" costs amount to 15 percent of the total, which brings the aggregate cost of poor quality to 46.8 percent, half again as much as the 30 percent that has been used for illustrative purposes throughout *The Banking Revolution.* Only 34.3 percent is being spent on "prevention" with another 18.9 percent for "inspection and detection." The message? Extrapolating the reported cost to the full budget, only 53.2 percent is needed to process 100 percent of the transactions coming to the cash management area. By doing what the customer wants in a way that it is wanted, the bank could save $225,000 in this department alone.

With the numbers displayed like this, the workforce can see the economic consequence of the way they spend their time, which makes it easy to question why they spend it that way. This is where you find the root causes: in whatever activity, task, or function that makes people spend their time in "failure" and "correction." With this information, everyone can ask, "Hey, why are we doing

TABLE 8–7

The Cost of Quality

Activity	Total Activity Dollars (in thousands)	Percent of Budget	Prevention	Inspection/ Detection	Failure	Correction
Managing	$63.0	9.6	$15.75	$15.75	$15.75	$15.75
Customer inquiries	46.6	7.1			23.30	23.30
Collection work	43.8	6.7				43.8
Meetings attended	32.5	5.0	8.12	8.12	8.13	8.13
Client management	27.2	4.2	27.20			
Transaction processing	24.9	3.8	24.90			
Report preparation	20.8	3.2		20.80		
Research	18.8	2.9		18.80		
Clerical work	18.5	2.8	18.50			
Complaints	17.2	2.6			8.60	8.60
Total activities—10	$313.3	47.9	$94.47	$63.47	$55.78	$99.58
Inquiries (internal)	$14.5	2.2			$7.25	$7.25
Account reconciliation	13.0	2.0				13.00
File maintenance	11.3	1.7	5.65			5.65
Customer inquiries (written)	11.1	1.7			5.55	5.55
Data entry	11.0	1.7	11.00			
Account opening	11.0	1.7	11.00			
Planning	10.9	1.7	10.90			
Internal consulting	9.6	1.5	9.60			
Proofing reports	9.5	1.4		9.5		
Statement rendering	8.0	1.2	8.00			
Accounts receivable	7.4	1.1				7.40
Exception items	7.2	1.1				7.20
Application analysis	6.9	1.0		6.90		
Photocopying	6.7	1.0		6.70		
Training	6.5	1.0	6.50			
Total activities—10	$457.9	69.9%	$157.12	$86.57	$68.58	$145.63
Percentage	100.0		34.3	18.9	15.0	31.8

that?" But make it fun as you do. Be positive and encouraging even if the answer is, "Well, gee, I guess it's because we have always done it that way" or "I really don't know."

In the case of cash management, here is the relationship that the data have established:

- Service quality gaps are large.
- The culture smacks of command and control.
- People are involved in activities that do not add any value.
- The cost of poor quality is high.

That is the correlation between the cost of poor quality, as represented by the behavior of the staff, and the size of the gaps between customer expectations and perceptions. The larger the cost of poor quality, the larger the service gaps. Conversely, the smaller the cost of poor quality, the smaller the service gaps. The task is to eliminate the errors and mistakes, effectively changing the behavior so that the effort currently expended in failure and correction can be applied to prevention. That results in better service and reduced cost. It is a fundamental of the revolution: equating customer attitudes, the behavior of the workforce, and cost—and then, most important, doing something about it.

Looking at the bank this way, even with the storms of environmental change swirling around, allows the leadership and the people to really understand what's going on and why. Moreover, in special situations like mergers, it allows them to see where there is true duplication of effort between the two organizations and to design and position the resulting one to be better able to service customers.

Having been in merger and acquisition activity for several years, it would have been great to have information like this about our bank's delivery system and that of the bank we were acquiring. As we sought to drive out duplicated functions and costs, I am sure that at times we cut things that were of value to customers. I know that we never gave a thought to eliminating mistakes and the resulting correction activities, but that's where the gold is.

"X" MARKS THE SPOT

The key to the treasure is understanding what the people of the bank are doing and why they are doing it. It is continually asking the question, "What value does your customer receive from what you are doing?" It makes no difference whether it is an internal or an external customer. If you are doing something that nobody wants, don't do it any more. It's that simple.

There are some great books describing the elements of reengineering and other cost management techniques, but what I am suggesting is a completely different way to get at financial performance improvement. Start with customers to understand their opinions about the banking experience and work back through the organization to determine the institutional behavior that has caused it. When you do, all of these corrective activities will become very apparent and subject to serious question.

Incorporating analysis like this into the company's style goes a long way toward making the necessary behavioral and cultural change. That has been one of our main themes from the outset, changing the culture to be more customer-focused and with a long-term view. This means opening lines of communication throughout the bank, working collaboratively to understand what customers want and what the people are being asked to do, and cooperating on changing the way in which their work is done. It also means empowering people to make decisions in the service of their customers and holding them accountable for those decisions; means eliminating entitlement where people think that they are owed a living for just showing up every day; and means teamwork in the truest sense of the word. In other words, now that we have these unique data, we can continue to bash the bureaucracy.

Changing the culture begins by telling everyone the results of the data collection process. If the people have taken the time to tell the leadership what they think about the bank and its processes, they are owed a report. They know what is going on anyway, but the gesture is important. It tells them that their input has value, that they count, and that something is going to be done with it. I can remember when all of us were interviewed in an employee satisfaction survey in the late 1970s. We knew that the results were in and had been compiled for management, but we never heard anything about it. Paranoia ran high as the rumor mill churned out story after story about the supposed outcome and the punishment that was to be meted out. Morale tumbled like a rock going downhill. What management did not understand was that even bad news represented only the places where we thought we could get better. Who better to make that judgment? We were the people who knew because we worked with each other and with our customers every day. But management saw the results and apparently took them personally because they were never made public. That has to be avoided at all costs.

> Surveys require long-term improvement focus—applicable shifts in employee perception requires years of effort. Management must first commit to publishing the results—no matter what! Committing to act on the feedback and [to] resolve employee concerns follows.
>
> John W. Rosenblum, chair of business administration at the University of Virginia, describes employee satisfaction surveys as "implicit contracts" whose powerful questions heighten employees' expectations. A firm's failure to live up to its part of the bargain can have dramatic negative impact on morale.[2]

The most critical element of the revolution is unlocking the potential of the people of the bank, effectively eliminating the burdensome structure and debilitating style that have shackled them. The word that describes it best is "empowerment." It is an overused term these days, but it is exactly what is needed. For the bank it cannot be a buzzword or a fad because it is the key to being competitive. People have to feel free enough to make the decisions and to take the actions that they believe they must in the service of their customers.

There are various definitions of *empowerment:*

- "To give authority to authorize."
- "We have an underlying purpose . . . We have to commit to achieving that purpose, now."[3]
- "The willing and open transfer of resources and power from one level of an organization to another."[4]
- Empowerment means sharing power, increasing autonomy, throughout the organization. It means giving everyone—instead of just people in certain positions and certain job titles—the legitimate right to make judgments, form conclusions, reach decisions, and then act.[5]

If the bank really wants to improve, it has to give its people the resources they need to do their jobs and the freedom to do them. As we saw in our cash management example, it is management exchanging its command-and-control style for servant leadership. However, as that process begins, some pitfalls need to be understood. First, it is highly unlikely that the leadership of the bank can simply let go of its power and transfer it to the people who work for them. The inability to "let go" is a cultural problem that manifests itself in the inability to serve. It is a matter of style.

Decisions in the bank have been made at the top for so long that this behavior is part of the culture: Always look to the corner office when a choice has to be made. Because of that, I am not going to suggest that the leadership walk into the bank in the morning, gather the troops, and say, "OK, gang, you're empowered. We'll be here if you need us." Neither group could handle such an abrupt change. This has to be a long-term learning process for both the leadership and those who would follow.

Leadership have the data about what's going on. Sit down with the staff and explain it. Tell references "the staff" that there are some opportunities to improve and that together you are going to try a new style to take advantage of them, one where they will have the freedom to act in the service of their customers. Go about it slowly. Agree with them about the approach or the task at hand and about their accountabilities, exactly what they can do and what they can't. How much change can the staff make? Who will make what decisions?

As these choices are being made, remember the severity of the service gaps, the culture that you want, and the cost of poor quality. Document the agreements that you reach and make them part of your formal position descriptions. Just as you ask your customers about what they expect, come to agreement with the staff about what you, and they, expect. Set some targets and help them along.

Empowerment without those boundaries can result in chaos. Just ask the people at Barings Bank and at Daiwa Bank about their derivative problems. Having clear boundaries precludes people from running all over the bank unchecked, doing whatever they please, and tripping over one another. Establish the limits before you let them go. As you do, make sure that there are checkpoints along the way where they can tell you about their progress. Then, as all of you get comfortable, give them more empowerment. Good two-way communication is the key. It eliminates the problem of staff stepping over their boundaries and having to be counseled about it. Give them a chance and watch them grow, but this is where it gets tricky for the leadership. Saying that they are empowered without a corresponding change in leadership style won't produce the results that can be achieved. That is what held the cash management people back.

Educators William Smitley and David Scott call this "extrinsic empowerment" because it is offered to the people and is not really their idea. On the other hand, intrinsic empowerment means that you want to be freed from your compartment and to be accountable for your actions. It is something that you want to do. Smitley and Scott give us four suggestions by which to make the transition from extrinsic to intrinsic empowerment.[6]

First, starting with the CEO, the people of the bank must be educated not only about their jobs, but also about the new leadership style and the desired cultural environment. It will take time away from the immediacy of the task at hand for formal training and informal coaching, but it is a vital part of making the change. Everyone has to learn about the new approach and the overall goal of the change and how they can fit into and prosper in the new organization.

The second ingredient is the development of an atmosphere of trust and confidence, rather than one of resentment and fear. This is a tough one, especially if there has been downsizing at the bank. It is very difficult to establish trust once it has been violated, and a variety of reasons explain why the bond has been broken.

- A friend was a victim of a cost-cutting program when he had been assured that he would survive.
- You were promised a position, and someone else got it.
- The leadership says that the bank will focus on customers, but it doesn't.

It all comes down to keeping your word, even if the news is bad. Once that fails to happen, the trust factor is gone along with morale and motivation.

Third, there must be freedom of information instead of the leadership hanging onto it as a source of power. As the data from customers and employees come in, the people who need it should have it; otherwise they cannot analyze their work flows to make the improvements that their customers say will make the service better. And, because the employees have shared their thoughts about the situation, the leadership is obligated to share that information with them.

The last suggestion has to do with motivation. People do their best when they feel appreciated. From top to bottom in the organization, they need to understand how they are contributing to the success of the organization and to that of their own delivery system. This is true regardless of the level of the organization in which people find themselves.

We need a caveat here. Not everyone wants to be empowered. Some people want to express their entrepreneurial spirit and cannot wait to get going. They have made the decision to learn and to be responsible for their own actions. These are the people who bash bureaucracy, the "state of mind . . . not to take responsibility for what is happening. Other people are the problem."[7]

However, other people like to be told what to do and to be supervised. That's OK, but the leader has to be aware of it and the consequences on his or her time. Still, these people should at least be given the opportunity. If they choose not to take advantage of it, that's fine. In essence, though, they have made an empowered decision about their own work and their future. Once, however, they see others enjoying their freedom, they may have a change of heart.

It is interesting to see that as the empowerment process plays out, the workforce spends less time in "failure" and "correction," and more in *kaizen* as they see new ways to get the work customers want done right the first time. Working together, staff can make use of the data to see the interrelationships of behavior and service gaps, and can work to close them. That allows the leadership more time for scouting what's "out there" and planning for the future.

THE OPPONENT

We need to be very realistic here. Bashing the bureaucracy is exactly what has to happen because your bank must be agile to compete in the new environment. The advances of technology and the new competition demand it. The key, however, is empowerment, but every banker in the country faces a formidable and dangerous opponent called entitlement: a mind-set where we give people what they expect even if their performance does not warrant it and we do not hold them accountable for carrying out their responsibilities.[8]

From Chapter 3, we know that for roughly 30 years after World War II, U.S. companies made so much money and had so little competition that quality did not matter. This environment also created an attitude whereby people expected to be promoted, to get a raise every year, and to be awarded a bonus just because they came to work every day, not because of their work effort and contribution. People began to take those things for granted, and there are a lot of them still around who think that way.

Starting in the executive suite and working all the way down, performance has not been graded accurately and fairly, if at all, principally, because we are afraid to hurt someone else's feelings. I have watched it happen as friends in the bank were asked to fill out their own annual evaluations for their bosses to sign. I never understood how that would do any good, because I am sure that there were things that could have been done better or differently. What the self-evaluations did was send a message that employees could get a 10 percent raise every year and a tidy bonus if they did not get into too much trouble and accomplished the objectives they had set for themselves. Yes, employees were also at fault for not asking bosses to grade them, but that flew in the face of the culture and they certainly were not about to do that.

Seldom was there coaching about behavior, which meant obviously that whatever was going on was OK. Oh, there might have been some hollering when something really went bad, but most of the time, a great deal of effort was aimed at keeping the peace. That's the legacy of the 1950s and 1960s; many people in the bank still believe in it. "The organization exists to take care of me," is the thinking, not "I had better produce so I get a raise and don't get fired." These kinds of people don't want to be empowered; they want to stay secure in their jobs. That means that they won't take a risk, won't venture too far from the gates of the fort, and at the first sign of trouble, will scurry back inside where it is familiar and comfortable.

People used to come to the bank as a career because they thought it was a safe place. Even with the cost cutting of the 1980s, it's still fairly sheltered because profits are high and there is no reason to rock the boat. But remember the disintermediation that's going on, the advances of the competition, and the estimates that 40 percent of all commerce will be done on the Internet by the year 2005. Remember too the parable of the boiled frog: The water in the pot may be warming up. So, how can we recognize entitlement? Here are some signs that indicate that the temperature of the water is rising and that entitlement is creeping in:

- Informal tenure for everyone.
- An appraisal system that has no real impact.
- A promotion system that doesn't reflect individual merit.

- An emphasis on precedent.
- Lots and lots of rules.
- Lots and lots of paper.
- A compensation system that doesn't reflect what people do.
- Committees with no authority.
- Rewards for fine-tuners and punishment for innovators.
- A formal hierarchy in which differences in power dictate permissible behavior.
- Talk about pushing power down without real empowerment or delegation.
- Layers of people whose jobs are making sure no mistakes are being made.[9]

There's a wake-up call. Start looking around the bank. If it is any or all of these symptoms, there is an entitlement problem. How big or small? That's up to you to decide. Stick your toe in the water and see for yourself. If there are a lot of rules and a lot of people and processes in place to make sure that those rules don't get broken and lots of paper is being shuffled from one desk to another as people play "CYA" and other games, it is a real good sign that the front burner is on, the water's starting to bubble, and frog's legs are on the menu.

It is just good business sense to empower people and to expect them to take risks and to be innovative. Whether or not they are held accountable for their actions will make or break the bank. We have established that the world is a faster, more competitive place, which means that the bank can't afford to have people hanging around who aren't pulling their own weight. Technology is bringing companies like Bank of America into the backyards of even the smallest communities. Charles Schwab provides access to the stock market over the wire wherever and whenever you want. With all that, the sheer pace of business means that there isn't time to run things up and down the hierarchy or to watch over people as we seek to make sure that no mistakes are made. It makes empowerment a necessity, even with the obstacle of entitlement. But there is another powerful reason for it as well.

On August 29, 1995, *The Plain Dealer* contained articles with the following headlines:

CHASE AND CHEMICAL TO MERGE

National City Becomes 17TH LARGEST BANK WITH PURCHASE

HUNTINGTON BANK PLANS FLORIDA DEAL

CINCINNATI'S FIFTH THIRD BUYS BANK IN KENTUCKY

Four deals, all made over the same weekend, are an indication of things to come as Merger Mania II gets into full swing. How well the people of the bank are performing may mean the difference between whether they have a job or not. Merger Mania II will be a formidable foe for entitlement as the aggressive acquirers expect their people to perform. At least that is what we are being told.

The Chase-Chemical deal sent the banking community a powerful message. At the press conference announcing this biggest banking merger in the history of the United States, Walter Shipley, chairman and CEO of Chase Manhattan, said that a significant number of jobs would be lost, about 12,000 worldwide. He said that it would be like merging the New York Giants and the New York Jets: He plans to take only the best players from both teams and go to the Super Bowl. Some of the starters from both teams would, by definition, become reserves on the new team. Some of the reserves on the old team would not be picked to be on the new one. The message from statements like Shipley's is that even the biggest banks in the country have an emerging antientitlement spirit, and that people who don't perform will not be picked for the new team. That puts pressure on the workforce to want to change and to become empowered when the opportunity is presented. Chase-Chemical is not a combination, Shipley asserted, with room for marginal performers.

It is entirely possible that this could be politically correct rhetoric—what the leadership thinks the world wants to hear. Further, there is also the potential that the actual integration of the two banks will not play out this way. Still, they are the fourth and sixth largest banks in the country, and the chairman is saying that only the brightest and the best will survive. That means that people at all levels are under the microscope.

The message: As the bank determines strategies, critical success factors, value disciplines, and action plans, it has to do one more thing. It must make sure that the people are aware of their responsibilities and are accountable for their actions. They have to know what is expected of them and to be free to achieve great things. Empowerment and accountability are in; entitlement is out.

THE NOAH PRINCIPLE

"You mean that promotions and raises should be based on performance and contribution to achieving the bank's vision?" You betcha. That's another requisite of the revolution. Whether it is the CEO who is leading the planning process, the marketing department that is conducting customer research, or the people in data processing who are experimenting in new technologies in response to a consumer request, everyone in the bank has to know:

- What he or she is responsible for.
- The boundaries within which they can work.
- The measures that will be used to see how they are doing.
- The rewards that will be given when they achieve their objectives.

Gone are the days when people get raises regardless of how well the bank does.

> It may be difficult to work up much sympathy for anyone who gets paid a
> million or two a year. And, in 1995, without question, U.S. chief executives
> will bring home more money than ever before. But finally, corner office
> denizens are starting to learn a lesson: When they fail to deliver the goods for
> shareholders, their own paychecks suffer.
>
> There could be no starker evidence than that contained in Banker's Trust
> New York Corp's proxy statement. Stung by a host of derivative debacles,
> Chairman Charles S. Sanford Jr. saw his pay package fall by 57 percent to
> $3.95 million in 1994. The reason: Banker's Trust stock languished in the mar-
> ket, as return-on-equity was sliced nearly in half, to 13.5 percent last year.[10]

But that is not the least of Sanford's worries now that the allegations of racketeering have been made by Proctor & Gamble. In any event, $3.95 million is a
lot of money, but the action at Banker's Trust may be an indication of a new
mood of accountability. It looks like the concept of pay for performance may be
gaining in popularity. The board of directors has to take an active role in holding the CEO and other executive officers accountable for the bank's performance and for compensating them accordingly. If entitlement has crept into the
boardroom, there is trouble ahead. Making the change has to start at the top. If
it doesn't start there, it isn't going to work because the workforce will perceive
the practice as unfair, which is exactly what it would be.

There cannot be things such as "no-cut" contracts where people get paid
regardless of how well they perform. That's been one of the big problems, but
that's also the essence of entitlement. What is meant by "accountable"? Being
accountable is:

> an attitude of continually asking "What can I do to rise above my circum-
> stances and achieve the results I desire?" . . . It requires a level of ownership
> that includes making, keeping, and proactively answering for personal com-
> mitments. It is a perspective that embraces both current and future efforts
> rather than reactive and historical explanations.[11]

Accountability means that we own our circumstances, and we make it or
we don't based on our actions. In its truest sense, it is like being in business for
yourself where the amount you make depends on what you produce for your
clients. It can be scary at times, but I can assure you that it keeps one motivated
to find customers and to do work that they like.

When one is truly accountable, no one else can take the blame or the
credit. It's just you and the people you serve. In a large organization, however,
it is unlikely that things will ever happen this way because there are few, if any,
services that are delivered to external customers by only one person. Value
chains contain many people. Therefore, the whole team is accountable externally;

internally, the members of the team are accountable to each other. That is why knowing the expectations of the next person in the chain is so important. But we have seen that mistakes and errors do reach customers; after all, 25 percent of us change banks every year because of them. Fingers get pointed and blame is assigned, but seldom does anyone step up and say, "This kind of stuff is going to continue unless we make some changes around here." Command-and-control and the desire to look good prevent it. However, that is exactly what is needed.

How do we get people to be accountable? The first step is to tell them that they have to be. Have that dialogue with them about their responsibilities, boundaries, deadlines, measures, and rewards. Work with them to clarify their questions and concerns. Then, help them along. As with empowerment, you can't walk into the office one day and say, "OK, gang, you are now accountable. See you later." That would be irresponsible. Rather, there has to be an emphasis on coaching the behavior that you want, and that will require some change in your own style. It is explanations of what is to be done, not just giving orders. The required change, though, has to be definite.

> Gradual change cannot work. There has to be a total break with the past, however traumatic it may be. This means that people cannot report to both their old boss and their new coach, conductor, or team leader. And, their rewards, their compensation, their appraisals, and their promotions must be *totally dependent on their performance* in their new roles on their new teams. But this is so unpopular that the temptation to compromise is always great. [italics added][12]

For the transition to work, the leadership has to break the traditional thought process. Everyone has to see the current situation as it really is. That is the reason for gathering data about the attitudes of customers and the staff. The results of the data have to be accepted and action plans have to be developed to make the changes in the organization that will narrow those service gaps. That is the break that Drucker refers to. There can be no ostrich syndrome. There has been too much of that already.

When there is accountability, people are free to get together to solve the problem or to make the improvement. They can cross organizational lines at will and can work with the appropriate people regardless of rank or title. They want to do this because they want to provide good service for their customers and because that is what they are paid to do. They have all the data they need so the task becomes the elimination of the root causes of the problems. They have to keep asking, "Why does this keep happening?" and "What can we do about it?"

In the words of Lou Gerstner, chief executive of IBM, "We need to adopt that legendary Noah principle: no more prizes for predicting rain. Prizes only for building arks."[13] Where we see something wrong, it is incumbent upon us to

fix it. Just talking about it does not make it anymore. Get the right people together and fix the process. As Noah found out, being empowered and accountable was OK, but it was the action of building the boat that really mattered. It
was the leader, the patriarch, who spurred the rest of the family to work. It is
the same today.

For the organization as a whole and for all the individuals within it, there
will be no purpose, no energy, no accountabilities, and no growth unless the
leadership makes that expectation very clear. Without it, mediocrity will reign
supreme and the stock price will follow suit. Furthermore, the ability of the
bank to attract new, talented people will be hampered because such people
don't want to work in an ordinary place these days. The new generation in this
country, which is to crucial to the bank's future, wants to be accountable and to
make a difference. Their motives are different from those of their grandparents.
Security is important, to be sure, but not at the expense of wearing a gray-flan-
nel suit into the bureaucracy every day. They have looked at bureaucracy and
don't want any part of it. To get the most talented people, which is what the
bank needs, there will have to be some more organizational change. How serious is this problem? It deserves prompt attention.

In February 1995, *Fortune* published an article titled "Kissing Off Corporate America." It told the stories of business school graduates who had entered
and then dropped out of corporate life in the United States. It contained some
interesting statistics:

- Of 1,000 adults surveyed by Opinion Research Corp., 1 percent
  responded that they would choose to be corporate managers.
- In 1990, 25 percent of Columbia University's graduating MBAs went to
  work at large manufacturing companies; in 1994, 13 percent did.
- In 1989, 70 percent of Stanford University's MBAs joined large
  companies; in 1994 about 50 percent did.
- It may be difficult for recruiters from large organizations arriving at the
  Kellogg School at Northwestern University to find enough interested
  students to fill a day's slate of interviews.[14]

To provide the best possible service, the bank has to have great people. Not
only is there new competition for customers, but also there is a battle for talent.
If customers don't find what they want at First National, they will simply go
somewhere else. Here are some things to be avoided:

What the New Generation Hates

The best bureaucrats, not the best performers, are more likely to get
ahead.

It's too easy to get pigeonholed or stuck in a dead-end job with no way out.

It takes too long to get enough responsibility, authority, and rewards.

There's not enough flexibility about where and when you work.

Top managers say they want risk takers, but they don't.[15]

Quite a dilemma, but it is another of the new realities. It is apparent that command and control won't work any more. It can be practiced, but a lot of people are not going to put up with it. They want an entrepreneurial model. They want the freedom to do their jobs, to be accountable for the outcome, and to be rewarded accordingly. That's the new workforce contract and it will require teamwork.

BETWEEN THE LINES

Research has shown that the concentrated efforts of committed groups of people produce far better results than individuals can working alone. There are many benefits to be gained from teamwork, but the preeminent ones are better thought processes and faster response time. With teams, there are fewer organizational lines to fight through, both up and down as well as sideways. Empowered, accountable people, working together toward a common goal, are able to provide the expected service to their customers and to make organizational improvements rather than having to expend energy working through the bureaucracy to get something done. They come together in natural working circumstances instead of being compartmentalized and stifled in their jobs. Quality and productivity improve. Morale increases, as people realize that they are making a real contribution. Then, when rewarded for that effort, they provide even better service. The organization flattens out with all of it adding to ever-increasing returns to the bottom line.

Let's start with a definition:

A team is a small number of people with complementary skills who are committed to a common purpose, performance goals, and approach for which they hold themselves mutually accountable.[16]

The literature says a great deal about the value of teamwork, extolling the successes of companies like Motorola, FedEx, Ford Motor, Texas Instruments, and Hewlett-Packard, among others, but the potential of their worth is not being maximized.

The Center for Effective Organizations at the University of Southern California recently conducted a study of Fortune 1000 companies showing that 68 percent use self-managed or high performance teams. Sounds like a lot—but the study also shows that only 10 percent of workers are in such teams, hardly a number betokening a managerial revolution.[17]

Our independent, pioneering spirit being what it is, and recognizing the influence of 100 years of corporate bureaucracy on our behavior, it is hard to get people to perform as a team:

- We all bring different mind-sets to the task at hand.
- Our egos often don't subjugate themselves for the good of the group.
- We may find that we simply don't like some of the other people in the room.
- Some of us work better alone.
- There are some tasks and functions that do not require a team of people to do them.
- Some of us would rather be productive than to sit in a team meeting, bored to tears and doodling on a legal pad.

As with the other concepts presented in *The Banking Revolution,* teamwork is an attitude that manifests itself in organizational behavior. Even if there are tasks and functions that can be carried out by one person, that does not mean that the organizational attitude precludes being part of the team. Remember the definition: a common purpose with goals, an approach, and accountability. What distinguishes the different types of teams is the degree of dependency, but attitude is the key.

What we need to do is establish an organizational environment that fosters teamwork and lets various kinds of teams assemble when it is the right time and circumstance. That is what most people miss. It is creating a climate where people like and are encouraged to collaborate on projects and tasks. It is one where there is a great deal of cooperation and communication like we see at Microsoft and other such "product leaders." It is a mood, an attitude, that says that the people of the organization can work together in whatever way is necessary in the service of their customers. The secret? To have a culture where teamwork is the expectation and to know when to form specific working teams.

To do that, the leadership has to understand that different kinds of teams work for different purposes. Drucker suggests that there are three types, each of which has a different structure, behavioral expectation, strengths, vulnerabilities, requirements, and purposes.[18] First, there is the baseball team concept in which players are part of a team, but they do not play as a team. It is the same idea that most business people have about teamwork; they may say "Good morning" to each other as they get on the elevator, but that is about as far as it goes.

In baseball, the shortstop doesn't help the pitcher by telling what to throw. The catcher does that, and none of us ever got any help when we went up to bat except for some verbal encouragement. There are specific roles that people are asked to play, but as they perform their tasks, they do them alone. But there can be a great deal of self-satisfaction when what you do helps the next person do his or her job. It is that encouragement and support that makes you want to do your best in the service of your internal customer.

The baseball concept relies upon the individual, though, for communicating expectations. The first baseman has to tell the other infielders where he wants them to throw the ball. As such, it permits breakdowns in those kinds of communications where people in product development design a new product, coordinate with operations to produce it, and fail to get the input of marketing, which might just tell them that they are wasting their time. The "football concept" keeps that from happening. On a football team, people have fixed positions, much as they do in the symphony orchestra and for that matter, on a baseball team. The difference is the degree to which each one is dependent upon the others in pursuit of the objective, whether it is playing the symphony as Beethoven wished or following the diagram in the playbook correctly and scoring a touchdown.

Under this concept, there is an expectation that each player is skilled and will play up to the best of his or her abilities. All have to do their jobs, or the team won't be successful. In baseball, the second baseman can make some errors, but if the pitcher throws a no-hitter, the team can still win. Under the football concept, the dependency is greater. The wide receiver can run the pass route perfectly, with the offensive line keeping the defense away. But if the quarterback doesn't throw the ball correctly, all that work will be for nought. The same thing happens if the receiver drops the ball or if the defensive end eludes his blocker and sacks the quarterback. Plays are drawn up for 11 people to execute, and all of them must carry out their assignments to complete the pass.

In the football concept, there has to be a great deal of communication and coordination. Plays have to be timed, people have to know where they are going to be, and then they have to execute. Before each play, they have a meeting in the huddle where the leader explains what they are going to do, but then it is up to each member of the team to carry out his specific responsibilities. It's the same in business. Using this concept, product development, operations, and marketing get together to plan and implement new service ideas. There is increased dependency, but each group has to use its unique skills and talents to do its specific job. It is not like the "tennis doubles concept."

When playing doubles, there is complete dependency upon one another if the team is to be successful. It's like the 4×100 meter relay team. Each person has to run as fast as he or she can and then execute the handoff perfectly. A split second can spell the difference between winning and coming in second. In tennis doubles, if you don't hit the shot, your partner had better hustle to try to get it. Each of us has a general area that we are supposed to cover, but that doesn't mean that we stay planted there. We should be all over the court as we help each other. There is a great deal of communication on a doubles court about how the ball will be served and "I've got it." It is like beach volleyball where you dive face first into the sand to dig the ball out, doing whatever it takes to keep it alive.

In business, tennis doubles isn't played very much. It would be the self-directed work team in which only 10 percent of the people in the University of Southern California survey participate. These kinds of teams have a degree of reliance and communication that differentiates them. In baseball, the left fielder doesn't have to talk to the first baseman if he or she doesn't want to. In football, the defensive back doesn't have to explain his expectations to the left guard. But, in tennis doubles, the two players need to have a continuing stream of conversation. There isn't much structure either. That is the kind of environment that is needed in the bank.

> I was talking with a friend the other day about life at the bank. "Oh, it's still there," she said with a sigh. "We're still consolidating and cutting back at the expense of customer service. And management wants earnings to be high for the analysts, so we can't get what we need to service our customers.
>
> "They have a short-term view, and there's really no loyalty anymore. Everyone is pretty much out for himself. I really don't know why anyone would want about work in a big company anymore."

That seems to tell the story of why teamwork doesn't happen. When people are out to protect themselves, they won't commit to a common goal. It gets back to trust and a true sense that the organization respects the people who work within it and can go forward together. If people can't trust each other, they will not give their best to the job. They will be more concerned about themselves than they will about the good of the team.

The essential elements for teamwork to happen are the environment and culture. Having the concept of servant leadership firmly in place can really assist as the senior people help and nurture the others to become great performers. A true sense of teamwork cannot happen without it.

The first task is the establishment of the climate. We have talked about that before. Second, we have to know the kind of team to use and when it is appropriate to use it. The study at USC helps again because it identified the five most common types of teams.[19] First, there are quality circles, or groups of working people who get together to talk about problems in the workplace. The study noted that 65 percent of the respondents use quality circles, a bit less than was reported in 1987. Perhaps they are being replaced by more effective types. The problem with quality circles is twofold. First, they are departmental or functional, which means only that they cannot influence activities farther down the value chain. Second, quality circles do not have customer-focused goals or measures, so they could never hope to analyze and diagnose issues deeply enough to get to the root causes of any service problems. Quality circles did help companies solve some of the more superficial quality matters, but for the most part their activity was limited.

The second type of team is a management team, a crucial element. The members of these teams have a chance to make the others work. They contain the sponsors of the bank's various value chains and the key officers who work within them. They also have the people who are in charge of key areas such as data processing, marketing, planning, and other functional areas, which gives all areas of the bank the opportunity and the forum in which to have their say. It is hoped that management teams have the big picture in mind and can work together to coordinate and help the people who work for them interface with one another. This is the quality council, the management committee, and most of the other committees in the bank. The problem is getting the people to work together.

There may be different and competing agendas going on; there may not be a common goal; ego may be getting in the way; standards of performance may be lacking as debate is based on emotion, not facts; and a sense of organizational provincialism may characterize management teams. These types of things have to be eliminated, or at least overcome, as the bank seeks to create its new culture. It also helps those at lower levels to mold their behavior; if they see collaboration and a sense of partnership at the top, they will be more likely to incorporate those characteristics into their own styles. Here is another "baseball" team, but at the very least management teams should be migrating toward the "football concept."

Third, there are problem-solving teams. These are cross-functional teams, which is a popular concept these days even though the USC study suggests that they don't involve many people. A problem-solving team is assembled to work on closing the gaps between the expectations and perceptions of the bank's customers. The players on these teams are the people within the value chain who can get things done regardless of their rank or title. They see the matter clearly, realize that they can make a demonstrable difference, and have the people skills and wisdom to make it happen.

Even with problem-solving teams, some work is required to make them real teams. As they begin their work, the presence of individuality indicates that not all team members understand that they are all accountable for the results of their work. The problem solvers are diplomatic, creative, responsible, energetic folks who come together to make improvements, but they may not be quite sure why they are there. Once, however, they see the service gaps and the data supplied by the workforce, they get the idea and soon become committed to solving the problem. They learn the value of *kaizen* and they work hard at it.

Once the specific assignment has been completed, the problem-solving team may disband, getting together once each quarter to review the latest rounds of survey data. If issues arise again, the members may meet more frequently, but the team does not take on a life of its own. Problem-solving teams demonstrate the "football concept" because the members bring their expertise to the table, communicate effectively with each other, and realize that without the help of others the hope of victory is nil.

It is possible that problem-solving teams may have another fate. They may transform into work teams and take on ownership of the process in question. This means that not only are they working to close any service gaps that may appear, but also they are responsible for putting the product in customers' hands on a daily basis. They have a common goal, a solid approach for achieving it, an understanding that all of them are accountable, and they live and breathe continuous improvement every day.

The people of a branch could also be a work team. So could the people in the credit department if there is a reluctance to split it up among the lending value chains. It could be the accounts payable staff and the people from purchasing who come together to become the procurement value chain. It could also be the people from the mail room who work together to make sure that deliveries are on time.

When empowered, all of them can do surveys and organize the way in which their work will be done to meet their customers' expectations. Basically, the work teams are responsible for the entire function, carrying it out each and every day, measuring their performance against their standards, and knowing that a common reward awaits. Tennis doubles for sure in this case as each team member understands that he or she has to work closely with others to ensure that there is no failure in customer service.

The last kind of team, the virtual team, is a variation of the problem-solving team and the work team. It is comprised of the people involved in the delivery of service to the bank's customers, but when problems or opportunities occur, people from other areas can be brought onboard. It is like a virtual corporation where specialists are asked to handle matters outside the experience and know-how of the regular members. It could be that a person from data processing might be needed to fix a teller terminal. Maybe someone from marketing has to be brought in to create a special retail advertisement. Perhaps someone from cost accounting is needed to recalculate a price. Virtual teams are football teams where the punter comes in when it is fourth-and-twelve or when the placekicker comes out to kick the game winner.

Whether it is a management team, a problem-solving team, a work team, or a virtual team, the ideal is to be a "high-performance" team.[20] These are real teams, but with a difference. The members are deeply committed to achieving great results for the bank and truly wanting to help each other grow and be successful. These desires become the beacon that guides all thought and action because they put the welfare of the others before their own, knowing that the team will be even more successful because of it. To have high-performance teams, the bank needs to create a culture where that kind of expression can flourish. It has to develop an environment in which people really care about each other and their success, as well as that of the bank as a whole.

Thus, as the bank seeks to bash the bureaucracy, you must pick the right team for the right job, make sure that the interfaces between them are known, and work together toward the goal of serving customers.

SPRING TRAINING

As the teams come together in an appropriate format, you should be alerted to some dangers. They come from a 12-year study about organizational effectiveness that began in 1980 and encompasses over 1,000 organizations:[21] The dangers include:

- Calling work groups "teams" in the belief that team language alone will change the way in which the work is done.
- Removing frontline leaders as a shortcut to developing teams. This leaves team members with no leader to help them set standards, plan the work, coach, and give feedback.
- Assuming that teams can develop on their own without strong, visible support from senior management.
- Overlooking the need for a clear vision and for the clarification of expectations for teams.
- Assuming that setting up teams is an isolated act, with little or no implication for systems or other functions in the organization.
- Overlooking the need to teach the skills that everyone (senior leaders, frontline leaders, and team members) will require for a successful transition.

Teams require a new way of thinking to consider these kinds of things: the reverse of these assumptions is what makes them work. A completely new and different notion about the way work is organized is now based on a long-term commitment to letting people serve. It is the opposite of the old command and control, and the migration to it won't be easy. "Companies make the investment [in teams] because they have realized that in a fast-moving brutally competitive economy, the one thing sure to be harder than operating with teams is operating without them."[22] The companies that use them understand that empowered, accountable people, working together as a unit, have a better chance of success than a bureaucracy with all of its rules and regulations. It calls for change, but that is what the revolution is all about.

Establishing a true team will not happen just because the leadership has issued the order that teams will be the new organizational structure. As with empowerment and accountability, progression will occur, which requires coaching and patience. It is a sensitive and serious task which cannot be taken lightly. We have seen that there are people in the bank who do not want to be empowered. We have seen that entitlement may be winning out over accountability. Pick up your bugle and sound the charge. The competition is attacking the bank's customer base just like a herd of buffalo on the stampede, and we have to respond.

The people who hear the call to arms first are the prime candidates for the initial teams. Their objective? To take the data from the surveys and to design delivery systems that will close the service gaps.

Invite the people who can really help to join the team. When they sign up, reward them. Give them identity by means of a T-shirt with the team's name on it, which is to be worn at team meetings, or a coffee mug bearing the team logo. People cannot be forced to join. Encourage the reluctant ones who have that special skill that is needed. Help them see the value of the effort and coach them about why their contribution is so important. If necessary, make the commitment a limited one. Tell them that they will only have to be on the team for a short while, but if they are crucial to *kaizen,* get them there.

Once they have assembled, they have to know the goal. It is vital that they understand why they are there, what they are expected to accomplish, the deadline for achieving it, and the rewards that await them when they are done. The role of the leader is that of the head coach. To make the required changes, the team must learn how to work with each other in spite of individual idiosyncracies. Understanding the mission and goal is a help; so is realizing that the team is greater than the individuals that make it up; and so is having a recognition system that will reward them for the right behavior. It all comes down to leadership and helping people to learn about and from each other, so that they can help the team. The job of the coach is to be sensitive to the differences of all the players and to mold them into a high-performing group that can achieve great things.

PLAY BALL!

Many years ago, my father gave me a plaque that is labeled "Commitment to Excellence." It still hangs above the desk in my office. I don't know where he got it, nor do I know the source of the quotation. On the plaque is a photograph of Vince Lombardi, the legendary coach of the Green Bay Packers, considered the dominant team in the National Football League in the 1960s. Whether you are a football fan or not has no bearing on it. It is the coach's message that is important. I include it here because there is little more that can be said about the necessity for service excellence in this fast-paced, merging, competitive, changing, global economy. Now, it's time for action.

> I owe most everything to football, in which I have spent the greater part of my life. And I have never lost my respect, my admiration or my love for what I consider a great game. And each Sunday, after the battle, one group savors victory, another group lives in the bitterness of defeat. The many hurts seem a small price to have paid for having won, and there is no reason at all for having lost. To the winner there is one hundred percent elation, one hundred percent laughter, one hundred percent fun; and to the loser, the only thing left . . . is one hundred percent resolution, one hundred percent determination. And it's a game, I think, a great deal like life in that it demands that one's personal commitment be toward excellence and be toward victory, even though you know that ultimate victory can never be completely won. Yet it must be pursued with all of one's might. And each week there's a new encounter, each year a new challenge. *But all of the rings and all of the money and all of the color and all of the display, they linger only in memory. The spirit, the will to win and the will to excel, these are the things that endure and these are the qualities that are so much more important than any of the events that occasion them.* And I'd like to say that the quality of a man's life has got to be a full measure of that man's personal commitment to excellence and to victory, regardless of what field he may be in. [italics added]

That is the challenge for all of us.

A P P E N D I X   8-1

Culture Survey Results
The ABC National Bank
October 1995

OVERVIEW OF FINDINGS

Cash Management Services

Survey results are grouped into eight categories to identify any structural blocks or barriers that preclude the delivery of service excellence and isolate the cultural issues that impact daily performance and contribute to the severity of any service shortfalls.

MISSION

There is a very clear understanding of the mission of the cash management services staff: to provide timely and accurate service to its customers. They have some difficulty relating it to other departments where the mission is not so clear. They also understand how important their work is to the overall mission of the bank.

LEADERSHIP

The leadership also understands the mission very well. However, there is a tendency on the part of the officers to want to take control of daily activities to ensure that all tasks are completed properly. The staff is somewhat resentful and expressed the desire to be able to do their jobs on their own. This action would go a long way toward relieving the pressure felt in the department and also would provide more time for planning, sales, and process improvement. There is a large gap between the leadership and the staff that must be closed.

COMMUNICATION

The structure and the leadership style preclude effective communication. It is top-down with little ability to cross lines or for feedback to go back up the chain of command. This is a serious problem that must be alleviated.

EDUCATION

The expertise of the staff is good. They believe that they have been educated sufficiently to perform their tasks and assignments well. That is why the officers can afford to "back off" as there will be no deterioration of service; rather, it is expected to improve.

ENDNOTES

1. Helene F. Uhlfelder, "Why Teams Don't Work," *Quality Digest,* June 1994, p. 47.
2. Clare Krulikowski, "Employee Satisfaction," *Quality Digest,* Sept. 1994, pp. 59–60.
3. Peter Block, *The Empowered Manager* (San Francisco: Jossey-Bass, 1991), pp. 69–70.
4. Lawrence Holpp, quoted in William Smitley and David Scott, "Empowerment: Unlocking the Potential of Your Work Force," *Quality Digest,* Aug. 1994, pp. 40–41.
5. Judith M. Bardwick, *Danger in the Comfort Zone* (New York: AMACOM, 1991), p. 119.
6. Smitley and Scott, "Empowerment," p. 40.
7. Block, *The Empowered Manager,* p. 6.
8. Bardwick, *Danger in the Comfort Zones,* p. 18.
9. Ibid., p. 21.
10. John A. Byrne, "Deliver—Or Else," *Business Week,* March 27, 1995, p. 36.
11. Roger Connors et al., *The Oz Principle* (Englewood Cliffs, NJ: Prentice Hall, 1994), p. 65.
12. Peter F. Drucker, "There's More than One Kind of Team," *The Wall Street Journal,* Feb. 11, 1992, p. A16.
13. Quoted in Connors etal., The Oz Principles, p. 171.
14. Kenneth Labich, "Kissing Off Corporate America," *Fortune,* Feb. 20, 1995, p. 44.
15. Ibid., p. 50.
16. Jon R. Katzenbach and Douglas K. Smith, *The Wisdom of Teams* (Boston: Harvard Business School, 1993), p. 45.
17. Brian Dumaine, "The Trouble with Teams," *Fortune,* Sept. 4, 1995, p. 86.
18. Drucker, "More than One Kind of Team," p. A16.
19. Dumaine, "Trouble with Teams," pp. 86–88.
20. Katzenbach and Smith, *The Wisdom of Teams,* p. 65.
21. Dumaine, "Trouble with Teams," p. 92.
22. Kate Ludeman, "Using Surveys to Transform Groups into Teams," *Quality Digest,* March 1994, p. 43.

CHAPTER 9

A Better Way

The service of others should be fun. That means working in the bank should be fun. Knowing that we have done something that pleased someone else or made their life easier should make us feel good. But, from what I see and hear, that doesn't seem to be the case in most banks these days. Many friends and colleagues have indicated that working in the bank right now is not as much fun as it used to be, which is probably the case in most other declining industries as well. This situation may be the legacy left by most of the recent "improvement" programs that financial institutions have undertaken. There's so much to do, and because of the cost cutting, there are fewer people than necessary to do it.

Furthermore, most compensation programs are productivity based, so the job becomes very task oriented. Finish one as quickly as possible, throw it over the wall to the next person in the line, and continue to attack the pile which always seems to be getting larger. That leaves little time or incentive for creativity, innovation, or even finding out if what you are doing really satisfies the requirements of your customers, which really is what has to happen. So, the behavior we need is not what the bank is telling its people to do.

A friend is executive director of a group that matches people who want to volunteer their time and talent with the needs of nonprofit organizations in the community. We talked about the supply of people who want to give of themselves; she told me that currently they have more people than ever who want to help out in these kinds of organizations. I asked her why. She told me that a majority of these potential volunteers are looking for ways to use their creativ-

ity and energy to make something positive happen, and they find it difficult to
do that in the workplace.

> Across America, more people than ever before are volunteering for commu-
> nity work. Altruism plays its part, of course, but you can't help wondering
> how many people are doing this because they do not feel appreciated at work
> and think they can make a contribution there. [Kevin] Cooney's [division
> vice president at Whirlpool] point is simple: Why not siphon off some of this
> creative energy, this untapped leadership ability, and put it to work at work?
> In such a demanding decade, can you afford not to?[1]

It is this kind of creativity that the bank has to unleash. The people who
deliver the mail to your customers every day know what they want and there's a
good chance they know how to get it to them. All they need is an opportunity to
express it. But, once again, that's contrary to the way things have been done in
the bank. The bureaucratic structure and style have prevented it. With its boxes
and rules, true creativity hasn't happened. But, if my friend and Kevin Cooney
of Whirlpool are right, and I think they are, this is the secret to success. All we
have to do is listen to them, for service excellence is impossible without a special emphasis on the people who are being asked to deliver it.

In this chapter, we will focus on the importance of the people of the bank
and will see how to initiate the improvement process. We will also see how to
have some fun. It is not a cookbook or a paint-by-the-numbers. It cannot be because every bank in the country is different, even within the same markets.
What works for Chase Manhattan might not work for Citicorp. What works for
First Union may not work for NationsBank. What works for Star may not work
for Fifth Third. Cultures are different, as are markets, niches, employees, customs, visions, and the like. Therefore, it is impossible to write out a standard
prescription of things to be undertaken in sequence which, when accomplished,
will guarantee that the expectations of your customers are being met.

However, there is a basic and fundamental discipline that can be followed
that will ensure success regardless of the personality of your bank. As your
bank engages in this discipline, the features that differentiate it in the market
will create an improvement process that is yours, and yours alone. It must fit
with what the bank is in the communities and markets that it serves. That is
why a manual that was used to restructure any other bank will not work for you
unless the mandate is to cut expenses by 15 percent across the board. Following
the methodology of *The Banking Revolution,* what is necessary and what works
for Central State Bank in Muscatine, Iowa, may not be required at Penn Central
National Bank in Huntingdon, Pennsylvania; but, because of the inherent flexibility of it, both banks will be successful.

This chapter will give you some parameters and guidelines, the elements of which will contribute to your own personalized initiative. It will require thought, creativity, teamwork, and innovation—a spirit of entrepreneurship. These attributes are different from those included in most "improvement" programs. This is a positive, action-oriented way to achieve sustainable improvement, and it can be a great deal of fun.

BLOW IT UP?

The literature is filled with prescriptions for success, judging by the extensive coverage of downsizing, rightsizing, and reengineering. Those techniques have been seized upon by U.S. corporations like Little Leaguers attack their ice-cream cones at the Dairy Queen. Millions of dollars have been saved. Millions of jobs have been lost. There are three problems that preclude the success of these techniques: (1) the focus on cost reduction, not revenue enhancement; (2) the basic work remains the same despite downsizing and restructuring; and (3) the conflict among bank leaders about what to do.

1. The first and major issue is that most of the "improvement" techniques focus on reducing cost, not enhancing revenue. They occur because the overhead ratio has crept up to an unacceptable level or because the forecast for earnings per share is short of the projections given to the analysts. With that, management tells the people of the bank to come up with ideas concerning how to reduce costs in order to save something like 40 percent of their budgets or more. And management gets it. The problem? How could 40 percent of what everyone in the bank does not render some value to customers? I have been involved in cost cutting like this, and at no time did we reflect and say, "Gee, I wonder what our customers will think about that."

A well-known bank hired a major consulting company in 1992 to help reduce cost. Three thousand jobs were cut and, in the short term, earnings improved. The stock market, however, did not reward that behavior; the price of the bank's common stock has not moved much. Millions of dollars were spent, customer service went to pot, and morale sank like a stone. The main topic of conversation among bank officers was how to get out and not about ways to beat the competition.

Here's a more specific example. As part of the cost-cutting initiative at another bank, the manager of the retail division knew that he had to carve out that 40 percent of noninterest expense. In reviewing the branch network, he spied the drive-up teller function. I'm not sure how many drive-ups there were, but when the manager saw that some cost could be jettisoned, he decided to close them. Another friend related the following story that occurred as a result of that action. As she was standing in line waiting to see a teller (for which she would be charged a fee), another customer came into the branch with two small children, all bundled up to protect them against the cold and the snow of a typical January day in the Upper Midwest. They began a conversation, during which my friend learned of the frustration.

> "I used to use the drive-up. It was so much easier with the kids. Now, I have to find a parking space, which is harder now, get their gloves and scarves on, and come in here where I have to wait." Naturally, the children were squirming about, looking for something to do, which further increased the anxiety level of not only their mother, but of the other customers in the line. "Why do you suppose they closed it?"

OK, so this was just one customer, but if we think about it, she was complaining to everyone in the line. Those folks might be annoyed at having to stand in line with a couple of active children. They might look for another banking alternative. Furthermore, they might tell a few of their friends about the "poor, young mother at the bank." The mother will certainly relate the story to her husband who might be a successful businessman who could find another institution that will serve his family in a more satisfactory way.

That is one example. Here's another.

> A survivor of the latest cutback at one company commented, "My job is driving me over the edge! Our company restructured last year, and I was one of the 'lucky' survivors. Now I do the job of four. I'm working 60 hours a week without extra pay, and I'm taking work home. Weekends are spent catching up, and my family life is in ruins.
>
> "Meanwhile, the morale in the plant has been destroyed, people hate and mistrust each other, and fear dominates every action because job security and loyalty is gone. A cloud hovers, spraying the you-may-be-next virus into everyone."[2]

The focus that causes this to happen is wrong. Instead of saying "How much cost can we wring out?" the questions should be, "What value do customers, internal and external, place on what you are doing?" "What is the error rate in your area of responsibility?" "How much does it cost to correct the errors?" "How many accounts have we lost because of it?" and, "What can we do to prevent mistakes from happening in the first place?"

2. Restructuring and downsizing do nothing to change the basic work. People at the bank seem to accept the notion that processes always have to have the characteristics they have had in the past. Who says accounts payable has to be labor intensive and dependent on forms and other pieces of paper? What once was a cumbersome, awkward process is really a simple one with the advances of technology. Just look at Digital Equipment. The company evaluated the accounts payable function, designed some new processes within the framework of what "accounts payable" is supposed to do, and, as of November 1992, realized savings of $15 to $20 million annually by streamlining over 150 duplicate systems. However, the fundamental reason for having an accounts payable process has not changed. It is there to pay the bills, but Steve Behrens of Digital added, "as efficiently as we can." That means changing the tasks and functions within the process.[3]

Furthermore, because managers do not think of the bank in systemic terms, departmental efficiencies reign, suboptimizing the final delivery of service to the customer. Another letter to the editor read: "One of Corporate America's greatest deficiencies has been the failure to realize and act meaningfully on the concept that all areas and all employees must operate together with a common goal as stated in organizational and departmental charters."[4] Like Digital Equipment, we have to think systemically because the accounts payable function is available to all departments and divisions around the world.

There are elements of reengineering, in its truest sense, that may enable the necessary changes to be made in the work processes. From the results that we have, however, the way that it has been implemented must not have followed the intended design. Even the originator of reengineering, Michael Hammer, has felt it necessary to defend it.

> "Much of the criticism is based on a misconception of what reengineering really is," he asserted, "and much of the rest reflects a limited assessment of its significance." Earlier, of course, Hammer had helped muddy the waters by asserting on more than one occasion that 70 percent of reengineering projects fall short of their stated goals.[5]

In a survey performed by the consulting firm of Arthur G. Little, Inc., in the summer of 1994, only 16 percent of the executives questioned were completely satisfied with their reengineering programs. The survey revealed that 68 percent were having "unanticipated problems." In similar research by the Institute of Management Accountant's Controllers Council, 45 percent of the respondents said that it is too early to tell whether the promises that reengineering makes were actually fulfilled.[6] None of these techniques—downsizing, restructuring, or reengineering—has really looked at the behavior that is needed to provide service to customers. Did the manager of retail really think about the ramifications of closing the drive-up window, other than to think about cost? With the bank's culture concentrated on the overhead ratio, probably not.

3. The third problem is the conflict over what should be done. Should the bank blow up its current delivery systems and start over as "reengineering" suggests or should it capitalize on the good things that have been done in the past? There is a school of thought that says you should order the dynamite, but think of the residual cost involved if you were to start from scratch. Banking transactions are governed by generally accepted accounting principles (GAAP). The Securities and Exchange Commission, the Internal Revenue Service, and the Fed, among others, demand it. That means that the basic rules for installment loan transactions, those in wholesale lockbox, and trades in the trust department have to be handled in accordance with established convention. I don't think any CEO would be predisposed to writing off millions of dollars of unamortized computer software or hardware that crunches thousands, even millions, of transactions according to those rules.

Furthermore, it just does not make much sense to throw out the good things that work, especially if there are no better alternatives out there. That's why I don't think you can be, in the words of Michael Hammer and James Champy, "tossing aside old systems and starting over."[7] In a perfect world, perhaps that's feasible, but the world isn't perfect. There are things in our banks that work well. Those that do should be left alone; those that don't, because they are outdated or have been patched beyond recognition, may need to be blown up. Just be careful with the hand grenades, and let some common sense prevail.

It makes a lot of sense to eliminate those things in the banks that add no value. Question the way that service is delivered. What do our customers want? How do they want it? That's at the very heart of the revolution. Question whether you need branches or will the Internet do? But question it from the customer's perspective because the objective is to close the back door and then to have such good service that customers want to buy even more from your bank. That's revolutionary thinking. That's what this has been all about: changing the way bankers think about how they serve their customers. It has to do with challenging how things have always been done and the apparent basic conflict of a philosophy of service excellence as compared with the traditional economic model of the firm.

If the bank is to change structure and style to be more customer focused, it has some historical opposition. Table 9–1 shows the fundamental differences between the two philosophies that will compete with one another as the journey begins. The basic problem with the economic model is focus. It says that the bank should do whatever is necessary to increase shareholder wealth. It apparently ignores the notion that without customers, there is no wealth to be had.

How the bank is able to deal with customers depends on the strength of the prevailing culture and its willingness and ability to embrace change. That is what reengineering misses because it goes only after cost. This merely reinforces the culture of the past, which must be changed to reflect the wishes of the customer. Moving away from the economic model to the service model will be hard because we will be changing the bank's culture, which, as we have seen, has been created by the accepted modes of behavior for the last 60 years. When you choose to attack, realize that it is going to take time.

Even with the mounting pressure caused by the disintermediation, the new competition, and the advancement of technology, you must understand the

T A B L E   9–1

Service Model and the Economic Model of the Firm

	Service Model	Economic Model
Organizational goals	Serving customer needs by supplying goods and services of the highest possible quality.	Maximizing profit (i.e., shareholder wealth).
Individual goals	Individual motivated by economic, social, and psychological goals relating to personal fulfillment and social acceptance.	Individuals motivated only by economic goals; maximization of income and minimization of effort.
Time orientation	Dynamic; innovation and continual improvement.	Static optimization; maximizing the present value of net cash flow by maximizing revenue/ minimizing cost.
Coordination and control	Employees are trustworthy and are experts in their jobs—hence emphasis on self-management. Employees are capable of coordinating on a voluntary basis.	Managers have the expertise to coordinate and direct subordinates. Agency problems necessitate monitoring of subordinates and applying incentives to align objectives.
Role of information	Open and timely information flows are critical to self-management, horizontal coordination, and quest for continual improvement.	Information system matches hierarchical structure; key functions are to support managers' decision making and monitor subordinates.
Principles of work design	System-based optimization with emphasis on dynamic performance.	Productivity maximization by specializing on the basis of competitive advantage.
Firm boundaries	Issues of customer-supplier relations, information flow, and dynamic coordination common to transactions within and between firms.	Clear distinction between markets and firms as governance mechanisms. Firm boundaries determined by transactions costs.

Source: Robert M. Grant et al., "TQM's Challenge to Management Theory and Practice, *Sloan Management Review* (Winter 1994), p. 33.

power of the mind-set that is prevalent in the bank. It is a formidable foe, but the longer the bank waits, the stronger the culture becomes. That says that the improvement initiative has to start today. Don't be like the banks that give the following excuses:

- Our bank is different—always has been, always will be.
- Our market is truly unique—the only one like it on the planet.
- Our expenses are high, but we'll grow into them.
- We promised not to let anyone go . . . ever.
- We'll just increase prices to cover expenses.
- Our profits have been the highest they've been in history, so why worry?
- Our customers are loyal, so let's not discuss how old they are.
- Our customers don't follow interest rates and don't do business with any other service providers. They also don't read newspapers, watch cable TV, or talk with friends.
- We can't let anyone go. Half the town is related to somebody who works here, and the percentage is growing all the time.
- We need these employees to give all our customers highly personalized individual attention all the time, and you can never have enough controls.[8]

Sounds like David Letterman. My favorite? "Our customers don't follow interest rates and don't do business with any other service providers. They don't read newspapers, watch cable TV, or talk with friends." I have some colleagues in some pretty small banks in some pretty small towns who have told me that their customers have received calls from Merrill Lynch and have been tempted to withdraw their deposits. The kind of thinking represented in that statement has allowed the competition to jump in and the disintermediation to happen.

We have to turn that thinking around. We have to come at improvement in a different way. So far in *The Banking Revolution,* we've changed a little because we have empowered the staff and are holding them accountable for serving their customers with excellence. We have determined the expectations of our customers, and we have a good idea about the culture and how people are spending their time. We know the value of teamwork and using different kinds of teams for different purposes. And we have just found out that there is no improvement manual sitting on the corner of our credenzas to provide the sequence of events that will result in long-term and sustainable improvement. What do we do?

We're going to draw on a variety of techniques that we have put together in an overall improvement process which is aimed at changing the thinking and resultant actions of the bank. We are not going to blow up what we have and start over again. That doesn't make any sense. Furthermore, recognizing that we have to start the process, we must also acknowledge that people are reluctant to change what they do and how they do it, even if there are better ways. Economist John Kenneth Galbraith put it well: "Faced with the alternative between changing one's mind and proving it is unnecessary, just about everybody gets busy on the proof."[9]

This is where the CEO comes in. Don't let the staff exhaust themselves in the development of data that might, in some way, reinforce the status quo. There isn't time. The scouts have seen the trail of dust, and if you put your ear to the ground, you might be able to hear the rumble of the oncoming herd. Tell these people who really want the bank to do well that it is time to change the focus. Encourage them to be open-minded about what has to happen. The old way, focused on cost, needs to be put aside in favor of one that concentrates on meeting the needs of the bank's customers.

As the process begins, we have to recognize that two things are happening simultaneously: changing the culture, slowly and deliberately, and improving the way in which the bank provides service, which happens somewhat more quickly. Let the leadership work with the former. There are some truly talented people elsewhere in the bank who can handle the latter.

WHAT DO WE DO FIRST?

The first thing on the agenda is to understand that we are dealing with processes and not tasks and routine assignments. The vast majority of service problems are caused by outdated and patched processes or the ones that were designed for a completely different time and function. *Process* is a particular way of doing something and usually involves a number of steps. It is everything that is involved in the delivery of service to customers, whether inside or outside the bank.

To make the improvements that those customers have told the bank are necessary, we must view the bank from the perspective of its processes. Instead of looking at organizational units like the "retail division" or a "teller," we have to study services that the bank offers. For the retail division, services may include:

- Installment loans, both direct and indirect
- Mortgage loans
- Demand deposits
- Time deposits
- CDs

TABLE 9-2

Service Excellence Report
Retail Banking Services
2nd Half, 1995

Service	Gap
Installment lending—direct	−1.274
Installment lending—indirect	−0.989
Mortgage lending	−1.765
Demand deposits	−0.009
Time deposits	−0.123
CDs	−0.310
Home equity lines of credit	−1.199
Credit cards	−0.781
Debit cards	−0.652

- Home equity lines of credit
- Credit cards
- Debit cards

The particular services listed may or may not be offered by your bank. All that you have to know is what you are offering to your markets. Make a list of them. The next step is to develop surveys for the customers of each of these products, making each questionnaire very specific about the expectations, perceptions, and priorities in the five service dimensions. Let's assume that was done. The service improvement council has authorized surveys throughout the bank. The CEO has asked the major lines of business in the bank to document any gaps— and the priorities customers place upon them—in the services that each of them provides and to report back at a subsequent meeting.

With that direction, the leadership of the retail side works with operations and marketing to identify their primary processes and to create the survey documents. They are mailed to a random number of customers, sufficient to ensure statistical validity. A focus group or two is assembled for each service line, at which time the participants complete their own questionnaires. Marketing is declared to be on the point in the data gathering effort. The results are in. The director of the marketing department presents the data to the leadership of retail (see Table 9–2).

Using Table 9–2 for illustrative purposes, the bank can begin to think with a process orientation. The results could have been for trust or for the commercial side. I chose retail for no particular reason except that more banks offer retail services than the other lines.

T A B L E   9-3

Retail Banking Services
Service Quality Gaps

Service Line	Gap
Deposit products	
Demand deposits	−0.009
Time deposit	−0.123
CDs	−0.310
Plastic	
Debit cards	−0.652
Credit cards	−0.781
Consumer loans	
Installment lending—indirect	−0.989
Home equity lines of credit	−1.199
Installment lending—direct	−1.274
Mortgage lending	−1.765

What does the chart tell us? First, it turns out that the sizes of the gaps correlate with the various service lines. Let's rearrange them as shown in Table 9.3.

Grouping them this way, we can see that deposit products have the smallest gaps. Plastic has the second smallest ones. And, the consumer lending area has some pretty severe ones. These data suggest that little can be done to improve the delivery of CDs, savings products, or demand deposit accounts. The bank's customers have indicated that their perceptions almost meet their expectations; if there are any complaints at all, they might think that the interest rate being paid should be higher or that the fees that are being charged should be lower. However, that would probably be true of any other bank in town as well, so we should not consider them too serious, especially in light of the other gaps.

Debit and credit cards may be a problem. The gaps are less than −1.000 so there is some uneasiness on the part of customers. The leader responsible for them should be concerned. There's a little bleeding present. He or she should ask to see the results by service dimension, both gaps and priorities, to find whether the problems reside in reliability, responsiveness, assurance, empathy, or tangibles. There has to be something wrong somewhere; that analysis will help the leader to understand where to look.

The head of consumer lending, on the other hand, has a real problem. Stitches are needed here. These gaps call for immediate action, but what should be done? It's the same answer. Dig into the survey results and find out where the gaps are the most serious. Find out which dimensions customers think are the most important. That will provide a clue about what to do next, but when the detailed information arrives, don't shoot anybody. Those with the data are only the scouts who have been "out there" talking with customers. It is, however, time to round up the troops because there is work to be done.

> A bank that has a process orientation has a horizontal view of itself. The processes are a group of logically related tasks that use the resources of the entire organization to achieve defined results. The primary emphasis in the process focus is how something is done; management is organized to be accountable to accomplish these results. In contrast to an organization focus, management looks at how the work is to be done in order to satisfy a particular customer's needs or a particular target market. Consequently, management adopts the customer's point of view rather than the organization's point of view.[10]

The senior leadership, most visibly the CEO, the COO, and the people who report to them directly, cannot react negatively to this information. They have to resist the temptation to take charge and to try to fix the problem. As we saw in *Flight of the Buffalo,* the senior leadership must give this information to the people responsible for it, asking, "What do you need from me to fix it?" In other words, "How can we in senior management help you?"

That becomes a visible sign that the culture is changing and gives the people who are equipped to fix the problems the authority to do so. We all know that they are the right ones to be entrusted with that assignment; besides, senior people have some important tasks of their own to accomplish. First, the CEO has to explain to everyone in the organization that the surveys are back, that there is work to do, and that everyone is expected to be involved in the improvement process. He or she has to impress upon the organization that merely tinkering with their processes isn't going to make it. Some will require more radical surgery than others, but all of them will result in positive service gaps. That's a much more optimistic and affirmative target than "we will reduce expenses by 40 percent."

Boeing CEO Frank Shrontz heard from his customers that delivery schedules were too slow. Besides, the faster the company could build an airplane, the less it would cost. He asked that the time required to build a 747 or a 767 be reduced from 18 months in 1992 to 8 months by 1996. In late 1994, Boeing could build a plane in 10 months.[11] Note the difference. Shrontz focused on the process and the wishes of his customers and challenged the people at Boeing to come up with better ways of building airplanes, knowing that there would be economic benefit as well. Once he did that, I'll bet he got out of the way and let the experts go to work. He invited his people to be creative, effectively saying that he just expected them to use their God-given talents to meet his expectation. That's what has to happen in the bank.

The CEO has to be fair, to encourage everyone to participate, and to live and breathe the challenge every day. Do like the CEO who walked around each day asking people what they had done to improve the service to their customers. Now's the time to leave the office. The results will be astounding. They start with the service improvement council. The first time the head of the trust department is asked, "Say, Dave, what have you done today to improve the service to your customers?" the response may be a blank stare. But, when Dave sees that the question is for real, attitudes change, and service takes a new place on the agenda. "Uh, well, Bill, we got our statements out on time," won't be good enough anymore.

The members of the service improvement council, or service excellence council, as it is known at the Savings Bank of Utica in upper New York state, become the champions. These are the people who report and review progress each week, making it the highest priority of their agenda. It may be the only item on the agenda as the bank works diligently to close those service gaps. The critical nature of their jobs cannot be emphasized enough. The CEO can't be everywhere, but if the expectation is made very clear, he or she might as well be omnipresent as the members of the service improvement council fan out into the bank. These are the CEO's assistant coaches who begin to ask the questions:

- What prevents you from being a great performer?
- How can I help you become a great performer?
- How can I help you remove the obstacles that prevent you from being a great performer?

These are the people who have looked at the survey data and who can prioritize the improvement effort. In the example from "retail," the members of the council know that it is the lending side that needs attention because the gaps are so high. Without any finger-pointing or levying of blame, the head of retail must accept sponsorship of the improvement initiative. It is his or her responsibility to do whatever is necessary to close those gaps because they mean that earnings are walking out the back door. The head of retail must become a leader in the truest sense of the word.

We know that the necessary attributes are designer, steward, and teacher, those essential elements of servant leadership. But there also has to be some vision, some courage, and that can-do attitude that says, "C'mon, I'm not sure where we're going, but it sure beats where we are now."

Moses was a visionary leader. He persuaded the Children of Israel that they should go forward toward a land of milk and honey when all they could see around them was sand. One man couldn't force a whole people to set off into the desert; he had to inspire them with his vision. He also set a personal example. When they arrived at the Red Sea, Moses said, "Here's the plan.

We're going to march into the sea, the Lord will part the waters, and we'll walk though on dry land." His followers looked at the Red Sea and said to him, "You first." He went, and they followed. Being out front when risk presents itself is part of leadership. (This story also demonstrates the value of having the boss on your side, as Moses certainly did.)[12]

The message for the CEO and the person who has stepped forward to coordinate the improvement initiative on the consumer loan side? Together, the effort can be successful. However, it is essential to have the full and complete support of the boss, just as Moses did. Moses knew that he was in good hands, and so must those who are charged with the responsibility for closing the gaps. They must be free to devote 100 percent of their time to the effort and to help those below them to remove the obstacles that are preventing great performance and which are resulting in those gaps. Therefore, when the head of retail has problems in mortgage, installment, and home equity lending, he or she must find owners for each of these processes and fully empower them, in turn, to make the required changes.

ENOUGH TALK . . . IT'S TIME TO ACT

To be frank about it, even before the survey results were in, the heads of mortgage, installment, and home equity lending had to know that there were problems. They were rushing from meeting to meeting and slopping the water from their buckets on the stairs, which didn't leave them much to put out the next fire. Now, however, there are some data and some urgency because the head of retail and the CEO think that the gaps have to be closed, and fast. Their job? Quite simply, to do whatever is necessary to close them, spending as much time as possible, preferably 100 percent, on it.

At the outset, some things have to be done. First, they need an internal customer survey, culture survey, and workforce activity questionnaire for each of these lending processes. They have to find out what the people are thinking, how they are spending their time, and the amount of the corresponding costs. The sponsors have a good idea about what's going on, but without data, they may end up chasing ghosts.

Second, we're going to need teams of people who can analyze these data, diagnose the problem, suggest innovative solutions, and implement them. These people can be found in positions of responsibility within the service delivery system in question, and they must be the first ones to be asked to join the team. There also should be representatives of unrelated value chains who may not know anything about installment lending, mortgage lending, or home equity lending, but who have some positive service quality gaps in their own processes and can lend some of their expertise to the improvement effort. There will also be a need for some functional specialists, people who know the latest technology or have the latest demographics, for example. We are creating a hybrid between the problem-solving team and the virtual team by finding the people who are needed wherever they are working in the bank. There's a herd of buffalo stampeding the wagon train, and there is little time to waste.

With the CEO's stated expectation out there, getting people to become part of the teams is made much easier, even if the process sponsors have to cross organizational lines to get them. However, that's why they were chosen: They know how to navigate through the politics of the organization. They can go to the members of the service improvement council for help or they can ask their specific council member for help. However it is done, the right people need to be on the team, even if it will take them completely away from their jobs. That is what should happen anyway. They will design a new and better way of serving customers and then will be responsible for it. For many, their old jobs will disappear anyway, so they should be glad to sign up. Writer Rita Mae Brown sums it up nicely: "A good definition of insanity is doing the same old stuff in the same old way and expecting different results."[13]

The third thing that has to be done—and it is frequently overlooked in much of the literature—is that customers must still be served. Just because there is a team being assembled that will be devoting half to three-quarters of its time to the improvement process doesn't mean that transactions don't have to be processed accurately and on a timely basis. The sponsor will be challenged to accomplish it, but accomplish it he or she must. If the sponsor is like the manager in our example of cash management, he or she may find it convenient to back off.

Fourth, another task generally forgotten is that process sponsors need some education. They are being asked to do something new and different, so they have to learn how to be effective team leaders or facilitators. Simply because one of them is the manager of the installment loan department, for example, does not mean than he or she has the skills and talent to lead a newly recruited band of warriors in the improvement effort. There are some definable differences between the two leadership roles. As such, it is almost impossible to fill both roles at the same time. Each role requires some specific behavior. Let's look at Table 9–4.

The facilitator is there to make sure that things run smoothly and that everyone has a chance to participate on an equal footing, not letting those with dominant personalities suppress those who might be more quiet, yet have some great things to contribute. The facilitator also works closely with the team leader to make sure that the whole process stays on track, acting as an advisor when things start to get stalled or off on a tangent. He or she can also tell the leader to back off when the natural tendency to lead starts to assert itself. Facilitating a group requires a person who can put the ego away, has the good of the

TABLE 9-4

TABLE 9-4

Team Leader or Facilitator?

Team Leader	Facilitator
Focus the effort of the team on its objectives and overall purpose.	Foster active participation of all team members, including the leader.
Guide the team without dominating it.	Provide feedback to team members.
Assist in the education of the team.	Help members to stay focused on the agenda.
Be an active participant, providing ideas and encouraging others.	Educate the team on applicable problem-solving techniques.
Establish and communicate the agenda and meeting objectives.	Take advantage of the strengths of all team members.
Make sure that responsibilities are clear for all team members.	Make sure that the team stays motivated and on track.
Ensure that assignments are completed on time.	Ensure that all conflicts are resolved as soon as possible.
Make sure that the minutes of each meeting are published and distributed on a timely basis.	Be neutral at all times.
Report regularly to the service improvement council.	Encourage others to contribute technical ideas and suggestions.
Recommend changing the makeup of the team, if necessary.	Refrain from evaluation of ideas or making suggestions.
Make sure that all team members are involved, both in meetings and with assignments.	Help the team to reach consensus, making sure that all dissent is heard.
	Clarify feelings and questions back to the team.

organization in mind, and can encourage the team members to find innovative and workable answers to some fairly complex issues. You have to be able to mediate in the midst of disagreement, to work toward effective compromises, to set objectives, and to hold the team accountable.

The team leader makes it all happen. He or she must encourage team members to have confidence in what you are trying to achieve, help them remove any obstacles that are in their way, establish their boundaries, and get out of the way. First and foremost, however, make the team your number one priority, doing whatever is necessary for it to be successful. Don't dominate team meetings, but be an active member as the facilitator guides you along. Work closely with the facilitator and with the service improvement council; those folks can give you, the team leader, all the resources you need to make the changes that your customers are asking you to make. Above all, try to make it fun for those who have volunteered to be a part of the effort. Reward their efforts. Recognize their achievements. Help them succeed, and you will succeed at the same time. Your reward? It could be a financial one, but more than that, there will be a great sense of satisfaction.

As the team leader and the facilitator begin their roles, the members of the team also need some education about what is expected of them. Their own private agendas have to be put aside. There is no room for any turf battles. Egos must be left at the door. "Leave your business card here on the receptionist's desk," is the way one of my clients puts it for team members who are going to their working sessions. Like the players in baseball, football, and tennis, the members of the improvement teams have to realize that they are dependent upon one another. They must understand that without cooperation, regardless of their departmental loyalties, little change will occur.

What may prove most difficult of all for improvement team members is that they have to learn how to follow. They have had little education in being followers. They may be leaders in their own departments and divisions, and they may take leadership roles while on the team, but they have to be able to follow when not in a leadership position.

Effective followers do their best to:

- Subjugate their own feelings for the good of the team.
- Listen to other members of the team, trying to understand where they are coming from.
- Understand and be committed to the mission of the team.
- Be interested in the lives of other team members.
- Cooperate and communicate with others about their assignments.
- Acknowledge conflict and confront it.
- Reach consensus, not imposing their will on the decision-making process.
- Understand and respect differences among team members.
- Contribute ideas and solutions when called upon.
- Value the ideas and solutions of other team members.
- Encourage and appreciate feedback about the team and its performance.

Being followers is one thing, but they also have responsibilities to the team, the team leader, and the facilitator. When followers agree to become members of the team, they contract their active participation to its success. They have been asked to be there because they have something to contribute, and that is what they have to do. Take a look at Table 9–5.

Team members are there to add value. The last thing that you want is someone sitting there in team meetings who has not done his or her assignment, thereby impeding the progress of the whole team. Team membership can be an

TABLE 9-5

Responsibilities of Team Members

Attend and participate in team meetings.

Provide functional expertise about the process under study.

Suspend assumptions and bias.

Offer dissenting opinions; play "devil's advocate."

Be objective.

Complete assignments accurately and on a timely basis.

Support the efforts of members of other teams, offering assistance whenever asked.

exhilarating and productive experience if those chosen to be on the team will let it happen. They can challenge all sorts of things, asking why things are done the way they are, but they have to be willing to be challenged themselves. What assumptions and biases are they bringing in? "Finance people aren't creative," say the folks in marketing. "All they care about is making sure that the rows and columns balance." People from finance might have a little trouble with that assumption. Team members have to be able to look at their own thoughts about others, and be big enough to admit that, in some cases, they may have been mistaken.

While the teams are getting organized, the council has to consider a couple of other matters. First, there is the communication plan. The people of the bank and external stakeholders deserve to know what's going on. In what can be one of the most effective marketing campaigns ever, announce that the bank is undertaking process design, the objective of which is to serve customers better. Tell them that it is a new way of organizing according to the demands of the new economic environment in the financial services industry. Once that is said, make sure it happens because false promises are quickly discovered.

In most banks, a vehicle is already in place by which to communicate with shareholders and customers. Don't blow it up and start over. Rather, change what those people are saying and how they may be saying it. Make the communication regular and let them know how the bank is doing. The important thing for customers to see is the bank's concerted effort to follow up on what they have said while the shareholders and the analysts would certainly be interested in the reduced cost of quality and increased market share.

Internally, there should be regular communication about team progress and some of the specific success stories that have occurred. Use whatever mechanisms work for your culture: newsletters, staff meetings, bankwide meetings, or reward and recognition banquets. The leadership has a responsibility to tell everyone about the new direction and how well it is going.

The second matter also concerns communications. Because people will invariably be uprooted in their jobs even in a process like this, there has to be a solid, well-thought-out human resource communications strategy to deal with it. Some people may not be able to handle the change. There has to be a strategy for that. Jobs will be eliminated. There has to be a strategy for that. However, as the bank seeks to minimize those numbers, the leadership has to remember that in all likelihood customers will cause an increased demand for people in other areas.

Thus, using the concept of resource reallocation, one way to mitigate the financial and psychological costs of separation is to take those whose jobs have been eliminated and to educate them with the new skills required in a new area of responsibility. There can also be a hiring freeze as the bank seeks to fill open positions from within. The idea is to avoid the trauma of layoffs by putting loyal people to work in another area of the bank, which solves a staffing problem and creates even greater dedication on the part of workers.

As the teams begin their work, another matter of concern that muddies things up for the bank requires some very creative thinking. The typical bank organization structure is full of complicated interdependencies. Look at the branch and the number of value chains of which it is a member. Transactions of all types flow through this single collection point. Is it a deposit gatherer? Yes. But it also handles loan payments, credit card transactions, ATM withdrawals, and the like. The branch is a moment-of-truth. It exists to make the bank available to customers. It should, like Wal-Mart, be able to take care of the needs of your customers. That means that the installment loan team, for example, has to recognize that however it may change what branch personnel do, it could have an impact on the credit card team. Throughout the entire improvement process, the team has to think systemically and to watch out for suboptimization.

Then there is the matter of operations, which has to be able to process all of the bank's transactions. However, operations typically reports to someone who isn't responsible for the frontline customer service of the branch system, which suggests a fractionalization at the same time as there are these complicated dependencies.

Many banks have established separate divisions to sell different products to the same clients—large corporations, for instance. One division sells traditional lines of credit; another, asset-base finance; a third, letters of credit; and a fourth, pension fund management . . . In this fractionalized structure, everyone is looking at narrow slices of the market, but no one is looking at the customer as a whole, so important aggregate issues may fall between the cracks.[14]

As the teams get together to close the gaps, they have to be aware of the dangers of suboptimization and fractionalization. They have to think of the bank as an "open system" where change in one process means a corresponding change in one or more other processes, and they have to be sure that they understand the implication of one kind of transaction on another. Above all, they have to view it from the perspective of the customer. With competition so stiff, they have to look at their processes as ways to get customers in the front door and then to satisfy their needs for service.

That brings us to a subtle difference in motivation. Why are the teams here? What are they supposed to do? The literature says that they should have a cost-reduction target, something like that 40 percent number we saw before. Having such a goal is supposed to make people really creative as they get together to reduce cost. In a bank, however, 40 percent of noninterest expense means people. The goal then becomes one of how many people to cut out. It is reducing capacity to meet current demand or it is reducing capacity period, regardless of the demand.

> Profitable companies use customer intelligence as the cornerstone of their [service improvement] programs to deliver more of the right values at the right time. A recently published study concludes that "strong market leaders" deliver 15% more satisfaction than their competitors and that increasing customer satisfaction by 3% adds 1% to ROI.[15]

There is a different target that the teams should have: closing the service quality gap. Wouldn't it be better to hear, "Guys, your task is to improve service so that the gaps are closed. Yes, we want you to reduce cost, but attack the cost of quality, don't just cut. Our main concern is getting our service levels to where we don't have much customer attrition. We want to improve revenues as a result of streamlined, customer-friendly delivery systems. That's your charge!" Having a goal like that makes things a lot easier and much more positive.

BATTER UP!

As with much of what is contained in *The Banking Revolution,* I have used examples and stories about one area of the bank that are intended to apply to other areas. Teaching in this way lets people relate to a particular situation and then think about how it fits in with their own areas. Now it's time to talk about a service excellence team; I do so in a generic sense. Installment lending is the subject this time, but the same principles apply for any of the bank's processes.

In our example in this chapter, the manager of the retail division has created three teams. One is to look at the mortgage loan processes because it has a negative gap of over −1.700. Those folks have a lot of work to do in a hurry with a gap that large. Installment lending also needs help because the gap on the direct side is over −1.200 while that of indirect is almost −1.000. Home equity lending is under study as well. The manager of consumer lending has been chosen as the process sponsor for installment. There is a representative from the branch network, a calling officer or two, someone from credit, the manager of installment loan operations, an auditor familiar with the commercial loan process, a person skilled in loan accounting and accruals, the marketing director, and the head of deposit operations.

The people you ask to be on the team really depend on your bank. If it is a small institution, maybe these kinds of people don't exist or they serve in dual functions. If the bank is larger, additional people may be necessary. Whatever the size, the people who are critical to the delivery of installment loans or any product have to be on the team.

A word of caution for the process sponsor who has now assumed the mantle of team leader: the people on your team have been assembled to help you improve things. They are not there to be commanded; several of them may be your equal in title and some may be higher. As you assume the leadership role, remember what it is to be a servant leader. Your job is to facilitate the improvement process, providing the grease to make it run as smooth as possible.

There will be regularly scheduled team meetings with a set agenda at which progress reports will be given. There will also be brainstorming sessions which may last all day. The task of the leader is to be perceptive to the needs of the team and to help it along. There is a deadline now and a target. It is time to move on.

For the team to be effective, it needs data. It needs an accurate representation of exactly what is going on within the process that led to the service quality gaps that were placed before them at the first meeting. The head of retail has attended the first meeting and set out the ground rules, effectively empowering the team to action. The task is to look at the process by which installment loans are sold to and serviced for customers. Obviously, with the wide gaps between expectation and perception, those customers think there is room for improvement. The assignment for the team is to create ways to close the gaps.

The next data are the survey results from those involved in making installment loans and servicing them on a daily basis. We know that external customers have given the process a rating of -1.200 on direct lending and -1.000 on the indirect lending. Now we have to find out what the people who are delivering that service think. In this example, the results from the internal customer surveys for direct and indirect are about the same, -1.350, telling us that the perception in the market is better than it is inside the bank, but we still don't know why. On to the culture survey, the results of the workforce activity questionnaire, and the classification into the four dimensions of the cost of quality. The team also reviews customer attrition rates retrieved from the installment loan system. They are able to determine how many loans were put on the books, how many went to maturity before they were closed, how many were closed early, and the costs and revenues for each grouping.

Using these data, the team can "drill down" quickly to identify the amount of time and money spent on corrective activities in the aggregate. Then it can dig all the way to the individual level to find out why specific people within the installment loan chain are so unproductive. They are looking for two things. Why are customers leaving the bank? Why are more leaving than coming in the front door?

The team has to begin to see the cause-and-effect relationships within the process. They have to remember that the bank is an open system wherein every activity is offset somewhere else. That is why they cannot simply cut cost or change things on the surface. They have to understand the ramifications of any changes before they are made. Therefore, they need to visualize the work flow as it really is, which is usually a difficult and disorganized endeavor.

Decisions have to be made about where one process ends and the next one begins as well as the level of detail that needs to be examined as the root cause analysis gets under way. To do that, the team needs to make those decisions and to document exactly how the process in question works. The result is a process work flow, or flowchart, which depicts all of the steps within a given process and allows the members of the team to see how transactions and paper wind their way through the bank. In most cases, this is an eye-opening experience.

A number of fine software programs are commercially available by which to develop this process map. They are easy to use and will guide the development of similar ones for the functions within the process under study. For every one of them, there are five components:

Supplier → Input → Mechanism → Output→ Customer

Each person in the chain can be considered a mechanism, that is, doing something to add value to the input received from the prior person in it. That is why it is essential for each one to know the expectations of the next person in the line. In any process, there is a critical dependency on the accuracy of the input. If it is not what is needed for use right away, time and money are lost in the correction process. Therefore, starting with the external customers' needs and expectations, the team has to work all the way through the process to identify the requirements of each function within it and then to assess how well those requirements are being met.

In this case, it could well be that the process starts with hiring people who can work well with customers, in the design of the application form, or in the rates and terms being offered. The team has to backtrack all the way to the absolute beginning, so that it can see all of the interrelationships and dependencies that the process contains before it starts to make any improvements.

To develop the process map, the team has to conduct field research. Making sure that they are not assigned their own area of responsibility, team members fan out into the bank to find out what the people actually delivering the service are really doing. They have the results from the workforce activity research. They can see how each person in the chain is spending his or her time. They need to verify that and, at the same time, to understand all of the steps involved in each of the functions within it.

Two members of the team hit the branches or wherever customers fill out application forms. Two others interview the people who do the credit review. Another pair is dispatched to the installment loan operations area. Still more make an appointment in accounting to map what happens there. They need to visit every organizational unit that has been identified as touching upon the installment lending function, asking questions such as the following:

- What is the purpose of this activity?
- What triggers action, that is, what is your input (forms, reports, deadlines, etc.)?
- Who supplies the input to you?
- What do you do with that input?
- What steps happen according to a deadline?
- What steps happen every day? Are there some that happen only once in a while?
- What do you do with the output?
- Is it stored someplace? Do you send it to somebody else? If so, to whom?
- Are there any delays in this activity?
- Are there any redundancies?
- Do you know exactly what the next person in the chain does with the output? Are you supplying it according to expectations?
- Does the input you receive meet your expectations?

As team members conduct their research, they are doing three things: (1) they are finding out what is happening that causes the service quality results to be as they are; (2) they are asking how things should be in the minds of the people directly accountable for it—they know, but they may never have been asked; and (3) they are finding out about individual expectations, whether they have been communicated and are being met.

As the research continues, each group can use a technique called a "force-field analysis" (see Table 9–6). The analysis can be used to document what is happening with the current procedure and to record ideas about better ways to provide the service. The difference between the two is the gap that the team has to close.

T A B L E 9–6

Installment Lending Service Excellence Team
Force-Field Analysis

Function: _____	Task: _____
What Is	*What Should Be*

There is an additional benefit from this technique: People from different areas of the bank are crossing organizational boundaries as they research their processes and are suggesting that others do the same to improve communication and cooperation between the various units. They encourage those with whom they meet to see the people for whom they provide input to find out whether their expectations are being met. This will further blur the traditional organizational lines and boxes.

Once the research has been completed, the process map, or flowchart, can be drawn. It is best to have one central software system for the team to use to ensure consistency of approach and to allow the linkages of the various functions to be made. When the process map is generated, note the points that are those essential moments-of-truth and take the applicable pieces back to those who were interviewed to make sure that the way the process is functioning was captured accurately. If it was, great. If not, change it. This can be a time-consuming and difficult process, so approach it with curiosity and patience.

EXPLORATION

Armed with the process map, the gap analysis provided by customers and the people in the chain, the cost of quality analysis, and the results of the culture and workforce activity surveys, the team can really get down to work. Team members can start to look for things that are problems in the delivery of service to customers:

- Layers of management that add no value.
- Places where effort is replicated.
- Unclear or complicated handoff points.
- Inabilities to meet schedules and deadlines.
- Frequent corrective activities.
- Time spent clarifying or changing input.
- Places where work stacks up.
- Effort that adds little or no value to the process.
- Lack of communication within activities or the process.
- Volume in excess of capacity.

The team can start to hone in on the dimensions that customers say are the most important, looking at these potential problem areas, asking the questions:

- What is this activity? Why is it being done? Is there a customer for it? Do we need to do it? Who else could do it?
- Where are we doing this activity? Is there a good reason why it is done there? Is there a more appropriate place to do it?
- When does this activity take place? Does that make sense? Could it be scheduled at a better time? Does it fit in a natural sequence?
- How much is being processed? How much effort is spent in rework or corrective activities? Do we have enough capacity? Do we have too much capacity?
- Who is accountable for this activity? Where does he or she report? Why there? How do these people add value to the process? Would it be better positioned somewhere else?
- Why is this activity being done this way? How could it be done better?

As these questions are being asked and answered, remember that we are after process improvements because 85 percent to 95 percent of the problems that occur in the bank are a function of process design. Working with the people who are continuing to provide service and using research techniques such as the Pareto analysis or scatter diagrams, the team can see how often a specific problem is occurring and relate it to the other pieces of the process.

When that is done and the team has a clear understanding of the breakdowns that are causing the gaps, they can begin to fix them. Team members have some options. First, they can eliminate a step or an activity altogether if it is adding no value or is detracting from the pursuit of excellence. Second, they may combine a step with a similar function as long as capacity is sufficient to prevent incurring any bottlenecks. Third, it may be best to change the person responsible for the activity if there is a more logical place for it to be conducted. The team may also want to rearrange the timing to make for a smoother operation overall. Finally, they may wish to change how a step is being accomplished if there is a more effective way to do so.

Thus, before they even think about innovative ways to deliver service differently, team members have to correct what customers are telling them needs work now. They have to concentrate on current customer attrition and do whatever is necessary to minimize it. Once determined, they can help the people who are working with their customers on a daily basis to make the required change.

As they analyze the process and the various functions within it, team members also need to work with the people within the process to make sure that it is under control; in other words, they have to establish measurement points, standards of acceptable performance, and ways to know if those standards are being met. They have begun to see the relationships between the functions; they are beginning to understand why cooperation is so important; now they have to make sure whether the expectations of the next person or persons in the chain are being met. As those expectations are documented, they become those measurement points. Each function within the process defines its output in accordance with the expectations of those next in line. Whether it is the percentage of the loan applications that are completed properly and on time, or the disbursement that was made in accordance with customer wishes, whatever is important to the effective running of the process becomes the metric to be used.

A new study by The Conference Board, a business research firm in New York, notes that senior managers today realize that to compete effectively they have to keep tabs on investments in "vital intangibles," such as processes to improve quality and customer satisfaction.

> "Traditional measures lack predictive power," says Carolyn Brancatao, The Conference Board's director of corporate governance and author of the report. "They do not capture key business changes until it is too late. They reflect divisional, not cross-functional processes within a company . . . a small, but growing number of companies in the United States and abroad are explicitly developing key performance measures that incorporate both financial and non-financial measures to augment the more traditional [ones]."[16]

Now, don't go hog-wild on me here. No more than five measures per function. They are your critical success factors, so don't get to the place where all you are doing is measuring stuff. That will take you away from designing your processes to meet your customers' expectations. Work with them to find out what things are critical to their success, then measure those. No more, no less. As you go through this exercise and find that you are doing things that your customer doesn't want or need, there's a good chance you can discontinue them. But talk with your customers, even if they happen to be the regulators or the independent auditing firm. Remember, whatever it is may have an impact farther down the chain. Don't change anything until you know what that effect really is.

FIRST SIGNS OF A TURNAROUND

The team has brought installment lending to the point where the key players understand all of the relationships involved in providing the service to the bank's customers. The inefficiencies in the process have been corrected, and the latest survey data are beginning to show that the service quality gaps are narrowing. It has taken some time, probably close to six months, but customer attrition has not increased. In fact, it has begun to decline. Where it was not a great deal of fun in the beginning to report to the service improvement council, the team leader actually looks forward to making the monthly report.

The people in the branches are measuring their accuracy for the people in loan administration, making sure that they beat the standard. It may not be six sigma yet, but it's on the way up. The folks in Loan Administration are making sure that the loans get put on the books, funds are disbursed, and coupon books are issued. The people involved in the process have been educated about the importance of service excellence; they have coordinated with their customers and know their expectations, and they have told their suppliers in the chain what they need to produce their own piece of it right the first time and every time.

> In the words of M. D. "Mal" Hepburn, president of Ozaukee Bank, Cedarburg, Wisconsin, "I cannot over-emphasize the long-term benefit of investing in your people. In our bank, we enjoy low turnover, high morale and productivity, and a waiting list of quality applicants. There's no doubt in my mind that we are in the top ten in earnings in our state because of our people first philosophy."[17]

Error rates are coming down; the cost to provide the service follows because fewer mistakes are being made. The savings can be applied to an advertising campaign that emphasizes quality service, no ifs, ands, or buts. People involved in the improved delivery system are rewarded for meeting their quality standards, not just because they managed to survive another year. They share in the wealth that they have created, and the leaders at the top of the house show their appreciation with a semiannual recognition ceremony.

The word is getting out all over town. More and more people start to apply for the bank's installment loans. Market share starts to increase. External customer surveys say that the gaps between expectations and perceptions are narrowing even further. They aren't positive yet, but the trend is definitely in the right direction. Whenever problems arise, the team knows it before anyone else. Things are good. Now what?

It's time to challenge the entire process by which installment lending is accomplished, looking for better ways to do it. This is where the fun really begins. This is where team members have the time to think about new concepts for providing the lending service. They aren't fixing current problems. There aren't any because the people of the chain have set their standards, let their suppliers know what they expect, and are measuring performance. Now the team can challenge every assumption in the process. Team members can say, "Why do we do it that way? What would happen if . . .?" It's a process called brainstorming.

For the facilitator and the team, a few rules of brainstorming need some amplification. They should be repeated every time a brainstorming session takes place to remind the participants of the code to be followed. First, say whatever comes into your head. Censorship is outlawed by the First Amendment, and that applies to the bank as well. Further, this is no time to be bashful. Some of the greatest ideas have come when people brainstorm from what others have said. Go for it.

Second, there are no real boundaries. Everything is fair game, regardless of how stupid it might sound. This is where people from outside the process can be a big help. Even if there is only a remote connection, say it anyway.

Third, don't worry about offending anyone. We're concerned about creativity here. Trip over each other, interrupt if you have to, but always say, "Excuse me, but I may have something here." If politeness is a virtue, write your thought down, holding it until the proper opening happens. When it does, jump in, fast!

Fourth, don't commit "ideacide" or "firehosing." Those terms mean that someone kills an idea before it is evaluated. Evaluation happens later. It is the entire team's job to "boo" anyone who commits these dastardly crimes. Every idea is a great one. Every idea has possibilities. Don't let anyone throw water on any of them. The one that got wet might be the very one that lets you outdistance the competition.

Here's a familiar story. Maggie, a merchandising manager for a large supermarket chain, is excited about a new idea that would change and expand the chain's marketing approach to appeal to the increasing number of double-paycheck families. Her boss listens to her enthusiastic and well-prepared presentation and from time to time interrupts, saying things such as:

"If it's not in the budget, where's the money going to come from?"

"Who'll do all the extra work to set it up?"

"It's going to decrease our quarterly numbers."

"It'll never work."

"It's not practical."

"Why change? Things are working the way they are."

"Yeah, but . . ."

"We've never tried anything like that before."

"That's not the way we do things around here."

In an attempt to cling to the familiar and stay on safe ground, Maggie's boss responded like a fireman hosing down a fire. He effectively "firehosed" her, dousing her ideas, enthusiasm, and spirit.[18]

Nothing will kill the spirit of the team faster than the firehose. Both team leaders and the service improvement council must have open minds when ideas and suggestions are brought to them. They need to be encouraging coaches who help the team members nurture their ideas into reality.

As the brainstorming comes to an end, the team can begin to compress the process into fewer steps, using the benefits of technology in new ways. Maybe loan approvals can be communicated using one of those computers that prints your bill at the airport when you return your rental car as you are taking your attaché case out of the back seat. Maybe they can use the Internet to advertise the greatness of the lending process: "No Hassle Lending," and mean it. In doing so, they continue to provide more value to the bank because the fewer the steps in the process, the fewer chances there are for errors to occur. It also makes the whole process faster to accomplish as there are fewer handoffs and reasons to have to stop the process to get a decision from somebody higher up the corporate ladder.

The team can start to ask questions like the following:

- Is the work being done by the right people?
- Are the core tasks that require the unique expertise of the bank being done in-house?
- Are those that aren't done in-house being contracted to trusted third parties who may even be customers?

- Are the people who are doing the work selected in a way that matches their skills, talents, and desires with the requirements of the task or the job?
- Are the people compensated in the fairest, most appropriate way?
- Is everyone involved in the process given the information they need to understand their part in the system?
- Does the way in which people are organized help them to fulfill their responsibilities?
- Or does it tie them to outdated expectations and assumptions that were valid only in another time?[19]

As all of this happens, the new process begins to take shape naturally. Ideas surface about better ways to serve both inside and outside the bank. The teams are encouraged not to think about the potential consequences of resource reallocation opportunities but about how to improve customer relationships and to keep the competition at bay. At this point, when there are no more suggestions, each idea is subject to rigorous evaluation in terms of volume, quality, and time. The new work process should allow the production of the greatest amount of volume, at the quality level specified by the customer, in the least amount of time. Therefore, the team has to test and verify each alternative suggestion and include only those that pass.

Once done, the suggestions that remain are then ordered into the new process. In doing so, the team should look to reduce the number of steps by 30 percent to 50 percent. As it does so, be sure to document how the new process works compared with the previous one. There are three reasons for doing this.

1. Removing tasks and activities from a delivery process means that the bank will have some excess human capacity. Anyone whose job depended on those unnecessary tasks becomes a candidate for additional education and skill development and subsequent redeployment to other positions. Some centerpost in the bank, probably the human resources department, will need to track this procedure, reporting regularly to the service improvement council.

2. The team must calculate the economic impact of the changes. It may have developed its own financial target during the improvement process. Therefore, a simplified transaction flow will result in cost savings, other things being equal. Documentation of the new process cost allows the team to compare it against the old and to share in some of the difference.

3. The standards that were set before will have to change. The team and the people in the chain will have to see if the metrics established before still apply, and add to or change them as they see fit. They must make sure that the measures are consistent with the chain's critical success factors. And they need to be incorporated into the bank's performance measurement system and tied to individual and group rewards.

The team has capitalized on the processes and systems that the bank has had in place to bring new ways of providing excellent service to its customers, but it has used revolutionary thinking, style, and structure to do it. It has designed a process that provides regular feedback about customer and workforce attitudes. It can see what the people within their value chains are doing and how that relates to the cost of quality.

The team knows that the expectations of customers are communicated throughout the ranks of those who are providing lending services and that actions are regularly and routinely taken to make sure that they are being met, even if they change. Attacking the service quality gaps as a way to improve financial performance is a much more positive approach than expense productivity where the cost side of the ledger is the focus. This way, the concentration is on customers, the people who provide them with service, and the reasons for being in business.

INSTALLING THE NEW PROCESS

It is time to install the new process. As with anything new, implementation has to be controlled. Using the PDCA (plan, do, check, act) cycle, developed by Walter Shewhart in the 1930s, the team can assure itself that the change process is being done in an orderly way.

The first step in the cycle is to develop and document the implementation plan. In the plan, the team details the problems to be solved, citing the benchmarks gained from the data collection effort with customers and the workforce. Team members describe the actions they want to take, the results they expect to achieve, the measurements they will use, and the standards of performance that will ensure that the expectations of their customers are being met. They make sure that the process is organized around the value chain and that communication channels are wide open.

The plan outlines who is to do what, the time frame for completion, and the resources that are necessary to implement it. The plan also includes a section on potential negative outcomes, if any; the projected impact the changes will have on quality and customer service; and a contingency plan in case the proposed solutions fail. In short, the team must think through all the changes that they want to make and plan thoroughly and accordingly.

Next, they "do." The team presents the plan to the service improvement council in what should be a mere formality. Presuming that communication has been good throughout the process, the council should be very well aware of the progress of the team and the likely changes that will be proposed. There should be no surprises, so think through the installation in terms of tools, education, and physical relocation. Then test the change on a small scale, if possible. Do a pilot test in one branch, but make sure to document what happens: What was done? How was it done? What was the effect on the customer? What was the impact on the organization?

Third, they must "check." After the change has been implemented at the test site, the team must check the results to make sure that it worked and to determine what was learned. As a word of caution, though, processes temporarily improve simply because people are paying attention to them. So, the team must be very careful. They must measure objectively, making sure that it is the change that has caused the difference and not the extra attention that has been given. Once that has been determined, and based upon the results, the design of the change may need some refinement, or it might have to be scrapped altogether as unworkable. If it has failed, the team will need to review the plan to determine what happened and to reconvene to chart a new course.

Finally, the team "acts." If the change meets with the success criteria of the test, the team can take the final step to adopt and incorporate it into the rest of the operation. Make sure that the metrics are working because they are the only way to know that the service your customers want is what they are getting. It is very tempting to rush through this final step, because (1) it is exciting and (2) you are about to get results. Nevertheless, it is important to take things slowly and carefully. A little preventive thinking at this stage will avoid numerous problems down the road. It is a different way of operating. I hope you can see that. It focuses first and foremost on your customers and next on the designing processes to meet their expectations. It also takes advantage of the bank's greatest resource, its people, who come in every day and work hard to make the place better.

Downsizing, restructuring, reengineering? They have the wrong target. They are after cost as the bank tries to improve earnings. Process mapping, teamwork, innovation, service to others—that's the best way to improve earnings. Costs come down naturally. Revenues go up, but they do so because the people are working together. It is the senior leadership that serves as the beacon, listening to the scouts, planning for a better future, and giving those who would follow the time and the resources by which to achieve it. It is the teams who diligently analyze data, brainstorm crazy ideas, and help those in their value chains to understand the new order. And it is the people of the chains themselves, who see customers every day and experience those real moments of truth. It is all of you, working together in the service of your customers.

My friend, Ken Heiser, president and CEO of First National Bank in Hudson, Wisconsin, summed it up well:

A key factor in our success . . . has been our stable, experienced staff. It is impossible to build long-term customer relationships with short-term employees. High turnover hurts our bottom line because of lost training dollars and lost customers. *Paying attention to our employees makes the difference between remaining in first place and coming in second.* [italics added][20]

Ken knows that he and the bank will be successful because of the workforce. He understands the value they bring to First National Bank every day. They may not have gone through an improvement process like the one described here. They may not have needed to. The point is that guys like Ken Heiser and Mal Hepburn put people first. They realize the importance of customers, how crucial it is to serve them well, and the only way to do that is with a highly motivated, happy workforce. Their banks prosper because of it, and I'll bet they are having fun in the process.

ENDNOTES

1. Rahul Jacob, "TQM: More than a Dying Fad," *Fortune,* Oct. 18, 1993, p. 72.
2. Letter to the editor, *CFO,* Oct. 1995, p. 11.
3. Steven A. Behrens, "The 4 R's of Finance: Re-think, Re-engineering, Re-tool, Re-energize," speech at Digital Equipment Corporation Corporate Leaders Forum, Nov. 16, 1992.
4. *CFO,* Oct. 1995, p. 9.
5. Stephen Barr, "Grinding It Out: Why Reengineering Takes So Long," *CFO,* Jan. 1995, p. 27.
6. Ibid.
7. Michael Hammer and James Champy, *Reengineering the Corporation* (New York: HarperBusiness, 1994), p. 31.
8. Alex Sheshunoff, "Reengineering the Bank," *Bank Director,* Fourth Quarter 1993, p. 15.
9. Quoted in Michael Hammer, "Beating the Risks of Reengineering," *Fortune,* May 15, 1995, p. 106.
10. John H. Wolfarth, "Focusing on Processes Improvement," *Bankers Magazine,* Jan.-Feb. 1995, p. 51.
11. Shawn Tully, "Why to Go for Stretch Targets," *Fortune,* Nov. 14, 1994, p. 146.
12. Hammer and Champy, *Reengineering the Corporation,* p. 105.
13. Quoted in Hammer, "Beating the Risks of Reengineering," p. 106.
14. Hammer and Champy, *Reengineering the Corporation,* pp. 63–64.
15. "Reader's Report," *Business Week,* Aug. 29, 1994, p. 8.
16. Quoted in Bill Birchard, "Making It Count," *CFO,* Oct. 1995, p. 44.
17. Quoted in Bob Romano and Barbara Sanfilippo, "The People Factor: 6 Ways to Energize Your Service Quality Process," *Bank Marketing,* Dec. 1993, p. 29.
18. Robert J. Kriegel and Louis Patler, *If It Ain't Broke . . . BREAK IT!* (New York: Warner Books, 1991), pp. 21–22.
19. William Bridges, "The End of the Job," *Fortune,* Sept. 19, 1994, p. 74.
20. Quoted in Romano and Sanfilippo, "The People Factor," p. 26.

CHAPTER 10

Final Thoughts

The purpose of *The Banking Revolution* has been to show how the pursuit of excellence leads to improved market share and revenue streams. It also results in increased organizational efficiency and reduced costs. Truly, it is the best of all worlds. To achieve this market and financial success, we have learned about five organizational imperatives: the importance of a customer focus that is not an internal one always aimed solely on the overhead ratio; the necessity to consider the long term instead of the next 90 days and what the analysts might think; the efficiency that a flattened, nonbureaucratic, horizontal organization affords; a culture that encourages and rewards continuous improvement of the processes within the bank; and a style that is based on servant leadership, where team leaders and other managers change their approach from command and control to servant leadership—designer, steward, and teacher.

This may be a tall order for many banks and their bankers whose structures and styles are so embedded in history that change of this kind cannot happen. Furthermore, with the rapid pace of Merger Mania II, I am afraid that for some banks there won't be time. However, for those that have enough, my purpose has been to acquaint you with these ideas so that you might develop a new understanding of the organizational and personal behavior necessary to survive and prosper as we head into the next century. The hope is that these ideas can find their way into your bank if they are not already there, or that they can be strengthened if this kind of change process has already begun.

THREE CONSTANTS

We have talked in great detail about the economics of such a strategy, learning that service excellence results in lower operating costs, greater customer retention, more cross-sales to them, increased sales to new customers, and reduced marketing costs. We have learned how to eliminate the errors that result in poor service by gathering data from customers and the workforce, and using that data to change what the people of the bank do each and every day. That process must become the way of life at the bank as all of your delivery systems must be subject to endless study and improvement.

We have seen why it is so important to understand what customers want and to organize in such a way that the bank can meet their expectations. The advent of the incredible nature of competition within the financial services industry and the new technology have made that evaluation a must, and there is no pat answer. Yes, customers may be telling a bank, such as Huntington in Ohio, that the branch system as we know it may be obsolete; yet, it may be the lifeblood of First of America, which has offices throughout the Midwest. Yes, customers may be suggesting to Wells Fargo that the Internet is the perfect distribution channel for that bank, but your customers haven't said that to you. That's what makes the industry so intriguing. It is extremely diverse as America's bankers seek to find and establish their niches. Nevertheless, throughout all of this turmoil, there are three constants.

First, and without question, the successful financial institution will serve its customers better than any other financial institution in its markets. It will know their expectations across every external and internal service line, and it will do whatever is necessary to meet them. These organizations will place the value of the customer first, even before the shareholder, for they realize that without customers there is no need for shareholders. As a result, they do not place the efficiency ratio and earnings per share at the forefront of their culture, which means in turn that they do not get into the kinds of deals that were made in previous years in the developing countries of Latin America, in energy in Texas and Oklahoma, in commercial real estate in Massachusetts, and the like. They will understand their niches, strengths, and weaknesses, always remembering why they are in business and making the continuous improvement of the way they serve the corporate way of life.

Second, if the last 10 years are any example, the pace of change will accelerate in the banking industry. Who even heard of the Internet five years ago except the nation's academicians? And now we will be using it to look for the best rates and terms on loans worldwide, to pay bills, to move funds into the best alternatives, and who knows what else. It may not happen overnight, but it is going to happen.

To be sure, full blown home banking isn't just around the corner. Fewer than 1 percent of all bank customers currently manage their money on-line, and it will take time to persuade more to do so. . . . According to Jupiter Communications LLC, a Manhattan research firm, there are currently about 700,000 active users of home banking services in the U.S. . . . Jupiter predicts that the home banking market will grow by five million users by the turn of the century. By 2005, it says, 75 percent of all U.S. homes will be doing some form of home banking. By 2010, the company forecasts, 95 percent of homes will be banking in cyberspace.[1]

It used to be that the "turn of the century" was a long way off, but it will occur in four years. What Jupiter Communications is suggesting is that in the first decade of the 21st century, a technological explosion will occur in banking, the size of which we have never seen before: from 1 percent of all homes enjoying home banking in 1995 to 95 percent some 15 years down the road. Of course, the actual dates might not be exact and the percentages may be off a tad, but there is no denying that it is going to happen, big time. That means the bank will have to become knowledgeable about these new distribution channels and will have to be able to operate within them, presuming of course that they are what its customers want. But if Jupiter is right and the number does approach 95 percent, Americans in even the smallest towns will avail themselves of this technological innovation.

A second element of change is also becoming more evident as each day passes. As we turn the corner to 2000, there will be significantly fewer banks in this country. We spoke of the merger of Chase Manhattan and Chemical Bank. First Bank System will stay active, as will PNC. There is some smoke starting to be seen in San Francisco and Charlotte as Bank of America and NationsBank are talking merger to create America's first $400 billion banking giant. First Interstate, the nation's 14th largest bank, will disappear in 1996.

The conventional wisdom says that costs have to be cut to pay for the deal. That means people. Very few acquirers talk about revenue enhancement except to say that they haven't reached their targets. What that means is that it is harder to improve income levels than it is to cut costs, so the attention stays firmly focused on the expense side of the ledger. Some people think there will be only 2,500 banks in this country by 2010, down from the 11,000 that we have now. That means even more turmoil.

Finally the bank needs great people, but that creates a dilemma. Banking has always been a "people business," so the institutions that survive will have to have first-rate, top-notch people who have been educated in how to serve customers better than anyone else. Still, will transacting business in cyberspace fundamentally change that, making it obsolete? Maybe. But, even though we will witness the marvels of technology, it will be the people of the bank that make it work. They may have different roles than they do now, but service requires people even if it only means having the technology in place to make sure that statements are available when customers ask for them.

As technology impacts jobs and how people serve, there will be even more profound change as the consolidation starts to occur. Here's the problem: Mergers mean that people are let go. That suggests that few people will want to come to work in a place that may disappear in the next year or two. If they don't, there won't be any fresh, new ideas coming in. The thing is, you never know when the tender offer from the outside is going to occur. The people at First Interstate thought they were safe. Then, boom, here comes the hostile offer from Wells Fargo that put the bank in play.

To complicate matters further, the legacy of the cost cutting of the 1980s, which pervades the industry, also might scare those talented people whom you need. In essence, it will be very difficult to keep the people that the bank will need to provide the services that customers want, and perhaps it will be even more difficult to attract new ones. This may be the most fundamental problem that U.S. bankers face: how to get talented, professional people to come to work in a place that may not be around very long or might be subject to another round of cost cutting.

Coming up with the answer to that will be a challenge, and the answers will be as different as there are banks in this country. How one bank approaches it may not be appropriate for another, but rest assured, the people in human resources in your bank need to face up to it right now. As they do, two things are clear. One, it will be difficult to make very many promises until the frenzy is over. That makes it hard for people to embrace the long-term view as they look for some economic security. Second, because that is the case, the bank has to take care of those who stay.

REWARDS!

As we have seen, the banking revolution is about change, change in the way the people of the bank think and act in the service of their customers. Throughout it, we have talked about freeing up people to analyze data from customers and themselves about the way that service is provided. The motivation is that serving others makes them feel good about themselves and spurs them on to continue the behavior that resulted in it. Although social psychologists will tell us that the nonfinancial reward is more important than the financial one, for the most part we respond to money. Simply put, people will do what they are paid to do. It is the reason we go to work in the first place. We have things to buy, the mortgage payment, the tab at the grocery store, and other bills to pay. We also have to think about the education of our children, and, frankly, we deserve to be paid fairly for our time and effort. Therefore, the leadership must make sure that the compensation program rewards people equitably, and stimulates a behavior pattern that contributes to the well-being of customers and ultimately to that of the bank. It should be a "win-win-win" situation. Unfortunately, it doesn't always happen.

The promise of the big return is what made the bankers of the 1960s and 1970s invest in the highly speculative real estate investment trusts (REITs), loans to developing countries, and energy-related credits. The promise of windfall profits fosters dreams of more cash in the wallet and may cloud the use of sound judgment. It is what made commercial real estate deals and leveraged buyouts so attractive in the 1980s, even though, in general, they failed. It is what made Nick Leeson gamble at Barings and lose everything in the process, including the bank itself. It is also what caused Daiwa's Toshide Iguchi to roll the dice to cover his losses, which resulted in his indictment and the expulsion of Daiwa from the United States and the possibility of a forced merger with another Japanese institution. In what may be the most troubling lack of judgment, it is what caused Procter & Gamble to charge Bankers Trust with "broad, systemic fraud" and "racketeering" as the bank "engaged in a pervasive pattern of fraud spanning a number of years and involving numerous victims."[2] The motivation is wrong in these cases. It is not focused on improving the welfare of the bank's customers. It is concentrated on personal gain, which the traditional compensation system encourages.

The typical bank uses the conventional system which, with the cultural emphasis on cost, rewards the workforce according to the amount of the merit increase budget rather than on the basis of their performance. That, in all reality, pits the members of the staff against each other as they fight to see who can get the highest raise. The pie is only so big, so the people, even within the same department, compete with each other to see who can get the biggest slice. Presumably they are doing what their customers want, but more likely than not, they are completing assignments to please the boss, which may or may not be contributing any value. Therefore, when the big raise arrives, not only is there financial satisfaction knowing that you got the largest one, but psychologically you are on a high because you think that you're better than everyone else. That kind of incentive really precludes a sense of teamwork and any hope that the workforce will ever come together in the pursuit of a common objective.

The big contributor to this way of thinking is the bell curve, which forces the classification of people into three general performance categories. Twenty percent of the people are allowed to be excellent, 60 percent are told that they are average, and 20 percent are either on probation or ready to be fired. Even if your value chain is providing the service that meets your customers' expectations, you are forced to rate the majority of the staff as merely adequate or less, which is hardly a positive motivator.

A couple of observations. We have established that the bank has to attract the finest, most talented people it possibly can to be creative and innovative in the service of its customers. By doing so, it establishes a talent bank that is highly motivated and works hard to serve. It also takes these talented individuals away from the competition. Is it not better that the bank have them onboard than Merrill Lynch or First Boston?

By using the bell curve approach, the bank immediately says to those high-powered people that it has hired, "Oh, by the way, 60 percent of you are just average and will get only a 3 percent raise, if that much. For the bottom 20 percent, you're in trouble; maybe you made a mistake and should find a job someplace else." In those cases, before the axe can fall, it's off to Merrill Lynch where creativity and industriousness are appreciated.

> By using the bell-shaped curve in labor-force decisions, organizations impose an unnatural constraint on the workforce and productivity in order to support an outdated competition/conflict mentality. Many managers force employees into the curve because it once again gives them the opportunity to neutralize potential competition. They presuppose that there must be losers when having all winners is ultimately better for the bottom line. . . It also creates a group of "B" and "C" grade employees who eventually begin to accept and believe in their inferiority.[3]

Thus, being forced into the bell curve is a huge demotivator even for great performers, but that has been part of the command-and-control style for decades. Its subtle message? There are two. First, people will do whatever they think is necessary to move from a "B" to an "A" because that's the way to get more money. Second, and make no mistake, management is in charge. If you make a mistake of any kind, you certainly will not be rewarded, and it is quite possible that management will drop you from a "B" to a "C." It is quite the opposite of servant leadership. This emphasis on cost does little to add to an infectious spirit of service. What we really need is value chains that contain nothing but "A's," who are then rewarded according to their customer satisfaction ratings.

The bell curve poses a management problem, too. Those at the lower end of senior management and those in middle management have to figure out how to get great work from their people, knowing that there is going to be little reward at the end. "I'm sorry, you have done a great job this past year, and I got you all the money I could," is the refrain employees hear as supervisors try to explain away a 2 percent raise to people who have been determined to meet the customer expectations all year long and have the measures to prove it. Great performance is exactly what the bank must have to compete, but the typical compensation system blocks it.

It is the same with promotions. Considering the subjective nature of business, little thought is given to measurement of contribution when raises are passed out or promotions are given. Goals and objectives set at the beginning of the year are obsolete within weeks or months due to the speed of change in the industry, which makes it almost impossible to use them as a performance metric. Furthermore, having individual goals does little to foster a sense of teamwork as we climb over each other on the way up the corporate ladder.

The traditional promotional legacy is to advance those who behave like the boss and do what the boss wants. It is a very political activity that penalizes those who may be contributing a significant amount of excellent work but who may not fit the "corporate image." We also promote those who are the best technicians and who may not give a hoot about being managers. They become unhappy and demotivated because, in effect, they have been set up to fail when previously they were valuable contributors to the success of the organization. They just don't want to be managers. I have known some brilliant financial people in the bank whose effectiveness died when they were made part of management. They did not want to be there and have that responsibility. The best strategy to deal with them? Give them what they need to do their jobs, and like Shrontz at Boeing, get out of their way.

There is another powerful influence on the promotion decision which gets back to the whole issue of cost. In many banks, promotions instead of a raise are used as a motivator. It is thought that organizational prominence is more important than rewarding people for what they have done. This policy keeps the overhead ratio low, but it is the opposite of what people really want. People would rather have a little extra in their pockets, but the traditional line is, "Let's make Jack an assistant vice president" with little or no added responsibility, authority, or dollars.

Thus, everyone in the bank has a title, whether it be senior executive vice chairman or installment loan operations credit review supervisor. It all gets back to the military, the hierarchy, and all that. In reality, people don't care about titles because everyone has one. What they care about is financial well-being and the satisfaction that they have done a good job.

Along with raises and promotions, we also need to think a little about incentive plans. I have previously mentioned the $800 million dollar bank that had 66 different incentive compensation programs. Many of them were in the same organizational unit, were diametrically opposed to one another, and caused a great deal of confusion about what the workforce was really supposed to do. Another problem with incentives is entitlement. If we are lucky enough to be included in an incentive program, we get used to being there and begin to think that the annual bonus is our due.

> "In a recent quarter, the people of my area got 96 percent of their total bonus because their work was so good—and the reaction was, 'Why was I docked 4 percent?'" says Andy Dumaine, senior financial manager of Fiberspar, a composite-materials manufacturer in West Wareham, Massachusetts."They seemed to focus more on what they lost, not on what they gained."[4]

When people perceive that something has been taken away, they won't be happy. As a result, their work will suffer. In what was thought to be a great motivator, the concept and practice of incentives may have backfired. In a 1993 study of 663 companies by the Consortium for Alternative Reward Strategies Research, satisfaction levels with incentive plans were well short of being what they were thought to be.[5]

- 12 percent were terminated after three years.
- 46 percent failed to achieve payout measures.
- 30 percent did not succeed because corporate strategy changed.
- 29 percent suffered from lack of employee acceptance.
- 28 percent had management changes.
- 26 percent lacked support/acceptance of management.
- 24 percent were too expensive.

People seem to forget that these programs used to be a reward for a job well done. As a result, entitlement creeps deeper into the organization.

Another big problem with incentive compensation is the downside. What happens when the profits of a particular unit or the company as a whole don't measure up to the plan or whatever standard has been set? The people get less than what they got before, which leaves them resentful of the way they have been treated when, in reality, every one of them has contributed to those results. Everybody has to recognize that going in. They have to realize that when the measure is not met, the bonus is not there. When it is not, they have to avoid the finger-pointing that invariably starts as teamwork, not the bureaucracy, gets bashed.

Finally, another big problem is the promise of a bonus for individual contribution to the bottom line. People can get greedy, and if the proper internal control systems are lacking, like we saw at Continental Illinois, there is no telling what can be done or hidden as huge sums of money are traded. That's what causes people to cut corners on documentation, to add two or three basis points to a derivatives deal, to take unnecessary risks in the bond market, or to speculate unwisely in foreign exchange. They know that there can be a huge reward for them if they pull it off, but history instructs that may only happen for a short time.

The way that the workforce is rewarded and recognized is the key driver to the behavior that the bank wants. It just needs some new thinking. We have talked about organizing horizontally according to the bank's service delivery systems. When that happens and when the people of each value chain know the requirements of its customers, the bank needs to tie some portion of their compensation to how well they serve. We have seen how to measure it. Measures should relate to things such as customer retention, accounts opened and closed, reduced cost of poor quality, increased sales to new customers, and greater market share. They should not be limited to profitability alone.

The ideal is an even compensation split based on individual performance, team performance, and the results of the company as a whole, giving the staff a piece of the economic benefits which they have created. If the installment lending team is able to reduce the cost of operations by 15 percent, give them some portion of it in appreciation for their efforts. If some people continually do more than the rest in the service of customers and that effort relates to increased sales or higher retention rates, give them a piece of that pie. And when the company's profit margins exceed what was planned, give everyone some of that. It is the concept of pay for performance, only this time we apply it to the entire organization.

A client of mine, a law firm, closed its books on the 29th of December 1993. The annual Christmas bonus had been paid according to plan along with the normal year-end expenses. When the accounting staff computed net income for the year, they found that the firm had done much better financially than had been expected. When the managing partner and the controller met to look at the numbers, they decided that since everyone had contributed to that result, everyone should share in the reward, As the staff left the office at the close of business the next day, there was the managing partner handing out another set of bonus checks, every one of them in the same amount. Needless to say, morale at the firm skyrocketed.

Everyone who worked at the firm knew that it was a one-time deal and felt very good about the contribution that he or she had made. Their feelings showed as the managing partner returned their smiles. The same thing can happen at the bank, but it also means that the folks in mortgage lending could get higher bonuses than those in trust, even the senior people, based on how well they perform. It is not entitlement; it is based on contribution. People know that there is a portion of their salary based on how well they work together to serve customers. That's the right focus, not getting something simply because they showed up for work each day, or were able to cut 15 percent of noninterest expense, or swung a deal of undue risk.

As the bank goes about reviewing its compensation program, it might be a good idea to start over again. It may be necessary to rethink the whole thing since the outcome of most current plans is more than just paying people every two weeks. The real outcome is the attitude that the people develop and their resultant behavior. We have seen that the bank's success depends on its people and how well they service their customers. That means that we need to change the emphasis of the compensation system. Three modifications need to be considered.

1. Pay people on the basis of what they do and how they perform. Remember, the bank is in serious competition for talent and needs to develop a reputation of rewarding people on the basis of their contribution. To do that, the evaluation process itself has to change. Use the "360" approach where all members of the team have the opportunity to rate the performance of everybody else. This approach results in a much more objective view. Base part of the merit raise on that. For the rest, consider how the bank did as a whole and how the team/value chain did in the service of its customers.

Also, there can be spot rewards for completing a self-development class; awards for the teams that are able to streamline their delivery systems; incremental bonuses for the value chains that exceed the expectations of their customers; profit sharing for everyone; and the like. Whatever you do, make sure that everyone knows both the upside and the downside of the plan. Tell them how much they have a chance to earn, but make sure that the goals and targets are the right ones: focused squarely on the necessity to improve customer satisfaction levels, and thereby to increase market share, and to decrease cost as a result. All of these can be quantified, which provides an objective basis for evaluation to those who are involved in the review process.

2. Think hard about titles. What do they really add to the value of the service the bank provides?

> The major argument in defense of titles is that the customer demands to deal with a vice president. But is that really true? Has anyone asked customers recently? Most people deal with tellers [or customer service specialists, these days], and they certainly don't carry vice president titles. And, the majority of customers are savvy enough to understand the game that is played with titles; they don't take them seriously. . . Corporate titles could be replaced with functional titles that better describe what the employees actually do and their experience in doing it.[6]

In your bank, is a teller really a "customer service rep" when their real mission is to move people through the line as fast as possible? The best titles are the ones that describe what people do: "left fielder", "point guard", "quarterback", "goalie", and so on. If the compensation program is right and with functional titles, a person can have a certain role on one team and a different one on another. This enhances the ability of the team to work together as it eliminates the hang-up with being vice president and being asked to do something that is considered beneath what a "vice president" is supposed to do. There is too much pomp and ceremony in hierarchical organizations. We need to lighten up and to focus on the team. Then, when people are given an assignment or a responsibility, there is the right incentive to do it, knowing that everyone on the team will be rewarded for accomplishing it.

Eliminating titles goes a long way toward achieving the horizontal structure. Without them, decision making is done by the team and does not have to be done by someone up the ladder or in the corner office. It is probably a scary thought, but think about it. Use titles to describe activity, not as a substitute for the compensation that people deserve.

3. The third suggestion has to do with promotions, and it is just as tricky as the other two. Instead of making them political appointments that have to be repaid in one way or another, base them on objective review and evaluation of measured results. Get the most talented people with the best leadership skills into the critical positions of the bank. Then, give these people the education that they need to become servant leaders. They may not conform to the way things have always been done before, but that is exactly what the revolution needs. They are the risk takers who look at the sand and the sea and say, "Come on, gang. It's going to be all right."

Take a chance. Promote someone who is not in your own image. Promote someone who has demonstrated an unconventional, but uncanny way of getting things done. Better yet, let the teams decide who their leaders are in a natural selection process. "First among equals" is the best way to describe it. For those who show that talent and ability, the promotion becomes a challenge, not a reward, and should be made with the approval of the others. That eliminates the suspicion and becomes a very positive influence on the morale of everybody in the group.

How the bank treats this greatest of its assets, its people, tells a lot about its future. Get the best people you can find, educate them, set objectives and measurable performance standards, evaluate their performance objectively, and reward them. If all of them are "A's," then all of them are "A's." That is what we should want from the people in our value chains. Why in the world would we want any "C's"?

Then, promote on the basis of talent and watch out for "title inflation." Following these suggestions will send a powerful message to everyone in the bank and to your customers. It is one more step in the transition from lead buffalo to lead goose: servant leadership at its best.

HERE IT COMES AGAIN!

We have seen that the younger generations joining the American workforce want to be empowered, accountable, and free to contribute to organizations that are unencumbered by bureaucracy and hierarchy. We have also learned that traditional compensation methods do not contribute to that kind of atmosphere, which limits the ability of the bank to attract the talent that it will need to be able to compete in this ever-faster, global environment.

There is another barrier in the way of the retention and recruitment process, one that I have struggled with for several years since I first got *the* call. In early December 1982, the phone rang. It was the chairman.

"Tom, this is Tim. Can you come up to my office right away?" His voice was unmistakable.

"Yes, sir," I replied, "I'll be there right away." Grabbing my suit coat and picking up my latest financial reports and a legal pad, I was off to the third floor. There was no question as to why the call had come.

When I arrived, there was Tim Treadway, chairman of the board of Union Commerce Bank; Frank Wobst, chairman of Huntington Bancshares; our auditor; our legal counsel; our CFO, who was my boss; and two or three people I had never seen before. After we had exchanged pleasantries, Tim looked at me and said,

"Tom, I'd like you to put the banks together." The room was very quiet. I paused and looked at the others, as I tried to understand the significance of what was happening.

"Yes, sir," I responded. "Is there anything else?"

"No. Not right now."

As I walked back to my office, I paused to look over the main banking floor from the top of the stairs. I thought to myself, "Gee, I think I've just been fired."

We had been engaged in a hostile takeover battle with Huntington for the past year, most of which had been fought in *The Wall Street Journal.* Huntington had tendered for Union Commerce a year before, and now the fight was over.

When I got back to my office, I called my boss: "Hey Brian, did I miss something or am I the first casualty of the merger?"

"You've always been pretty perceptive," came the answer, "but at least you have nine months to find a job."

My initial responsibility was to assist in the financial combination of the two banks while their respective systems departments figured out how they were going to consolidate everything. It then became my duty to coordinate the conversion of the products that Union Commerce offered to those of the Huntington, the development of effective operating procedures, and the education about those new services and procedures for the people of the retail, commercial, and trust departments.

We did not think systemically about what this merger really meant back then or what the current combination of Chase and Chemical means. We did not consider what the act of merging did and is doing to those who would seek a career in banking. The question that has to be asked is why anyone would want to work in a bank these days faced with the prospect of a firestorm of mergers and combinations that is predicted by nearly everyone who is close to the industry.

The second question is similar to it and goes something like this: How motivated can the people of the bank be when that prospect is evident? What are they thinking about? Making the bank better or how to survive? I have seen this human side, both from the CEO's office and from the perspective of good, hardworking people who have jobs at lower levels. Much of the officer staff is taken care of when a merger takes place, but those below them typically are not so lucky. They need their jobs to survive, literally. Their fear is real.

As I helped dismantle Union Commerce Corporation, I watched my friends pack up their belongings in those heavy cardboard storage boxes and leave. I watched as everything that we had worked so hard to build went away. There was no "merger manual" back then, so we made it up as we went along using as much common sense as we could to bring the banks together. It was very exciting doing something that had never been done before, but that excitement masked my true feelings to most of my associates at the bank.

However, I was fortunate to have the chance to reflect about the meaning of what we were doing with trusted colleagues like Elaine Geller and Dick Wild who had served the bank very well and were now dealing with their own fears about the future. Somehow, even back then, we could not see how destroying the bank would create value even over the long term. This feeling was intuitive because there was little data about bank mergers, but to us, it did not make sense. In the short term, our shareholders were enriched, but I could not help wondering how much more they would have made if we could have kept the bank independent.

Mergers appear to be artificial economic events that companies rush into for the promise of big returns. As banks such as Union Commerce and First Fidelity disappear, I wondered whether it should be the market that determines their fate rather than the recommendation of the investment bankers who stand to make a tidy profit on the deal. As I helped with the disappearance of Trust-Corp in Toledo, Ameritrust in Cleveland, Central National in Cleveland, Third National Bank and Trust in Dayton, and Harter Bank in Canton, this thought kept nagging at me.

During that time, some support for it started to appear. Some studies were published that questioned whether mergers were creating value for the shareholder. The *Baltimore Sun* carried an article in August 1991 titled "Pitfalls of Bank Mergers," which contained the following paragraph:

> History suggests that people can be pared quickly, but doing so often provokes low morale and chaos. Turf wars erupt. Employees begin printing resumes rather than business proposals. Credit officers familiar with accounts leave. Loyalty dies. Files get bungled. Irate customers are left on hold, disconnected because of telecommunications problems stemming from office shifts and the firing of familiar old operators.[7]

About the same time, *Fortune* ran a story titled "Do Bank Mergers Make Sense?" which led with: "Customers won't get the sweet deals they used to as competition wanes."[8] *Business Week*'s April 22, 1991, issue had a special report, "If Mergers Were Simple, Banking's Troubles Might Be Over." All of that occurred after Merger Mania I. Now Merger Mania II is in full swing. NationsBank and Bank of America are supposed to be getting together. First Interstate is history. In the first nine months of 1995, mergers worth $248.5 billion were made all across the United States and not only in banking, which surpassed the record of $246.9 billion set in 1988. The editorial in the October 30, 1995, issue of *Business Week* read, "Mergers: Will They Ever Learn?"

> This historic surge of consolidations and combinations is occurring in the face of strong evidence that mergers and acquisitions, at least over the past 35 years or so, have hurt more than helped companies and shareholders. The conglomerate deals of the 1960s and 1970s that gave rise to such unwieldy companies as ITT Corp. and Litton Industries have since been thoroughly discredited, and most of these behemoths have been broken up.
>
> The debt-laden leveraged buyouts and bust-ups of the 1980s didn't fare any better, and many did a whole lot worse. That era ended not with a whimper but with a bang: In October 1989, when bankers couldn't raise the money for the ill-conceived buyout of UAL Corp., the deal collapsed, dragging the stock market down with it.[9]

Business Week had commissioned a study of 150 mergers of over $500 million that had been done in the first half of the 1990s. Analysis of the data revealed that half of them lessened shareholder value with another third only adding marginally to it, as follows:

- 30% reported "substantial erosion" of shareholder value.
- 20% "some erosion"
- 33% a "marginal return"
- 17% a "substantial return" [10]

These conclusions were drawn based on the performance of the company three months before the acquisition was announced contrasted with returns up to three years later and then compared against the Standard & Poor's 500 industry indexes.

Why don't mergers work? On paper, they might, but there's a fallacy in the thinking that gets back to the heart of the revolution. Conventional wisdom says that combining two complex organizations is easy, but it isn't. The reason? As we have seen before, it is the strength of each one's structure and style. Organizational paradigms are difficult to change, especially when the change is of a radical nature. That's when it gets emotional and people lose their sense of reason.

That was what happened at Union Commerce, and I have seen it over and over again. The people being taken over don't want to be part of another, unfamiliar organization, so heels can be dug in to the point of total gridlock. They have their own ways of doing things (style) and their own departments and divisions (structure), and they don't want that to change even if the power at the top sees some potential synergies.

When Society Corporation bought Centran in 1984, it made good sense, we thought, for we were a retail bank while Centran concentrated on the commercial side. The merger would let both organizations take advantage of each other's strengths. That was the synergy that the leadership saw. However, because of those strengths, each bank had its own culture—and bang, they ran right into each other head first. Their way was contrary to our way, and ours did not fit with theirs. Even though we were told to get along and to figure out how to make it work, much of what we did was foreign to them and vice versa.

Even so, in the integration, we were told to mix up our departments, making sure that we had people from both banks represented. As with the Chase-Chemical merger, some people from both banks did not make the cut. In cases like that, resentment can run pretty strong, especially if one of the people who reported to you didn't make it and you ended up with a less qualified person doing that job. People talk about how the lack of a cultural fit impedes these kinds of transactions, but they may not fully appreciate how powerful that insight might be.

There can be a lack of planning, a less than accurate view of the strategic fit, or a blue-sky estimation of the economies that can be achieved, but the two biggest impediments are the strengths of the competing cultures and the focus, once again, on cost. Cost reduction becomes the order of the day so that the acquisition can be paid for, but as we have seen, that results in the "maybe I'm next syndrome" and weakens trust levels throughout the organization. When that kind of attitude on the parts of both merger partners is brought together, every person truly is out for himself or herself, which is hardly the atmosphere that is needed to compete with all of the new entrants. Nor does it let talented people from the outside with new, fresh, and different perspectives join the bank. Perhaps, they would not want to.

There is another factor about mergers that has an impact on the people: price. The initial bid by Wells Fargo for First Interstate was a nearly unheard of three times book value. We used to think 1.5 times book was a lot. The higher the price that is paid, the more cost that has to be taken out or the more revenue that has to be generated, and banks have fared poorly in the latter. That means back to the old standby: cost cutting, which makes the cloud hanging over both organizations blacker and blacker. Perhaps, Wells Fargo can afford to pay that much, but it sends an unhealthy signal to the rest of the industry that three times book is OK. A lot of banks should not bid that high; unfortunately, they probably will.

As with downsizing, restructuring, and reengineering, the emphasis of the way mergers have been done in the past is wrong, and the results of the *Business Week* study, among others, support that contention. BancOne was heavily involved in mergers in the 1980s, leaving the acquired banks alone to serve their customers. Its unique approach was called the "uncommon partnership with customers," but now core earnings are flat and the growth by acquisition strategy that seemed to work so well is being seriously questioned.[11] The people at KeyCorp admit that the acquisition of Society has not produced the results they thought were there. And Bank of America had a very hard time digging out from under the burden of Security Pacific.[12]

Since the advent of Merger Mania II, we have seen First Union acquire First Fidelity, CoreStates buy Meridian, NationsBank purchase AmSouth and BankSouth, PNC buy Midlantic, National City gobble up Integra, and even the Bank of New Hampshire, acquired by Peoples Heritage Financial, will disappear. The primary motivation for these deals appears to be the notion that sheer size will assure independence or will provide an opportunity to reduce fixed cost. If Bank of America and NationsBank get together to form a $400 billion company, all of a sudden size is not an issue. That makes all banks potential targets.

The message? Even though the evidence suggests that mergers don't work, be prepared to be acquired. However, try to do it for the right reason, to serve customers better. It does not appear that the rush to merge can be stopped, but it can be slowed if the good of the market is the primary motivator. Instead of worrying about synergies with a potential merger partner having a different culture, think more about the bank's markets and how to serve them better. That is what lowers the cost of operations; closes the back door, thus increasing retention rates; offers the opportunity to sell more to current customers; and provides greater appeal to noncustomers.

It is a focus on increasing revenue, not decreasing cost, that will also be rewarded by the stock market. That, as I have tried to show, requires both personal and organizational change. Gather the data about customers and the staff. Analyze it carefully to see where the opportunities lie. As you do, consider the following:

- Realize and understand the competitive nature of the industry and the disintermediation that it has caused.
- See how technology is changing the expectations of your customers and the methods of distribution for meeting them.
- Remember that the key to the bank's success is its people of the bank who want to do a great job every day.

It is their creativity that is critical. That is one of the greatest assets that the bank has. Why?

> After companies have downsized and rightsized, improved quality and reengineered themselves—after they have made themselves very, very fit, a central question will emerge: fit for what? On the new competitive playing field, with what cudgels will players batter one another? How about . . . ideas? Competition doesn't get any more basic than that.[13]

TO CHANGE

Initiating the required behavioral and organizational changes will not be easy, but the process must begin. Where do we start? What follows is the Change Index (see Table 10–1), which addresses 17 elements that will either enhance, or inhibit, the bank's ability to change. We found the Change Index to be helpful as organizations take their first steps on the journey. Copy it for everyone who is critical to your organization's initiative and have them fill it out. When there is a representative sample of responses, tally them; calculate the average for the organization in question, whether it is a business unit or the bank as a whole; and communicate the results to the service improvement council or quality council.

THE CHANGE INDEX, THE PACE

It has taken nearly a year to write *The Banking Revolution,* during which time some remarkable things have happened: (1) the emergence of the Internet and World Wide Web; (2) the opening of markets in places that many of us had never heard of before; (3) the advent of Merger Mania II in which even the largest banks are getting together; and (4) the continued, significant inroads of the new competition. First, the Internet and the World Wide Web surfaced, and CompuServe began to get a workout every day from my office. Who would have believed that millions of Americans would converse daily with one another with their PCs and the Internet? In November 1995, *Bank Marketing* published another cyberspace article, "Setting Up Your Bank Marketing Web Site," following its September 1995 article, "Direct Marketing Goes On-Line." The forecasts call for staggering growth in the use of the Web as people in all corners of the country begin to take advantage of it. Banking services offered by Barnett Banks in Jacksonville may now be available to customers in places like Gallup, New Mexico; Kalispell, Montana; and Petosky, Michigan. That creates a new and different challenge for the banks in those communities. It also presents an opportunity to provide the human side of the banking equation, something its new competitor cannot render over the wire.

We have also seen world markets open significantly, perhaps in response to the improvement in communication afforded by the Internet. Since this book was begun, and as mentioned before, I have traveled to the Russian Far East twice to teach Asset-Liability Management and Strategic Planning to representatives of the banking system there. Our Russian friends realize that global trading activity is the key to their success and have entered into joint ventures with Canadian, Malaysian, and Korean companies, in addition to those in the United States. That will increase quickly as the value of the vast amount of natural resources in the Russian Far East becomes known.

TABLE 10-1

The Change Index

The left-hand column lists 17 key elements of the ability to change. There is a space provided in the right-hand column for you to rate your organization on each one. Give three points for a high opinion, two for an average one, and one point for a low opinion.

Sponsorship

The sponsor of the change is the bank's visionary, the person who can make things happen. Give your organization three points—change will be easier—if the sponsor is the CEO or the COO, or the head of a major, independent business unit. _____

Leadership

Change is more likely to happen if the leadership is at a high level and has a good idea of the result to be achieved. Lower levels that are not well connected or come from staff areas have less of a chance for success and should be scored lower. _____

Motivation

Give three points where the leadership provides a heightened sense of urgency which is understood and embraced by the rest of the organization and,where a culture already emphasizes *kaizen*. Give low points for a culture that discourages risk taking and is based on outdated traditions and paradigms. _____

Direction

Does the senior leadership have a clear understanding of what the future should be and do they have a road map for success? Can they get the right people together to start the journey? If so, score the bank high. If not, and management thinks only minor change is needed, score the bank low. _____

Measurement

If your organization has set performance standards within its value chains based on the expectations of customers and measures against them, and if you are measuring the cost of quality, give three points. Give two points if the measures are in place but compensation is not tied to them. For no measures, one point. _____

Organizational Context

How well does the change fit in with other strategic initiatives that are happening at the bank? High points if it is linked very closely or is at the center of everything that is going on. Low points if there is no connection. _____

Processes and Functions

If the pyramid structure precludes effective cross-functional communication and cooperation, or if turf is guarded carefully, give a low score. Give a high score if there is a willingness to collaborate on improving entire service delivery systems and to join together as teams. _____

Competitor Benchmarking

If the bank is surveying customers of other institutions and doing research on the competition, give high marks. Give a low score if there is little factual information about competitors.

Customer Focus

Score high if everyone in the bank has identified who their customers are, understands their expectations, and works to meet them. Give a low score if the workforce acts in a vacuum, effectively "throwing things over the wall."

Rewards

Give yourself a low score if the bank continues with a traditional compensation system that rewards individual accomplishment above all else or emphasizes continuity over change. If there is a spirit of entrepreneurism and risk taking for which the workforce is rewarded, give three points.

Organizational Structure

Give a low score if the pyramid is firmly in place and has not been changed in the last five years. Give three points if the lines are blurred and cross-functional teamwork is the norm.

Communication

Give a high score if there is effective communication up, down, and sideways. Give a low score for the organization that features one-way, top-down communication.

Organization Hierarchy

If there are several layers in the pyramid that stifle effective communication and decision making, give one point. If the bank has made the transition to the horizontal organization, give three.

Previous Change

Score three points if the company has been able to deal with and implement major change in the last five years. If that change caused a decline in morale, lack of trust, or resentment, give one point.

Morale

If the members of the workforce are empowered, accountable, and responsible, give three points. If team spirit is low, little extra effort is expended, and the workforce has an attitude of "I may be next," give one point.

Innovation

If it takes forever to get a new idea implemented, give one point. If experimentation is expected and people try out new ideas, getting them implemented quickly and easily, give three points.

Decision Making

Score three points if decisions are made quickly, close to the customer, and by the right people. Give one point if decisions have to be made by someone higher up or in the corner office.

Total Score
Scoreboard
41–51   The bank is likely to be successful in implementing change. Note the areas where the score is one or two. Those need some additional work.
28–40   It is possible for the bank to change, but it will be difficult, especially if scores are low in the first seven elements. Bring those up before trying to implement change across the board.
17–27   Change will not be successful. Start to work on the elements with the lowest score or empower small groups to start a "grass roots" campaign.

Source: Thomas A. Stewart, "Rate Your Readiness to Change," *Fortune,* Feb. 7, 1994, pp. 108–10.

I had been asked to teach a week-long course in Magadan, a city in the northern stretches of the Primorsk region of the Russian Far East. Many of my students were from the Kolyma Bank, which has offices throughout the region. On the first day of class, one of them came up at a break and asked, "Can you tell me about credit cards?"

She told me that she was from a town 600 km north of Magadan called Omsukchan which has 25,000 residents. It is near the Arctic Circle where it gets cold during the winter: –48 degrees Celsius which translates to well over –100 degrees Fahrenheit. That sure would keep me from going outside. Nevertheless, mining technology has progressed to the point where there are both Russian-Canadian and Russian-U.S. joint ventures working in the gold mines there. All of this data prompted my question of "Why credit cards?"

Her response was that Russia is a cash society, but the Americans and the Canadians who are in Omsukchan working in the gold mines don't want to carry a lot of rubles. They want to use their credit cards, and she wanted to be able to provide that service.

There were some lessons there. First, trade is finding its way to some extremely remote places in the world and banks have an opportunity to facilitate it. Second, with technology, the bankers in the Russian Far East can offer the same services that are provided in New York City. All they need is a satellite dish and some advanced telecommunications equipment. Third, my student recognized an opportunity that her customers presented and was trying to figure out how to meet it. When the class reconvened, I asked if all of them would like to learn about credit cards. The material that I had prepared for the afternoon stayed closed as we talked about the theory and practice of credit cards and how they could be introduced in their markets. As the world moves closer together, there will be many more opportunities to serve in places about which we know little today.

The third thing that has happened in this very short period of time is the advent of Merger Mania II. Merger and acquisition activity will continue to rock the financial services industry for the next five years. By the turn of the century, or shortly thereafter, there will probably be only 12 to 15 national banks in this country, but that will leave a lot of room for the community banks. If we take a Darwinian approach, perhaps this is what is supposed to happen. However, we can only hope that it is being done to serve customers and markets better and more efficiently than in the past. By definition, mergers and acquisitions can't go on forever, and the banks will be back to the same basic problem, a dwindling number of customers. Consider the following:

> Consolidation could well make the banking industry more productive. But merging and slashing expenses give only a short-lived boost to earnings. Eventually the merger boom will peak if for no other reason than that deals will get too expensive. Recently banks have been bidding for one another at more than two times book value, well above the multiple of 1.5 that prevailed just three years ago. And in the end, these bigger banks will be stuck with the same problem—fewer and fewer people who need them.[14]

The Banking Revolution opened with a description of the threat of nonbank competition. The continuing disintermediation is number four, and it is getting worse. John Alden, senior vice president and director of corporate marketing at PNCs understands that. "One of the things I've come to appreciate is the constant reminder . . . that our major competitors are from outside the industry, not from other banks."[15] American Express has signed up with Intuit to offer on-line services; those 6:00 P.M. phone calls from Prudential Securities continue to come in from brokers offering to take just a moment of our time to acquaint us with this or that retirement fund; Merrill Lynch still provides a higher yield on its money market funds than the bank. Even with markets opening up all over the world, the intensity of the domestic competition will continue to increase.

We started with some statistics about the advance of the nonbank competition. As we near the finish, here are some more.

> In 1980, banks and thrifts accounted for 54 percent of the total financial assets of financial institutions in the United States. By last December, that share had dropped to 33 percent and by June it had slipped to 32 percent. Fifteen years ago consumers left about 34 percent of their assets in checking and savings accounts and CDs. Now we bank about 17 percent of savings. Over the same period, the share of financial assets that individuals hold in investment accounts like stocks and mutual funds has jumped from 28 percent in 1980 to 37 percent.

Bank rivals are pressing from all directions. Over the past five years, loan activity at GE Capital—already one of the country's biggest lenders—has climbed 11 percent a year, while the banking industry's loan growth has crept along at a 3 percent annual rate.

Take credit cards, long a lucrative business for banks. Since 1991, First USA, a credit card company no more than 10 years old, has prospered furiously, raising its card receivables 650 percent, to $15 billion, during a period when growth in overall card debt grew just 36 percent.

The same holds true for consumer savings. At Charles Schwab, assets in money market mutual funds with check-writing privileges have been rising 35 percent a year since 1989, and now stand at $28 billion. Conversely, deposits at NationsBank grew just 3 percent a year—only half the average for all U.S. commercial banks.[16]

The only way to counter it is with the service that your customers want.

Whether the bank chooses a strategy of operational excellence, product leadership, or customer intimacy does not matter. What does matter are your skill sets, the understanding of your customers' expectations, and the ability of the bank to meet them. The pace of the world of financial services will continue to get faster, which makes the willingness and ability to serve ever more important.

THE CHALLENGE

Listen to your scouts whoever they might be. Keep an eye on the horizon at all times, measuring the expectations and perceptions of your customers and understanding what the competition is doing. Limit the amount of time spent looking at the profitability scoreboard and the overhead ratio. Capitalize on the strengths of your institution and be ready to take on the weaknesses. Create an organization full of empowered, accountable, team-oriented people who can and want to serve. Then let them go.

Profitability follows performance. To quote James Burke, CEO of Johnson & Johnson throughout the late 1970s and the 1980s, "I have long harbored the belief that the most successful corporations in this country—the ones that have delivered outstanding results over a long period of time—were driven by a simple moral imperative—serving the public in the broadest possible sense better than their competitors."[17]

We have covered a lot of ground here since we first learned the definition of service. We have seen the changes taking place in the financial services industry and the economic opportunities awaiting the bank that adopts a strategy of service excellence. We have learned about the legacy of structure and style that today's bankers have inherited from their predecessors and about the need to change it. We have focused on customers and their critical and fundamental importance to the bank, and we have learned a technique by which to change the behavior of the people of the bank to ensure that their expectations are being met.

My purpose has not been to provide answers to all of the questions that you have raised as you read these pages. Rather, it has been to provide you with information and observations that I hope have helped you to ask them. It is impossible to write a cookbook of the steps that could be taken by every banker in the country to compete in this fast-paced world. But it is possible to raise the critical issues that every bank faces and to ask that you and your teams deal with them as creatively as you can. That is what the banking revolution is all about. New ways of thinking. New ways of behavior. Both in the service of your customers.

ENDNOTES

1. Timothy L. O'Brien, "On-Line Banking Has Bankers Fretting PCs May Replace Branches," *The Wall Street Journal,* Oct. 25, 1995, p. A1.
2. Kelly Holland et al., "The Bankers Trust Tapes," *Business Week,* Oct. 16, 1995, pp. 106–107.
3. William Roth and Douglas Ferguson, "The End of Performance Appraisals?" *Quality Digest,* Sept. 1994, p. 55.
4. Lynn Brenner, "The Myth of Incentive Pay," *CFO,* July 1995, p. 28.
5. Ibid., p. 33.
6. Janet L. Gray and Thomas W. Harvey, *Quality Value Banking* (New York: John Wiley & Sons), pp. 12–13.
7. Thomas Easton, "Pitfalls of Bank Mergers," *Plain Dealer,* Aug. 4, 1991, p. 2E.
8. Gary Hector, "Do Bank Mergers Make Sense?" *Fortune,* Aug. 12, 1991, p. 70.
9. Philip L. Zweig, et al., "The Case against Mergers," *Business Week,* Oct. 30, 1995, p. 122.
10. Philip L. Zweig, et al. "The Case Against Mergers," *Business Week,* Oct. 30, 1995. p. 125.
11. Terence P. Pare, "Clueless Bankers," *Fortune,* Nov. 27, 1995, p. 152.
12. Kelly Holland and Sam Zuckerman, "A Bank-Eat-Bank World with Indigestion," *Business Week,* Oct. 30, 1995, p. 130.
13. Alan Farnham, "How to Nurture Creative Sparks," *Fortune,* Jan. 10, 1994, p. 95.
14. Pare, "Clueless Bankers," p. 151.
15. John E. Alden quoted in Tanja Lian, "BMA Board Says Nonbanks are the Biggest Threat," *Bank Marketing,* Sept. 1995, p. 87.
16. Pare, "Clueless Bankers," p. 151–52.
17. James E. Burke quoted in Robert H. Waterman, Jr., *What America Does Right* (New York: Penguin Books USA, 1994), pp. 297–98.

INDEX